Qualitative Reading Inventory-5

Lauren Leslie

Marquette University

JoAnne Schudt Caldwell

Cardinal Stritch University

Boston • Columbus • Indianapolis • New York • San Francisco • Upper Saddle River
Amsterdam • Cape Town • Dubai • London • Madrid • Milan • Munich • Paris • Montreal • Toronto
Delhi • Mexico City • Sao Paulo • Sydney • Hong Kong • Seoul • Singapore • Taipei • Tokyo

Editor-in-Chief: Aurora Martínez Ramos
Editorial Assistant: Amy Foley
Vice President, Director of Marketing: Quinn Perkson
Executive Marketing Manager: Krista Clark
Text Designer: Omegatype Typography, Inc.
Cover Coordinator: Linda Knowles
Cover Designer: Jennifer Hart
Senior Managing Editor: Elaine Ober
Manufacturing Manager: Megan Cochran
Full Service Project Management: Omegatype Typography, Inc.
Composition: Omegatype Typography, Inc.

Credits and acknowledgments borrowed from other sources and reproduced, with permission, in this textbook appear on appropriate page within text or on page 499.

Library of Congress Cataloging-in-Publication Data

Leslie, Lauren.
    Qualitative reading inventory. 5 / Lauren Leslie, JoAnne Caldwell.—5th ed.
        p.   cm.
    Includes bibliographical references and index.
    ISBN-13: 978-0-13-701923-6 (spiralbound)
    ISBN-10: 0-13-701923-8 (spiralbound)
  1. Qualitative Reading Inventory.   2. Reading comprehension—Ability testing.   I. Caldwell, JoAnne (JoAnne Schudt)   II. Title.
    LB1050.75.Q34L47 2010
    372.48—dc22

                                                    2009038336

Printed in the United States of America

7   8   9   10   11   V011   17   16   15   14   13

www.pearsonpd.com
www.pearsonhighered.com

ISBN-10: 0-13-701923-8
ISBN-13: 978-0-13-701923-6

Contents

QRI-5 Video and Resource DVD Contents

Part I: Video Clips

These demonstrate the administrative procedures for the *QRI*-5.

VC1: Demonstrates Introduction to a Story and Directions for Concept Questions and Prediction

VC2: Demonstrates Retelling Directions

VC3: Demonstrates Lookback Procedure

VC 4A: Demonstrates Think-Aloud Procedure

VC 4B: Demonstrates Think-Aloud Procedure

Part II: Audio Tape Recordings and Corresponding Scoring Protocols

Student #1: Devonte: A beginning reader. Audio tape recording of oral reading, retelling, and answering comprehension questions

Student #2: Katrina: A beginning reader. Audio tape of oral reading, retelling, and answering comprehension questions

Student #3: Pam: Reading 4th grade story. Audio tape of oral reading, retelling, and answering comprehension questions

Student #4: Cynthia: Reading 3rd grade story. Audio tape of oral reading, retelling, and answering comprehension questions

Student #5: Miranda: Demonstrating retelling and thinking aloud on high school narrative

Part III: Forms & Figures from the QRI-5

These are arranged according to the sections of the QRI-5.

Scored Protocols for students reading aloud in the audio section of the DVD

Section 4: Uses of the *Qualitative Reading Inventory-5*

    Uses of the *Qualitative Reading Inventory-5*

Section 5: Administration and Scoring of the *Qualitative Reading Inventory-5*: Preparation for Testing

    Guidelines for Administration • Scoring Guidelines

Section 6: Administration and Scoring of the *Qualitative Reading Inventory-5*: The Word Lists

    Pattern for a Word List Window Card • Examiner Word Lists • Reading by Analogy Test

Preface

The fifth edition of *Qualitative Reading Inventory* continues the emphasis on authentic assessment of children's reading abilities, from the earliest emergent readers to advanced readers. Like other informal reading inventories, it provides graded word lists and numerous passages designed to assess a student's oral reading accuracy, rate of reading, and comprehension of passages read orally and silently. However, the QRI-5 has several unique features. The QRI-5 contains narrative and expository passages at each level from pre-primer through high school. All are self-contained selections highly representative of the structure and topics of materials found in basal readers and content-area textbooks. For example, passages at the pre-primer through second grade levels are presented with and without pictures. Maps and illustrations are part of expository selections at fourth grade through high school levels.

Prior to reading, knowledge of concepts important to an understanding of the passage is assessed, which allows the examiner to label a passage as familiar or unfamiliar to each student. The QRI-5 measures comprehension in several ways: through an analysis of the student's retelling; through the student's answers to explicit and implicit comprehension questions; through the use of look-backs, which separate what readers remember from what they comprehend; and through the use of think-alouds at the sixth grade level and above to analyze the student's thoughts during reading.

NEW TO THIS EDITION

There are at least eight goals that have directed the design of the fifth edition of the QRI. One goal is to present a current, condensed research review that provides an up-to-date research rationale for all elements of reading assessment. Sections of the QRI-5 have also been rewritten to make it easier for those with less background in assessing children's reading ability. For example, new tables and charts have reduced the amount of written explanation needed to convey how to interpret the results and plan interventions. A sample report format has also been included with a completed report on the DVD as an example of how the sample could be applied. A simplified system of oral reading miscue analysis has been developed that focuses on students' self-correction behavior. New narrative passages that are easier for the very beginning reader have been included at the request of those who are assessing kindergarten and first grade children. In addition, a new measure of decoding ability has been developed. Also, the rating of the difficulty of all QRI passages has been provided using readability formulae, lexiles, leveled books, and student performance. An additional narrative passage at the first through third grade levels has been included and extensive piloting provided data on the comparability between new and previously included passages. An expansion of this summary follows.

- The current and condensed research review allows the user to quickly identify an updated research rationale for each element of the *QRI-5*. The references include classic studies in the areas of prior knowledge, text structure, and reading fluency, as well as recent research. Theoretical views of retelling and current research on how culture affects a student's understanding of the structure of narrative text have also been included.
- New tables and charts reduce the amount of written explanation needed to assist the user in interpreting results and designing appropriate interventions. For example, Table 3.1 provides suggested interventions for students with specific needs identified by the *QRI-5*.
- A simplified miscue analysis system was developed to focus the user on an analysis of the conditions under which students self-corrected miscues that did or did not change meaning.
- Passages with very few words and high picture support have been developed to make the assessment of very beginning readers more precise. These passages were piloted and revised to provide an estimate of their difficulty for kindergarten and first grade children.
- A new decoding assessment, called "reading by analogy" has been designed to assess whether children can use words they already know to decode less frequent words that they don't immediately recognize. The words used to assess reading by analogy contain the most frequent rime elements (i.e., phonograms) and the difficulty of each rime for first and second graders has been provided from our pilot data.
- The difficulty of all passages has been assessed using readability formulae, lexiles, and Fountas and Pinnell Guided Reading Levels. The table presenting these comparisons allows users to align the results of *QRI* testing to the leveled readers or advanced lexiled materials appropriate for the student's instruction or independent reading.
- An additional narrative passage at all levels through third grade has been added and piloted to ensure comparability with previous stories on the *QRI*. These additions bring the number of narrative texts at the primary levels to at least four (five on the pre-primer level). The narratives have been added because many school districts are using narratives to monitor student progress four times per year. The same genre should be used when monitoring progress over time because students often comprehend one genre better than another.
- The revised DVD is more user-friendly and includes many new features. As requested, examples of students reading orally are included to provide practice for the novice user. Scored protocols accompany these readings. In addition, the directions for administering each segment of the *QRI* are presented on one page, and tables or charts that increase the consistency of administration, scoring, and interpretation are included. Finally, all student and examiner copies are included on the DVD.

The DVD icon indicates materials are on the DVD.

USE AND VALIDITY OF THE *QRI-5*

The *QRI-5* provides a number of diagnostic options that serve a variety of purposes. Whereas the administration of standardized tests remains identical for all students, the *QRI-5* provides the user with choices that depend on the goal of assessment. The *QRI-5* can be used to identify reading levels and to match students to appropriate text. The *QRI-5* may also be employed to verify a suspected reading problem, determine reader strengths and needs, and suggest directions for intervention instruction. In addition, the *QRI-5* can be used for charting growth across a school year or after completion of a special intervention program, an important function in these times of increased focus on accountability. Unlike many standardized tests, the *QRI-5* provides a tool for observing the reading behavior of a student in a relatively natural context that approximates a real reading situation. Each examiner is encouraged to decide which of the *QRI-5*'s components meet his or her diagnostic purposes.

We have designed the *QRI-5* for students in graduate education courses, reading-assessment specialists, and school district personnel who offer in-service work in reading assessment or who are involved in choosing assessment procedures for a school or district. If the *QRI-5* is used with pre-service education students, an instructor will need to acquaint the students with recent research on factors affecting the reading process. In addition, the *QRI-5* presumes a basic knowledge of informal reading inventories.

ACKNOWLEDGMENTS

We extend our appreciation to the following persons who aided in testing, scoring, and interpreting the *Qualitative Reading Inventory-5*. We especially thank Casey O'Keefe of Cardinal Stritch University for sharing her expertise regarding language and dialect patterns. The following individuals were extremely helpful in many aspects of the revision process.

Cardinal Stritch University

Lori Ladiges
Molly Shiffler

Marquette University

Kit Engbring
Marge Laughlin
Mary Taft
Susan Glass

Betsy Caughie, Battleground School District, WA
Terri Brecklin, Brown Deer Public Schools, WI
Mary Pat Lucy, Brown Deer Public Schools, WI
Margaret O'Connor Plotkin, Mequon-Thiensville School District, WI
Eric Dimmit, Mequon-Thiensville School District, WI
Leanne Giese, St. Joseph's Parish School, Grafton, WI
Mary Stallman, St. Joseph's Parish School, Grafton, WI
Adrienne Hansher, Urban Day School, WI
Peter Johnston, Urban Day School, WI
William Anderson, Wauwatosa Public Schools, WI
Jeni Berthold, Wauwatosa Public Schools, WI
Beth Erenberger, Wauwatosa Public Schools, WI
Linda Forbord, Wauwatosa Public Schools, WI

Michael Leach, Wauwatosa Public Schools, WI
Lori Lester, Wauwatosa Public Schools, WI

Also, we extend our appreciation to the following reviewers: Katherine L. Anderson, Univesity of South Dakota; Nancy Horstman, Central Michigan University; Karen A. Jorgensen, University of Kansas; Tabatha Scharlach, University of Central Florida; and Roslyn Woodard, California State University, San Marcos.

1 Description of the *Qualitative Reading Inventory-5*

General Description of the *Qualitative Reading Inventory-5*

The Word Lists

The Passages

    Pre-Primer, Primer, First Grade, and Second Grade Passages

Third Grade though Fifth Grade Passages

Sixth Grade Passages

Upper Middle School Passages

High School Passages

Use of the Passages

Measures of Comprehension

GENERAL DESCRIPTION OF THE *QUALITATIVE READING INVENTORY-5*

The *Qualitative Reading Inventory-5* (*QRI-5*) is an individually administered informal reading inventory (IRI) designed to provide information about (1) conditions under which students can identify words and comprehend text successfully and (2) conditions that appear to result in unsuccessful word identification or comprehension. The *QRI-5* continues a long history of informal reading inventories, which for forty years have been used to identify subjects' reading levels—independent, instructional, and frustration— and to provide valuable diagnostic information. Like other informal reading inventories, the *QRI-5* provides graded word lists and numerous passages designed to assess the oral and silent reading and listening ability of students from the pre-primer 1 through the high school levels.

The *QRI-5* provides a number of assessment options. Results can be used to estimate students' reading levels, to group students for guided reading sessions, or to choose appropriate books for literacy circles, reading workshops, and independent reading. The *QRI-5* can provide information for designing and evaluating intervention instruction. Finally, the *QRI-5* can be used to document student growth.

The *QRI-5* is not a norm-referenced or standardized instrument. Norm-referenced tests provide comparative data; that is, an individual's score is evaluated in terms of the scores of the norm group. Standardized instruments are administered identically for all students. Users of an informal reading inventory, on the other hand, make their own decisions as to the number and type of passages to administer and which assessment options to use. While the *QRI-5,* like other IRIs, uses traditional percentages to determine independent, instructional, and frustration levels, student scores are interpreted only in regard to the individual and not to any norm group.

THE WORD LISTS

The pre-primer 1 word list has 17 words; all of the other word lists contain 20 words that we have selected from *QRI* passages at the same level of readability. For example, the primer word list contains words from the primer passages. The word lists are designed

1. To assess accuracy of word identification
2. To assess speed and automaticity of word identification
3. To determine a starting point for reading the initial passage

The *QRI-5* includes a new feature. Some words on the pre-primer 1 through first grade lists contain phonetically regular vowel patterns. However, because these words are high-frequency words (as is appropriate at these levels), students may still pronounce them as memorized sight words and be relatively unaware of the sound patterns they contain. Therefore the *QRI-5* provides an additional list of low-frequency words that contain the same phonetically regular phonograms. This additional feature allows the examiner to determine two things. First, does the student actually recognize phonograms as phonetic units? Second, does she or he know the more common or frequent ones? This can suggest a beginning point for phonics instruction.

THE PASSAGES

The passages to be read orally or silently assess the student's ability to read and comprehend different types of text. Passages can also be used to assess a student's listening level.

Pre-Primer, Primer, First Grade, and Second Grade Passages

At the pre-primer levels, there are six passages of increasing difficulty. Five are narratives and one is expository. Narratives usually involve stories while expository text is written primarily to inform, as in textbooks, newspapers, and much magazine writing (Pearson & Fielding, 1991). Three of the narratives and the expository passage are presented with pictures. The primer, first, second, and third grade readability levels have six passages—four narrative and two expository. At the primer and first grade levels, three narrative passages and one expository passage are presented with pictures. At second grade there are two narratives with pictures. Research suggests that emergent readers depend on picture context for both word identification and passage comprehension. In addition, text with pictures more closely approximates the type of selections presented to beginning readers. However, good readers are not dependent on pictures for word identification (Stanovich, 1991b), and it may be important to ascertain whether word identification differs when pictures are present as opposed to when they are absent. The examiner can assess the effect of pictures on a student's word identification or comprehension by contrasting performance on passages with and without pictures.

Because children often have difficulty making the transition from narration to exposition, we felt that it was important to include expository material at all levels. The inclusion of expository material also makes the *QRI-5* more usable by teachers working with adult beginning readers who might be put off by children's narratives. Examiners who give passages from pre-primer through second grade will be able to ascertain the reader's relative strengths in recalling and comprehending narrative versus expository material. In addition, we have included enough passages to assess differences between oral and silent reading, which, if they occur, should be more predominant at these early reading levels.

All passages contain concept questions that are designed to measure prior knowledge of three or four major concepts within each passage. While the topics of pre-primer 1 through third grade passages are generally familiar, scores on the concept task will help the examiner determine whether the student possesses knowledge of basic concepts necessary to comprehend the selection. All passages are also accompanied by a short prediction task where, given the title of the passage and the concepts included in the prior knowledge measure, the reader is asked to predict passage content.

Third Grade through Fifth Grade Passages

The passages for third grade through fifth grade include three narrative and three expository passages at each level. The narratives for fourth through fifth grades are biographies of famous people who vary in their familiarity to students in these grades (e.g., Johnny Appleseed versus Amelia Earhart in fourth grade and Martin Luther King, Jr., versus Patricia McKissack in fifth grade). We chose biographies in order to provide a more controlled assessment of prior knowledge. For example, it is easier to assess prior knowledge of a real person than the content of a fictional narrative. Because both familiar and unfamiliar people are included, *QRI-5* results can be useful in suggesting why students are having trouble in comprehension.

The expository passages are descriptive science and social studies materials on various topics, modeled after or taken from representative textbooks. We include passages that, according to our pilot data, offer a range in familiarity because of research suggesting that familiarity, which is measured by students' prior knowledge, is an important determinant of reading comprehension.

Sixth Grade Passages

At the sixth grade level, we have included three narrative passages, two social studies passages, and two science passages. The two expository passages are on the same topic —ancient Egypt, including The Nile River and Building Pyramids. The second of the two passages has been formatted to allow the examiner to engage in the think-aloud process with students, and the examiner copy provides a scoring grid to help the examiner keep track of the type of comments made by the reader. If the examiner does not wish to use think-alouds, a student sheet without think-aloud formatting is provided on the accompanying DVD. Because the second passage focuses on the same general topic as the first, it can be used as a pre–post assessment as long as the student's prior knowledge is considered. It can also be used for other purposes such as contrasting oral and silent reading and assessing note-taking ability.

Upper Middle School Passages

At the upper middle school level, there are six passages. Two passages representative of middle school literature selections are biographical or autobiographical in nature, two passages represent science content, and two represent social studies content. Like the sixth grade level, the two social studies (Immigration 1 and 2) and science passages (Life Cycle of Stars 1 and 2) are on the same topic, with the second passage in each category formatted for the use of the think-aloud process. As in the sixth grade level, the second passage can also be used for pre–post assessment of progress or other purposes. All the passages were taken from published literature, science, and social studies texts, so they are representative of classroom materials. Prior knowledge tasks allow the examiner to determine whether comprehension scores were due, in part, to the subject's level of prior knowledge.

High School Passages

At the high school level, there are three passages taken from representative literature, social studies, and science texts used at that level. The passages within each content area are sections of a biography in the case of literature or a chapter for social studies and science. Readability formulas for determining text level are not particularly useful at the high school level and different formulas provided us with a wide range of readability levels for a single selection. We reasoned that readability levels mattered less than the content typically chosen for high school textbooks. We have therefore included selections that were especially representative of high school content across several publishers.

All high school passages represent relatively unfamiliar topics: the Vietnam War, World War I, and viruses, and each passage is divided into three sections. The second section can be used for post-testing, for assessing note-taking ability, or for other similar purposes. The third section of each selection is formatted so it can be used for engaging in the think-aloud process.

We do not provide guidelines for scoring word identification on the high school passages. Our rationale is that students should read passages at this level silently. However, if a student demonstrates lack of comprehension after silently reading a high school passage and the examiner wishes to evaluate word identification, we suggest two options. The examiner can administer the high school word list, or the examiner can drop back to an upper middle school passage and ask the student to read it orally.

Use of the Passages

The passages are designed

1. To determine a student's independent, instructional, or frustration levels for word identification in context (pre-primer 1 through upper middle school)
2. To determine a student's independent, instructional, or frustration levels for comprehension
3. To assess a student's ability to read different types of text: narrative and expository text, text with and without pictures (pre-primer 1 through grade two), and text of varying familiarity
4. To assess a student's ability to comprehend in different modes: oral and silent (pre-primer 1 through upper middle school)
5. To assess a student's ability to use look-backs to locate missing or incorrect information (grade three through high school)
6. To assess the variety and quality of a student's think-alouds (grade six through high school)

Measures of Comprehension

The *QRI-5* assesses comprehension of all passages in two ways: retelling and questions. In addition, for passages at the third grade through high school levels, the examiner may utilize look-backs to evaluate the quality of comprehension further. In sixth grade through high school levels, the examiner may employ think-alouds as a further assessment of comprehension quality.

The comprehension measures are designed

1. To assess the quality of the reader's unaided recall
2. To assess the reader's understanding of the text when prompted with questions
3. To examine the quality of a student's comprehension during reading

Retelling. After reading the selection, the student is asked to retell the passage as though telling it to someone who never heard it before. The student's retelling is scored from a map of important idea units contained in the passage. Retelling for narrative passages is coded according to setting or background, goal, events, and resolution. Coding for expository passages focuses on main ideas and details. What the student is able to retell and the organization of that retelling can provide information about the reader's ability to recall important ideas that are structured in some logical way.

Questions. Next, the examiner asks the student two types of questions. Questions with answers stated explicitly in the text are called text-explicit questions. Questions with answers that the subject must infer from information in the text are called text-implicit questions. Answers to text-implicit questions must be tied to information in the story and not simply derived from prior knowledge. Independent, instructional, and frustration levels for comprehension are derived from scores on the question measure.

Look-Backs. At the third grade through high school levels, the examiner may use look-backs to assess comprehension further. After scoring the questions, the examiner can ask the student to look back in the text to locate missing information or to correct erroneous answers. Look-backs allow the examiner to differentiate between comprehension during reading and memory after reading. Students may understand a concept while reading but then forget it. As a result, they are unable to answer an explicit or implicit question. Look-backs are particularly informative when the student has read unfamiliar or difficult, concept-dense text. While skilled readers can generally employ skimming or rereading to locate information, less skilled readers are unable to do this successfully.

Think-Alouds. At the sixth grade through high school levels, the examiner can ask the student to think aloud while reading. The examiner asks the student to pause at designated segments of text signaled by the word **STOP** and describe what he or she is thinking at that point. A think-aloud scoring grid is provided to help examiners keep track of the type of comments made by the reader. A passage that examiners can use to model the think-aloud procedure is also included.

In summary, the *QRI-5* consists of graded word lists and narrative and expository passages. The word lists and passages, which range from pre-primer to high school levels, vary in familiarity, and prior knowledge is assessed before the student reads each passage. Comprehension is assessed through retelling, questions, look-backs, and think-alouds.

2 A Research Perspective

Since the first edition of the *QRI* was published, we have continued to read and conduct research on factors affecting word identification and comprehension as well as those related to usage of an IRI. Chapter 2 provides a brief summary of this research base.

READING ACQUISITION: A DEVELOPMENTAL PERSPECTIVE

Developmental descriptions of the reading process have been provided by Adams (1990), Chall (1983), Ehri (1991), Ehri and McCormick (2004), Gough and Juel (1991), Spear-Swerling and Sternberg (1996), and Stahl (2006). These descriptions suggest that the knowledge sources children use to construct meaning from text and the aspects of constructing meaning that give them trouble vary depending on their stage or level of reading acquisition. Children tend to move through several stages as they learn to recognize words and construct meaning. The first level has been termed the logographic stage (Ehri, 1991; Ehri & McCormick, 2004), the stage of visual-cue reading (Spear-Swerling & Sternberg, 1996), or the awareness stage (Stahl, 2006). Children understand that print stands for language and for meaning and they attempt to identify words; however, they do so using visual cues as opposed to sound cues. They may use the shape of a word or letter or the presence of a logo as a cue. For example, they can recognize "McDonald's" but only in the presence of the familiar golden arches. They might call any word that ends in *y* as "monkey" because the word has a tail at the end, just like a monkey.

Children then move to the next level, called the semialphabetic stage (Ehri, 1991; Ehri & McCormick, 2004), the stage of phonetic-cue word recognition (Spear-Swerling

& Sternberg, 1996), or the accuracy stage (Stahl, 2006). At this point, children recognize that sounds within words are represented by letters. Supported by developing phonemic awareness and emerging knowledge of grapheme–phoneme relationships, they begin to focus on letters and sounds usually in the initial and final positions. However, they have difficulty acquiring meaning directly from print without the aid of context, and they use context to facilitate word identification (Jett-Simpson & Leslie, 1997; Stanovich, 2000; Sulzby & Teale, 1991).

Gradually, children move to a phase of controlled word recognition (Spear-Swerling & Sternberg, 1996), where they make full use of letter–sound relationships but often do so slowly and laboriously. Aware that letters represent sounds in a consistent manner (Beck, 2006), they rely less on context. They become more economical in their word identification efforts and begin to use word chunks (i.e., *ap, ick*) to pronounce unfamiliar words (Chard, McDonagh, Lee, & Reece, 2007). They recognize that printed words contain onsets or beginning consonant sounds (*fl* as in "flip") and rimes or the chunk beginning with the first vowel in a syllable (*un* as in "fun"), and the use of known word patterns to identify unknown words becomes an important development in reading acquisition (Adams, 1990; Stahl, Duffy-Hester, & Dougherty Stahl, 2006).

The next stage has been termed sight word reading (Ehri, 1991) or automatic word recognition (Spear-Swerling & Sternberg, 1996). Children recognize many words accurately and automatically without the need of "sounding out." When they encounter unfamiliar words, their word recognition is rapid and automatic and context no longer plays a meaningful part. Instead, context becomes a "mechanism in the comprehension process" (Stanovich, 1993–1994, p. 282) and is often used to assign meanings to unknown words.

Spear-Swerling and Sternberg (1996) described the next level as the strategic reading stage. Students have mastered basic word-recognition skills. They can read familiar text with fluency and comprehend it fully and now focus on learning how to apply those same strategies to more difficult text and less familiar genres (Chall, 1983).

This developmental perspective does not imply rigid stages through which children pass at prescribed rates. Nor should it be inferred that at any point in learning to read, children are focused only on one aspect of reading. Stanovich (1980) described the interaction of different sources of information that students have available to them as they read. Beginning readers, having less knowledge of phoneme–grapheme relationships, use picture cues and other contextual elements to aid the word recognition process. A pronounced word may be a semantic fit but bear little resemblance to the actual word with regard to letters and sounds. When reading "Who do I see on the plant?" one child read, "Who do I see on the leaf?" As readers begin to develop knowledge of letter–sound patterns, pronounced words may resemble the actual words with regard to letters and sounds but not fit within the meaning of the text. When reading *Marva Finds a Friend,* one child read "looked" as "locked" and "cried" as "cared," both mispronunciations that seriously changed the meaning of the text. When readers develop automatic word identification, they are able to focus attention on learning different strategies for comprehending and remembering information from text.

We believe that assessment should observe developmental differences in learning to read. The *QRI-5* includes passages for assessment of the stages of beginning word identification. Pre-primer through third grade passages contain high-frequency words as well as words that contain regular and common letter–sound patterns. The passages focus on familiar topics and some include pictures. Our pilot data indicated that at the pre-primer and primer levels, texts with pictures were read more accurately by readers at these levels (Leslie & Caldwell, 1995). At the primer through second grade levels, pictures assisted retelling and comprehension, which suggests emerging use of context as an aid to comprehension as opposed to being a factor in word identification. Timed administration of the word lists and the determination of reading rate during passage reading allows for evaluation of a student's move into the stage of sight word reading. The gradual rise in reading rate on emergent through third grade passages suggests the students are taking less time to decode words and/or there are less words that need decoding. All levels in *QRI-5* include both narrative and expository text. Expository selections were taken from or modeled after representative classroom texts, which allows for assessment of a student's move to the stage of strategic reading.

FACTORS RELATED TO COMPREHENSION

Text Structure

Research has described the structures of narrative (Graesser, Golding, & Long, 1991; Johnson & Mandler, 1980; Stein & Glenn, 1979) and expository text (Meyer & Rice, 1984; Weaver & Kintsch, 1991). Narratives that follow the structure of fables (setting–character–goal/problem–events–resolution) have been found to be easier for children to recall than narratives without the major story components (Brennan, Bridge, & Winograd, 1986; Stein, 1979) and, throughout the elementary school years, narrative text is easier for children to recall and comprehend than expository text (Berkowitz & Taylor, 1981; Leslie & Caldwell, 1989; Leslie & Cooper, 1993; Pearson & Hamm, 2005). Paris, Carpenter, Paris, and Hamilton (2005) suggested that a "genuine predictor of reading comprehension is children's narrative reasoning, the ability to understand the elements and relations in goal-directed narratives" (p. 153).

It is highly likely that readers' familiarity with the structure of narratives is greater than their familiarity with the structures of expository text. Children have probably been read more narrative than expository texts. Primary grade instructional materials are predominantly narratives and the narrative texts with which children have the most experience tend to have a single common structure (Graesser, Golding, & Long, 1991; Graesser & Goodman, 1985; Mulcahy & Samuels, 1987). Another reason that narrative text is easier to comprehend may be related to readers' knowledge of content. Students tend to know more about the topics discussed in narrative writings compared to those usually presented in expository texts. Pearson and Hamm (2005) suggested that the difference between narrative and expository comprehension may actually be a function of assessment. The way in which understanding of the two genres is assessed may create "an artifactual difference," that is, we may test more central ideas in narratives than in nonfiction (p. 61).

In contrast to children's rather stable knowledge of narrative structure, their knowledge of expository structures is more variable (Englert & Hiebert, 1984; Klingner & Vaughn, 2004). Children may be less familiar with any single structure of expository text because of the variety of expository structures—sequence or time order, listing or description, compare and contrast, cause and effect, and problem and solution (Caldwell, 2008b). Skilled readers recognize and use these patterns to facilitate comprehension and memory (Goldman & Rakestraw, 2000) even though they rarely appear in pure form. While authors do not always clearly signal the pattern and may combine two or more patterns into a single text segment, skilled readers tend to structure their recall according to the dominant structure (Meyer, 2003).

Different languages and cultures have different structures for telling stories. Although all cultures have stories with episodic structures, the number of episodes may vary (Westby, 2004). Cultural groups also vary in the importance that they give to different components of the story. Several cultures emphasize settings and often omit the event sequence. Matsuyama (1983) reported that 80% of Japanese folktales did not have a goal for the main character. Although many cultures speak Spanish and the structures of their stories differ, one common feature is omission of pronouns when retelling important story segments, under the assumption that the character can be easily inferred from the story (Mahecha, 2003).

When an expected narrative structure is not present, the reader may reorganize the retelling to fit the anticipated structure. Students who encounter a story structure different from what is familiar to them may retell the story according to their cultural format. For example, Japanese children accustomed to folktales that do not include goals for the main character might not include goals in their retelling. Other readers may reduce the number of narrative episodes or combine two episodes into one (Kintsch & Green, 1978). Users of an IRI must be aware that a student's native language can influence recall of English stories and that such retelling is not necessarily inaccurate or poorly organized.

QRI-5, like previous editions, offers both narrative and expository texts at all levels. This allows the examiner to contrast comprehension following narrative text with comprehension following expository text. Our experience suggests that students may attain higher instructional levels in narrative text than in expository text.

Prior Knowledge

It has been shown repeatedly that readers with greater prior knowledge, consistent with the content in the text, recall and comprehend better than those with less prior knowledge (Alvermann, Smith, & Readance, 1985; Lipson, 1983). This finding is true for adults (Anderson, Reynolds, Schallert, & Goetz, 1977) and children (Pearson, Hansen, & Gordon, 1979; Taft & Leslie, 1985). Furthermore, the results can be generalized to poor readers as well as good readers (Stevens, 1980; Taylor, 1979). In fact, research has found that good and poor readers' ability to recall and summarize did not differ significantly if the groups were similar in their levels of knowledge (Recht & Leslie, 1988). The implications of these findings for assessment seem obvious (Johnston, 1984). A student with high knowledge of particular content that is consistent with the information presented in the text will be able to recall more information and answer more questions correctly than on material of the same readability about which the student had less or inconsistent knowledge.

There are many ways to measure prior knowledge (Holmes & Roser, 1987): multiple-choice tests, interviews, oral free associations, written free associations, open-ended questions, and oral or written predictions. Valencia, Stallman, Commeyras, Pearson, and Hartman (1991) concluded that different prior knowledge assessments may measure different aspects of prior knowledge. Free-association tasks have been shown to be significantly correlated with comprehension of narrative (Langer, 1984; Leslie & Caldwell, 1989, 1990; Leslie & Cooper, 1993) and expository text (Hare, 1982; Langer, 1984; Leslie & Caldwell, 1989, 1990; Taft & Leslie, 1985). Research (Leslie & Cooper, 1993) also has suggested that instructions for a free-association task, which ask for precise responses rather than general associations, were more predictive of sixth graders' comprehension and retelling of narrative text. Also, prediction tasks have been shown to correlate somewhat with comprehension, although the findings are less consistent than those using free-association concepts (Leslie & Cooper, 1993; Valencia & Stallman, 1989).

We have often been asked why we do not include questions that assess vocabulary after each *QRI* passage. While we acknowledge the importance of vocabulary knowledge as a critical component of comprehension (Paris, Carpenter, Paris, & Hamilton, 2005), what information is actually acquired by asking for the definition of a single word following the reading of a passage? If the word was explicitly defined in the passage, a correct answer suggests the reader can comprehend literal elements. If the word was not so defined, it suggests an ability to draw an inference. However, the correct definition of a single word does not offer any indication of the scope of a reader's vocabulary knowledge. We believe that our key concept questions are a more sensitive measure, not of a reader's total vocabulary base, but of vocabulary that is relevant to the comprehension of a specific selection.

The *QRI-5* measures prior knowledge by asking children to answer questions that tap their understanding of key concepts (Langer, 1984). In addition, a prediction task based on the concepts and the title of the selection is provided. Our pilot data suggested that at the first grade level and above, both conceptual knowledge and prediction were significantly correlated with some form of comprehension, be it retelling, answers to questions without look-backs, or answers to questions with look-backs.

Oral and Silent Reading

Although overall differences in oral and silent reading comprehension may be minimal, some children may comprehend better in one mode than in the other. Results of research examining differences between oral and silent reading comprehension are mixed. The most consistent findings appear to be that poor readers at the fourth grade level and below tend to comprehend better when reading orally (Burge, 1983; Swalm, 1972). Rate differences may also suggest the reader's stage of reading development. Children for whom oral and silent rates are similar may not yet have moved into the stage of automatic word recognition. Generally, fluent readers read faster silently than orally.

In the *QRI-5*, multiple passages at the same level allow for a comparison of comprehension following oral and silent reading with regard to retelling and question answering. Multiple passages also allow for examination of possible rate differences between the two modes.

Questions and Look-Backs

Question content is broadly categorized as literal or explicit questions and inferential or implicit questions (Applegate, Quinn, & Applegate, 2002; Bowyer-Crane & Snowling, 2005; Caldwell, 2008b; Ciardiello, 1998; Graesser & Person, 1994; Kintsch & Kintsch, 2005). Literal questions focus on what was explicitly stated in the text and usually begin with such words as "who," "what," "where," and "when." There are several variations or levels of inferential/implicit questions (Caldwell, 2008b; Leslie & Caldwell, 2009). Low-level inference questions have relatively obvious answers. These may be stated in the text but in different language than the question stem or they may require connecting text segments that are not signaled by grammatical markers such as "because." Higher-order inferential questions ask students to move beyond the text in order to predict, hypothesize, reconstruct, form opinions, or offer rationales. Applegate, Quinn, and Applegate (2002) also described response items that ask the reader to address the significance or meaning of the passage as a whole. They examined eight published informal reading inventories and differentiated inferential questions into low-level, high-level, and response items. The percentages for low-level inference questions ranged from 6.6% through 36.6%; high-level inferences ranged from 0.8% to 17.5%. Percentages for inference questions on *QRI-4* were 23.7% for low-level inferences, 17.5% for high level inferences, and 18.4% for response-based inferences. Questions that ask students to engage in higher-order reasoning tend to be indicative of a deeper form of comprehension than that revealed by literal questioning (Graesser, Baggett, & Williams, 1996; Kintsch, 2005; McNamara, Kintsch, Songer, & Kintsch, 1996).

Little research has been done on the quality of questions. Few studies of technical adequacy exist (Hamilton & Shinn, 2003) and these generally take the form of correlations with standardized measures (Fuchs, Fuchs, & Maxwell, 1988). A serious issue with using questions is their passage dependency, that is, whether they can be answered correctly without reading the passage. This generally occurs when students already know much of the text content prior to reading and can infer answers based on extensive prior knowledge.

Another issue concerning question usage is whether students answer the questions from memory or have access to the text (Leslie & Caldwell, 2009). Looking back in the text to answer questions clearly changes the nature of the question-answering task (Johnston, 1984). However, it also differentiates between understanding during reading and memory for what was read and understood (Leslie & Caldwell, 2006). While research suggests that students younger than eighth grade rarely use spontaneous look-backs (Garner & Reis, 1981), Leslie and Caldwell (2001, 2006) found that students with levels above third grade were able to use look-backs effectively; that is, they were able to skim the text, find the location of the answer, and respond with a correct answer that was unavailable to them without looking back. Palincsar, Magnusson, Pesko, and Hamlin (2005) asked fourth graders to return to the text in order to answer questions and described the process as "one of constructing and revising coherent and sensible meaning" (p. 275). If looking back increases comprehension, this suggests that assessments that do not allow look-backs may actually underestimate a student's level of comprehension.

The *QRI-5* includes the option of asking students to engage in look-backs after answering questions in order to resolve comprehension failures. We recognize that asking students to look back is not the same as spontaneous look-backs but we believe that examining whether students, when prompted, can look back and correct or add to answers provides valuable information for instruction. Our pilot research indicated that students with instructional levels at or above third grade were able to increase their explicit and implicit comprehension scores by looking back in the text. Prior to this level, a focus on word identification frequently resulted in the student rereading the entire text rather than looking back and locating the section that contained the relevant information.

Retelling

Measuring retelling after reading has taken different forms. Kintsch and Van Dijk (1978) measured recall as the percentage of propositions retold by the reader with a proposition defined as a predicate and one or more objects such as agent, object, or goal. Others have broken sentences into clauses that consist of a main verb (Kendeou & van den Broek, 2005; Magliano, Trabasso, & Graesser, 1999; van den Broek, Lorch, Linderholm, & Gustafson, 2001). Retelling has also been defined as the total number of words retold (Fuchs, Fuchs, & Hamlett, 1989; Roberts, Good, & Corcoran, 2005) and the percentage of words that are exact matches or synonyms of text words (Fuchs, Fuchs, & Maxwell, 1988).

The inclusion of retelling formats into recently published informal reading inventories (Bader, 2002; Burns & Roe, 2002; Leslie & Caldwell, 2006; Stieglitz, 2002) suggests that asking students to recall and retell text is a valuable assessment tool. Fuchs, Fuchs, and Maxwell (1988) found correlations between .76 and .82 for different forms of retelling scores and standardized reading comprehension tests. Leslie and Caldwell (2006) found significant correlations between retelling and comprehension as measured by questions for upper middle school and high school text.

However, retellings do present difficulties as an assessment tool (Leslie & Caldwell, 2009). They may underestimate the comprehension of some children because of linguistic demands required by the retelling process (Francis, Fletcher, Catts, & Tomblin, 2005; Palincsar, Magnussen, Pesko, & Hamlin, 2005). Retellings are difficult and time-consuming to score because the text must be broken into units to which the student's responses are matched. Because narrative and expository text have different structures, the quality of literal recall is often measured using story maps for narratives and text maps for expository selections (Pearson & Hamm, 2005).

In addition to breaking the text into units of some kind, using retelling as an assessment tool demands attention to extra text comments such as inferences. Students' retellings generally involve more than literal recall. They include inferences, personal comments or observations, and unrelated or erroneous remarks. Limiting recall scoring to literal components may provide an incomplete picture of the student's comprehension. In order to address extra text comments, retellings are often scored according to qualitative rubrics that include such components as gist/main idea statements, details/ story elements, interpretive ideas, generalizations, retelling coherence, retelling completeness, use of linguistic/language conventions, and inclusion of additional information not in the passage (Brown, Pressley, Van Meter, & Schuder, 1996; Hall, Markham, & Culatta, 2005; Irwin & Mitchell, 1983; Romero, Paris, & Brem, 2005). Few numerical guidelines exist for describing the completeness of recall. Our pilot data indicated that the amount of retelling comments varied across passages and passage types with higher recall evident in narrative passages.

The *QRI-5* provides retelling scoring grids that are based on narrative and expository structure. Narrative retellings are scored according to recall that addresses setting/ background, goal, events, and resolutions. Expository retellings are scored according to recall that focuses on main ideas and details. In all passages, space is provided to record nonliteral elements of recall such as inferences and reader comments.

Think-Alouds

Asking readers to read a selection and think out loud as they do so provides valuable information about the strategies that readers use as they attempt to comprehend text. It offers the opportunity to gather observations about the thinking that occurs during the reading process. Over a decade ago, Pressley and Afflerbach (1995) provided a comprehensive summary of studies that have examined this think-aloud process.

There is evidence that skilled readers and those with higher levels of prior knowledge employ more and varied think-aloud strategies than poorer readers or those struggling with unfamiliar text. Goldman (1997) noted that individuals who used a variety of strategies and attempted to build relationships between text ideas demonstrated better recall. Similarly, Crain-Thoreson, Lippman, and McClendon-Magnuson (1997) reported that successful comprehension was associated with "knowledge-transforming activities" during the think-aloud process (p. 586). Readers who connected the text to their background knowledge, constructed inferences, and integrated information across the text demonstrated higher comprehension. Similar results were noted by Chou-Hare and Smith (1982), Kavale and Schreiner (1979), Myers, Lytle, Palladino, Devenpeck, and Green (1990), and Zwaan and Brown (1996). In light of this, we have decided to emphasize a think-aloud component as one possible alternative for identifying why a student may demonstrate inadequate comprehension.

Readers of varying ages have engaged in think-alouds: university students (Garner, 1982); high school students (Olshavsky, 1976–1977; Rogers, 1991); middle school students (Bereiter & Bird, 1985; Caldwell & Leslie, 2003/2004; Chou-Hare & Smith, 1982; Kavale & Schreiner, 1979); and primary school children (Coté & Goldman, 1998; Coté, Goldman, & Saul, 1998; Myers, 1988; Myers, Lytle, Palladino, Devenpeck, & Green, 1990). Apparently, with appropriate instructions and modeling, learners of most ages can effectively engage in thinking aloud while reading.

Researchers use a variety of coding systems to classify think-alouds (Bereiter & Bird, 1985; Coté, Goldman, & Saul, 1998; Crain-Thoreson, Lippman, & McClendon-Magnuson, 1997; Myers, Lytle, Palladino, Devenpeck, & Green, 1990; Olshavsky, 1976–1977). Many of these systems are quite similar, varying only in the language used to describe the think-aloud comment. For our pilot study, we devised a coding system based on those comments identified most often in the literature.

Is there a link between the assessment and identification of think-aloud strategies and reading comprehension instruction? Instruction in many classrooms actively teaches readers to engage in many of the strategies identified in the think-aloud literature, such as predicting, self-questioning, summarizing, and checking understanding (Nist & Kirby, 1986; Pressley & Afflerbach, 1995).

Traditional assessment measures often have predictive validity; that is, good performance on these measures tends to predict average or above-average classroom performance. However, such measures do not assess process and offer no suggestions for increasing learning. Think-aloud data may be a process measure that can suggest instructional directions. For this reason, we have included think-alouds in the *QRI-5*. In our pilot, we carefully modeled each of the think-aloud strategies that we intended to score before asking the students to think aloud on their own. A recent study (Caldwell & Leslie, in press) found that, on the sixth grade and upper middle school level passages, thinking aloud increased the proportion of text-based associative inferences in retelling. However, the more text-based associative inferences made in retelling, the *lower* the student's scores on comprehension questions. This surprising finding indicates that the associative inferences, which tend only to embellish the text, may interrupt students' processing of complex text and therefore, the text base necessary for answering our comprehension questions is impoverished.

FACTORS RELATED TO WORD IDENTIFICATION

Speed and Automaticity

As readers practice the accurate identification of words, they begin to read these words with less conscious attention to letter–sound matching and therefore more rapidly. Although automaticity and speed in word identification are different constructs (Stanovich, Cunningham, & West, 1981), reading rate can suggest the presence of automaticity.

Perfetti's (1985, 1988) verbal efficiency theory hypothesizes that children who do not develop the ability to read words accurately and quickly will encounter difficulty in comprehension. Because most of their attention is directed toward identifying individual words, they are unable to access word meanings efficiently and integrate sentence meanings across an entire passage. LaBerge and Samuels (1985) also stressed the importance of fast and accurate automatic word identification. Both word identification and comprehension require attention on the part of the reader. Because attentional resources are limited, if more attention is directed to word identification, less is available for comprehension.

The *QRI-5* measures word-identification speed (and automaticity) in two ways. The timed portions of the word lists provide one measure. Our pilot data showed that the number of words read within one second predicts reading rate in context better than the total number of words read correctly.

Some may argue that the use of word lists for assessment is not an authentic task. We agree. Readers do not curl up with a good list of words. However, the ability to identify words accurately and quickly out of context is a characteristic of the skilled reader (Perfetti, 1985, 1988; Stahl, 2006; Stanovich, 1980, 1991b). Therefore, using word lists may provide an important piece of assessment information. Readers who take more than one second to identify a word accurately may not have achieved automaticity for that word.

The *QRI-5* provides another measure of word-identification speed: rate of reading as measured in words per minute or correct words per minute on the passages. Reading rate is affected by a variety of factors (Carver, 1990). Rate varies with the purpose of the reader and the process chosen. Text difficulty, as determined by the structure of the text, the familiarity of the content, and the difficulty level of the author's vocabulary, can be important determiners of reading rate. Reading rate can also vary according to the mode of reading (oral versus silent), the age of the reader, and reading skill. Finally, reading rate is also determined by individual cognitive processing speeds. The complexity of variables affecting rate suggests that hard-and-fast norms may be impossible to formulate. In Section 9, we offer some general suggestions for evaluating reading rate based on our pilot data.

One might argue that rate of reading as measured in words per minute (WPM) is primarily an indicator of speed. Another measure of rate that is an index of both accuracy and speed is correct words per minute (CWPM) (Fuchs, Fuchs, Hosp, & Jenkins, 2001; Kame'enui & Simmons, 2001). The concept of correct words per minute (often termed oral reading fluency) has its origin in the field of curriculum-based measurement (Deno, 1985; Fuchs & Fuchs, 1992, 1999; Fuchs, Fuchs, & Maxwell, 1988; Good, Simmons, & Kame'enui, 2001). Curriculum-based measurement is the process of using grade-level classroom materials to assess students at regular intervals throughout the year. The number of CWPM has been described as a valid and reliable measure of student progress (Fuchs & Fuchs, 1999; Fuchs, Fuchs, & Maxwell, 1988) and as an indicator of general reading competence (Kame'enui & Simmons, 2001). Good, Simmons, and Kame'enui (2001) and Hasbrouck and Tindal (1992, 2006) have determined classroom norms for correct words per minute.

Fluency has become an important and popular concept. Many articles and even books are devoted to explanations of how to assess and develop it and the majority of early reading assessments contain some measure of oral reading fluency (Caldwell, 2008a; Caldwell & Leslie, 2009; Johns & Berglund, 2002; Kuhn, Schwanenflugel, Morris, Morrow, Woo, Meisinger, Sevcik, Bradley, & Stahl, 2006; Morrow, Kuhn, & Schwanenflugel, 2006/2007; Pikulski & Chard, 2005; Rasinski, Padek, McKeon, Wilfong, Friedauer, & Heim, 2005; Samuels, 2007; Southwest Educational Development Laboratory, 2008; Walczyk & Griffith-Ross, 2007). Why is fluency so popular? Fluency is highly correlated with comprehension; that is, fluency rates tend to predict comprehension at least on standardized assessment measures. Unfortunately, some have erroneously interpreted prediction as causality and have assumed that assessing and developing fluency will automatically lead to increased comprehension. (Certainly assessing and practicing fluency is an easier task than designing and delivering effective comprehension instruction.) However, increase of fluency may or may not lead to similar increases in comprehension. Although fluency suggests that the student has cognitive capacity for paying attention to comprehension, it does not indicate how or if that capacity is used (Caldwell, 2008b). Paris, Carpenter, Paris, and Hamilton (2005) cautioned that "fast and accurate word identification does not always lead to high levels of comprehension, and neither does slow, less accurate word recognition necessarily imply poor comprehension" (p. 136). The disappointing results of Reading First grants that tended to emphasize fluency assessment and practice suggests that stressing fluency above or in lieu of comprehension instruction may be a mistake (Glenn, 2008).

Knowledge of Letter–Sound Matching

A common assessment practice in many recent IRIs is to qualitatively evaluate knowledge of letter–sound matching through a process called *miscue analysis*. This was originated by Goodman (1965, 1967), who referred to word pronunciation errors as miscues influenced by three possible cue systems. The graphophonic cue system refers to the relationships between graphemes (letter and letter combinations) and phonemes (units of sound). If a reader pronounces "jump" as "junk," one can infer that the reader is utilizing sound cues in the initial and medial positions. The syntactic cue system refers to the position of the word within the syntax of the sentence. If the reader reads "Mary sat on his chair" as "Mary sat on a chair," one can infer that sentence syntax influenced the substitution of an indefinite article for a pronoun that is at variance with the feminine subject of the sentence. Semantic cues are meaning cues obtained from the content of what is being read. For example, if a reader reads the sentence "I received six presents for my birthday" as "I got six presents for my birthday," one can infer that the reader is using semantic information in saying "got" for "received." Goodman's theory was that reader use of context, as exemplified by the semantic and syntactic cue systems, was an important and strong influence in word pronunciation (1965, 1967). He believed that, as readers develop word recognition skill and speed, they use less graphophonic cues. Therefore, miscues that indicate context usage are strengths because they indicate developing expertise on the part of the reader and a focus on meaning. On the other hand, overreliance on letter-sound cues suggests a poor reader or one who may be headed for trouble.

While the majority of IRIs presently on the market offer some form of miscue analysis that focuses on the three cue systems, the viability of extensive reliance on such an analysis has been questioned. First, additional research has called into question Goodman's theory regarding the role of context in efficient word identification (Nicholson, Lillas, & Rzoska,1988; Stahl, 2006; Stahl & Hiebert, 2005; Stanovich, 1991b, 2004). Rayner and Pollatsek (1995) believed that the graphophonic cue system takes precedence over the syntactic and semantic ones. Stanovich (2004) explained that when letter–sound knowledge is emerging or deficient, readers compensate by use of context. Word-identification skill does not depend on contextual prediction but rather "the level of word recognition skill determines the extent to which contextual information will be relied on" (p. 466). To put it another way, as readers develop skill in using the graphophonic cue system, they use context less and less to identify words. Finally, context becomes a factor in the comprehension process as opposed to the word-identification process (Stanovich,

1993/1994). In line with this, McKenna and Picard (2006/2007) suggest that meaningful miscues, those that retain meaning but have little similarity to the letters in the text, may not reflect a strength on the part of the reader. They may actually be evidence of inadequate decoding skills as the reader attempts to compensate for weak decoding by use of context. This suggests the need to reevaluate the miscue analysis process and interpretations drawn from it. We believe that miscue analysis can be helpful but only if interpreted in accordance with current research.

Can letter and sound patterns drawn from miscue analysis provide information on a reader's skill needs in the area of decoding? McKenna and Picard (2006/2007) did not believe so, because such needs may be "masked by context" (p. 379). Miscue analysis, as traditionally used, describes miscues made during oral reading of passages. A reader aided by context may be able to offer a pronunciation that is similar to the passage word while unable to identify the same word or word unit in a different situation. To put it another way, the same letter and sound patterns may or may not be an issue if presented in a list devoid of context. This suggests that phonics must be evaluated apart from context.

Users of QRI-5 can examine oral reading behavior quantitatively and qualitatively. The quantitative criteria used to determine independent, instructional, and frustration levels follow the recommendations of Harris and Sipay (1985) and Betts (1946). Our pilot data suggested that the best predictor of instructional-level comprehension is 95% for Total Acceptability, the measure of accuracy attained when only uncorrected meaning-change miscues are counted. While we include Total Acceptability as an option for those who believe that semantically acceptable miscues should not be counted as errors, we recommend the use of Total Accuracy in determining reading levels, a practice endorsed by McKenna and Picard (2006/2007). We do this because counting all miscues takes less scoring time than deciding whether a miscue did or did not substantively change meaning. In addition, counting all miscues represents a more reliable practice because examiners can vary in their interpretation of what constitutes a meaning-change miscue. For example, while many individuals might not consider the substitution of "a" for "the" as a miscue that changes meaning, others might disagree and distinguish between the indefinite ("a") and definite ("the") articles. In our classes, we have noticed similar disagreements regarding whether meaning is changed by miscues such as the following: "song" for "singing"; "broken" for "old"; "find" for "get"; "drop" for "die"; "special" for "precious"; and "shiny" for "waxy." In Section 9, we offer guidelines for determining whether a miscue did or did not change meaning.

In addition, we encourage qualitative miscue analysis to ascertain how much attention the reader is paying to the graphic elements of the text and to meaning. We caution, however, that miscues focusing on the graphophonic cue system represent a strength, not a weakness. We also suggest, based on pilot data, that reader self-correction may indicate whether the reader is paying attention to decoding or to overall passage meaning. We examined the self-correction strategies of children reading pre-primer through third grade passages. We distinguished between miscues that changed meaning and were corrected and miscues that did not change meaning but were also corrected. In levels pre-primer through two, there were little differences between the two. Children were as liable to correct a miscue that distorted meaning as they were to correct one that did not. In level three, there was a change; children tended to correct significantly more meaning-change miscues than those that did not change meaning. While our pilot data needs to be validated with larger numbers of children, we do suggest the following. At instructional levels of pre-primer through grade two, children are still focused on pronouncing words and, as a result, little distinction is made between meaning-change or non-meaning-change correction attempts. However, at the third grade instructional level, developing word-pronunciation skill and increased fluency allow them to focus more on overall passage meaning. Thus they correct more meaning-change miscues. We have revised our miscue analysis worksheet in Section 9 to reflect this alternative interpretation.

At the lower levels (pre-primer through level three), we encourage the examiner to differentiate between words that contain common and regular letter units such as vowel phonograms versus words that contain irregular or uncommon sound patterns. For example, the word "hill" contains a very common vowel pattern, *ill,* found in approximately 26 single-syllable words (Fry, 1998). In *QRI-5,* we have differentiated word list words at the pre-primer through first grade levels into two general kinds: those containing regular sound patterns and those that do not. Why is this important? Children who learn a regular sound pattern in one word can easily transfer this knowledge to other words (Beck, 2006; Cunningham, 2000; Fry, 1998; Gaskins, Ehri, Cress, O'Hara, & Donnelly, 1996; Stahl, Duffy-Hester, & Dougherty Stahl, 2006). The recognition and use of such common patterns can provide a critical element in phonics instruction.

The *QRI-5* provides a list of low-frequency words that contain 18 frequent phonograms (Beck, 2006; Fry, 1998; Gaskins, Downer, & the teachers of the Benchmark School, 1997). These phonograms are present in words on the word lists and in from three to 13 passages at the pre-primer through first grade levels. The words that contain the phonograms in the lists and passages are high-frequency words as is appropriate for those levels. However, Leslie & Calhoon (1995) found that the ability to read a phonogram in a high-frequency word may not indicate that the child has fully analyzed the word into constituent phonemes. To put it another way, the child may recognize the word by sight, not by knowing its spelling pattern. Our list of low-frequency words containing frequent and common phonograms allows the examiner to determine if the child actually knows the phonogram and is approaching economy of word identification that is characteristic of the stage of controlled word recognition.

Role of Dialect in Coding Miscues

Oral reading accuracy is a determination of how accurately someone reads a specific text, and practitioners must make distinctions between the oral language pronunciation of a word and a reading error (or miscue). Sometimes this is quite difficult. First, humans do not always hear exactly what is said. Also, distinguishing between a miscue and an acceptable pronunciation often depends on whether the listener or teacher is familiar with the dialect patterns of the reader. If not, differences in pronunciation may be mistaken as oral reading errors or miscues.

This becomes seriously problematic when teachers who use Standard American English (SAE) are listening to children who use a nonstandard dialect, such as African American English (AAE), or whose pronunciation reflects the sound system of another language, such as Spanish. Teachers who are not sensitive to variations in the sound patterns of the students' oral language may tend to score such differences as miscues. Therefore, it is incumbent on all teachers to understand the patterns of a student's oral language to accurately interpret oral reading pronunciation and discern a student's miscue patterns in reading. This is not a small task, for teachers typically listen to the meaning of what children say and not the many forms (phonologic, morphologic, and syntactic) in which meaning is communicated.

Much research has focused on the structure and usage of AAE. The context of use determines the form of language and thus, children who speak AAE vary their dialect patterns across language contexts (Thompson, Craig, & Washington, 2004). Preschool and K–5 AAE speakers vary their use of AAE features in free-play contexts versus picture descriptions (Washington, Craig, & Kushmaul, 1998). Additionally, third grade speakers of AAE were found to use AAE dialect patterns in oral language tasks, such as picture description, to a greater degree than when engaged in oral reading or writing tasks. Picture description tasks appear to be a more sensitive method than spontaneous conversation to obtain a representative sample of a student's oral dialect patterns for comparison of miscues in oral reading (Thompson, Craig, & Washington, 2004).

Craig and Washington (2004b) listed 24 morpho-syntactic examples of AAE that are common in school-aged children. The most frequent seem to be the zero copula and auxiliary form of "to be" ("Where the dog?") and subject-verb agreement ("Now she need some candy"). However, AAE dialect changes across grade levels (Craig & Washington, 2004b), and as children become more competent readers, use of AAE features decreases during oral reading. This shift has been found to be most dramatic between second and third grade.

Research on child AAE is incomplete in that it has primarily focused on morpho-syntactic characteristics. Less attention has been paid to phonological features, and it is often difficult to distinguish dialect patterns from developing sound production (Craig & Washington, 2004a). In addition, interpreting dialect forms is often considered apart from vocabulary knowledge. For example, does a child mispronounce a word because of dialect or because that specific word is not part of his or her oral vocabulary base? Early research determined that dialect during oral reading was unrelated to reading comprehension; however, Craig and Washington (2004a) questioned acceptance of this conclusion because such research was based on features of adult AAE that are different from the AAE produced by children. Craig and Washington suggest that it may not be the specific types of AAE features produced by the child that are related to literacy but the frequencies with which they are produced. They refer to this as *dialect density* and suggest that there may be a relationship between dialect density and literacy acquisition.

What does this mean for users of *QRI-5?* Certainly, interpretation of miscues during oral reading should reflect the teacher's awareness of the child's spoken language whether it be AAE or Spanish. In Section 9 on the DVD we provide some guidelines for doing this.

FACTORS RELATED TO THE USE OF AN INFORMAL READING INVENTORY

Passage Leveling

What makes one selection more difficult than another? A common method to describe text difficulty is the use of a readability formula. There are a variety of readability formulas. Some are meant to be used on primary or elementary text. Others focus on higher-level text and adult readers. However, all are based on two components. One is word difficulty estimated as the frequency of the word. For example, "matriarch" is much less frequent in our language than "mother," so a text containing "matriarch" might have a higher readability level. Word length is another aspect of word difficulty. "Received" is a longer word than "got" and its inclusion in a text would increase the readability estimate. Another readability component is sentence complexity, often measured by sentence length. Thus, "Because she needed sugar, Mary jumped in the car and quickly drove to the store" would increase text readability more than "Mary needed sugar. She jumped in the car. She quickly drove to the store."

Readability formulas provide a general estimate of difficulty level but many other components contribute to the complexity of a text. Is the text coherent and well written? Does it include pictures? Do headings accurately indicate content? Is it on a familiar topic? Is the topic interesting to the reader? Is the structure of the text clearly signaled? Is the purpose of the text to entertain or to inform? To what extent does the language of the text parallel spoken language or does the language represent a stylized and formal form of writing? Readability formulas do not account for these components and a text leveled as appropriate for the fifth grade level may be very easy for some fifth graders and extremely difficult for others. Readability formulas provide very rough estimates of difficulty and are aptly described by Allington (2001) as "crude." And yet, he defended readability formulas as "providing a ballpark estimate of text difficulty. Even a ballpark estimate is better than none at all" (p. 48).

In attempting to level passages for multiple editions of the *QRI,* we have subjected each passage to a variety of readability formulas using the technology available at the time. We moved from counting words, syllables, and sentences and using a handheld calculator for applying the formula to a computer program that did all the calculations for us and insured a greater degree of accuracy. Passages were leveled using Readability Calculations Windows version 7.0 (Micro Power and Light Company, 2007) using the following formulas: the Powers-Sumner-Kearl Formula, the Flesch Reading Ease Formula, the Dale-Chall Formula, the Spache Formula, and the Fry Graph. We have also used the Harris-Jacobsen Formula for passages below grade three. At every level, we found wide fluctuations in the grade levels assigned by different formulas. We chose the level agreed on by at least two out of three appropriate formulas and then tested the appropriateness of the level through extensive piloting. Passages were included in the *QRI* if readers at a specific grade level achieved instructional-level scores in word identification or comprehension and if piloting indicated that the passage was more difficult than the next lower level and easier than the next higher level. Thus, third grade passages were more difficult than second grade texts for our pilot sample; similarly, they were easier than the fourth grade selections.

Since the first edition of the *QRI,* additional ways of determining text difficulty have emerged. Beginning texts used in guided reading have been grouped according to such characteristics as length, print size and layout, difficulty of vocabulary and concepts, language structure, genre, text structure, language patterns such as predictability, and support offered by illustrations (Fountas & Pinnell, 2006). Fountas and Pinnell described 16 guided reading levels crossing kindergarten through third grade: nine levels for kindergarten and first grade text, four levels for grade two, and three levels for grade three. Because of many requests from teachers, we have designated guided reading levels for our pre-primer through third grade passages (see page 461 and Section 15 on the DVD). However, we must issue a word of caution. While the guided reading levels assigned to our passages were not piloted and they represent professional judgments on the part of the levelers, we can provide data to show that adjacent passages are easier or harder.

A relatively recent measure, the Lexile scale, has been developed based on the readability measures of word frequency and average sentence length. What makes the lexile unique is that a reader's ability and text readability are on the same developmental scale (Stenner, Burdick, Sanford, & Burdick, 2006). The Lexile scale is a transformed logit scale where 1 logit equals 180 lexiles (L). Therefore, when we say that a reader has an

L of 500, it means that he or she is predicted to be able to comprehend a text with a 500L with 75% comprehension on a multiple-choice test. The process for determining a reader's lexile is very different from what most of us consider a valid measure of reading comprehension. A text of 125 words of some difficulty is given to a student and comprehension is assessed with one question. This process continues with different segments of 125 words from various texts (there is no indication that these texts are contiguous). In a study of the accuracy of lexiles, Stenner et al. (2006) tested over 1,000 students in grade three, 893 in grade five, and 1,500 in grade eight. Each item writer developed one question on each of 30 text passages, for a total of 90 items. The standard error of measurement (SEM) is reported to be 32L for a short text (i.e., 500 words), but is reduced significantly by a much longer text (e.g., a text of 900 words would have a SEM of 2L).

To determine the lexile of a reader requires the student to read a series of 125-word text segments and answer one question on each. Then, given the lexile of the segments the mean text lexile on which the student can read with 75% accuracy (on a multiple-choice test) is considered to be the student's lexile. The *QRI-5* requested lexile levels from Metametrics Corporation on each of our passages at second grade difficulty and above (see pages 468–469 and Section 15 on the DVD). Second grade was chosen because the lexile scale does not evaluate the role of pictures or predictable text, as well as other graphic features. Therefore, we determined that a lexile is inappropriate for first grade materials. How to interpret these texts is a bit of a challenge. The lexile is an index of the difficulty of a text, but can we say that a student who scores 75% or higher on the most difficult passage has a lexile equal to that of the passage? That, of course, is what people want to conclude, but because we have not obtained student lexiles for our pilot group such a conclusion is highly questionable. Section 15 explains readability issues in more detail.

Response to Intervention

In 2004 the Individual with Disabilities Education Act (IDEA) was reauthorized to give schools and districts the option of identifying students as learning disabled based on their response to instruction. In the past, identification of a learning disability rested on an observed discrepancy between intelligence as measured by an individually administered IQ test and classroom performance. Now, if a student's performance "is dramatically inferior to that of his peers, the student may be determined to have a learning disability" (Bender & Shores, 2007, p. 7). Why is this important? Schools receive federal money to provide instruction for students with special needs and funding is closely tied to the identification of a learning disability. This new initiative has been termed *Response to Intervention* or *RtI.*

RtI embodies three tiers. The first is classroom instruction. The teacher implements screening measures to identify students who are achieving below the level of their peers. These students then move into the second tier of instruction involving additional assessments to identify specifics of the problem and provision of small-group instruction to address student needs. A student who still fails to respond adequately moves into the third tier of instruction, which is usually individualized in format. At this point, a learning disability is generally identified. It is very probable that an IRI could be used as a screening measure or progress monitoring tool for all three tiers.

At the present time, explanations of student progress in RtI emphasize "short, quick and easy-to-administer probes" (McCook, 2006, p. 14). This does pose a problem for use of an IRI which, unfortunately, is not short, quick, and easy to administer. The most popular RtI assessment is oral reading fluency, the number of words read correctly in one or two minutes (CWPM). Other RtI probes include the number of sounds and letters recognized and number of words correctly spelled within a one- to three-minute time frame (Wright, 2007). For comprehension assessment the student orally reads a passage for one minute and then retells it with retelling scored as the number of words in the passage offered within a one-minute time frame. A second form of comprehension assessment is a three-minute cloze or maze task where the student supplies missing words in a passage or selects them from three or four choices.

At the present time, the RtI assessment and intervention model primarily centers on early reading performance (Bender & Shores, 2007; Brown-Chidsey & Steege, 2005; McCook, 2006; Wright, 2007) and involves sound-based/phonological measures and reading fluency, which are predictive of future reading performance. However, Gersten and Dimino (2006) stated that while such assessments are not inaccurate, they are incomplete and "only one part of the picture" (p. 104). Other measures also predict future reading performance, such as oral language proficiency, expressive vocabulary, and understanding of narrative structure (Paris, Carpenter, Paris, & Hamilton, 2005). However, these do not necessarily lend themselves to short, quick, and easy-to-administer RtI probes.

RtI is basically quite new and it remains to be seen how various schools and districts will interpret and implement the fairly general federal guidelines. As presently conceptualized, RtI is primarily focused in the early elementary grades; however, there is certainly a chance that the initiative will extend into the upper elementary, middle, and secondary levels, especially given the large numbers of students above grade four who struggle with reading. Perhaps it is at these levels that an IRI would be most effective as a progress monitoring tool and, because an IRI is informal in nature, teachers can adapt the process to fit their needs. In Section 4, we provide descriptions of various ways in which the QRI-5 can be used to address the increasing accountability issues in our schools.

3

Information Provided by the *Qualitative Reading Inventory-5*

FINDING READING LEVELS

The *Qualitative Reading Inventory-5* can be used to provide appropriate information in three areas:

1. To identify a student's instructional level
2. To determine areas of reading in which the student is having difficulty
3. To document growth based on a type of instructional program or intervention

Identifying Reading Levels

When used to determine a student's reading levels, the *QRI-5* can help find the levels at which a student can read independently, read with instructional guidance, and read with frustration. The *QRI-5* can also be used to determine if a student's reading levels are below his or her chronological grade level.

The Independent Level

This is the level at which a student can read successfully without assistance. Oral reading should be fluent and free from behaviors such as finger pointing and overt signs of tension. The student's accuracy in word recognition while reading orally should be 98% or higher. Silent reading should also be free from finger pointing. For both oral and silent reading, comprehension should be excellent. The reader should be able to answer 90% or more of the questions correctly.

An examiner should choose materials written at this level for the student's free-reading pleasure or for tasks that the reader is expected to perform independently. It is also wise to choose materials at an independent level for reading-strategy instruction or fluency practice. This allows the reader to learn and practice a strategy on relatively easy text before transferring to more challenging material.

The Instructional Level

This is the level at which a student can read with assistance from a teacher. Both oral and silent reading should be free from behaviors that often indicate serious difficulty, such as finger pointing or tension. Although oral reading may be less fluent at this level than at the independent level, it should retain some sense of rhythm and expression. The examiner should use a criterion of 95% accuracy when counting only those miscues that changed the meaning of the passage. Our pilot data revealed that 95% Acceptable Accuracy best predicts comprehension at the instructional level. The examiner who is counting all miscues should use a criterion of 90% accuracy, and the student should correctly answer 70% of the questions asked.

Materials written at this level should be chosen for reading and content-area instruction. This placement assumes that the teacher will introduce words and concepts that are likely to be unfamiliar to the readers. She or he presents the identification and meaning of these concepts and provides appropriate background knowledge necessary for understanding the material. Obviously, when students are placed at the instructional level, the teacher should not say, "Read Chapter 5 and we'll have a test tomorrow."

A student's instructional level, once determined, can be compared to the student's chronological grade placement. Is it below the level of materials that are appropriate for that grade level? Such information will allow the examiner to estimate the severity of a reading problem. Assessment specialists once believed that a student had a reading problem if there was a substantial difference between expectancy level or reading potential and instructional level with familiar material. Expectancy level or reading potential was generally based on IQ; however, this practice has been seriously questioned (Aaron, 1997). The reauthorization of the Individuals with Disabilities Education Act (2004) conceptualizes reading problems in terms of lack of response to instruction and it may be more appropriate to talk of serious reading problems in terms of a discrepancy between the student's reading level and his or her chronological grade level. Spache (1981) described severe reading problems as follows: The problem is severe if a first, second, or third grader is a year or more behind or if a fourth, fifth, or sixth grader is two or more years behind. For students in seventh grade and above, a severe problem means three or more years behind their grade level.

The Frustration Level

At this level, the student is completely unable to read the material with adequate word identification or comprehension. Signs of difficulty and tension are evident. Oral reading lacks fluency and expression; a word-for-word, halting style is common. Accuracy of word recognition is less than 90%, and less than 70% of the questions are answered correctly. Teachers should avoid materials at this level.

Level Variety

Although once common, it is now simplistic to talk about a single independent, instructional, or frustration level for an individual. The act of reading is highly complex and contextual. When students possess extensive prior knowledge about a topic, they can read and comprehend at a higher level than when dealing with unfamiliar material. This is well illustrated by the difficulty that mature readers often have with an income tax form or the language of an insurance policy. Text structure also affects a student's reading ability. The diverse structure and concept density of expository material makes it more difficult to comprehend than narrative text. Whether a student reads orally or silently can affect comprehension, depending on the age of the student. Younger, less-fluent readers generally do better in oral reading, whereas older readers are often constrained by the performance aspect of oral reading, and their comprehension suffers accordingly. The variety of passages in the *Qualitative Reading Inventory-5* allows the examiner to evaluate the effects of background knowledge, text structure, and reading mode on the independent, instructional, and frustration levels of the reader. It is not inconceivable that a single reader may have different levels for familiar and unfamiliar text, for narrative and expository material, and for oral and silent reading modes. The presence or absence of pictures may affect performance. Levels may also vary depending on whether the examiner is assessing comprehension with or without look-backs. A student may be at a frustration level for answering questions without referring to the text but may achieve an instructional level when allowed to utilize the look-back strategy.

Which reading level is most important? Given the constraints of time, few examiners would be able to determine all possible reading levels that a student might have. Based on individual purposes and needs, each examiner will have to choose which reading level to isolate for a given student. Which level best estimates the overall reading ability of the student? Determination of the familiar narrative reading level seems most essential. Because reading familiar narrative text is generally easier than dealing with expository and unfamiliar material, the familiar narrative level probably represents a reader's best effort. However, in unfamiliar, concept-dense, and lengthy texts, the level attained after look-backs may represent the reader's best effort.

DETERMINING READER STRENGTHS AND NEEDS

Another purpose of the *QRI-5* is to indicate the conditions under which a student would perform successfully or unsuccessfully in reading. For most readers with serious problems, strengths and needs in reading are evident. The *QRI-5* is designed to identify these strengths and needs by providing more information about why a student is not reading well.

Table 3.1 lists questions that the *QRI-5* is designed to answer. The table also provides suggestions for intervention strategies.

DOCUMENTING GROWTH AND CHANGE

The *QRI-5* can be used to assess a student's growth in the level of materials that he or she can read with at least 90% accuracy, 95% acceptable accuracy, and 70% comprehension. That is, the *QRI-5* can be used to determine a change in the student's instructional reading level as long as the pre-test and post-test use the same genre. Beginning readers are more often exposed to narrative text, and the differences in their comprehension of narrative and expository text are apparent. Students reading at pre-primer, primer, first grade, and second grade levels reliably comprehend narrative text better than expository texts (Leslie & Caldwell, 1989). Students above those reading levels reliably retell stories better than exposition. It is recommended that when materials are used to judge growth or change in a student's reading level, the same genre should be used at pre-test and post-test.

A number of published studies have used the *QRI* to document growth in reading based on a type of instructional program or intervention. These studies are found in the References and are marked with an asterisk.

Table 3.1 — Determining Reader Strengths and Needs and Providing Intervention

Student Strengths and Needs as Indicated by *QRI-5*	Suggested Intervention Strategies*	
Can the student identify words accurately?	Chapter 4: Phonological Awareness	• Sample lesson: Rhyming • Sample lesson: Onset-rime awareness • Elkonin boxes • Sample lesson connecting letters and sounds
	Chapter 5: Word Identification Instruction: Phonics and More	• Guidelines for exemplary phonics instruction • Teaching consonant sounds using shared reading • Teaching vowel sounds: Using spelling patterns to read by analogy • Cross-checking • Teaching high-frequency words by sight • Practicing sight words in isolation • Word cards and word sorts • Guided reading
Can the student identify words automatically?	Chapter 6: Word Identification Instruction: Fluency	• General principles for developing fluency • Reading aloud to students • Fostering wide reading • Providing modeling: Assisted reading; echo reading; paired reading; partner reading; structured repeated reading • Performance reading: Choral reading; reader's theater; radio reading • Lesson procedures for developing fluency: Fluency development lesson; supported oral reading; fluency-oriented reading instruction
What is the depth of the student's prior knowledge?	Chapter 7: Prior Knowledge and Concept Development	• Determining critical concepts • Building a knowledge base
Can the student comprehend successfully?	Chapter 12: General Interactive Strategies	• Directed reading-thinking activity • Visual imagery • KWL • Reciprocal teaching • Thinking aloud • Discussion cards
	Chapter 8: Vocabulary Learning	• General principles for developing vocabulary learning • Personalizing word learning • Clustering word learning • Building words • Comparing word meaning
Can the student answer questions? Can the student use look-backs to locate answers in the text?	Chapter 11: Comprehension Instruction: Answering Questions	• General principles for helping students to answer questions • Question–answer relationships • Content-free questions
What is the quality of the student's think-alouds during reading?	Chapter 12: Comprehension Instruction: General Interactive Strategies	• Thinking aloud

continued

Table 3.1   *(continued)*

Student Strengths and Needs as Indicated by *QRI-5*	Suggested Intervention Strategies*	
Does the student organize recall?	Chapter 9: Comprehension Instruction: Retelling Narrative Text	• General principles for developing narrative retelling • The importance of modeling
	Chapter 10: Comprehension Instruction: Expository Retelling	• General principles for developing effective expository retellings • Expository expectation grid • Expository idea map • Main idea map

*From Caldwell, J. S., & Leslie, L. (2009). *Intervention strategies to follow informal reading inventory assessment: So what do I do now?* Boston: Allyn & Bacon.

QUESTIONS REGARDING THE VALIDITY AND RELIABILITY OF *QRI-5*

Because *QRI-5* is an informal assessment instrument, questions may arise about the validity and reliability of the information provided. Although Chapter 15 addresses these issues in detail, a few comments are appropriate at this point.

Inter-Scorer Reliability

The *QRI-5* results are scored by different individuals. Analysis of prior-knowledge scores, oral reading miscues, and answers to comprehension questions all require judgment on the part of the examiner. Therefore, inter-scorer reliability becomes an issue. Can two independent examiners score the same answers in the same way? We believe that they can if they are trained using *QRI-5* guidelines. On prior knowledge scores of over 300 concepts, the agreement reached between two independent scorers was 98% (*QRI-3*, p. 436). Agreement between independent examiners on identifying oral reading miscues and miscues that change meaning was 99%. Finally, the reliability of scoring answers to comprehensions questions was 98% for both explicit and implicit items (Leslie & Caldwell, 1989).

Alternate-Form Reliability

This measure is used to determine the consistency with which an instructional level would be the same if two passages *of the same genre* were used. We examined the reliability of comprehension scores on two passages at the same readability level by asking how close the two scores were to the instructional-level cutoff score of 70%. The degree of consistency in comprehension scores on two passages of the same readability was always above .80, and 75% were above .90. Over 70% of the time the same instructional level would be obtained independent of the passage chosen, *as long as the same genre was used.* It should be noted, however, that some of the pre-primer passages include pictures and others do not. For the beginning reader, one cannot assume that the same instructional level would be obtained if pictured and non-pictured passages are compared, because beginning readers rely heavily on picture clues.

Reliability of Diagnostic Judgments

Two judges independently scored data from 108 children to determine the reliability of diagnostic judgments. The following data were available for all students: current grade placement, percent accuracy on word lists, percent oral reading accuracy on all passages read orally, and comprehension on all passages read. Judgments were made within type of text (i.e., narrative or expository). The judges classified the students' difficulties in reading as "word recognition" or " comprehension" within text types. The judges agreed on the diagnostic category of the students' abilities 87% of the time.

Concurrent Validity

What is the relationship between two scores on assessments that are given close to each other in time? For example, how do scores on the *QRI* compare to scores on norm-referenced achievement tests? Correlations between the two measures were all positive and statistically significant. Section 15 presents data illustrating that scores on the *QRI* are correlated with standardized norm-referenced tests to a significant degree. Positive correlations between the *QRI* and measures such as the Wisconsin Knowledge and Concepts Evaluation, the Iowa Test of Basic Skills, the Woodcock Reading Test, and the Measures of Academic Progress were all positive and statistically significant.

Construct Validity

Construct validity is determined by correlations between various types of data. We examined correlations between word identification on the word lists, oral reading accuracy on passages, semantic acceptability of oral reading miscues, and reading rate (in words per minute). For students with instructional reading levels at or below second grade, these variables were highly correlated. Word identification in a story was also significantly correlated with comprehension through the first grade instructional reading level. Beyond first grade there appear to be factors other than word identification at work, such as prior knowledge and text structure. That is, students could read a passage accurately enough to meet the oral reading accuracy criteria for instructional reading level but not meet the criteria for comprehension.

Classification Validity

We analyzed whether the comprehension scores of students whose word-list score were higher or lower than their instructional reading levels (good word identifiers vs. poor word identifiers) could be predicted by similar or different variables. The comprehension scores of good word identifiers with second and third grade instructional levels were predicted by text type (narrative vs. expository). The comprehension scores of good word identifiers with fourth through sixth grade instructional levels were predicted by prior-knowledge scores. Therefore, there appears to be developmental and individual differences in the factors that influence students' comprehension scores.

Uses of the *Qualitative Reading Inventory-5*

THE EXAMINER AS A REFLECTIVE DECISION MAKER

Using the *QRI-5* to Estimate Individual Instructional Reading Level

Using the *QRI 5* to Estimate Reading Level through Group Administration and Monitor Classroom Progress (Response to Intervention)

Using the *QRI-5* to Determine Reading Level

Using the *QRI-5* to Indicate Growth and Monitor Progress: Response to Intervention

Using the *QRI-5* to Verify a Suspected Problem

Using the *QRI-5* to Describe Specific Reading Behaviors as a Guide for Intervention Instruction (Response to Intervention: Tiers Two and Three)

In order to use the *QRI-5* to its best advantage without undue testing and interpretation time, the user must be a decision maker. The examiner must decide what information he or she wants to obtain about the student and how to use the *QRI-5* to obtain it. He or she need not determine a complete range of levels (independent, instructional, and frustration) or administer both word lists and passages or establish familiar/unfamiliar, narrative/expository, and oral/silent levels for each student. He or she need not use all options (recall, questions, look-backs, think-alouds, and miscue analysis). This would be extremely time-consuming and, in many cases, totally unnecessary. The examiner must decide beforehand what information will be most helpful and choose the passages and options accordingly. In some cases, he or she may administer only one or two passages to estimate a reading level or to confirm the existence of a problem in a specific area. In other cases, the examiner may choose to engage in a more complete assessment of a reader's strengths and needs.

Who might choose to use the *QRI-5* and for what specific purpose? The classroom teacher, the reading-assessment specialist, the special education specialist, and the literacy researcher can all use the *QRI-5* in different ways depending on their needs. The *QRI-5* provides each professional with an instrument for estimating or determining the reading levels of individual students. The *QRI-5* can also be used in a group format for estimating classroom reading levels. It can function as an instrument for charting growth across a school year or after completion of a special intervention program—an important function in these times of increased focus on accountability. Also, the *QRI-5* is an effective instrument for verifying and describing suspected reading problems.

In many school districts, scores obtained on standardized norm-referenced tests take precedence in describing a student's reading performance. However, these tests seldom present reading in a natural context. That is, they tend to include isolated word lists, multiple-choice vocabulary tests, and comprehension assessments based on brief, decontextualized passages. In addition, while some may provide a valid estimate of a student's instructional reading level (Blanchard, Borthwick, & Hall, 1983; Smith & Beck, 1980), others may be of limited use in ascertaining the level of text that a student can read successfully. Unlike such standardized instruments, the *QRI-5* provides a tool for observing the reading behavior of a student in a relatively natural context that approximates a real reading situation.

A classroom teacher, reading-assessment specialist, or reading researcher does not have unlimited time for assessment. Each must choose those parts of the *QRI-5* that will offer the most valuable diagnostic information for a given student or purpose.

USING THE *QRI-5* TO ESTIMATE INDIVIDUAL INSTRUCTIONAL READING LEVEL

The *QRI-5* can be effectively used to estimate the reading level of individual children. This is important for several reasons. First, while classroom reading instruction is characterized by different organizational formats, the success of a specific format depends on using materials appropriate to the children's reading levels. Second, some school districts require that a child's reading level be placed on a report card or in a cumulative folder and parents often ask for an estimation of reading level. In estimating individual reading levels, a classroom teacher does not have the luxury of ample time for assessment activities. Administration of the *QRI-5* should involve only a few passages. Choose a narrative at the appropriate grade level, for example, a third grade passage for use with third graders. You can use the word lists to estimate a beginning point for selecting a passage that corresponds to an instructional or independent level attained on the word lists. Have the child read orally or silently, depending on which mode is primarily utilized in the classroom. We recommend using oral administration for second grade and below and using silent administration for third grade and above. If the child reads orally, count all reading miscues and use a 90% cutoff score. It takes less time to count all miscues than to evaluate which ones represent meaning-change miscues and which do not. Again, because it is easier, ask the comprehension questions as opposed to scoring recall.

If the student achieves at an instructional level, you can estimate that the child is at least at grade level. You then have the option to move up to the next higher passage in order to determine whether the child can read higher-level passages. If the student is at a frustration level, administer the next-lower passage in order to determine the instructional level. Usually you need administer only two passages in order to determine reading level. It is not necessary to exercise other assessment options.

It is important to remember that this offers only an estimate of reading level, because many other variables affect whether or not a child can comprehend a specific selection. Above second grade, you will probably not find an instructional level that does not vary across genre, familiarity, and topic. For this reason, we have provided passages at each level that vary in these dimensions. Because a child can demonstrate acceptable word recognition, fluency, and comprehension in one fourth grade passage does not ensure similar success with all the fourth grade passages. For example a child who is successful with "Johnny Appleseed" may experience difficulty with "Plant Structures for Survival," both fourth grade selections. A student may be successful with the relatively short fifth grade selection on Martin Luther King, Jr., and experience difficulty with the Patricia McKissack reading, which is considerably longer. For this reason, we recommend that instructional level be interpreted in relation to the genre, topic, familiarity, and length of the passage that was read. Section 13 contains an example of using *QRI-5* passages to estimate reading level.

USING THE *QRI-5* TO ESTIMATE READING LEVEL THROUGH GROUP ADMINISTRATION AND MONITOR CLASSROOM PROGRESS (RESPONSE TO INTERVENTION)

Estimating reading level is appropriate in a silent reading group format for grades three and above. This option has been recently employed in several schools and districts. While procedures vary across sites, all follow a relatively similar format. *QRI-5* passages (grade three and above) are duplicated and given to students as a classroom group. The students silently read the passage and write answers to the questions on sheets provided for that purpose. The students are allowed to refer back to the passage to locate and verify answers. The teacher then scores the answers according to the guidelines provided in *QRI-5* and determines the student's estimated independent, instructional, or frustration comprehension levels. Group administration of leveled passages approximates the actual reading process as practiced in schools where students in third grade and above are expected to read silently on their own and demonstrate the ability to write answers to questions, often after looking back in the text. When answering questions on standardized measures, students are also allowed to look back. As explained in Section 2, answering questions while looking back in the text discriminates between comprehension during reading and memory after reading. The process of determining group reading level is delineated in the following step-by-step procedure.

- The teacher chooses a passage at a level corresponding to the grade level of the students. For example, third grade students would begin with a third grade passage. We suggest that the initial group administration involve narrative passages; these are generally easier for students. We also suggest that the same passage be chosen across all classrooms in a school or district; that is, all third grade classrooms would use the same third grade *QRI-5* passage. The chosen passage should be reflective of the district or school curriculum with regard to length and conceptual depth.

- The teacher hands out duplicated copies of a passage and question sheets about it. (Question sheets especially formatted for group administration are included on the DVD accompanying *QRI-5*.)
- The students read the passage and write their answers on the accompanying question sheet. If some students finish before others, the teacher asks them to read independently or engage in some other quiet activity and wait until all have finished. All question sheets are collected at the same time and ample time is given for the slower readers to complete the task.
- The teacher corrects the questions and does not count spelling, punctuation, and penmanship. The scoring of explicit questions poses few problems; however, written answers to implicit questions are often somewhat vague and, of course, the teacher does not have the luxury of probing. We recommend that answers to implicit questions be evaluated in relation to the text, that is, to concepts or information that direct or allow for a valid inference. After correcting the answers, the teacher then assigns group comprehension levels to each student: independent, instructional, or frustration, based on the passage guidelines in *QRI-5*.

- On another day, students who are independent or instructional at their grade level are given the next higher passage and the procedure is repeated until all students have attained their highest instructional level.
- For students who score at a frustration level for their grade placement, the group process can be repeated with a lower passage. That is, a fourth grader who is at a frustration level for his or her grade can be given a third grade passage.
- For students who are at a frustration level in a third grade passage, districts have pursued several options. One is to administer the same passage individually to evaluate the student's oral reading proficiency with regard to word identification and reading rate. Often students who struggle with silent reading achieve at an instructional level while reading orally, which suggests they have not yet made an effective transition to silent reading. Another option is to administer a second grade passage individually and move to even lower levels if needed. In some schools and districts, the reading specialist works with those students who are not able to achieve at an instructional level in third grade material.
- The procedure can stop with narrative text. However, some districts have repeated the procedure with expository text and found clear differences between student performance on narrative as opposed to expository selections at the same level.

This procedure can be repeated throughout the year as a way of monitoring progress. One district did this three times during the school year; another school did it at the beginning and end of the year. For the second administration, choice of passage was based on the highest level attained during the first administration. For example, if a student was instructional at the fourth grade level, he or she would be asked to read the fifth grade selection during the second session.

Results of the group administration informed instruction. In one district, because of lower scores on expository passages, teachers realized the need for inclusion of more expository material in reading classes. In another school, teachers recognized that there was a need for increased emphasis on writing. One district chose to share the results of the group testing with parents and grouped data across all classrooms as the percent of students at level, above level, and below level.

Because the *QRI-5* is an informal instrument, districts have modified the group administration to fit their needs. One district differentiated between silent and oral reading levels. If a student scored at a frustration level, he or she read the passage again in an oral format. If the student then attained an instructional level, this was marked with "o" for "oral" on the record sheet to differentiate it from levels attained through silent reading. When reading expository text, another school encouraged students to utilize strategies that they had been taught, that is, underline the text, take notes, or construct a graphic organizer during and after reading as an aid for answering questions. Another district engaged in a prereading discussion about key concepts in the selection in an attempt to reduce the variability in students' prior knowledge. The DVD that accompanies *QRI-5* contains a classroom record sheet for recording performance on group administration.

Some caution is in order. The group administration may underestimate reading level because of differences between individualized and group administration. For some students, writing is difficult. As a result, they may not include all they know in their answers, especially answers to implicit questions, and there may be difficulties with reading and understanding the questions themselves. In an individualized setting, the examiner can probe if an answer seems vague; this cannot be done in a group format. Attention and independent work habits can also play a part. However, having said this, group administration does parallel much classroom activity involving independent work following reading.

Determining reading level is usually the role of the assessment specialist. This person generally has several kinds of data to use in estimating which passages to administer in determining a student's instructional level. Because of time constraints, it is important to avoid administration of unnecessary selections. Classroom information may be a viable starting point. For example, if the student is not functioning successfully in the second grade classroom, this suggests that first grade may represent an appropriate instructional level, and the validation of level may begin with a selection at that level. The score on a standardized reading test may also provide a starting point. We suggest, however, administering a passage that is one or two grade levels below the grade equivalent attained on this test. By careful use of existing data, you can use a minimum number of *QRI-5* passages to ascertain level placement for the student. Of course, if time permits, the word lists can also be used as a guide for passage administration. Although the familiar narrative level is most important, in that it probably represents the student's best effort, you may choose to exercise one of the following options:

- If the familiar instructional level was obtained through oral reading, you may choose to verify this level in silent reading. A discrepancy between the student's oral and silent reading comprehension may suggest which mode to stress during instruction.
- If the reading level was obtained by reading a text with pictures, you may choose to compare this with performance on a text without pictures. If a student performs less well on the text without pictures, this may suggest excessive reliance on pictures for word identification.
- You may choose to determine the student's instructional level for familiar expository text as a guide to the type of classroom or intervention instructional materials to select. For example, a lower level for expository text may suggest that this type of material should receive primary emphasis.
- Finally, you may choose to ascertain a level for unfamiliar text. Most readers do score at a lower level for unfamiliar material, but designation of a specific level for unfamiliar material can help the assessment specialist plan specific background enhancement activities for the student.

USING THE *QRI-5* TO INDICATE GROWTH AND MONITOR PROGRESS: RESPONSE TO INTERVENTION

Increased emphasis on accountability requires that students' growth be carefully documented across a school year. In addition, many schools and school districts have implemented the three tiers of Response to Intervention. As part of the reauthorization of the Individuals with Disabilities Education Act (2004), Response to Intervention allows diagnosis of a learning disability to be based on a student's response to instruction as opposed to the discrepancy between IQ scores and reading performance. The three RtI tiers are classroom instruction, small-group instruction for students whose performance ranks below their classroom peers with regard to specific components of reading, and individual instruction for those who do not demonstrate satisfactory progress in small-group instruction. In each tier, the student's progress is carefully monitored (Fuchs & Deshler, 2007; Hollenbeck, 2007). An individually administered *QRI-5* can be used for analysis of reading growth during all three tiers. Several studies have suggested that passages on the *QRI* are sensitive to immediate and long-term change. In addition, the *QRI-5* has also been extensively used by literacy researchers to evaluate student progress. Representative articles describing this use are found in the References and are marked with an asterisk. The group administration format described in the early part of this section can also be used to monitor progress in tier one.

Pre- and post-assessment can take two forms. You can administer a passage prior to an intervention, at the beginning of an RtI tier, or at the beginning of the school year and then administer the same passage as a post-test. You can also check progress at several points during the school year by noting a decrease in oral reading miscues, a rise in reading rate, or an increase in the number of questions answered and the number of ideas recalled. You can also determine the students' highest instructional level at a beginning point and then readminister the same passage at a later time or at the close of the intervention. Have students moved to an independent level in that passage? If so, you may want to administer the next highest passage. Of course, the pre- and post-intervention passages must be administered in the same way. Both should employ the same genre, either oral or silent reading, and focus on the same comprehension components (retelling, questions with look-backs, or questions without look-backs).

We are often asked about the validity of administering the same passage. Will students naturally perform better on the second administration just because they read the same passage previously? If the times of administration are spaced far enough apart, this may not be an issue. At one of our reading centers, the pre-test passage is routinely used as the post-test passage after the completion of an entire semester. We have noted that many children actually seem unaware that they had read the passage previously. However, if you are concerned about this and you feel that a student's performance on the post-test is suspect, we suggest the following. First, you can administer a different passage as the post-test. Or, after administering the same passage as a post-test, verify the student's performance by administering a second passage of the same kind and level.

A second option is to administer different passages prior to and after the intervention or at different times. This may be a more viable option if the duration of the intervention is relatively short and if you are concerned that memory for the initial passage may confound comprehension performance on the same passage. If you choose this option, the two passages should be as similar as possible. They should be at the same readability level, of the same structure (narrative or expository), and of the same level of familiarity. Table 15.13 presents pilot comprehension scores for all passages, thus illustrating the difficulty of passages *within* each level.

USING THE *QRI-5* TO VERIFY A SUSPECTED PROBLEM

In some cases, a teacher or assessment specialist may suspect that poor performance in science, social studies, or other content classes may be due to a specific reading difficulty. You can use appropriate passages from the *QRI-5* to verify the existence of such a problem.

A Possible Problem with Expository Text. Choose an expository passage that is probably familiar to the student and that corresponds to the reading level of the content textbook used in the class. Because most content reading is done silently, have the student read the passage in this mode and then ask the accompanying questions. You can employ look-backs if you choose.

A Possible Problem with Unfamiliar Topics. Choose a narrative or expository passage that is probably unfamiliar to the student. Select this passage to correspond to the reading level of the textbook used. The student should read it orally or silently and answer the questions that follow. We strongly suggest that the student be encouraged to look back in the text to correct erroneous answers or find forgotten information. It is common for students to demonstrate poor comprehension after the first reading of an unfamiliar text. However, comprehension often improves when the student looks back in the text. If time permits, it may be helpful to contrast this passage with a familiar one at the same level in order to note whether comprehension differences are indeed present in familiar and unfamiliar text with or without look-backs.

A Possible Problem with Silent Reading Comprehension. Choose a narrative passage that is likely to be familiar to the child. Many children who are effective oral readers and comprehenders often experience difficulty in making a transition to independent silent reading. Ask the child to read the passage silently and then ask the accompanying questions. If time permits, contrast this with a similar passage read orally, timing both. If the child's rate of silent reading is similar to his or her oral reading rate, this may indicate that the child is not engaging in effective silent reading strategies.

A Possible Problem with Ineffective Note Taking. Choose a familiar expository passage at a level that corresponds to the level of the content textbook. Ask the student to read silently and take notes on the important parts of the passage. An alternative would be to have the student underline the important parts while reading. Then examine these notes or underlinings to ascertain whether the reader has internalized effective note-taking strategies for finding important elements in the text.

A Possible Problem with Recall Following Reading. Choose a familiar passage at a level that corresponds to the textbook being used by the student. Ask the student to read silently and then ask for unaided recall. Compare this recall to the retelling scoring sheet in order to evaluate the quality of the reader's memory for what was read. Ask the accompanying questions and contrast the student's ability to give correct answers with his or her ability to offer unaided recall of a selection.

You can utilize the *QRI-5* effectively to verify the existence of a suspected problem. Because of time constraints, you will rarely employ all the diagnostic options provided by the *QRI-5* but will instead choose one or two passages to serve a very specific purpose.

USING THE *QRI-5* TO DESCRIBE SPECIFIC READING BEHAVIORS AS A GUIDE FOR INTERVENTION INSTRUCTION (RESPONSE TO INTERVENTION: TIERS TWO AND THREE)

Selected passages and assessment options on the *QRI-5* can be used effectively to isolate areas for intervention emphasis. Again, it must be stressed that you are a decision maker. You should ask, "What do I want to know about this student?" and then choose *QRI-5* components accordingly. Some possible assessment questions are presented next, and the *QRI-5* components that can be used to answer each one are listed. Guidelines for using these components are given in greater depth in later sections of the manual.

How Accurate Is the Student in Identifying Words?   The total score on the word lists and the number of miscues made during oral reading of the passages can provide accuracy information.

How Automatic Is the Student in Identifying Words?   The timed administration of the word lists can suggest a level of automaticity. Automaticity can also be inferred from the student's oral and silent reading rates on the passages.

What Word-Identification Strategies Are Used by the Student?   You can evaluate the nature of the miscues made on the word lists or when reading the passages by engaging in miscue analysis (see Section 9). Does the student use graphic or letter cues? Does the student self-correct miscues that do not make sense, suggesting a focus on passage meaning? Does the student correct miscues that do not change meaning? This may suggest a focus on word pronunciation as opposed to comprehension. A student's performance on the list of low-frequency words containing common vowel patterns can also suggest word-identification strategies (see Section 6).

Is There a Difference between a Student's Ability to Identify Words in Isolation and Words in Context?   If the student has a higher level of word-identification skill when reading passages than when reading word lists or when reading text with pictures than when reading text without pictures, this may suggest effective use of context by a beginning reader or excessive use of context by an older, less-skilled reader. Context-free word identification is a characteristic of a skilled reader, whose word-identification levels in isolation and context should be similar (Perfetti, 1985, 1988; Stanovich, 1980, 1991b). You can also contrast the student's ability to identify specific words on the word lists with her or his ability to identify those same words in the passages. All list words are underlined in the passages wherever they occur at that level. For example, the word "in" on the pre-primer list is underlined wherever it occurs in the pre-primer passages.

Which Types of Text Can the Student Handle Most Successfully?   You may compare narrative and expository text. This is probably more important for middle and high school students. You may also compare content areas for middle and high school students. Does the student perform more effectively in social studies, science, or literature passages? For younger children and those reading at pre-primer through second grade levels, the examiner can contrast reading when pictures are present and reading when they are absent.

Which Modes of Reading Represent a Strength for the Student?   You can compare oral and silent reading comprehension to determine which mode to emphasize during instruction. You can then compare comprehension following listening with that following reading. Listening comprehension is often regarded as representative of a child's comprehension potential in the absence of decoding problems (Gough & Juel, 1991; Stanovich, 1991a). If a child does not attain an instructional level in pre-primer text, we strongly advise that listening comprehension be assessed.

How Does the Student Perform on Familiar and Unfamiliar Text? You can note any differences between performance on familiar and unfamiliar text. Students may not comprehend as well on unfamiliar text, but you can note whether this difference represents a change in instructional level. Lower levels in word identification on unfamiliar text may suggest that the student is overly dependent on familiar context for word identification.

Does the Student Effectively Use Look-Backs? You can compare the student's ability to answer explicit and implicit questions with and without look-backs. The ability to look back in the text and locate information is a characteristic of effective readers. At the upper levels and in unfamiliar, concept-dense text, performance in answering questions without look-backs is less important than answering questions accurately when allowed to look back. Memory constraints placed on students who are struggling with such text argues that effective use of look-backs may represent a more realistic picture of a student's reading performance.

What Comprehension Strategies Does the Student Employ While Reading? The use of think-alouds can offer evidence of the comprehension strategies used by the student during the act of reading. Does the student self-question? Does the student construct inferences? Does the student recognize his or her understanding or lack of it? Does the student summarize or paraphrase parts of the text before moving on to the next segment? The presence of such strategies can suggest an interactive and involved reader. Conversely, their absence can suggest the need for a metacognitive instructive focus.

You will have to decide which of the above questions will be most helpful in describing the reading behavior of an individual and in planning suitable intervention instruction. No two students are the same, and it is likely that you will use different components for different students. Because the *QRI-5* is not a standardized instrument, you can decide which options to choose, given the constraints of time and the needs of each individual student. A summary of these questions can be found in Section 4 of the DVD.

5 Administration of the *Qualitative Reading Inventory-5*

PREPARATION FOR TESTING

Summary Guidelines for Administration
Guidelines for Administration

To ensure the best possible testing environment, the examiner should administer the *QRI-5* in a quiet place that is free from distractions. Before meeting the student, the examiner should gather all materials and place them in the testing room: word lists, passages to be read, accompanying sheets for examiner recording, audio recorder, stopwatch or timer, clipboard, paper, and pencils.

It is often difficult to determine how many scoring sheets to prepare, especially if the examiner has never met the student. It is better to prepare too many than not enough; otherwise, the examiner may have to leave the room to obtain more. We recommend that the examiner prepare a kit of scoring sheets for all the passages and organize them according to grade level. The examiner can then be assured of having the correct passages on hand. It may be advantageous to laminate the student's copy of each passage or to encase it in a plastic cover for protection.

Before beginning the testing, the examiner should strive to put the student at ease. Engaging in conversation about the student's interests, feelings toward school and other subjects, or favored activities can act as an effective icebreaker as well as provide valuable information. Some students are concerned with the use of a stopwatch or with the examiner writing. Sitting across from the student can make the act of writing somewhat less noticeable. Using a clipboard that rests on the examiner's lap and a stopwatch that rests on a chair placed to one side can also make these items less obtrusive.

We highly recommend that the entire testing session be recorded, especially in the early stages of learning how to administer the *QRI-5*. Even experienced examiners often find a recording helpful in scoring. Some students are upset by the use of an audio recorder. Explaining the need for this and allowing the student to experiment with it may help to alleviate anxiety.

An examiner who is using the word-identification lists to estimate a starting point for passage administration gives those to the student first and scores them immediately in order to estimate which passages to administer. Next, the examiner administers the prior-knowledge task for a passage before the student reads it, which allows the examiner to determine whether the content of the passage is familiar to the reader. It need not be scored before proceeding; however, the examiner should estimate familiarity with the text topic. Third, the examiner gives the student the passages. If the passages are being used to determine an instructional level, the examiner must score oral reading accuracy and responses to comprehension questions in order to know what additional passages to administer. We recommend that during the actual administration, the examiner determine oral reading accuracy by counting all errors or miscues. This allows for a quick estimation of the word-identification level so that the examiner can ascertain which passage to administer next. After the administration, if desired, the examiner can determine passage level by counting only those miscues that change meaning.

Finally, the amount of time spent in administering the QRI-5 will vary depending on the assessment questions posed by the examiner. It is important that the examiner be sensitive to the student's energy level and attention span. Frequent short breaks are often helpful. If somewhat lengthy testing is required, there is no reason why testing should not be scheduled across several days, if this can be arranged.

SUMMARY GUIDELINES FOR ADMINISTRATION

As we have worked and interacted with novice users of past editions of the *Qualitative Reading Inventory,* we have recognized the need for a simplified administration summary that new examiners can use as they work with their students and score the results. Although detailed instructions and scoring guidelines are present in QRI-5, these occur in different sections and it can be awkward to locate a specific piece of information during the administration and scoring process. For this reason, we include an administration summary below and again with Scoring Guidelines on the accompanying DVD.

Guidelines for Administration

Materials to Have Ready. Student copies, examiner copies, clipboard, pencils, stopwatch, audio recorder

Word Lists. Introduce the word lists to the student by saying, "I have some lists of words that I want you to read one at a time. Some of the words will be easy for you, and some I expect to be very hard. Don't worry. You are not expected to know all of them. If you don't know a word right away, try your best to figure it out. I cannot help you in any way, and I cannot tell you whether you are right or wrong. Just do your very best. Are you ready?"

Concept Questions. Introduce the concept questions by saying, "Before you read, I want to know what you already know about some ideas in the text. I will ask you a few questions to find out."

Prediction Task. If you choose to administer the prediction task, do so by saying, "Given that the title of the passage is _____, and it includes the ideas _____, _____, and _____ (naming all the concepts within the questions), what do you think the passage will be about? I want you to take a guess or make a prediction about what you think the passage will be about."

Passages. Introduce the passages to the student by saying, "You now get to show me how you can read on your own. We'll see how well I pick things for you to read so some you will read out loud and some you can read to yourself. Do you understand so far?

"Because my job is to make sure I remember all the things you do as a reader, I'm going to write notes and record this. This will make sure I don't miss any of the great things you do. Since this is your time to show me who you are as a reader, I can't give you any hints or any help. If you come to a word you don't know, do your best and keep on going. Do you understand so far?

"When you are done reading, I'll ask you to retell what you read. Your job is to pretend that I didn't hear you read this or that I didn't know the selection. So tell me as much as you can. After you tell me all you can remember, I will ask you some questions. Again pretend that I don't know anything about the selection so tell me all that you can. Do you have any questions?

"Ready? The first selection is called _____."

Retelling.   After the student has finished reading the selection, the examiner should remove the passage and ask the student to retell it as if to someone who had never read or heard it before. After the student has retold as much as he or she can, ask if there is anything else he or she would like to say. If the student claims to remember nothing, draw attention to the title and ask whether he or she can remember what the author wrote about. Do not offer any hints or direct suggestions.

Questions.   After the student has retold all that he or she can remember, ask the questions. You may choose to use or not to use the look-back procedure. However, be consistent.

6

Administration and Scoring of the *Qualitative Reading Inventory-5*

THE WORD LISTS

Purposes for Administering the Word Lists
- Estimating the Starting Point for Passage Administration
- Estimating Automatic Word Identification
- Estimating Knowledge of Letter–Sound Matches
- Examining Knowledge of Vowel Patterns
- Analyzing the Differences between Word Identification in Isolation and in Context

Procedures for Administering the Word Lists
- General Procedures
- Instructions to the Student

The Beginning Point
- Recording Student Responses: Accuracy and Automaticity

Procedures for Scoring the Word Lists
- Estimating the Starting Point for Passage Administration
- Estimating Automatic Word Identification
- Reading by Analogy: Comparing Knowledge of Low- and High-Frequency Vowel Patterns
- Additional Diagnostic Uses of the Word Lists

PURPOSES FOR ADMINISTERING THE WORD LISTS

Estimating the Starting Point for Passage Administration

The word lists provide a quick estimate of the student's word-identification ability. Because words on the lists are in the passages for that level, even if the examiner has little other information about a student's performance, the lists may help the examiner estimate the level on which to begin testing. If the student has problems with word identification, his or her performance on the word lists will indicate a realistic beginning point for passage administration. If, however, the student can identify words well but has problems in comprehension, the word lists may suggest a starting point that will be too difficult for the reader to comprehend. Our pilot data suggested a relationship between performance on the word lists and word recognition in context (see Section 15).

Words in the passages are underlined if they are present on the word list at that level as well as the preceding level. For example, words in the third grade passages are underlined if they appear on either the third and second grade word lists. This underlining allows the examiner to compare a student's word recognition in two situations, with and without context. Increasing the number of words that are present in both situations improves the reliability of determining context usage.

Estimating Automatic Word Identification

The examiner can estimate automaticity of word identification by counting the number of seconds it takes the student to read each word on the word lists. If a student reads a word within one second, we can assume that the student has identified the word automatically without needing to sound it out by applying decoding rules. The more words that a reader identifies automatically, the more likely she or he will be a fluent reader in the corresponding level of passages.

Words that are automatically identified have often been termed *sight vocabulary*. It was thought that a direct link occurred between the visual aspects of a word and word meaning. However, automatic word identification involves a strong sound component (Ehri, 1992). Therefore, *sight vocabulary* may be a misnomer, and we prefer to use the term *automatic word identification*.

Estimating Knowledge of Letter–Sound Matches

All other words that the student reads correctly beyond a one-second limit are probably read via decoding ability; that is, the student is matching letters and sounds in order to identify the word. The examiner can examine correct and incorrect pronunciations in order to assess the letter–sound matches that the student knows and those that might need emphasis in an intervention program.

Examining Knowledge of Vowel Patterns

The *QRI-5* also provides examiners with the opportunity to specifically examine the student's knowledge and use of 18 frequently used vowel patterns, often called phonograms (Beck, 2006; Fry, 1998; Gaskins et al., 1997). If children learn a regular sound pattern in one word, they can easily transfer this knowledge to other words. For example, if a students knows the word "can," then the student can use the vowel pattern *an* to decode "pan." The students must delete the sound represented by the letter "c" from "can" and replace it with the sound represented by the letter "p." This is called *reading by analogy* (Gaskins, Downer, Anderson, Cunningham, Gaskins, & Schommer, 1988), and not all readers do this without instruction. Because of the usefulness of reading by analogy, the *QRI-5* offers examiners insight as to whether or not a student is using the strategy. Teaching students to recognize and use these common patterns is a useful component of phonics instruction.

In the pre-primer through first grade word lists, the 18 frequent vowel patterns are present in high-frequency words such as "make" and "at." However, children may identify these words as sight words, that is, as words that they have memorized. In order to determine if a reader recognizes and uses vowel patterns for word identification, the *QRI-5* provides a list of low-frequency words that contain the same vowel patterns as the word list words. It is less likely that readers at the pre-primer through first grade levels will have encountered the low-frequency words and thus have opportunity to memorize them. Section 15 describes our pilot data regarding recognition of high- and low-frequency words containing common vowel patterns.

Analyzing the Differences between Word Identification in Isolation and in Context

The words on the word lists were taken from the passages and the words underlined in the passages appear on the word list of the same or previous readability level. Thus, the examiner can determine if the reader is dependent on context by examining whether the student can identify words in a passage that she or he could not identify in isolation. Beginning readers often rely on context to determine word pronunciation and, at early levels, this can be regarded as a strength (Stanovich, 2004). However, at levels three and above reliance on context for word identification may be evidence of inadequate decoding or sight vocabulary as readers attempt to compensate for such deficiencies by use of context. If the reader identifies more words in context than on the word list and the words are within a frequency range appropriate for his or her instructional reading level, then instruction on word identification and/or practice in sight vocabulary may be in order.

PROCEDURES FOR ADMINISTERING THE WORD LISTS

General Procedures

The student is given the list of words and asked to pronounce them. The examiner records the answers on the accompanying scoring sheet, carefully differentiating between words identified automatically and those identified after some delay. Those identified automatically are marked in the Identified Automatically column; those identified after some delay are recorded in the Identified column. There are several ways to administer the lists. Each may seem awkward at first, but with practice, the examiner will soon choose the method with which she or he is most comfortable.

The examiner can sit next to the student and cover each word with an index card, which is then moved down to reveal the word. Immediately after the word is completely exposed, the examiner says mentally "one thousand and one." This acts as the equivalent of one-second timing. If the student has not pronounced the word within that time frame, any attempt, correct or otherwise, is marked in the Identified column. Many students may choose to move the cards themselves, and the examiner must watch when the word is uncovered and say mentally "one thousand and one." Another alternative is to use a window card. When the examiner places the card over each word, the student only sees one word at a time. The examiner may find it more comfortable to dispense with the card and simply hand the list to the student to read at his and her own pace. The important thing is to keep track of automatic pronunciation by saying "one thousand and one." A pattern for the window card is present on the DVD.

As the examiner juggles the word lists and the timing, recording the student's answers may seem difficult at first. Until she or he becomes more accustomed to timing, listening, and recording all at once, the examiner should audio-record the entire session. A recording also helps if the examiner is unsure of how to score a miscue. Asking another individual to listen to the audio and offer input can be very helpful.

Instructions to the Student

The examiner should introduce the word lists to the student by saying, "I have some lists of words that I want you to read one at a time. Some of the words will be easy for you, and some I expect to be very hard. Don't worry. You are not expected to know all of them. If you don't know a word right away, try your best to figure it out. I cannot help you in any way, and I cannot tell you whether you are right or wrong. Just do your very best. Are you ready?"

The Beginning Point

Whether the examiner is using the word lists to estimate automatic word identification or to suggest a level for passage administration, she or he must determine a realistic beginning point. In order to avoid initial frustration, the examiner should begin with a word list two or more years below the student's chronological grade placement. This is especially important if the examiner suspects a serious reading problem. For example, the pre-primer or primer list is a good starting point for children in first through third grades. Likewise, the second or third grade list is appropriate for students in grades four through six. The fourth and fifth grade lists can be beginning points for those in sixth grade and above. It is better to begin too low than to place the student in a frustrating situation immediately. Little time will be lost if the list is too easy, and the initial experience of success may put the student more at ease.

Recording Student Responses: Accuracy and Automaticity

There are two things for the examiner to keep track of while administering these lists: accuracy of identification and automaticity of response. *Accuracy* refers simply to whether or not the student reads the word correctly. If the student makes an error, the examiner should write down the phonetic equivalent of the mispronunciation. For example, if the student reads "live" with a long "i" sound, the examiner should use the – mark above the "i." If the student changes the word quite a bit, the examiner should write the best phonetic equivalent. This information provides an indication of how the student approaches word identification. If a student immediately self-corrects an error, the examiner should write "SC" and count it as correct. If the student skips a word, the examiner should write "d.k." (don't know).

Automaticity of response refers to whether or not the student gives a response (correct or not) within one second. To provide a realistic estimate of one second, the examiner can say mentally, "one thousand and one." Any response begun within one second is recorded in the Identified Automatically column. If the response is correct, the examiner should simply put a "C" in the column.

If the student takes more than one second to begin a response, the examiner should record the response in the Identified column. If it is a correct response, the examiner should put a "C" in the Identified column. If it is incorrect, she or he should write the phonetic equivalent. It is possible for a student to give an incorrect response within one second but then correct it. In this case the word is a correct decoded word. Figure 6.1 contains an example of recorded and scored word lists.

PROCEDURES FOR SCORING THE WORD LISTS

Scoring procedures vary depending on the purpose for administering the word list. Finding a beginning point for passage administration simply involves counting the number of correct responses in both the Identified Automatically and the Identified columns. Independent, instructional, and frustration levels are determined from this total. Guidelines for determining levels are included on each word list.

Estimating the Starting Point for Passage Administration

The examiner should administer the first list and score it immediately to determine which level it represents. If the student scores at an instructional or frustration level, the examiner should move down until the student attains an independent level. Then the examiner should continue upward until the student reaches a frustration level. The examiner may also stop before the frustration level if the student reaches a word list that corresponds to his or her chronological grade placement. These levels suggest what passages may represent a realistic starting point. Word identification in isolation is a rough predictor of the level of passage that a student can decode reasonably well. If a student scores at an independent or instructional level on a word list, she or he will probably decode a passage of similar readability level successfully.

Students often score at an independent or instructional level across several lists. For example, a student may score at an independent level for the primer and first grade

Figure 6.1

Examiner Word Lists

Second

	Identified Automatically	Identified
1. morning	c	
2. tired	tried	
3. shiny	c	
4. old	c	
5. trade	c	
6. promise		c
7. pieces	c	
8. suit	c	
9. push	c	
10. though	through	
11. begins	c	
12. food	c	
13. light	c	
14. visit	c	
15. clue	c	
16. brĕathe		
17. insects		c
18. weather		c
19. noticed	not iced	sc
20. money	c	

Total Correct Automatic _13_ /20 = _65_%
Total Correct Identified _4_ /20 = _20_%
Total Number Correct _17_ /20 = _85_%

Third

	Identified Automatically	Identified
1. lunch	c	
2. celebrate	c	
3. believe	belief	
4. confused		c
5. motion		c
6. rough	rug	sc
7. engines	c	
8. tongue		c
9. crowded	c	
10. wool	c	
11. remōved		sc
12. curious		kircus
13. silver		c
14. electric		c
15. worried	worry	
16. enemies	enemy	
17. glowed		DK
18. clothing		c
19. interested		c
20. entrance	entray	

Total Correct Automatic _5_ /20 = _25_%
Total Correct Identified _9_ /20 = _45_%
Total Number Correct _14_ /20 = _70_%

Level 2

Level 3

LEVELS		
Independent	Instructional	Frustration
18–20	14–17	below 14
90–100%	70–85%	below 70%

lists and at an instructional level on lists for grades two through four. If the examiner wants to be safe and present an initial passage that will ensure success, she or he should choose one that corresponds to the lowest instructional level attained on the lists.

Word-list scores for Chris, a third grader, provide an example of how to estimate a starting point for passage administration. Initially, Chris was asked to read the first grade list. He scored at an independent level. The second grade list was administered, and again, he attained an independent level. Chris scored at an instructional level for the third grade list and reached frustration at the fourth grade level. The examiner chose to administer a second grade passage first in order to ensure that Chris met with success with his initial attempt at oral reading. (However, a third grade passage would also have been a viable starting point.) Chris scored at an independent level in second grade text and attained an instructional level in third grade text.

When Joe, a fifth grader, read a third grade list, he scored at frustration level. The examiner moved to lower levels, and Joe scored at an instructional level for second grade and at an independent level for first grade. The first passage chosen for Joe to read was at a second grade level, which was his anticipated instructional level.

There are two types of readers whose levels the word-list scores will not predict accurately. One is a reader who makes exceptionally good use of context and, thus, whose capabilities in context far exceed her or his word identification in isolation. The word-list scores will underestimate this reader's capabilities. The other type of reader has comprehension problems but also has excellent word-identification capabilities. This student's abilities will be overestimated by the word-list scores.

Estimating Automatic Word Identification

A student's ability to identify words automatically is estimated as the number of words correctly read within one second. On each list this number is written in the column marked Identified Automatically. The examiner should compare the words read automatically and words identified after one second in order to decide whether automatic word identification represents a weakness for the student.

Caution: The graded word lists do not represent a natural reading situation and do not assess a student's comprehension ability. Also, some students identify words more effectively in context than in a list format. Therefore, a student's scores on an isolated list should never be used to estimate his or her overall reading ability.

Reading by Analogy: Comparing Knowledge of Low- and High-Frequency Vowel Patterns

Children who learn regular letter–sound patterns can transfer this knowledge to unfamiliar words. For example, child who knows "make" can probably use this knowledge to decode "rake" or "sake." This is called *decoding by analogy,* using known letter–sound patterns to pronounce new and unfamiliar words.

The Reading by Analogy Test contains 18 less-frequent words that share the same vowel patterns as the high-frequency words on the pre-primer through first grade lists. If a high-frequency word is read correctly on the word list, we cannot determine if it was decoded or read as a memorized sight word. However, if the student also correctly identified the accompanying low-frequency word, we can assume that decoding by analogy was probably used. To put it another way, a child who correctly identifies "make" but is unable to read "rake" probably reads "make" as a memorized sight word. However, the child who correctly identifies both "make" and "rake" probably decoded "rake" by using the known vowel pattern *ake.*

You can administer the test as a stand-alone measure, that is, administered apart from the word list tests. In this case, ask the child to read both the high-frequency words from the word lists and the 18 low-frequency words. You have the option to administer all four levels (PP1, PP2/3, Primer, and First) or just ask the child to read words matching his or her reading level. If a child correctly identifies *both* the low-frequency and high-frequency words containing the same vowel pattern, you can assume knowledge and use of vowel patterns as an aid to pronunciation.

If the word lists have already been administered, fill in the number of high-frequency words that were correctly identified and just ask the child to read the low-frequency list. Only administer the words that correspond to those from the word list. If the child did not read primer-level words, do not present the primer low-frequency words. Figure 6.2

Figure 6.2 **Reading by Analogy Test**

PP 1

High-Frequency Words from the Word Lists	Correct	Low-Frequency Words	Correct
can	c	pan	c
in		pin	
see	c	bee	c
at	c	rat	

PP2/3

High-Frequency Words from the Word Lists	Correct	Low-Frequency Words	Correct
make	c	rake	c
same		fame	
like	c	bike	c
place	c	race	
play		bay	
look	c	book	c

Primer

High-Frequency Words from the Word Lists	Correct	Low-Frequency Words	Correct
keep		peep	
need		seed	
thing		sing	
went		rent	
jump		bump	

First

High-Frequency Words from the Word Lists	Correct	Low-Frequency Words	Correct
sound		pound	
knew		chew	
brain		stain	
Total		Total	

contains an example of a recorded and scored Reading by Analogy Test. The test itself follows the word lists on page 104.

The student read PP1 and PP2/3 word lists during word list administration and correctly identified seven of the high-frequency vowel pattern words. Therefore, the examiner asked the student to only read the corresponding low-frequency words with the same vowel pattern. The student correctly identified five of these. This suggests that the student may be using knowledge of vowel patterns to decode other words, specifically those containing -an, -ee, -ake, -ike, and -ook. However, the student was not able to identify low-frequency words containing -at and -ace and may not have internalized these patterns as helpful in decoding words.

The value of this test is not in obtaining a score but in identifying characteristics. First, has the child internalized any letter–sound patterns or is she or he approaching each unfamiliar word as a completely new phenomenon unrelated to any previously known words? Second, which vowel patterns are known? Which are unknown? Answers can offer insights into the type of phonics instruction that will best help the reader. The child can be shown how to use known sound patterns to pronounce new words. Known vowel patterns can be applied to unfamiliar and multisyllabic words and phonics instruction can focus on identifying and using unknown patterns as aids to pronunciation.

Additional Diagnostic Uses of the Word Lists

Because many of the words on the lists are contained in the passage of corresponding readability, the examiner can choose to note whether a word missed on the list was identified correctly in context. Although this may involve only a small number of words, it can reveal a reader who is not utilizing context effectively.

The examiner can also note the accuracy of the student's decoding attempts within the untimed format. For example, are there any consonant or vowel sounds that are missed consistently? Does the student attempt to apply phonetic strategies to irregular words? Which phonetic principles are applied erroneously? Word-list administration can provide the examiner with a tool for probing into the student's strategies for pronouncing words. For example, the examiner can direct the student to various parts of unknown words and model word-analysis strategies to see whether she or he can take advantage of them. The examiner can cover up parts of words and uncover them sequentially for the student to pronounce. The examiner can contrast an unknown word with one of similar spelling or pronunciation to see whether the student can transfer knowledge to the unknown word. Any success achieved through examiner aid should be noted on the scoring sheet, but a student should not receive credit for it when the diagnostician is determining independent, instructional, and frustration levels for word identification in isolation.

Caution: A student's ability to decode words in isolation may be very different from her or his ability to identify words in context (Nicholson, Lillas, & Rzoska, 1988). Therefore, any diagnostic decisions made on the basis of word-list information should be corroborated by the student's performance while identifying words in the context of *QRI-5* passages.

7

Administration and Scoring of the *Qualitative Reading Inventory-5*

ASSESSMENT OF PRIOR KNOWLEDGE

Assessing Prior Knowledge
    Concept-Questions Task
    Prediction Task

ASSESSING PRIOR KNOWLEDGE

Because students' knowledge has such a powerful effect on comprehension, it is important to determine whether the selection read by the student contains familiar or unfamiliar concepts. Understanding what students know and do not know about important concepts or ideas in the selection allows the examiner to evaluate comprehension difficulties in relation to students' knowledge base. The *QRI-5* provides two methods for assessing prior knowledge: concept questions and predictions. Before reading a passage, a student should be asked to participate in one or both activities so the examiner can assess the student's familiarity with the topic of the selection. Lack of knowledge or a different knowledge of the concepts from that reflected in the text may explain difficulty in comprehension. Engaging in the concept questions and/or prediction tasks prior to reading can also serve to activate any background knowledge that the student has for the information contained in the selection. If this knowledge is consistent with text information, facilitation of comprehension will occur. Our pilot data suggested a strong relationship between prior knowledge and comprehension at the first grade level and above. In fact, prior knowledge predicted passage comprehension more frequently than did a general measure of reading achievement. This latter finding illustrates the value of measuring prior knowledge in reading assessment. See Section 15 for more on these findings.

Concept-Questions Task

General Procedures. For each passage there are three to five questions judged to be important to comprehension of the passage. Some questions were chosen because they represented the topic of the selection (such as a class trip, soccer, or viruses) or because they represented the person the selection was about (such as Martin Luther King, Jr., or Amelia Earhart). Other questions were included because we believed that if students understood them, they would be more likely to answer the implicit comprehension questions correctly (for example, questions involving animal defenses in the fifth grade passage "The Octopus" and changing seasons in the second grade passage "Seasons").

The questions are on the examiner's copy of the passage, directly under the title of the passage. The examiner should ask all these questions before the student reads the passage. The examiner should also ask all questions for each passage that the student reads.

Instructions for the concept-questions task are as follows: "Before you read, I want to know what you already know about some ideas in the text. I will ask you a few questions to find out." Additional examples are on the DVD.

3 Points: A Precise Definition, or a Definitional Response to a Phrase, or an Answer to a Question Specifically Related to Passage Content

Examples:

Why do people work? to get money for their families

What is "learning to read"? pronouncing and understanding words

What is the brain? we think with it or it runs our body

When do you see turtles outside? in summer when it's hot, because turtles like the sun

What do flowers need to grow? sunlight, water, and food

Why do people sing together? they like to do this; they like making music with other people

What are things to pack if you are going on an overnight trip? clothes, pajamas, and a toothbrush

What does it mean to be adopted? you get new parents

A Synonym

Examples:

What does "coiled" mean to you? twisted or wound in a circle

What is a puppy? a baby dog

What are claws? nails

What is the fall? autumn

What is a horn? a musical instrument

What is a streamliner? a train

What is a ratio? a fraction

What is a pharaoh? a king

What is a biography? a life story

2 Points: An Example of the Concept

Examples:

What is working at home? cleaning house, washing dishes

What happens when someone gets very tired? my baby sister fusses and moves around a lot and then starts crying but finally falls asleep

What is an animal care center? well when our dog hurt his paw, we took him to a place where they bandaged it and made it well so I guess that is a care center

What does it mean if something is lucky? you win the lottery or you find some money on the street

What does it mean to communicate with another person? you wave your arms at them so they know you are there; you write notes

A Specific Attribute or Defining Characteristics

Examples:

What does it mean to have a shy personality? you kind of hang back and don't talk to
  people first
What does the word "survive" mean? if something bad happens like a tornado you are
  still alive
What is a settlement? it's land but it has homes on it
What do nuclear reactions produce? a very big blast like an explosion
What do you know about Vietnam? the U.S. was in a war there

A Function

Examples:

What is Washington, D.C.? a city where Martin Luther King, Jr., did his "I Have a Dream"
  speech
What is wool used for? you can make coats and pants and scarves
What does the word "imagination" mean? it helps you when you are bored because you
  can pretend you are somewhere else
What is an autobiography? you can learn about people by reading them

1 Point: A General Association

Examples:

What does "going to work" mean to you? leaving the house
What does it mean when something is found? it's a good thing
What are seeds? you can buy them in a store
What happens when someone gets very tired? it's not good to get tired
Why wouldn't a child get everything that he or she wanted for her birthday? maybe she
  forgot to tell her parents
What does the word "celebration" mean? it's a happy word
Why do people go to libraries? to get something

Isolation of Prefix, Suffix, or Root Word

Examples:

What is a streamliner? it moves like a stream
What is a repairman? someone who repairs
What is an advancement? it advances
What do we mean by hardship? something hard
What does "unrestricted" mean? not restricted
What does "reeducation" mean? educate again

Firsthand, Personal Associations

Examples:

What happens when a car or bus breaks down? my dad fixes it
What is learning to read? I learned to read in first grade
What is a school trip? my mother came on our field trip
What does "an old house for sale" mean to you? we just sold our house
What happens when someone gets very tired? my mother makes me go to bed

0 Points: **Sound-Alikes**

Examples:

What is a bear? wear
What is fall? wall

Unconnected Responses

Examples:

What does "looking for something" mean to you? Batman
Who was Martin Luther King, Jr.? wears a crown

No Response or I Don't Know

Interpreting the Concept-Questions Scores.   Generally, we have found that students who score at least 55% of the points possible on the concept task score above 70% on comprehension questions on the related passage. See Section 15 for details.

Prediction Task

General Procedures.   After administration of the concept-questions task, the examiner may choose to administer the prediction task. If so, the examiner should say, "Given that the title of the passage is _____, and it includes the ideas _____, _____, and _____ (naming all the concepts within the questions), what do you think the passage will be about? I want you to take a guess or make a prediction about what you think the passage will be about." For example, on the third grade selection "The Trip to the Zoo," the instructions would be phrased, "Given that the title of the passage is 'The Trip to the Zoo' and that it has the ideas 'class trip,' 'taking notes,' 'being by yourself,' and 'why people use maps,' what do you think the story will be about?" If the student simply restates the title of the passage, the examiner should provide a *general* probe for more information. For example, if the student says, "Amelia Earhart," say, "What about Amelia Earhart?"

Scoring the Prediction Task.   Leslie and Cooper (1993) examined three ways of scoring the prediction task and found that one of them significantly correlated with retelling and comprehension among sixth graders. Further piloting of the task at other reading levels and ages found that the same method of scoring was related to retelling and/or comprehension at second and third grade reading levels. Thus, we have chosen to score the prediction task by counting the number of idea statements the student predicts *that are contained in the passage either explicitly or implicitly.* By idea statements, we mean any proposition (verb and accompanying nouns) contained in the selection or implied by the selection. The following list, which is also on the DVD, provides students' predictions and our scoring from passages at diverse levels. The idea statements are in italics.

Pre-Primer Story: "Just Like Mom"
2 Ideas:

— *Mom is going to work,* and having a good day. Dad is doing something at the end. *The girl does everything the Mom does.*
— *Mom is working at home* and *going to work.*

1 Idea:

— *Mom is working.*
— What a mom is and *mom going to work.*
— *Working with Mom*

0 Ideas:

— Mom

Primer Story: **"The Pig Who Learned to Read"**

2 Ideas:

— *The pig that just learned to read* and *he liked it.*
— *A pig that heard people read; learned to read.*

1 Idea:

— *A pig learning how to read*
— *A pig that learns to read*

0 Ideas:

— The pig who told the boy how to read

Level Three Passage: **"The Trip to the Zoo"**

5 Ideas:

— *Somebody is going to a zoo on a field trip; gets lost; looks at a map; and finds his way back*

3 Ideas:

— *Taking a trip; taking notes; and having a map for directions*

1 Idea:

— *About going to the zoo*

0 Ideas:

— Things you can see, touch, or use

Level Four Passage: **"Early Railroads"**

2 Ideas:

— *About steam engines and traveling on them*

1 Idea:

— *About railroads*

Level Five Passage: **"How Does Your Body Take in Oxygen?"**

2 Ideas:

— *Why you need oxygen and about air in your blood*

1 Idea:

— About breathing

Level Six Passage: **"The Lifeline of the Nile"**

2 Ideas:

— *About the Nile flooding and how this helped the harvest*
— *About harvests and floods*

1 Idea:

— *About floods*

Upper Middle School Passage: "Immigration—Part 1"
2 Ideas:

— *About immigrants* and *how hard it was for them*

1 Idea:

— *Why immigrants leave*

Upper Middle School Passage: "Life Cycles of Stars—Part 1"
3 Ideas:

— *What stars are made of; the life of a star;* and *what happens when there is a nuclear reaction*

1 Idea:

— *What makes up a star*

Interpretation of the Prediction Scores.   As you can see from the predictions made by students, most students gave only one or two idea statements in their predictions. There seem to be three levels of quality in predictions. First, there are young readers, who only restate the title and do not integrate the concepts at all. Second, there are students who integrate some of the concepts and make a prediction using them. For example, on "The Trip to the Zoo," a student predicts, "taking a trip and taking notes and having a map for directions." Finally, there is the occasional student who is so knowledgeable about the concepts as to make a prediction that sums up many main ideas contained in the selection. For example, such a student might answer the concept questions for the sixth grade passage "Building Pyramids" by predicting, "It's about how they built the pyramids in Egypt. It will probably say how long it took and what they were made of. And how they turned their pharaohs into mummies and put them in the pyramid and why they did it and about what the archaeologists discovered."

In summary, predictions should be evaluated in light of the examples, which are from our pilot data on average readers. Qualitative judgments can be made by examining whether or not students have integrated any of the concepts with the title in order to make predictions. Recognize that this skill, like all other skills, is learned and is subject to instruction. If we want children to make good predictions, we have to teach them how by modeling.

8

Administration and Scoring of the *Qualitative Reading Inventory-5*

THE PASSAGES

PURPOSES FOR ADMINISTERING THE PASSAGES

There are three main purposes for administering the passages.

1. Determination of a Student's Independent, Instructional, and/or Frustration Levels. This involves two steps: determining levels for word identification in context and determining levels for comprehension.

- *Word Identification in Context.* The examiner determines levels for word identification in context by asking the student to read graded passages orally. The examiner records the errors/miscues made and counts them to designate the level. The miscues can be counted in two ways, depending on preference or philosophy. The examiner can count all miscues regardless of quality and use this total to determine the level. We call this *Total Accuracy.* Alternatively, the examiner can choose to count only miscues that change or distort passage meaning, referred to as *Total Acceptability.* Section 9 explains how to identify, count, and score miscues.

- *Comprehension.* The examiner determines a student's independent, instructional, and frustration levels for comprehension by asking the student to read graded passages orally or silently and answer questions based on passage content. The examiner counts the number of correct answers to determine the designation of level. Section 10 explains the scoring of comprehension questions.

2. Assessment of a Student's Ability to Read Different Types of Text. The examiner can ask the student to read narrative and expository text, familiar and unfamiliar text, or text with and without pictures (pre-primer through grade two). He or she can determine independent, instructional, and frustration levels for each type of text depending on the diagnostic purposes. Not all levels should be determined for all passage types. To do so would require an inordinate and unrealistic amount of time. Determination of a familiar level is most important. For most students, determination of this level in narrative text is the primary concern. Narrative text is generally easier than expository text, so assessment of familiar levels in this genre tends to represent a student's best effort.

3. Assessment of a Student's Ability to Comprehend in Different Modes. The examiner can ask the student to read orally or silently. Then he or she determines independent, instructional, and frustration levels in oral reading from two scores: the number of miscues made while reading orally and the number of questions answered correctly. Guidelines for determining a total passage level for oral reading are explained later in this section. The examiner determines silent reading levels on the basis of the number of comprehension questions answered correctly. Section 10 contains guidelines for determining silent reading comprehension.

ASSESSMENT OPTIONS

Administration of the passages can also involve several diagnostic options.

1. Assessment of Prior Knowledge. There are two options for determining a student's prior knowledge for the topic of a passage: the concept-questions task and the prediction task. See Section 7 for an explanation of both.

2. Oral Reading Miscue Analysis. There are three types of miscues made while reading orally: whole-word substitutions, such as "tried" for "trade"; nonword substitutions, such as "trad" for "trade"; and omissions and insertions of words. See Section 9 for an explanation of analyzing and interpreting oral reading miscues.

3. Assessment of Comprehension through Unaided Recall. The examiner can ask the student to retell the passage as though telling it to someone who had never read it. The examiner can then record the number of ideas recalled and map them on a retelling scoring sheet. This recall can be evaluated for completeness, accuracy, sequence, and use of narrative and expository structure. (See Section 10 for guidelines on recording and interpreting unaided recall.) The quality of unaided recall can be contrasted with the student's ability to answer explicit and implicit questions about passage content.

4. Assessment of Comprehension through Look-Backs. After asking the student to answer questions, the examiner can then ask the student to look back in the text to locate answers to missed questions or to amend incorrect responses.

5. Assessment of Comprehension through Think-Alouds. In level six, upper middle school, and high school passages, the examiner can model the think-aloud process and then ask the student to think aloud while reading.

Examiners must choose purposes that are germane to their diagnostic needs. Seldom will an individual diagnostician utilize all the diagnostic options of the *QRI-5*. Examiners must ask themselves, "What are my purposes in administering the passages?" and choose the level and types of passages accordingly.

General
Administration
Guidelines

After choosing a passage for the student to read and using the concept-questions or prediction tasks to determine the student's familiarity with the topic of the selection, the examiner should then ask the student to read the passage orally or silently.

If the student reads the passage orally, the examiner should record the student's miscues (substitutions, omissions, and insertions) on the examiner copy of the passage. The examiner should also time the student's rate of oral reading. Once the student completes the passage, the examiner removes it and assesses comprehension by asking the reader to retell what he or she remembers, to answer explicit and implicit questions, or to do both. If the student reads the passage silently, the examiner obviously cannot mark oral miscues but can instead time the student's rate of reading and assess comprehension in the above manner.

The examiner should then determine whether the total performance on the passage represents an independent, instructional, or frustration level for the student. These levels are obtained from two scores. The total number of oral reading miscues determines the level for word identification in context. The percentage of questions answered correctly determines the level for comprehension. The examiner then compares these two scores to determine a general passage level.

Instructions to the
Student

"You now get to show me how you can read on your own. We'll see how well I pick things for you to read so some you will read out loud and some you can read to yourself. Do you understand so far?

"Because my job is to make sure I remember all the things you do as a reader, I'm going to write notes and record this. This will make sure I don't miss any of the great things you do. Since this is your time to show me who you are as a reader, I can't give you any hints or any help. If you come to a word you don't know, do your best and keep on going. Do you understand so far?

"When you are done reading, I'll ask you to retell what you read. Your job is to pretend that I didn't hear you read this or that I didn't know the selection. So tell me as much as you can. After you tell me all you can remember, I will ask you some questions. Again pretend that I don't know anything about the selection so tell me all that you can. Do you have any questions?

"Ready? The first selection is called _____."

PASSAGE SELECTION

As a decision maker, the examiner must choose, in accordance with his or her purposes, the number and types of passages to administer. Examiners can clarify this process by asking several questions regarding passage administration.

Which Level of Passage Should I Begin With?   An examiner can use the word lists to estimate a beginning point. This helps avoid starting too low or too high. If the passage is too difficult, the frustration at the beginning of a diagnostic session can prejudice the student against the entire process. The examiner should choose a level where the student has attained the independent level on the accompanying word list. (See Section 6 for an explanation of using the word lists to select a beginning point.) If there are data to suggest a viable starting point, such as test scores or reading-group placement, the examiner does not have to use the word lists for this purpose.

Must I Find Independent, Instructional, and Frustration Levels for All Types of Text? No. To do so would demand an unrealistic amount of time, and student fatigue would be a very real concern. Determination of an instructional level is of primary importance in most cases. Finding the instructional level in familiar text is more important than level determination in unfamiliar text. After obtaining the instructional level, the examiner can often estimate the independent and frustration levels.

Do I Have to Administer All Passages within a Readability Level? No. The passages chosen will depend on the examiner's purpose in giving the *QRI-5*. Assessment specialists may well use more passages than a classroom teacher attempting to determine an instructional level for text placement.

How Can I Select Passages for Pre- and Post-Testing? If you wish to use *QRI-5* for pre- and post-testing, you have several options. You can administer the same passage as your pre- and post-measure. Or you can administer two passages at the same readability level. For this option, select passages that are somewhat similar. They should both be either narrative or expository. They should be of roughly the same length and familiarity. However, even within a single readability level, passages can vary in difficulty. Table 15.13 in Section 15 indicates which passages tend to be more difficult at each readability level. You may wish to choose the easier passage as the pre-test and the more difficult one as the post-test. In this way, gains made on the post-test will tend to be a more accurate indicator of actual growth.

What Types of Passages Should I Start With? Determining the student's instructional level for familiar text is the first step. Within this parameter, an examiner can select either narrative or expository text. For younger readers, we suggest that text with pictures often provides an effective starting point. For students thought to be at levels six through high school, choice of narrative or expository text depends on the instructional needs and known capabilities of the student. Very often, students are performing acceptably in reading or literature classes but experiencing difficulties in content-area classes. For these students, expository text would be more crucial than narrative. If the examiner has no clear direction as to desired text type, familiar narrative assessment represents a good beginning point. Generally easier than expository text, narrative tends to lead to initial experiences of success for students and to represent their best efforts.

Which Mode Should I Use: Oral or Silent? We suggest that examiners use an oral reading format with younger children and with older students suspected of reading below the third grade level. The examiner can estimate this by the word-list scores. Students at this point are still learning how to read, and listening to oral reading performance can offer much valuable information. However, if time permits, asking younger children to read a familiar narrative silently can sometimes provide information about how well they are making the transition to silent reading.

For students reading at levels three through five, the examiner should use a combination of oral and silent reading. At these levels, oral reading miscues can provide important information. Once an instructional level is established for narrative material, the examiner may wish to change to a silent reading mode. It is better to evaluate ability in expository text through silent reading, because most students are expected to read expository material silently in school. For students reading at levels six through high school, silent reading is the best format because individuals do little oral reading at these levels.

HOW TO FIND AN INSTRUCTIONAL LEVEL

Finding the Instructional Level in Familiar Text

The examiner can use the word lists or knowledge of the student to choose a beginning passage that will probably offer an initial experience of success to the reader. The passage should be a familiar narrative. The examiner using the word lists can choose a passage of the same readability level as the lowest word list on which the student scored at an instructional level (see Section 6). The examiner should ask the student to read the passage orally and answer the questions. The count of oral reading miscues determines the level for word identification in context. (See Section 9 for guidelines for counting miscues and using this count to arrive at independent, instructional, and frustration levels.) The examiner then counts the questions answered correctly to determine the comprehension level. (See Section 10 for guidelines on scoring comprehension.) Once the examiner has the word-identification (WR) and comprehension (Comp) levels, he or she is ready to determine total passage level using the following guidelines:

WR: Independent	+	Comp: Independent	=	Independent Level
	+	Comp: Instructional	=	Instructional Level
	+	Comp: Frustration	=	Frustration Level
WR: Instructional	+	Comp: Independent	=	Instructional Level
	+	Comp: Instructional	=	Instructional Level
	+	Comp: Frustration	=	Frustration Level
WR: Frustration	+	Comp: Independent	=	Frustration Level
	+	Comp: Instructional	=	Frustration Level

If the student reads silently, the examiner can determine the total passage level by the comprehension score.

If the student scores within the independent or instructional range on the first passage, the examiner should choose another familiar narrative passage at the next higher level, continuing upward until the student reaches a frustration level. If the student reaches a frustration level on the first passage, the examiner should move downward until the student reaches an instructional level. There may be times when the examiner will not choose to find the highest instructional level. If the student reaches an instructional level at her or his chronological grade level, determining levels above chronological grade placement or ascertaining the exact frustration level may have little value.

Having found the student's instructional level, the examiner may choose to have the student read the other familiar narrative passage at that level. If the first passage was read orally, the student should read the second one silently, allowing the examiner to assess the student's ability in both oral and silent reading. If performance is different, the student may be experiencing discrepancies between the two modes. If the student read the first passage silently, the examiner may choose to verify the attained level by having the second one read silently also. Verification of levels and comparison of oral and silent reading provide for a more in-depth assessment; however, they are options that the examiner may choose to bypass in the interest of time.

Finding the Instructional Level in Other Types of Material

Having determined the familiar narrative instructional level, the examiner may wish to contrast it with other types of text: text with and without pictures (pre-primer through grade two), unfamiliar selections, and expository text. For expository text, the examiner should begin at the instructional level attained in familiar narratives and move up or down as indicated by the student's performance. For unfamiliar text, the examiner should begin one level lower than the level attained in familiar material. You will find two figures in Section 8 of the DVD that detail how to find an instructional level and the specific criteria for determining independent, instructional, and frustration levels.

Administration and Scoring of the *Qualitative Reading Inventory-5*

WORD IDENTIFICATION IN CONTEXT: ORAL READING

RECORDING ORAL READING MISCUES

When the student is reading orally, the examiner marks any miscues the student makes. It is helpful to record the oral reading segment; then the examiner will be sure to catch the miscues. As one becomes more proficient in recording student miscues, the audio becomes less important. We suggest the following system for recording miscues:

- *Substitution:* Write what the student said over the word as it appears in print.
- *Omission:* Circle the omitted word.
- *Insertion:* Write in the insertion and mark it with a $\wedge$.
- *Self-correction:* If a student corrects a miscue, write the miscue and mark it with "C."
- *Reversal:* If the student transposes two words or phrases, such as "Said John" for "John said," mark the reversal with a $\cap$ symbol.
- *Punctuation ignored:* Mark an "X" on any punctuation that the reader ignores.
- Mark miscues that change meaning as "MC."

Examples:

TEXT: Once there was a very (big) bear. ˣ

          loved ᶜ   *dark*
        He lived in the ᴧ woods.

        One day his father saw the big bear crying.

        Why are you crying, his father said.

In this example, the student omitted "big" in the first sentence and ignored the period by continuing to read. In the second sentence, the student said "loved" for "lived" and self-corrected. The student also inserted "dark." In the last sentence, the child read, "said his father" instead of "his father said."

Most IRIs allow the examiner to offer assistance to the student encountering an unfamiliar word. We do not recommend this. It is impossible to assess the effect of word identification on comprehension if the student is given the correct pronunciation for key words in the passage. If a student is unable to identify a word, gently ask him or her to move on. Figure 9.1 offers additional examples of recorded miscues.

| Figure 9.1 | **Example of Reading and Scoring Miscues** |

wet ¹ mc   *went* ² mc
It was a warm spring day. The <u>children</u> <u>were</u> <u>going</u> on a trip. The trip was

aminals ³ mc
to a farm. The <u>children</u> <u>wanted</u> to see many <u>animals</u>. <u>They</u> <u>wanted</u> to <u>write</u>

gone ⁵ mc   *the* ⁶
⁴ mc
down ⃝all⃝ <u>they</u> saw. <u>They</u> <u>were</u> <u>going</u> to <u>make</u> a book for their class. On the

pumpkin ⁷ mc
way to the ⌃farm the bus stopped ⃝moving⃝ ⁸ The <u>children</u> thought their trip

stepped ⁹ mc   ¹⁰
was over. Then a man stopped his car. He <u>helped</u> ⃝to⃝ fix the bus. The

won't c 11
bus ⌃started <u>again</u>. The <u>children</u> <u>said</u>, "Yea!" The <u>children</u> got to the farm.

was c 12   13 *hens*   *looked* 14 mc
<u>They</u> saw a pig. <u>They</u> saw a hen and cows. <u>They</u> <u>liked</u> petting the kittens.

looked 15 mc   *and* 16
<u>They</u> learned about milking cows. They <u>liked</u> the trip to the farm. <u>They</u>

<u>want</u>ed to go <u>again</u>. (119 words)

The following miscues were substitutions:
   #1, 2, 3, 5, 6, 9, 12, 13, 14, 15, 16

The following miscues were insertions:
   #7, 11

The following miscues were omissions:
   #4, 8, 10

The following miscues were meaning-changing miscues. They changed the meaning of the text or they were not self-corrected.
   #1, 2, 3, 4, 5, 7, 9, 14, 15

Examiners can count miscues in two ways. The examiner can determine independent, instructional, and frustration levels by counting all miscues. We call this *Total Accuracy*. Or the examiner may choose to count only those miscues that change or distort passage meaning. We call this *Total Acceptability*. It is not necessary to do both. Total Accuracy is perhaps the easier and less time-consuming to score. The examiner does not have to spend time deciding whether or not miscues distort meaning. However, the diagnostic philosophy of the examiner will determine which scoring system to use. If the examiner decides to use Total Acceptability, the examiner may still find it easier during the actual administration to record all miscues and only determine Total Acceptability after completing the test administration. In addition, the record of miscues that do not change meaning and the self-correction patterns of the reader can be used for later miscue analysis.

Counting Total Accuracy

Any deviation from the printed text is counted as a miscue. This includes

insertions
omissions
substitutions
reversals
self-corrections

We do not count repetitions, hesitations, and omission of punctuation because they tend to be scored unreliably (Hood, 1975–1976). Also, repetitions and hesitations may indicate uncertainty on the part of the student or a desire to clarify meaning that was missed. It can also be argued that repetitions and hesitations do not alter the text materially and therefore do not truly represent an error (McKenna, 1983).

Miscues made on proper names represent a special problem because of the extreme variability in pronunciation of some names. We recommend the following: If the student pronounces a proper name as a nonsense name—a name the examiner has never heard—and repeatedly calls the character by that name, the examiner should count it as one miscue. For example, if the student consistently refers to "Maria" as "Marin," these deviations count as one miscue. If, however, the student refers to "Maria" as "Marin," "Morin," and "Meres," each deviation is a separate miscue.

If a student makes the same miscue on the same word several times in the passage and it does not change the meaning of the passage, the examiner should count it as one miscue. For example, if a student consistently refers to "puppy" as "pup" or to "planes" as "airplanes," the deviations count as one miscue. If, however, the consistent miscue changes meaning, such as "poppy" for "puppy" or "please" for "planes," each pronunciation counts as a separate miscue. When a single word is repeated numerous times throughout a passage, students often pronounce it identically several times and then change to another pronunciation. How should this be scored? We recommend that each mispronunciation of the word be scored as a separate miscue. Examiners should assign *one* point to several miscues only if the mispronunciation does not change meaning and is consistent across the entire passage.

If a student omits an entire line, it is counted as one miscue because the omission represents a loss of place, not a conscious omission because of inability to identify words. Obviously, in this case, the student is not monitoring comprehension, and counting each omitted word as a separate miscue could distort the final level designation.

Variations in pronunciations due to articulation difficulties or regional dialects should not be counted as oral reading miscues unless the student has been observed to pronounce the word or word part correctly. For example, if a student who speaks a form of African American English (AAE) omits the "s" or "ed" marker sometimes but reads it in other cases, it should be counted as an oral reading miscue. The examiner should not assume that a student does or does not speak a particular dialect but should determine speaking patterns through casual conversation with the student before, during, and after testing.

Dialect differences vary signficantly among AAE speakers. You will find guidelines (adapted from Craig, Thompson, Washington, & Potter, 2003) that compare examples of AAE and Standard English on the DVD.

Individuals have questioned the inclusion of self-corrections as miscues that count toward Total Accuracy. We believe it is important to carefully record self-corrections and count them as miscues. First, they represent a deviation from the text and, even if self-corrected, can affect fluency and/or comprehension. A large number of self-corrections suggests a pattern of uncertainty on the part of the reader. If the examiner feels very strongly that self-corrections should not be counted, we recommend that Total Acceptability be used as the method of scoring and determining level.

The examiner should count the total number of miscues and use this result to determine whether the student's performance reflects an independent, instructional, or frustration level. For ease and accuracy in scoring, we recommend numbering the miscues. The following criteria determine level designations for word identification in context:

Total Accuracy

Independent Level:	98% accuracy
Instructional Level:	90% to 97% accuracy
Frustration Level:	less than 90% accuracy

The examiner can determine percentages by subtracting the number of miscues from the number of words in the passage (listed at the bottom of his or her copy of the passage). This yields the number of words read correctly, which is then divided by the number of words in the passage, rounding upward to find the percent of Total Accuracy. She or he may also wish to use the guidelines given at the bottom of each passage indicating how many miscues result in independent, instructional, or frustration levels. Examiners who use these will not need to determine percentages.

Example: "A Trip" has 119 words. A student made 8 total miscues.

$$\begin{array}{r} 119 \\ \underline{-8} \\ 111 \end{array} \div 119 = 93\% \text{ Total Accuracy}$$

For Total Accuracy, the student scored within the criteria for the instructional level of word identification in context.

Counting Total Acceptability: What Is a Meaning-Change Miscue?

Acceptable miscues are those that do not change or distort passage meaning. A meaning change miscue is any deviation from the text that results in an ungrammatical sentence or in a grammatical sentence that differs from the author's meaning. Meaning change miscues include substitutions or mispronunciations, insertions, and omissions.

Determining whether a miscue changes text meaning is not as clear-cut as one would wish. Some miscues are very obvious. Substituting a nonsense word for a text word ("rayvin" for "ravine") clearly changes meaning. The substitution of a synonym ("noise" for "sound") usually does not. However, other substitutions may or may not change meaning, depending on the preceding text and the structure of the sentence. For example, the simple substitution of the article "a" for "the" can distort meaning if it results in an ungrammatical sentence. Given the sentence "Ben had heard the songs before," a child who reads "Ben had heard a songs before," has produced an ungrammatical sentence in opposition to oral and written language conventions. We do not place a singular article before a plural noun. So this sentence would be scored as containing two miscues that change meaning. Consider the following sentence: "Come and listen to the music." If the child reads "Came and listen to the music," basic language conventions are violated because we do not generally include different verb tenses in the same sentence.

In determining whether a miscue changes meaning, it is important to consider both semantic acceptability and syntactic acceptability. *Semantic acceptability* refers to the meaning of the sentence. Does the sentence with the miscue differ from the author's meaning? Substitutions of nonsense word or words with different definitions than the text word change meaning. Meaning can be changed by the omission of a negative marker or by the addition of one. "Mouse did say a word" is very different from "Mouse didn't say a word." Meaning may or may not be changed by the addition or omission of a plural ending or the substitution of a pronoun for a noun. It all depends on the sentence as a whole. Given the sentence "The puppy put his paw on the cage," a miscue of "paws" for "paw" does not change meaning while the substitution of "in" for "on" does, given the preceding story context.

The next thing to consider is *syntactic acceptability;* that is, does the sentence follow the grammar conventions of oral and written language? For example, sentences contain a main noun and verb; omission of one of these changes meaning. The omission of an adjective or adverb may not. A change in verb tense may not change meaning as in "Ben and Ruth want something to do" for "Ben and Ruth wanted something to do." In judging syntactic acceptability, we suggest that you read the sentence to yourself. If a sentence sounds "funny," it can affect meaning because it probably differs in some way from language conventions followed both in speech and written text. For example, consider the sentence "Then Mr. and Mrs. Mayer adopted him and brought him to America." If a child reads "Then Mr. and Mrs. Mayer adopt him and brought his to America," the sentence does not sound right for two reasons. We do not mix different verb tenses in the same sentence ("adopt" is present tense and "adopted" is past tense) and possessive pronouns ("his") are followed by nouns. Earlier in this section, we made the case that miscues following the conventions of African American English (AAE) should not be counted as meaning-change miscues. The opposite is also true. For speakers of Standard American English (SAE), miscues that violate the linguistic conventions of standard English should be counted as miscues that change or distort passage meaning.

It is impossible to offer specific guidelines for all possible miscues students will make. Each miscue must be examined within the context of the sentence and, in some cases, the previously read text to determine whether it distorts the meaning or grammar of the text. We can, however, offer some general suggestions.

If a student mispronounces a proper name, do not count it as a meaning-change miscue unless the gender of the character is changed. The substitution of "Mary" for "Maria" does not change meaning; the substitution of "Mark" for "Maria" does. If a student substitutes a nonword for a proper name ("Rutz" for "Ruth"), it does not necessarily change meaning if the substitution is consistent throughout the passage. However, if the student pronounces the name differently each time it is encountered ("Rutz," "Reth," "Rath"), count each attempt as a meaning-change miscue. Use the same conventions for names of cities, states, and countries.

If a student consistently makes a meaning-change miscue on the same word throughout the text, we suggest that it be counted each time because each mispronunciation, however consistent, distorts the text in some way.

We recommend that examiners judge meaning-change miscues as strictly as possible. It is better to underestimate a student's level than overestimate it. We also suggest that you be as consistent as possible across passages. For example, if you believe that the deletion of the –ly ending in the sentence "Also, four people could never sing as loudly or joyfully as her whole family" does not adversely distort the syntactic acceptability of the text, then maintain this position across other texts and different children. If you believe that change of verb tense or omission of "is," "am," and other forms of "to be" preceding verbs ending in "ing" distorts meaning, maintain this position throughout. In scoring miscues for our pilot sample, we found it helpful to note these decisions as we went along so our scoring could be as consistent as possible across passages and children.

Mark each meaning-change miscue as "MC" or highlight it in some way. Count the number of meaning-change miscues and use the guidelines on the examiner copy of each passage to determine independent, instructional, or frustration levels for Total Acceptability. The following criteria determine level designations for word identification in context. (See Section 15 for a further explanation of these criteria.)

Total Acceptability

Independent Level:	98% Total Acceptability
Instructional Level:	95% to 97% Total Acceptability
Frustration Level:	less than 94% Total Acceptability

After counting the meaning-change miscues and subtracting the result from the number of words in the passage, the examiner divides this by the number of words in the passage, rounding upward to find the percentage of Total Acceptability. She or he may also use the guidelines given at the end of the passage, which indicate how many meaning-change miscues result in an independent, instructional, or frustration reading level.

Example: "A Trip" has 119 words. A student made a total of 8 miscues. Four of these were meaning-change miscues.

$$\begin{array}{r} 119 \\ \underline{-4} \\ 115 \end{array} \div 119 = 96.6 = 97\% \text{ Total Acceptability}$$

For Total Acceptability, the student scored within an instructional level for word identification in context.

ANALYZING ORAL READING MISCUES: MISCUE ANALYSIS

Recording Miscues   Examiners can qualitatively analyze miscues the student makes while reading passages orally. This analysis can provide information about a student's word identification strategies and suggest whether the student is primarily focusing on saying words or deriving meaning from the text. Such information can help in designing instruction that focuses on a student's strengths while addressing possible areas of need.

The Miscue Analysis Worksheet (Figure 9.2) provides a format for qualitatively analyzing the student's miscues. Miscue analysis works best with at least 15 to 20 miscues because patterns of behavior are not as evident with smaller numbers.

We recommend that you analyze only mispronunciations, not insertions or omissions. Insertions represented only a small part of the miscues made by our pilot group, ranging from 3 to 11% of the total miscues made in a passage. Insertions usually occur because the student is predicting what is coming next. For example, the student might read, "Marva went to . . . ," and pause before continuing, "out and picked up the cat." This insertion suggests that the student used prior meaning to predict that "to" would follow "Marva went." In our pilot sample of children reading primer through third grade selections, the majority of insertions occurred at the beginnings of sentences and were clearly predictive in nature. Predictive insertions suggest attention to meaning at least at the sentence level.

Omissions represented 10 to 23% of the total miscues made on a passage by students in our pilot sample. Omissions often reflect a loss of place by the reader. The largest number of omissions occurred at the third grade level and represented words omitted because the student was unable to pronounce them or unwilling to try. We suggest that you count omissions and insertions apart from the miscue analysis sheet and comment on them if they seem to represent a pattern such as prediction, inability or unwillingness to pronounce a word, or loss of place.

To use the chart, write the text word in the first column and the mispronunciation in the second column. Use check marks for the remaining columns. In column 3, evaluate the similarity of the mispronunciation to the text word by placing a check to indicate that the miscue represents one or more of the following patterns. Do the miscue and text word begin with the same letter or sound ("call" for "claw") or share a common consonant pattern ("broke" for "bright")? Do the miscue and text word share a common vowel pattern or phonogram ("then" for "when" or "hear" for "near")? Does the miscue resemble the text word in the final letter(s) or letter patterns ("fits" for "fins" or "decks" for "ducks") or do the miscue and text word share a common morphological ending ("looked" for "watched" or "going" for "sailing")? Some miscues may resemble the text word in one area, typically the beginning of the word, and others may resemble the word in more than one way.

In past editions of the *QRI,* we differentiated between miscues in the beginning, ending, or medial positions; however, we do not recommend that such patterns be analyzed separately. We believe it is sufficient for several reasons to indicate similarity as signaled by one, two, or three positions. First, our pilot data suggested similar percentages across primer through third grade levels at all three positions. Miscues with similar beginnings to text words were most prevalent with 72 to 73% of the miscues representing similar beginning patterns. Miscues with similar text word endings represented 30 to 50%, and miscues similar to the middle of text words represented 33 to 57% of the total miscues. Second, phonics instruction should involve attention to pronunciation of the entire word. For example, Beck (2006) suggests that beginning and ending sounds should be taught concurrently and that vowel sounds should be taught right from the beginning instead of waiting until a certain number of consonant sounds are mastered. Third, miscue analysis of sound patterns only offers general suggestions for instruction. It shows that the reader is paying attention to letter and sound patterns, but not which patterns have been mastered. Our pilot study suggested that students can miss a specific sound component in one word but successfully pronounce it in a subsequent one.

Figure 9.2   **Miscue Analysis Worksheet**

Student Name_____   **Selections** _____

1. Text Word	2. Miscue	3. Similar Letter–Sound Patterns	4. Changes Meaning	5. Corrected	6. Does Not Change Meaning	7. Corrected
Total Miscues		Similar Letter–Sound Patterns	Meaning-Change Miscues	Corrected Meaning-Change Miscues	Non-Meaning-Change Miscues	Corrected Non-Meaning-Change Miscues
Analysis: Columns Total						
Columns Total/Total Miscue Type = %						

Fourth, miscue analysis can take a large amount of time, something that is not always readily available to the reading specialist or teacher. Coding miscues as similar in sound without differentiating between the beginnings, middles, and ends of words is a faster process. It is also a more reliable one. Separating the beginning, middle, and end of a word may be relatively easy in a single-syllable word but not quite as easy in a multi-syllable one. While the miscue of "table" for "tablet" represents a relatively easy form of sound analysis, the same cannot be said for miscues such as "inspiration" for "expression" or "communicated" for "continued." While it is quite easy to identify the similarity of a beginning or ending sound, in the medial position we are often confronted with a miscue that retains the sound of the word but not its spelling or vice versa. For example, the substitution of "through" for "thought" retains the spelling of the word in the medial position but not the sound.

Use columns 4 and 5 to indicate whether the miscue changes the meaning of the text word and whether it is corrected. Correction of meaning-change miscues suggests that the student is paying attention to meaning during the reading process. An example is the substitution of "interrupted" for "introduced" in the following sentence: "Mrs. Wagner had introduced Ivan to the class about a week ago." Because the reader is comprehending during the reading process, he or she is able to note a miscue that distorts the author's meaning. As mentioned in Section 2, we noticed a significant increase in the number of meaning-change miscues that were corrected at a third grade level in our pilot sample as compared to correction of those that did not change meaning.

Use columns 6 and 7 to evaluate the number of corrections made to miscues that do not substantively alter the meaning of the text. An example would be the reader who self-corrects an acceptable miscue such as "put" for "divided" in the sentence "When they got to the zoo, their teachers divided the children into four groups." Other examples would be the substitution of "anyways" for "anyway" in the following sentence: "I'm going to wish for it anyway" or the substitution of "bookpack" for "backpack" in "Then he took the train book out of his backpack." What do such corrections suggest? We hypothesize that they imply that the student is still primarily focused on identifying the correct word. Such miscues can also reflect attention to comprehension but possibly at a sentence level as opposed to total passage level. As mentioned in Section 2, our pilot data suggested that readers at primer through second grade levels tended to self-correct both meaning-change and non-meaning-change miscues. However, readers at a third grade level demonstrated a focus on self-correcting miscues that clearly distorted meaning, suggesting that they were paying attention to passage meaning beyond the limits of a specific sentence.

Counting Miscues

Once you have recorded all miscues, total each column as indicated on the worksheet. First count the total number of miscues made by the student (column 2). Then count the number of checks in each of columns 3 through 6. You can determine the percentage of miscues that were similar in sound to the text word (column 3) by dividing the column total by the number of total miscues recorded in column 2. For example, if the student made a total of 23 miscues and 15 of these were similar in sound patterns, 15/23 = 65%. You can determine the percentage of miscues that changed meaning and were corrected (column 5) by dividing the column total by the total number of meaning-change miscues (column 4). Similarly, determine the percentage of non-meaning-change miscues that were corrected (column 7) by the total number of non-meaning-change miscues (column 6).

Analyzing the Miscues

The Miscue Analysis Worksheet can indicate the strategies used by the student when reading orally. Percentages should not be interpreted rigidly; no percentage limits are given. Rather, they should be used as a means of noting general patterns of reader behavior. The following guidelines may be helpful in interpreting the percentages.

1. If the worksheet shows a high percentage of sound similarity, the reader is clearly paying attention to letters and sound patterns in decoding words. However, to definitively identify which letter patterns are known or unknown, some form of added phonics assessment is necessary.

2. If the worksheet shows a high percentage of miscues that retain meaning, the reader is probably comprehending during the reading process. However, if a high percentage of these non-meaning-change miscues are corrected, the reader may still be focusing more on pronouncing words accurately than in deriving meaning from the text.

3. A high percentage of miscues that change passage meaning may suggest difficulty with comprehension. However, if a large number of these meaning-change miscues are corrected, attention to meaning is suggested.

Miscue analysis offers general suggestions for how students are processing text and such observations need to be made in relation to the student's comprehension score on the passages.

EVALUATING AUTOMATICITY

Rate of oral and silent reading can suggest automaticity of word identification. If a reader reads relatively quickly, one can assume that the words are no longer being decoded. Instead, the reader is processing the words as whole units. Words recognized in this way are often termed *sight vocabulary*.

The *QRI-5* provides the examiner with the means of determining oral and silent reading rates as measured in words per minute. The number of words in the passage multiplied by 60 and divided by the number of seconds it took to read the passage will yield a word-per-minute score.

Both oral and silent reading rates are quite variable. They vary across passages. More difficult or unfamiliar passages tend to be read more slowly. Reading rate also varies according to reader purpose. If the reader is reading in order to learn or remember text content, this is typically done at a slower rate than pleasure reading. Reading rate also varies across individuals. Some readers are naturally faster than others, a phenomenon that may be attributed to speed of cognitive processing (Carver, 1990). For these reasons, any guidelines for evaluating reading rate must be interpreted as general in nature.

Our pilot data reflect normal readers reading at their instructional level. We found that there was wide variation in the rates, despite a steady growth in rate as reading level increased. We offer these rates, based on means and standard deviations, as *suggestive* of the rates of typical readers when processing text at their instructional level. Some drop in silent reading rate occurred at the upper middle school and high school levels. We believe this was due to the increased length and difficulty of some passages, as well as the fact that the high school passages were being read by eighth graders.

Table 9.1	Ranges of Oral Reading Rate and Correct Rate of Students Reading at Instructional Level	

	Oral	
Level	Words per minute (WPM)	Correct Words per Minute (CWPM)
Pre-primer—P	23–59	13–55
Pre-primer—NP	22–64	11–59
Primer	28–66	10–52
First	37–77	20–68
Second	43–89	19–77
Third	56–104	53–101
Fourth	57–115	54–112
Fifth	65–121	62–118

Note: P = Pictured passages; NP = Non-pictured passages

Table 9.2	Ranges of Silent Reading Rate of Students Reading at Instructional Level

	Silent
Level	Words per minute (WPM)
Fifth	73–175
Sixth	91–235
Upper Middle School	
Narrative	119–233
Expository	105–189
High School	65–334

Note: Figures based on means and standard deviations

We also offer ranges for correct words per minute (CWPM) or words per minute (WPM) minus the number of errors or miscues made while reading a passage (see Tables 9.1 and 9.2). Kame'enui and Simmons (2001) have suggested that although a word per minute score measures rate or speed, a correct words per minute score addresses both speed and accuracy. Traditionally, CWPM has been used to measure a student's performance in grade-level text. Instead of determining an instructional level, the student reads text that is used in his or her classroom at his or her chronological grade level. Such text may be instructional but it may also represent a level of frustration. Measures of CWPM are taken at the beginning of the year and then used to plot progress throughout the year in classroom texts.

It is up to the examiner to choose which index of rate to compute. Much depends on the purpose of the assessment. If the purpose is to identify a student's instructional level, WPM will suffice. If, however, the assessment focuses on a student's ability to handle text at his or her chronological grade level, CWPM might be more appropriate.

10 Administration and Scoring of the *Qualitative Reading Inventory-5*

COMPREHENSION

Retelling	Questions
General Procedures	General Procedures
Scoring	Scoring the Questions
Analysis of Retelling	Criteria for Determining Reading Levels

An examiner can assess a student's comprehension of orally and silently read passages either by asking the student to retell the selection or by asking questions about the selection. The percentage correct on questions is used for assigning independent, instructional, and frustration levels. The examiner can evaluate the retelling qualitatively against a retelling scoring sheet composed of the important ideas contained in the passage. Examiners will use the questions more often than retelling; however, if an examiner should elect to do both, he or she should ask for the retelling before asking the questions. For that reason, we will look at retelling first.

RETELLING

General Procedures

After the student has finished reading the selection, the examiner should remove the passage and ask the student to retell it as if it were being told to someone who had never read or heard it before. After the student has finished retelling, the examiner should ask whether there is anything else the student would like to say. If the student remembers nothing further, the examiner can draw the student's attention to the title of the passage and ask whether he or she can remember what the author wrote about it. The examiner should not offer more extensive hints or direct suggestions, such as "Can you remember what Johnny Appleseed's journey was like?" The examiner will find it helpful at first to record the retelling and use the audio for scoring at a later time. After becoming familiar with the individual passages, the examiner can often score the retelling directly onto the Retelling Scoring Sheet as the student is talking.

Scoring

Scoring is determined by comparing the idea units recalled by the student with those on the Retelling Scoring Sheet. The scoring sheet was designed on the basis of an examination of the idea units most frequently recalled by students in our piloting sample, as well as a theoretical analysis of the important units. The scoring sheets for the high school passages were also designed from these two components, but we also used teacher judgments about the most important ideas in the passage as well as what they thought a student would normally recall after an initial reading. The examiner should place a check next to each explicit idea listed on the scoring sheet that was recalled by the student. As an option, the examiner may wish to indicate the sequence of the recalled ideas by using a number instead of a check mark; however, this is not necessary. He or she can write in any additional recalled ideas, such as explicit ideas not listed on the scoring sheet or inferences made by the student.

The following paragraph is Peter's retelling of "Johnny Appleseed"; it is accompanied by a scoring example in Figure 10.1.

Johnny, all the men nicknamed him Johnny Appleseed because he had planted a lot of apple trees, because he had lived in Massachusetts and he went down west to put in a lot of apple trees. While he was planting a lot of apple trees, miles and miles, he had crossed rivers and all that through the forest where Indians and that were there. His clothes were wet and torn in the knees and used his shirt for a pillow or something. He still didn't give up. And he didn't have any shoes or nothin'. He lived like raggy and then the apple trees that are here weren't really here before.

The following paragraph is Aaron's retelling of the expository selection "Early Railroads."

There was a . . . the railroads were made out of wood and then iron on top of them. There were tracks. First it started with horses pulling stuff but then Cooper got the idea of making an engine steam like train so the train could pull faster and more supplies. Weighed a ton, was very tiny. Even though it lost a race, it made 3,000 miles of railroad track in America, twice as much as Britain. All because of Peter there are trains instead of horses pulling our supplies to where they need to go.

Obviously, a student will not recall in the exact words of the text, and synonyms and paraphrases are acceptable. The examiner will have to decide whether the subject's recall matches the meaning of the text.

Our pilot data indicated that recall for the high school passages did not vary significantly among the three content areas of literature, social studies, and science. Students reading these lengthy and difficult passages recalled few explicit details. Their recall tended to take the form of summary or gist statements. For example, one student recalled the first part of "Where the Ashes Are" by saying, "It's about a boy caught in the middle of a war." Similarly, another student retold the second section of "World War I" by saying, "It's about how the war ended and what the guys who won wanted to get for themselves and the part that Wilson played with his ideas for peace." Such summary statements represent few ideas that are explicitly stated in the text, but they do demonstrate the student's overall understanding of the passage and should be written down. At the end of each Retelling Scoring Sheet, there is space to write in any summary statements that were part of the retelling.

Analysis of Retelling

Although the retelling is not used to determine independent, instructional, and frustration levels, it can provide valuable information with implications for instruction. For example, if the student does not retell the central parts of a narrative, he or she may not have an understanding of story structure. Similarly, if the student does not organize an expository retelling around the main idea and supporting details, he or she may not understand the structure of paragraphs in exposition.

Figure 10.1 Retelling Scoring Sheet for "Johnny Appleseed"

Setting/Background

____ John Chapman was born

____ in 1774.

____ He became a farmer

____ and grew crops.

____ John liked

____ to grow

____ and eat apples.

____ People were moving west.

____ Apples were a good food

____ for settlers to have.

Goal

____ John decided

_5_ to go west.

____ He wanted

_3_ to plant apple trees.

Events

____ John got many seeds

____ from farmers

____ who squeezed apples

____ to make a drink

____ called cider.

____ He left

____ for the frontier.

____ He planted seeds

____ as he went along.

____ He gave them away.

____ John walked miles.

_6_ He crossed rivers

_7_ and went through forests.

____ He was hungry

____ and wet.

____ He had to hide

_8_ from Indians

____ unfriendly Indians.

_9_ His clothes were torn.

____ He used a sack

____ for a shirt

____ and he cut out holes

____ for the arms.

_11_ He wore no shoes.

Resolution

____ John's fame spread.

_1_ He was nicknamed

_2_ Johnny Appleseed.

____ Settlers accepted seeds

____ gratefully.

____ Thanks to Johnny Appleseed

_12_ trees grow

_13_ in many parts

____ of America.

Other ideas recalled including inferences
4 lived in Massachusetts
10 didn't give up

The examiner should use the retellings to answer the following questions:

1. Do the retellings of narrative material retain the basic structure of the narratives? Is the most important information included?

2. Do the retellings of expository material retain the main idea and supporting detail structure of the selection? Is the most important information included?

3. Are the retellings sequential?

4. Is the recall accurate?

Peter's recall of "Johnny Appleseed" can be evaluated in the following way. Although his recall was not offered in a sequential manner, Peter included information related to all four categories of story structure: the setting/background, the goal, the events, and the resolution. This suggests that Peter has somewhat internalized the structure of the story and is using it to help his recall.

Evaluating the retelling of the longer selections at the upper middle school and high school levels poses a somewhat different problem. Because of the length of these selections and their concept density, it is unrealistic to expect a complete and lengthy retelling. We suggest that you use the following guidelines to evaluate the retellings of the longer selections:

1. Did the retelling contain appropriate summary/gist statements or main idea statements?
2. Did the retelling support the summary/gist statements or main idea statements with any details?
3. Was the retelling generally specific? Did it contain vague and general statements?
4. Was the retelling generally accurate?

Aaron's recall of "Early Railroads" can be evaluated in the following way. His retelling was both sequential and accurate. He primarily focused on details but he included one main idea statement. He also made a key inference tying Cooper's invention to modern railroads. Aaron's retelling suggests that he understood the passage.

Consider the differences between the following retellings of the sixth grade expository selection "The Lifeline of the Nile."

Gerardo's retelling:

The Nile is very long and it helped Egypt a whole lot. It flows from East Africa to Egypt. It fertilizes the land and during heavy rainfalls it floods. The land where it floods is very fertile and that is where they plant seeds. Sometimes it flooded too much and people died.

Sarah's retelling:

The Nile flooded. They grew papyrus so they could write. They grew crops. And they had to use sails. And there were roadblocks so they had to go a different way around it.

Gerardo's retelling was more extensive. It was also sequential and accurate. His recall primarily focused on main ideas: the Nile's value to Egypt, the result of its yearly flood, and a problem it posed. Sarah, on the other hand, focused on details and did not seem to connect flooding with the growing of crops, nor did she seem to understand why sails were a necessity. Finally, her explanation of roadblocks seems more related to prior knowledge of modern traffic than to the geography of the Nile River.

The contrast between Carol's and Terrie's retellings of the first section of "World War I" is instructive.

Carol's retelling:

How World War I got started in 1914 because Serbia killed some guy and what countries were involved like Britain, France, and Germany and how the U.S. got into it because Germany attacked supply ships and then asked Mexico to fight us.

Terrie's retelling:

It was about the reasons that started World War I and the countries that were involved and how they were fighting and who was fighting and what started it. The Serbian leader got killed for being too close to Serbia. It talked about Russia pushing Germany back. And it talked about what the empires were and where they were.

Carol's retelling contained three summary or gist statements: how World War I started, what countries were involved, and how the United States got into it. She expanded these with supporting details. Her retelling was generally specific and accurate.

Terrie mentioned two summary or gist statements: the reasons that World War I started and the countries that were involved. However, she repeated these in different words and offered few specific details. Her comments about the Serbian leader were inaccurate, as was her statement that Russia pushed Germany back. Her statement about "empires" indicates that she paid attention to the map but only in a very general fashion. Terrie's retelling suggests a less complete memory for the text than Carol's.

A comparison of Carl's and Mark's retellings of the first section of "Characteristics of Viruses" also illustrates differences in quality of recall on the high school passages.

Carl's retelling:

Viruses are not cells. They're infectious and harm other cells. They have two parts. Some contain DNA and others have RNA which are the hereditary genes. Viruses are simple and they don't eat. They only have five genes while humans have a lot. There was a diagram of the flu virus. It has an envelope which protects the virus.

Mark's retelling:

It told what viruses are made of and that there are different kinds. There are different layers of the virus and a middle part. They can infect people but not all are infectious but most of them are. They have DNA and some have RNA. There were a lot of scientific terms like "capsule."

Carl began his retelling by defining a virus. He mentioned two main ideas: that viruses have two parts and they are simple. For each, he recalled a few specific details. He also paid attention to the diagram and seemed to integrate this with the text. His retelling was sequential and specific.

Mark offered two summary/gist statements: what viruses are made of and that there are different kinds. He offered a few rather general comments in support of these, and he inaccurately stated that not all viruses are infectious. He confused the term "capsule" with "capsid" and seemed more aware of the terminology in the selection than of what it meant in relation to the topic. His retelling was less coherent than Carl's and suggests an incomplete understanding of the selection.

QUESTIONS

General Procedures	After the student has retold the story to the best of his or her ability, the examiner should ask the comprehension questions and score them according to the suggestions provided. There are two types of questions. *Explicit* questions have answers that are stated directly in the passage. These questions assess whether the student can understand and remember information stated directly by an author. For *implicit* questions, the reader must use clues in the passage to make inferences in order to answer correctly. These questions assess the reader's inferencing abilities.
Scoring the Questions	We suggest that answers be scored as either right or wrong with no half points given. This is because the awarding of half credit tends to be unreliable. In addition, our piloting was done on the basis of either right or wrong answers. Of course, the examiner should give credit for any answer that includes the same information in different words.

If the question is an explicit question, the answer *must* come from the passage. You cannot count as correct an answer that comes from prior knowledge (even if it is accurate). For example, on the third grade passage "Cats: Lions and Tigers in Your House," explicit questions ask the reader to name ways in which lions, tigers, and cats are alike. If a student says that they all have sharp teeth or all have fur, this would be an incorrect answer. Such information is accurate, but it is not stated explicitly in the passage.

Similarly, an implicit question cannot be considered correct if the answer is not related to a clue in the passage. Again, if the answer comes from prior knowledge only, it is not counted as correct. For example, for the "Amelia Earhart" passage, one implicit question is "Why do you think her plane was never found?" A student may answer, "Because it burned up," which is a reasonable answer drawn from his or her background. However, the clues in the passage suggest that it crashed into the ocean and probably sank. When the student's answer to an implicit question obviously comes from background knowledge, the examiner can acknowledge its reasonableness and then ask, "But what do the clues in the passage tell you?"

The pre-primer passages do not have implicit comprehension questions. However, the student may answer an explicit question by using information from the pictures. We have chosen to score such a response as a correct answer to an implicit question. For example, on "Just Like Mom," one question is "Name one thing that the girl can do just like Mom." One of the most common responses was "Water the flowers." That response comes from the fourth picture. However, the text says, "I can work at home." Thus, the child's response is an incorrect answer to the explicit question but is counted as a *correct* implicit response. A question asked about "People at Work" is "What is one thing that people do at work?" A common response was "Fix things." This is counted as a correct implicit response, because although the text says, "Other people make things at work," children interpret the picture as someone fixing a bicycle.

You must score the questions as you go along. The scores tell you when to move to higher passages and when to stop.

CRITERIA FOR DETERMINING READING LEVELS

Passages have five, six, eight, or ten questions. The following guide indicates the number of correct questions needed to attain an independent level (90% or above), an instructional level (67% to 89%), or a frustration level (below 67%). The following criteria for use on each passage are also provided on the examiner's question page.

Five questions:	Independent level: 5 correct
	Instructional level: 4 correct
	Frustration level: 0–3 correct
Six questions:	Independent level: 6 correct
	Instructional level: 4–5 correct
	Frustration level: 0–3 correct
Eight questions:	Independent level: 8 correct
	Instructional level: 6–7 correct
	Frustration level: 0–5 correct
Ten questions:	Independent level: 9–10 correct
	Instructional level: 7–8 correct
	Frustration level: 0–6 correct

Analysis of a student's ability to answer explicit and implicit questions can provide valuable information. An examiner should analyze a student's performance at independent and instructional levels separately from performance at the frustration level. For each grouping, he or she should count the total number of explicit questions asked of the student and the total number answered correctly. To arrive at a percentage, the examiner must divide the total correct by the total asked, repeating the procedure for implicit questions. A substantial difference between these two scores, such as 50% on several passages, may suggest that the student needs instruction either in remembering what the author stated explicitly in the text or in using clues in the text to make inferences, depending on which score is higher.

11

Administration and Scoring of the *Qualitative Reading Inventory-5*

ASSESSING STRATEGIC READING

Look-Backs

Think-Alouds
  Think-Aloud Statements That Indicate Understanding of the Text

Think-Aloud Statements That Indicate Lack of Understanding

Scoring Think-Alouds

Assessing Note-Taking Ability

The following procedures can offer valuable insights into a student's strengths and weaknesses in strategic reading. The examiner can choose to administer one or more of them in addition to or in lieu of the assessment measures explained in the preceding sections. The examiner must decide which procedures will offer the most meaningful information.

LOOK-BACKS

During normal administration procedures, the examiner asks the student to answer questions without the benefit of the accompanying text. Student success in answering is heavily dependent on memory for what was read. It is impossible to know whether an incorrect or missing answer resulted from poor comprehension during reading or poor memory after reading. As students read longer and more concept-dense text, such as the high school passages included in the *QRI-5*, memory constraints may interfere with the ability to answer explicit or implicit questions. This is especially true when the student is struggling with unfamiliar text.

Think about the last time you read a selection on a very unfamiliar topic. You probably comprehended what you were reading, but afterwards you may have been able to recall only a small portion of it. If someone asked you a direct question, you may not have been able to provide the answer. Did this mean that you were a poor reader? On the contrary, a quick skimming of the text would have improved your recall immeasurably. Similarly, looking back in the text would have allowed you to locate the answer to the question you were asked.

Skilled readers employ the look-back strategy naturally and efficiently as a way of increasing and maintaining comprehension. Our pilot data suggested that students with instructional levels at or above third grade could do this readily (see Section 15). For this reason, we recommend adding look-backs to the process of assessing comprehension.

After scoring the questions and determining comprehension level, the examiner can give the student the text and ask whether she or he can look back to locate answers that were unknown and to correct erroneous answers. Score the look-backs as correct or incorrect, and use this result to determine a level for comprehension with look-backs. The *QRI-5* provides space on the scoring sheet to record Comprehension without Look-Backs and Comprehension with Look-Backs.

A student who can locate answers and correct errors probably understood the text, at least after rereading it. The initial problem may have been one of memory or purpose. If, however, the student cannot locate or correct an answer, perhaps the problem lies with basic understanding of what was read.

Students vary in their ability to use look-backs. For some, it is an effortless procedure. They seem to know exactly where to look to find the information. Others do not seem to know how to begin. They begin to reread the entire selection laboriously or to stare helplessly at the page and look to the examiner for guidance. In such cases, the examiner may point to the area where the relevant material can be found. However, in order to receive credit for a look-back, the student should exhibit relatively independent performance. If the examiner has to point out where the information can be found or has to offer supportive hints, no credit should be given. For example, after reading a section of the high school passage on viruses, Sally was unable to look back to find the correct answer to an implicit question. The examiner pointed out where the information could be found (the illustration) and offered a few suggestions about what Sally knew and what information she should look for. Sally eventually arrived at the correct answer, but she did not receive credit for a successful look-back because it was not an independent performance on her part.

Answering implicit questions demands some background knowledge from the reader as well as identification of clues provided by the author. If a student look-back is unsuccessful, the examiner can probe to see whether the student's inability to answer an implicit question is due to lack of background or to lack of attention to the clues in the text. For example, the examiner can tell the student the correct answer and ask him or her to find the clue in the text. The examiner can also point out the clue and see whether the student can use it to arrive at the correct answer. Such procedures provide valuable diagnostic information, but the student should not be given credit for such examiner-supported answers.

Scoring comprehension without look-backs may underestimate a student's comprehension. For example, Jonah read the "Life Cycles of Stars" passage and, when answering questions without look-backs, attained a frustration score of 40%. When he was allowed to look back, he raised his comprehension score to 90%, an independent level.

Many students in our pilot study who read the high school passages attained frustration levels in their initial attempts to answer questions. However, the majority were able to raise their scores to an instructional or independent level following look-backs. For this reason, we believe that any determination of reading level on the high school passages *should be based on the use of look-backs*. In other words, comprehension with look-backs is most representative of reading performance on the high school passages. For all passages from third grade through upper middle school, we believe that a level based on a combination of questions answered without *and* with look-backs is more representative of what skilled readers do when faced with concept-dense and unfamiliar text. See Section 15 for more about comprehension.

There are other ways to utilize the look-back procedure to obtain information about a student's reading needs. The examiner can choose a passage that proved difficult to the student and ask him or her to look back and indicate specific parts that were especially troublesome. The examiner can either seek specific words the student did not know or can ask the student to identify "something you found hard or something you didn't understand." After isolating a segment of text, the examiner can ask a few questions to confirm that the chosen element actually was difficult and not selected at random. If the student says that everything was hard, the examiner should reverse the procedure and ask her or him to find one or two things that were a bit easier than the rest.

The examiner can ask the student to look back and define or explain certain key vocabulary words contained in a passage. This may be especially helpful if the student has evinced poor comprehension. The examiner can ascertain whether the student knows the meanings of words that were pronounced correctly, as well as words that were pronounced incorrectly, during passage reading. After silent reading, the examiner can ask the student to define and pronounce certain key words contained in the passage. Inability to do either may be an indication of why the student's comprehension was low.

THINK-ALOUDS

Think-alouds are a reader's verbalizations in reaction to reading a selection. They can be made before, during, or after reading. Think-alouds provide a way of "gathering information about individual readers' ongoing thinking processes and metacognitive behavior" (Brown & Lytle, 1988, p. 96). When using think-alouds during reading, the examiner asks the student to read the passage and stop at set points to "think out loud" and share efforts to understand, judge, reason, and monitor. Although this can be done in any text, we have designed expository passages to facilitate use of the think-aloud process at the sixth, upper middle school, and high school levels.

We have provided a passage, "The Mining Boom," that includes think-aloud statements the examiner can model to demonstrate how to think aloud during the reading process. We recommend that the modeling process be an interactive dialogue between the examiner and the student. The examiner shares his or her think-aloud comment and then asks the student to offer one in kind. However, the examiner can also read the entire passage and model the think-aloud comments without the student participating in the dialogue. We have found that both work. It is up to you to fit the modeling process to the needs of the student.

If you are going to use the think-aloud process as part of your assessment, we recommend that the student first read a selection without any attempt to think aloud. This allows for a comparison of comprehension in text with and without think-alouds. When asking students to think aloud, use the student copy that is marked with STOP signals. These signals indicate where the student should stop and think out loud. At this point, the student is basically on his or her own, reading the text silently and thinking out loud whenever the word STOP is encountered. The examiner can write the student's think-aloud comments on the examiner copy.

Based on the research literature on think-alouds (see Section 2) and our pilot study, we constructed a system for coding different types of think-alouds. The majority of think-aloud comments from students in our pilot involved paraphrasing or summarizing the text segment, questioning, and making new meaning, such as drawing an inference or a conclusion. Our pilot data indicated that questioning think-alouds tended to fall into two categories: questions that indicated understanding of the text and questions that indicated a lack of understanding of the text. Other less-frequent think-aloud comments involved indicating understanding or a lack of it; reporting a match, absence, or conflict with prior knowledge; and identifying personally. We divided the think-aloud comments into two categories: those that indicated understanding of the text and those that indicated lack of understanding. Our pilot data indicated the validity of this classification by the negative correlation between statements representing understanding and statements representing a lack of understanding for all content areas. In other words, students who made more think-aloud statements that indicated understanding made significantly fewer think-aloud statements that indicated lack of understanding (see Section 15).

Think-Aloud Statements That Indicate Understanding of the Text

Paraphrasing or Summarizing. The student repeats the content of the text segment and basically preserves the language of the author.

"Clouds and Precipitation"
> *Clouds are classified by how high they are. Their names kind of go with their shape. Like low clouds are like sheets so they are called strato or maybe it's stratus.*

"Building Pyramids"
> *The Egyptians built tombs for their kings called pyramids. They were made of stone. They put the dead kings in the pyramid with all their possessions so they could use them after they died. They thought they would keep on living.*

"Immigration—Part 2"
> *They thought the streets were gold but found out that wasn't real. So they looked for work because they needed money. They mostly got jobs and their friends and family helped them.*

Making New Meaning. The student makes an inference, draws a conclusion, or engages in reasoning.

"Life Cycles of Stars—Part 2"
> *The sun is going to be around for a very long time, which is a good thing.*

"World War I—Part 3"
> *Creating more countries and putting them under France and Britain will just create offspring, Little Frances and Britains. It doesn't seem logical.*

"Characteristics of Viruses—Part 3"
> *It's unusual that viroids have nothing, no capsid, to protect them. It doesn't seem like they would be able to survive.*

Questioning That Indicates Understanding. The student asks a question that is based on understanding of the text, such as questioning the motivation of a character, applying text content to a similar situation, or projecting text content into a future point in time.

"Clouds and Precipitation"

What makes some clouds stay low to the ground and others stay up high?

"Building Pyramids"

Why did they take out the brain? I think it would be just as important as the heart, maybe more important.

"Immigration—Part 2"

Did they all find jobs? I wonder what happened to someone who didn't.

Noting Understanding. The student recognizes that he or she understands what was read.

"Life Cycles of Stars—Part 2"

I know why they call the star a black dwarf because it's all burned out.

"World War I—Part 3"

At first I wasn't sure what they were doing but now I get it. If they cut up the big countries into little ones, they won't be that much of a threat.

"Characteristics of Viruses—Part 3"

It makes sense that some viruses only go into animals and not humans. After all, we are built differently from animals.

Reporting Prior Knowledge. The student reports a match with what was previously known or indicates that prior knowledge was absent or in conflict with the text.

"Clouds and Precipitation"

I thought clouds were all water but here it says they have dust in them. That seems strange to me.

"Building Pyramids"

I know a lot about mummies and how they wrapped them. We saw them in the museum.

"Immigration—Part 2"

Last year, we read about the Statue of Liberty and why France sent it to us.

Identifying Personally. The student relates the text to personal experiences, makes a judgment of some sort based on personal experiences, states interest or lack of it, or indicates like or dislike for topic.

"Life Cycles of Stars—Part 2"

I think stars are so neat. Some day I want my own telescope.

"Where the Ashes Are—Part 3"

I think it was really sad that he had to see his father tied up and taken away. He was just a little boy.

"Characteristics of Viruses—Part 3"

I feel sorry for the animals that die from these diseases.

Think-Aloud Statements That Indicate Lack of Understanding

Questioning That Indicates Lack of Understanding. The student asks questions about character motivation or the applications of a concept that indicate lack of understanding. The student also asks about the meanings of words or concepts.

"Clouds and Precipitation"
Why do they call a cloud stratus? (Indicates lack of understanding of the reason, which is stated explicitly in the text.)

"Immigration—Part 2"
Why did they stay where they landed? Why didn't they just go somewhere else? (Indicates lack of understanding that immigrants were poor and in a strange country.)

"Life Cycles of Stars—Part 2"
Why don't scientists have proof of black holes? (Indicates lack of understanding that black holes do not give off light.)

Noting Lack of Understanding. The student clearly states that she or he is confused about something.

"Life Cycles of Stars—Part 2"
I don't know what it means when it says the matter is denser than on earth.

"Where the Ashes Are—Part 3"
I don't get this whole part about the sister and why she kept wanting to wash her hands.

"World War I—Part 3"
I have no idea what a buffer zone is supposed to do. Is it a good thing?

Scoring Think-Alouds

Think-aloud scoring sheets are provided after each passage. Alys read the third section of "Where the Ashes Are." Her think-aloud comments were as follows:

Why would a little boy lead everyone into the basement? (Questioning that indicates understanding.)

The mother must be really very worried with her husband taken away and her one daughter mentally ill. (Making new meaning.)

I picture a lot of people all jammed into this room. What are the soldiers going to do to them? (Making new meaning and Questioning that indicates understanding.)

Did the boy wonder if his mother would come back? I would have been terrified. (Questioning that indicates understanding and Identifying personally.)

They don't sound too organized about helping the wounded. (Making new meaning.)

The mother is avoiding answering the boy's questions. (Making new meaning.)

The dirty water will be dangerous for her husband to drink. It's probably infected and I know that infection can spread fast. (Making new meaning and Reporting prior knowledge.)

The prisoners who were curled up might have been tortured. (Making new meaning.)

What did they do to him during those sixteen years? I don't know how the boy could stand it. If it was my father—well—I don't even want to think about it. (Questioning that indicates understanding and Identifying personally.)

Think-Aloud Statements That Indicate Understanding

Paraphrasing or summarizing	0
Making new meaning	6
Questioning with understanding	4
Noting understanding	0
Reporting prior knowledge	1
Identifying personally	2

Think-Aloud Statements That Indicate Lack of Understanding

Questioning no understanding	0
Noting lack of understanding	0

There were 9 STOP points in "Where the Ashes Are" but Alys made a total of 13 think-aloud comments, because she verbalized two different comments at several STOP points. For example, she commented, "I picture a lot of people all jammed in this room (Making new meaning). What are the soldiers going to do to them? (Questioning that indicates understanding)." All of her comments indicate that she was understanding what she was reading.

Does any one kind of think-aloud comment or any specific combination of comments indicate better comprehension as measured by retelling and answers to questions with and without look-backs? Think-aloud statements that indicate understanding, especially summarizing or paraphrasing and making new meaning through inferencing, are significantly correlated with retelling, inferences made during retelling, or comprehension with look-backs. See Section 15 for details. It would seem that what a reader thinks about during reading has some effect on comprehension, just as reader prior knowledge does. We believe that use of think-alouds, like assessment of prior knowledge, can offer an interesting and perceptive window into the reading process.

Students exhibit a variety of think-aloud patterns. Some use one exclusively, such as the student who only summarizes or paraphrases. Others, like Alys, exhibit a variety of patterns. There were a number of students in our pilot who could offer no comments whatsoever. The examiner must evaluate the variety and quality of a student's think-aloud comments in relation to several factors: the student's retelling and/or comprehension, the content area that was read, and the relative unfamiliarity of the text. If a student uses only one form of think-aloud and that student exhibits marginal comprehension, the examiner may be justified in suggesting that the student develop other think-aloud strategies. It is probably easier to identify personally in a literature selection than in a science or social studies text, so lack of this think-aloud comment should not be regarded negatively when students are reading science or social studies. In an unfamiliar text, summarizing or paraphrasing may be all a reader can do, at least during an initial reading. We suspect that think-alouds are very idiosyncratic to readers and affected by such things as difficulty level, familiarity, and interest. The examiner may have to evaluate each student individually in light of such factors.

Guiding students through the think-aloud process is time consuming. As with many of the options on the *QRI-5,* the examiner must be a decision maker and choose those components that will offer the information she or he feels is most meaningful.

Having determined an instructional level, the examiner can use a parallel passage to assess the student's ability to take notes. We recommend using expository text. This can be done in two ways. The examiner can provide a copy of the passage and ask the student to read with pencil in hand, underlining those parts of the selection that seem most important. Or the examiner can ask the student to read a selection and take notes as if studying for a test. Either procedure can identify a student who is unable to isolate the main ideas of a selection or engage in efficient note-taking procedures. The examiner may wish to map the student's note-taking efforts on the Retelling Scoring Sheet to indicate whether the more important points are included.

12

Summarizing the Results of the *Qualitative Reading Inventory-5*

Organizing the Data
    The Student Profile Sheet
    Describing Specific Reading Behaviors

Word Identification
Comprehension
Writing the Report

The major strength of the *QRI-5* is that it provides a profile of the strengths and needs of an individual reader across different types of text according to the student's prior knowledge. In order to facilitate such comparisons, we have provided a summary sheet referred to as the Student Profile Sheet (see Figure 12.1).

ORGANIZING THE DATA

The Student Profile Sheet

The examiner should fill out the Student Profile Sheet using the following abbreviations:

    Familiar: F   Unfamiliar: UF

    Narrative: N   Expository: E

    Pictures: P   No Pictures: NP

    Independent: Ind   Instructional: Ins   Frustration: Fr

Obviously, the completeness of the Student Profile Sheet will depend on the extent and complexity of the assessment. For some students, an examiner will enter data for only a few passages. Other students will be represented by a much more detailed profile sheet. In addition, examiners can choose not to fill in certain portions. For example, an examiner may choose to record levels, but not percentages, for Total Accuracy or Total Acceptability. An examiner may elect to determine levels from Total Acceptability only. In this case, the spaces for Total Accuracy would remain blank. Similarly, an examiner may elect to record the comprehension level without recording the number of explicit and implicit questions answered correctly. When recording the data, the examiner should

1. Begin with the lowest level of list or passage administered and move to the right with successively higher levels.

2. Organize the passages into groupings: narrative, expository, familiar, unfamiliar, pictures, and no pictures.

Figure 12.1   **Student Profile Sheet**

Name _____ **Age** _____ **Grade** _____

Sex _____ **Date of Test** _____ **Examiner** _____

Initial Testing _____ **Post-Testing** _____

Word Identification

Grade									
Level/% Automatic									
Level/% Total									

Oral Reading

Passage Name									
Readability Level									
Passage Type Narrative/Expository									
Concepts Familiar/Unfamiliar: %									
Level/% Total Accuracy									
Level/% Total Acceptability									
Retelling % Number of Ideas									
# Explicit Correct									
# Explicit Correct w/Look-Backs									
# Implicit Correct									
# Implicit Correct w/Look-Backs									
Level/% Comprehension									
Level/% Comprehension w/Look-Backs									
Rate WPM/CWPM									
Total Passage Level									

Silent Reading

Passage Name/Section									
Readability Level									
Passage Type Narrative/Expository									
Concepts Familiar/Unfamiliar %									
Retelling % Number of Ideas									
# Correct Explicit									
# Correct Explicit w/Look-Backs									
# Correct Implicit									
# Correct Implicit w/Look-Backs									
Level/% Comprehension									
Level/% Comprehension w/Look-Backs									
Rate: WPM									

3. When recording scores, record the information for familiar narratives first.

4. When recording scores, record the information from text with pictures before that from text without pictures.

5. After listing results for familiar narratives, record scores for unfamiliar narratives.

6. Record familiar expository scores, and then record unfamiliar expository scores.

7. If passages were administered to assess listening comprehension, group these to the far right on the Profile Sheet and draw a line separating them from passages administered orally or silently.

Section 13 contains an example of a completed Student Profile Sheet (p. 97), and a copy of the sheet is provided on the accompanying DVD.

Describing Specific Reading Behaviors

To facilitate comparison of a student's reading ability across different contexts, an assessment specialist might ask different questions about a student. Answering these questions can provide important information for planning intervention instruction.

Word Identification

How Accurate Is the Student in Identifying Words?   Total scores on the word lists and word-identification levels on oral passage reading allow the examiner to ascertain the student's accuracy in identifying words. The student's accuracy level should parallel his or her chronological grade placement. The greater the gap between word-identification accuracy and chronological grade placement, the more serious the reading problem.

How Automatic Is the Student in Identifying Words?   Reading fluency is dependent on an extensive sight vocabulary, or automaticity in identifying words. The timed score on the word lists gives the examiner one measure of word-identification automaticity. If the level for words pronounced automatically on the word lists is lower than the total level for word identification, the student may profit from procedures to increase automatic word identification. Reading rate attained on the passages is another measure that suggests automaticity of word identification. If a student reads very slowly, the examiner should recommend instructional interventions to increase fluency.

Is There a Difference between a Student's Ability to Identify Words in Context and Words in Isolation?   The examiner should compare the student's highest instructional level for words recognized in isolation with those recognized when reading within the context of a passage. For many readers, the instructional levels attained on the word lists will closely parallel the instructional levels achieved for word accuracy in familiar text. However, some readers recognize far more words in context. If the oral reading of these students is fluent and expressive, a lower score on the list probably does not represent a serious area of concern. However, if oral reading is slow and halting, lower scores on the word lists could indicate lack of automaticity in word identification. Occasionally a student will have better word-identification scores in isolation than in context. Also, some readers may be less threatened by a word list than by a passage. This is particularly true of beginning readers.

Comprehension

What Types of Text Can the Student Handle Most Successfully?   The examiner should compare the student's levels in narrative and expository text. Many readers, especially those below fourth grade, will score a year or two below their familiar narrative level when asked to read expository text. These readers will need instruction in expository text structure and strategies for dealing with their content-area textbooks. For levels pre-primer through grade two, the examiner can also compare a student's performance in text with and without pictures. Emerging readers naturally depend on a picture context for both word identification and comprehension. However, skilled readers are less dependent on such contextual aids. A student whose success in word identification is dependent on pictures needs to learn strategies for context-free and automatic decoding. A student whose success in comprehension is dependent on pictures should be exposed to instruction in prereading activities such as prediction and to self-monitoring strategies during reading.

What Modes of Reading Represent Strengths for the Student?   The examiner should compare the student's oral and silent reading comprehension. It is natural for young readers to do better in oral reading because of the emphasis on this mode during the early elementary grades. As the student moves through the grades, she or he must become increasingly efficient at silent reading. A middle school student whose instructional level for oral reading is higher than for silent reading will be at a disadvantage in coping with the demands of textbook reading. Such a reader needs practice in silent reading.

How Does the Student Perform on Familiar and Unfamiliar Text?   The examiner can compare levels in familiar and unfamiliar text. For levels three through upper middle school, the *QRI-5* provides passages that offer both familiar and unfamiliar content. Most readers will score at a higher level in familiar text for both narrative and expository material. It is likely that a student may score a year below the familiar instructional level when reading unfamiliar material. A fifth grade student reading at the fifth grade level in familiar text but only at the third grade level in unfamiliar material may have extreme difficulty with content-area subjects where she or he is less likely to be familiar with the material.

How Does the Student Perform with Look-Backs and without Look-Backs?   To what extent can the student raise his or her comprehension score by engaging in look-backs? Are look-backs more effective for explicit questions or can the student use look-backs to find clues that suggest correct answers to implicit questions? Does the student use look-backs more effectively with one type of text (narrative versus expository; familiar versus unfamiliar) or with one mode of reading (oral versus silent)?

What Comprehension Strategies Does the Student Employ While Reading?   Did engaging in think-alouds have any effect on comprehension? In other words, if the high school passages were administered, was there a difference in the student's comprehension between the first passage without think-alouds and the third passage with think-alouds? Do the types of think-alouds suggest effective or ineffective strategies? For example, reacting personally may be more appropriate in literature selections than in social studies or science text. Was the student even able to offer think-alouds? Some of the students in our pilot study were unable to construct a think-aloud statement independently. Did the student offer a variety of think-alouds or tend to stay with one type? Variety may indicate a more involved and interactive reader than one who reacts in the same way to different segments of text.

What Is the Extent of the Student's Reading Problem? To identify a serious reading disability, the examiner can compare the student's highest instructional level with her or his chronological grade placement. *Reading disability* was once defined as the discrepancy between reading level and a student's potential as indicated by IQ, but this definition has been seriously questioned (Aaron, 1997). It is more valid to define *reading disability* as a serious discrepancy between the chronological grade level of the student and the level at which the student can read familiar narrative material. A serious discrepancy is defined by Spache (1981) as follows:

One year for first through third graders
Two years for fourth through sixth graders
Three years for seventh graders and above

The seriousness of the disability is obviously dependent on the size of the discrepancy. For example, a third grader reading at a primer level would be more disabled than one reading at a first grade level. Another consideration is the grade level at which the student is reading. A student who cannot read primer material has not learned to read. A student who is having trouble at the second or third grade level may be able to read but lacks fluency and automaticity at that level. Children reading beyond the third grade level may have learned to read, but they may not have learned how to read *to learn*. An older student who has not learned how to read despite years of instruction is obviously more disabled than one who knows how to read but cannot handle the demands of reading to learn.

Writing the Report

In many cases, the Student Profile Sheet and the Miscue Analysis Sheet will be sufficient to describe a student's strengths and needs. However, a formal written report is sometimes needed. We suggest that the report be a brief as possible and utilize the following headings:

Background
Assessment Format
Word Identification Accuracy
Word Identification Fluency
Comprehension
Summary and Recommendations

An example of a completed report is presented on the accompanying DVD.

13

Examples of Using the *Qualitative Reading Inventory-5*

Using the *QRI-5* to Estimate Individual Instructional Reading Level	Using the *QRI-5* to Verify a Suspected Problem
Using the *QRI-5* to Estimate Instructional Reading Level through Group Administration and Monitor Classroom Progress (Response to Intervention)	Using the *QRI-5* to Describe Specific Reading Behaviors as a Guide for Intervention Instruction (Response to Intervention: Tiers Two and Three)
Using the *QRI-5* to Indicate Growth and Monitor Individual and Group Progress (Response to Intervention)	

USING THE *QRI-5* TO ESTIMATE INDIVIDUAL INSTRUCTIONAL READING LEVEL

Hallie is a fourth grader who never had any previous difficulties in school. However, when her parents moved and Hallie transferred to a new school, she immediately began to experience problems in reading class. Her parents became concerned when Hallie said she hated school and "being real dumb." After a conference with her teacher, the school reading specialist tested Hallie to determine her reading level.

Hallie read graded word lists on levels three through six and scored at an independent level for all four lists. In fact, she missed only five words across all lists. She recognized the majority of words immediately, suggesting that she was not decoding these words but recognizing them from memory. When she met an unfamiliar word, she used letter patterns to offer a similar albeit alternative pronunciation.

Hallie's strong performance on the word lists was duplicated when she was asked to orally read two narrative texts. On both a fourth and fifth grade passage, she scored at an independent level for word identification. Her miscues were few and similar in sound to the correct word, and she read the passages at acceptable oral WPM ranges for a fourth grader. Hallie scored at an instructional level for both selections. Her retelling was sparse but accurate and, in the fourth grade selection, it focused on important components of the text. While she was able to look back in the fourth grade text to locate answers, she was not as successful doing this for the fifth grade selection.

Hallie then silently read a fourth grade passage on Amelia Earhart. She was very familiar with the woman aviator as she had completed a unit on early aviation in her former school. Silent reading is generally faster than oral reading; however, in Hallie's case, oral and silent rates were almost identical. In addition, during silent reading, Hallie pointed to each word as she read, which had not occurred during oral reading. This suggests that she may not have made an effective transition from oral to silent reading and may be too focused on pronunciation of individual words as opposed to comprehension of thought units. After reading, she recalled six items present in the selection but in no coherent order. When asked questions, she placed at a frustration level, being only able to answer two of eight items.

Finally, Hallie was asked to silently read a fourth grade expository passage on plant structures to ascertain her ability to comprehend the type of text encountered in her classroom content textbooks. While she seemed relatively familiar with the concepts contained in the passage, she placed at a frustration level for comprehension.

The reading specialist determined that Hallie's reading level was above fourth grade for material that she read orally. However, she experienced difficulty in fourth grade text when asked to read silently in both narrative and expository material. Conversation with her parents revealed a strong emphasis on classroom oral reading in her former school both in reading and content classes. The opposite was true for Hallie's new school. The reading specialist agreed to work with Hallie on silent reading comprehension strategies such as self-questioning, thinking aloud, and building idea maps during and after reading.

A formal report on Hallie's performance that could be submitted to her parents or placed in her file is included in Section 13 on the DVD.

USING THE *QRI-5* TO ESTIMATE INSTRUCTIONAL READING LEVEL THROUGH GROUP ADMINISTRATION AND MONITOR CLASSROOM PROGRESS (RESPONSE TO INTERVENTION)

The school district of Woodland Glen initiated a group assessment process for grades three through five that focused on comprehension and provided a means of monitoring progress for older students as part of the district's Response to Intervention initiative. It also complemented the individualized phonological awareness, phonics, and fluency assessments that were administered in kindergarten through grade two. The district recognized that assessing comprehension was of critical importance as children moved into the upper grades; however, administration and teachers were concerned that individualized assessment would take a large amount of time and require additional staff support in order to free teachers for the task. Accordingly, they decided to administer *QRI-5* passages in a silent reading group format; that is, students would read passages silently as a group and write answers to the questions. The district reasoned that the ability to silently read grade-level text, look back in the passage to identify information, and write appropriate answers were important skills for third graders and above.

The third, fourth, and fifth grade teachers met to design a uniform process throughout the grades. They decided that students who were identified as having special needs would not be part of the group process. They agreed to use the same narrative passages across all classrooms and chose the following as most representative of their curriculum: "A Special Birthday for Rosa" (level three), "Tomie dePaola" (level 4), "Patricia McKissack" (level 5), "The Early Life of Lois Lowry" (level 6), and "Biddy Mason" (upper middle school). Next they laid out the sequence that would be followed. First, the teachers briefly discussed the vocabulary terms on the Key Concept Questions with the class in order to develop prior knowledge for the selection. Each teacher then distributed the duplicated passage at his or her grade level (i.e., third grade teachers handed out "A Special Birthday for Rosa," fourth grade teachers handed out "Tomie de Paola," and so on). The students read the passages silently and wrote their answers on specially formatted question sheets (see Section 14 on the accompanying DVD). Several of the QRI-5 questions that suggested further probing on the part of the examiner were slightly modified for group administration. For example, the first question for "Patricia McKissack" asks who she is. If the student simply says "an author," the examiner should ask the students what kinds of books she writes. Accordingly, the question was modified as follows: What kinds of books does Patricia McKissack write? (See Section 14 of

the accompanying DVD.) Prior to handing out the passages and questions, the teachers made certain that all students had a book to read independently if they finished before other students. When all were finished, the teachers collected the materials and scored the answers. Teachers at each grade level worked together to compare any answers that were somewhat ambiguous, which occurred primarily with implicit questions. If two or more teachers agreed that the answer was correct or incorrect, it was scored according to their joint input.

Once the answers were scored, all students who were independent or instructional at their grade level were given a second passage at the next higher level. This was repeated until all students met frustration or reached an upper middle school level. Students who met frustration at the third grade level were individually assessed to determine their word recognition and comprehension ability. In some cases, the regular classroom teacher did this; in most cases the reading specialist assisted.

The teachers recorded the results for their class on a class record sheet. (See Section 14 on the accompanying DVD.) Results were compiled according to grade level, not according to individual classrooms; that is, all third grade scores were grouped together in order to avoid any inappropriate comparison of individual classrooms. The data were converted to the proportion of students who scored below their grade level, at their grade level, and above their grade level Table 13.1 demonstrates how the data were reported to the teachers, administration, and parents. The district repeated this process in January and May and used the data to monitor progress and identify students who would profit from supportive help or additional challenge.

Table 13.1	**Proportion Correct for QRI-5 Group Administration of Narrative Passages**

September

Grade Three					
Below Level 3	At Level 3	Level 4	Level 5	Level 6	UMS
.007	.450	.337	.206	.000	.000

Grade Four				
Below Level 4	At Level 4	Level 5	Level 6	UMS
.161	.502	.294	.023	.000

Grade Five			
Below Level 5	At Level 5	Level 6	UMS
.126	.348	.375	.144

Because the process worked quite well, the teachers agreed to repeat it using expository text, because they recognized that ability in comprehending a narrative might or might not carry over to exposition. Dramatic differences were evident between narrative and expository scores. In some classrooms, the majority of students scored below their grade level for expository text, leading the district to initiate a stronger focus on expository material in reading instruction.

USING THE *QRI-5* TO INDICATE GROWTH AND MONITOR INDIVIDUAL AND GROUP PROGRESS (RESPONSE TO INTERVENTION)

Individual Progress.   Tamia is a first grader. Her school uses the *QRI-5* word lists and passages to monitor progress as part of their Response to Intervention initiative and to maintain an ongoing record of students' developing literacy skills. At the beginning of the year, Tamia read the pre-primer 1 word list. At that time, she knew only six words and scored at the frustration level. Tamia's teacher administered the pre-primer 1 list on two other occasions during the first three months of first grade. When Tamia approached an instructional level, her teacher asked her to read the pre-primer 1 text with pictures, "I Can," and she scored at an instructional level for both word identification (Total Accuracy) and comprehension. When asked to read a pre-primer 2 selection with pictures, "Just Like Mom," she met frustration.

Tamia's teacher administered the pre-primer 2 word list several additional times over the next months. When Tamia achieved at an instructional on this list, her teacher asked her to again read "Just Like Mom." Tamia was obviously aided by the predictable pattern and the pictures. By February, she had achieved a strong instructional level on the primer list and met success with "Fox and Mouse," a primer narrative with pictures. A month later, Tamia read a primer passage without pictures, "A Trip," and scored at an instructional level for both word identification and comprehension. When Tamia was able to read the first grade word list at an instructional level, her teacher asked her to read a first grade passage with pictures. By the end of first grade, Tamia experienced success on a first grade passage without pictures. Her teacher kept dated records of her progress throughout the year and determined that she had made appropriate progress.

Group Progress.   Two learning support teachers in a small urban elementary school were unhappily aware that some children in the school were not reading as well as they could. Accordingly, the two teachers designed structured lesson plans to be used in a tier two pull-out intervention program. The children, second through fifth graders, remained in their regular classroom for literacy instruction but were tutored four days a week. Each tutoring session lasted 30 minutes, and children were paired for these lessons according to their reading level. Each lesson involved repeated reading of familiar text, direct instruction in sound–letter matching, and the introduction of a new selection through supported oral reading and discussion of story structure.

The two teachers did not have unlimited time for testing. They knew their children exhibited difficulties in word identification, so they chose oral reading as the mode of assessment using Total Accuracy because it takes less time to score and is more reliable than Total Acceptability. The teachers determined the highest instructional level in familiar narrative text for each child for both word identification and comprehension. They used these as their pre-test measures.

The tutoring continued from October to the middle of May. At that time, the two teachers administered the same passages as a post-test, again using oral reading as the mode of assessment. For each child, they administered additional passages to determine the highest instructional level for both word identification and comprehension.

The teachers compared the pre- and post-*QRI* measures in several ways (Caldwell, Fromm, & O'Connor, 1997–1998). They assigned a number to each independent, instructional, and frustration level. Frustration on a preprimer passage was assigned 0. An instructional pre-primer level was assigned level 1, an independent pre-primer level was assigned 1.5, and so on. Using this scheme, they found that the average gain in levels was 2.8 for word identification and 2.0 for comprehension.

The two teachers also compared the pre- and post-percentages for word recognition (percent of miscues) and comprehension (percent of questions answered). They found statistically significant gains for word recognition but nothing significant for comprehension. Although the students raised their comprehension from one grade level to a higher one, they still tended to be at an instructional level and their percentage for questions answered remained basically the same. The teachers were well pleased with their intervention and felt that the *QRI* was a sensitive and valid measure of reading growth following tier 2 intervention.

USING THE *QRI-5* TO VERIFY A SUSPECTED PROBLEM

Thomas is in his first semester of high school. After the first grading period, his grades consisted primarily of Ds with the exception of English and physical education. The guidance counselor asked the reading specialist to evaluate Thomas's reading ability. The specialist asked Thomas to read the upper middle school word lists. He scored at an independent level. She then asked Thomas to read the high school lists. Again, he attained an independent level, reading the words fluently and with confidence.

Thomas then silently read a literature selection at the upper middle school level, "Biddy Mason." He obviously enjoyed it and, after reading, made several comments about the courage of Biddy and how times have changed since then. Scoring at an instructional level, his recall was extensive, and he was able to effectively look back in the text to locate answers to questions. Thomas indicated that he enjoyed reading novels, and he mentioned the Harry Potter series as a special favorite.

Thomas then read "Life Cycles of Stars—Part 1." Again, his reading rate indicated fluency, but he recalled little and scored at a frustration level for comprehension without look-backs. He managed to raise this to an instructional level when allowed to look back. The reading specialist asked Thomas whether he employed look-backs on a regular basis. He replied that he generally read assignments only once and seldom looked back because it "takes too much time." The specialist pointed out how looking back had improved his performance and suggested that he do it regularly.

The specialist then modeled think-alouds and Thomas seemed to enjoy the modeling process, often commenting "I thought that too." When thinking aloud on "Life Cycles of Stars—Part 2," Thomas kept his eyes on the page while thinking aloud and primarily offered extensive paraphrases. The specialist suspected that he was actually rereading the segment. When she asked him not to do this, Thomas' comments became very short and mainly consisted of comments about how difficult the text was.

Although Thomas has no problems in identifying words, he is not an interactive reader of expository text. He does not use look-backs effectively, and his inability to offer any independent think-aloud comments suggests that he is merely reading the words and hoping that comprehension will magically occur. Thomas needs to become more metacognitive as he reads. He needs to pause during reading and ask himself what he understood and what confused him and he needs to become more adept at using look-backs to refine his comprehension. Thomas could also profit from instruction in strategies for dealing with expository test such as identifying text structure and constructing visuals of text content.

USING THE *QRI-5* TO DESCRIBE SPECIFIC READING BEHAVIORS AS A GUIDE FOR INTERVENTION INSTRUCTION (RESPONSE TO INTERVENTION: TIERS TWO AND THREE)

Ethan was referred to a private reading clinic for evaluation of his reading ability. Presently a fifth grader, Ethan had been retained in second grade. Over the years, he had received occasional help from the school reading specialist and from volunteer tutors but he still continued to struggle in reading. His parents intended to place him in another school, and they wanted a complete evaluation of his reading to be part of his records. Figure 13.1 presents a summary of the results. Testing involved two separate sessions in order to avoid the factor of fatigue.

How Accurate Is the Student in Identifying Words?   The reading specialist knew from information provided by Ethan's present school that he was reading at a third grade level. He scored at an instructional level for the third and fourth grade word lists, although his score of 14 on the fourth grade list was close to the frustration cut-off. He met frustration on the fifth grade list.

The examiner chose a third grade familiar passage, "A Special Birthday for Rosa," for Ethan to read orally. He scored at an instructional level for word identification according to Total Accuracy. On the fourth grade passage "Tomie dePaola," he also scored at an instructional level for oral reading, but met frustration for word identification on the fifth grade "Patricia McKissack." Both the word lists and the passages suggest that Ethan's ability to identify words accurately is at a fourth grade instructional level.

How Automatic Is the Student in Identifying Words?   On the word lists, no differences were evident between the total number of words pronounced correctly and those pronounced automatically. Ethan's rate on the passages ranged from 30 to 40 words per minute, well below the ranges for these text levels. He read in a deliberate and monotone fashion and often pointed to words as he read.

What Strategies for Word Identification Are Used by the Student?   The examiner analyzed Ethan's mispronunciations on "A Special Birthday for Rosa" and "Tomie dePaola." At the instructional level, 83% of Ethan's miscues were similar in sound to the actual word, 67% changed meaning, and 32% did not. There was no pattern to Ethan's self-correction strategies. He was as likely to correct a meaning-change miscue as one that

Figure 13.1 **Student Profile Sheet**

Name _____Ethan_____ Age ___11___ Grade ___5 (retained)___

Sex ___M___ Date of Test ___5/12 5/14___ Examiner ___JC___

Initial Testing ___X___ Post-Testing _____

Word Identification

Grade	3	4	5						
Level/% Automatic	40 Ins	30 Fr	24 Fr						
Level/% Total	80 Ins	70 Ins	40 Fr						

Oral Reading

Passage Name	Rosa	Tomie	Patricia	Beavers					
Readability Level	3	4	5	4					
Passage Type Narrative/Expository	N	N	N	E					
Concepts Familiar/Unfamiliar: %	92 Fam	75 Fam	75 Fam	83 Fam					
Level/% Total Accuracy	95 Ins	95 Ins	88 Fr	95 Ins					
Level/% Total Acceptability									
Retelling % Number of Ideas	7%	9%	9%	4%					
# Explicit Correct	4	3	2	2					
# Explicit Correct w/Look-Backs				3					
# Implicit Correct	3	3	2	0					
# Implicit Correct w/Look-Backs				0					
Level/% Comprehension	88 Ins	75 Ins	50 Fr	25 Fr					
Level/% Comprehension w/Look-Backs				38 Fr					
Rate WPM/CWPM	41 WPM	35 WPM	30 WPM	33 WPM					
Total Passage Level	Ins	Ins	Fr	Fr					

Silent Reading

Passage Name/Section	John								
Readability Level	4								
Passage Type Narrative/Expository	N								
Concepts Familiar/Unfamiliar %	83 Fam								
Retelling % Number of Ideas	6%								
# Correct Explicit	3								
# Correct Explicit w/Look-Backs	3								
# Correct Implicit	2								
# Correct Implicit w/Look-Backs	2								
Level/% Comprehension	62								
Level/% Comprehension w/Look-Backs	62								
Rate: WPM	39								

did not alter text meaning. Forty percent of meaning-change miscues and 33% of non-meaning-change miscues were corrected. Ethan's primary strategy when meeting an unfamiliar word was to decode phonetically. Unfortunately, he did not check that the resulting pronunciation made sense either as an actual word or in the context of the passage. The Miscue Analysis Worksheet for Ethan is on Section 13 of the DVD.

Is There a Difference in the Student's Ability to Identify Words in Isolation and Words in Context? No differences were noted.

Which Types of Text Can the Student Handle Most Successfully? Ethan scored at an instructional level for both word identification and comprehension for the third and fourth grade narrative texts read orally. However, his retelling was extremely sparse and reflected only a few isolated ideas offered in a nonsequential manner. The examiner also asked Ethan to orally read the fourth grade expository passage "The Busy Beaver." Although he achieved at an instructional level for word identification, he met frustration for comprehension. When asked to look back in the text, Ethan was unable to improve his score beyond a frustration level. This suggests that expository text may present more of a problem for him than narrative.

Which Modes of Reading Represent Strengths for the Student? Ethan was asked to silently read the fourth grade narrative passage "Johnny Appleseed." He scored at the frustration level for comprehension and look-backs did not help, which suggests that silent reading may also pose a problem for him.

How Does the Student Perform on Familiar and Unfamiliar Text? Ethan experienced familiarity with the concepts contained in the narrative passages as well as the expository selection on beavers. However, because Ethan had experienced difficulty with expository structure in familiar text ("The Busy Beaver"), the examiner did not feel it was necessary to assess unfamiliar text.

Summary. Ethan needs instruction in several areas. His slow reading rate suggests that he has not developed automaticity of word identification but, instead, is still decoding words he has met many times before. Word-identification accuracy was at a fourth grade level, two years below Ethan's chronological grade placement if his retention in second grade is taken into account. His primary strategy for identifying unfamiliar words is to match letters and sounds but, because he pays little attention to the resulting meaning, the practice does not work well for him. Ethan seems more concerned with saying the words than with comprehending what he reads. His ability to comprehend familiar narrative text is two years below his grade placement, with problems suggested in silent reading and expository text.

The examiner suggested a program focused on silent reading accompanied by self-questioning and thinking aloud. She further recommended that Ethan receive tutoring in the structure of both narrative and expository text and in using this structure to summarize his reading. The examiner suggested that Ethan engage in much silent reading of easy text in order to develop automaticity in word identification. Repeated reading of text was also recommended as a way of building reading fluency.

14 Test Materials

Student Word Lists

Student Reading
by Analogy Lists

Examiner Word Lists

Reading by Analogy
Examiner Lists

Pre-Primer 1 Passages
  "I Can"
  "I See"

Pre-Primer 2 Passages
  "Just Like Mom"
  "People at Work"

Pre-Primer 3 Passages
  "Lost and Found"
  "Spring and Fall"
  Examiner Copies

Primer Passages
  "A Trip"
  "A Night in the City"
  "Fox and Mouse"
  "The Pig Who Learned to Read"
  "Who Lives Near Lakes?"
  "Living and Not Living"
  Examiner Copies

Level One Passages
  "Mouse in a House"
  "The Surprise"
  "Marva Finds a Friend"
  "The Bear and the Rabbit"
  "Air"
  "The Brain and the Five Senses"
  Examiner Copies

Level Two Passages
  "What Can I Get for My Toy?"
  "The Family's First Trip"
  "The Lucky Cricket"
  "Father's New Game"
  "Whales and Fish"

"Seasons"
Examiner Copies

Level Three Passages
  "The Trip to the Zoo"
  "A Special Birthday for Rosa"
  "The Friend"
  "A New Friend from Europe"
  "Cats: Lions and Tigers in Your House"
  "Where Do People Live?"
  "Wool: From Sheep to You"
  Examiner Copies

Level Four Passages
  "Johnny Appleseed"
  "Amelia Earhart"
  "Tomie dePaola"
  "Early Railroads"
  "The Busy Beaver"
  "Plant Structures for Survival"
  Examiner Copies

Level Five Passages
  "Martin Luther King, Jr."
  "Margaret Mead"
  "Patricia McKissack"
  "Farming on the Great Plains"
  "The Octopus"
  "How Does Your Body Take in Oxygen?"
  Examiner Copies

Modeling Passage for
Think-Alouds
  "The Mining Boom"

Level Six Passages
  "Pele"
  "Abraham Lincoln"
  "The Early Life of Lois Lowry"
  "The Lifeline of the Nile"

"Building Pyramids"
  (Think-Aloud Passage)
"Temperature and Humidity"
"Clouds and Precipitation"
  (Think-Aloud Passage)
Examiner Copies

Upper Middle School Passages
Literature
"Biddy Mason"
"Malcolm X"

Social Studies
"Immigration—Part 1"
"Immigration—Part 2"
  (Think-Aloud Passage)

Science
"Life Cycles of Stars—Part 1"
"Life Cycles of Stars—Part 2"
  (Think-Aloud Passage)
Examiner Copies

High School Passages
Literature
"Where the Ashes Are—Part 1"
"Where the Ashes Are—Part 2"
"Where the Ashes Are—Part 3"
  (Think-Aloud Passage)

Social Studies
"World War I—Part 1"
"World War I—Part 2"
"World War I—Part 3"
  (Think-Aloud Passage)

Science
"Characteristics of Viruses—
  Part 1"
"Characteristics of Viruses—
  Part 2"
"Characteristics of Viruses—
  Part 3" (Think-Aloud Passage)
Examiner Copies

Student Word Lists

1. can	1. make
2. I	2. same
3. of	3. like
4. me	4. doing
5. the	5. were
6. in	6. my
7. at	7. work
8. with	8. write
9. a	9. play
10. he	10. just
11. go	11. some
12. to	12. they
13. see	13. people
14. do	14. look
15. on	15. too
16. was	16. other
17. she	17. place
	18. where
	19. under
	20. help

Student Word Lists

1. keep	1. bear	1. morning
2. need	2. father	2. tired
3. going	3. find	3. shiny
4. what	4. sound	4. old
5. children	5. friend	5. trade
6. thing	6. song	6. promise
7. why	7. thought	7. pieces
8. again	8. run	8. suit
9. want	9. enough	9. push
10. animals	10. brain	10. though
11. sing	11. air	11. begins
12. went	12. knew	12. food
13. jump	13. put	13. light
14. read	14. heard	14. visit
15. said	15. afraid	15. clue
16. live	16. wind	16. breathe
17. there	17. choose	17. insects
18. one	18. without	18. weather
19. great	19. move	19. noticed
20. every	20. then	20. money

Student Word Lists

1. lunch	1. sunlight	1. attend
2. celebrate	2. desert	2. protest
3. believe	3. crops	3. movement
3. confused	4. engine	4. biography
5. motion	5. favorite	5. attention
6. rough	6. adaptation	6. capture
7. engines	7. weather	7. oxygen
8. tongue	8. pond	8. tales
9. crowded	9. illustrated	9. creature
10. wool	10. ocean	10. obstacles
11. removed	11. pilot	11. divorced
12. curious	12. fame	12. registration
13. silver	13. precious	13. arrested
14. electric	14. settlers	14. poison
15. worried	15. guarded	15. material
16. enemies	16. passenger	16. bulletin
17. glowed	17. memorize	17. giant
18. clothing	18. environment	18. fluent
19. interested	19. adventurer	19. pioneers
20. entrance	20. invented	20. pouch

Student Word Lists

1. sewed	1. businesswoman	1. armaments
2. controlled	2. settlement	2. alliance
3. championships	3. infrared	3. enzyme
4. possessions	4. fusion	4. hereditary
5. moisture	5. nebula	5. escalation
6. memories	6. emulate	6. convoy
7. abolish	7. articulate	7. opulence
8. pyramids	8. encyclopedia	8. armistice
9. emerge	9. persecution	9. idealism
10. temperature	10. inevitable	10. immunodeficiency
11. humidity	11. gravity	11. mediated
12. insistent	12. nuclear	12. mandates
13. irrigated	13. assimilate	13. infectious
14. thrived	14. riffling	14. nucleic
15. slavery	15. helium	15. chromosome
16. evaporate	16. migration	16. protestations
17. classified	17. immigrants	17. disinfectant
18. preserved	18. miserable	18. liberated
19. fashioned	19. berths	19. chauffeur
20. courageous	20. oppressed	20. retrovirus

Student Reading by Analogy Lists

1. can	1. pan
2. in	2. pin
3. see	3. bee
4. at	4. rat
5. make	5. rake
6. same	6. fame
7. like	7. bike
8. place	8. race
9. play	9. bay
10. look	10. book
11. keep	11. peep
12. need	12. seed
13. thing	13. sing
14. went	14. rent
15. jump	15. bump
16. sound	16. pound
17. knew	17. chew
18. brain	18. stain

Examiner Word Lists

Pre-Primer I

	Identified Automatically	Identified
1. can	_____	_____
2. I	_____	_____
3. of	_____	_____
4. me	_____	_____
5. the	_____	_____
6. in	_____	_____
7. at	_____	_____
8. with	_____	_____
9. a	_____	_____
10. he	_____	_____
11. go	_____	_____
12. to	_____	_____
13. see	_____	_____
14. do	_____	_____
15. on	_____	_____
16. was	_____	_____
17. she	_____	_____

Total Correct Automatic _____ /17 = _____%

Total Correct Identified _____ /17 = _____%

Total Number Correct _____ /17 = _____%

LEVELS		
Independent	Instructional	Frustration
15–17	12–14	below 12
90–100%	70–85%	below 70%

Pre-Primer 2/3

	Identified Automatically	Identified
1. make	_____	_____
2. same	_____	_____
3. like	_____	_____
4. doing	_____	_____
5. were	_____	_____
6. my	_____	_____
7. work	_____	_____
8. write	_____	_____
9. play	_____	_____
10. just	_____	_____
11. some	_____	_____
12. they	_____	_____
13. people	_____	_____
14. look	_____	_____
15. too	_____	_____
16. other	_____	_____
17. place	_____	_____
18. where	_____	_____
19. under	_____	_____
20. help	_____	_____

Total Correct Automatic _____ /20 = _____%

Total Correct Identified _____ /20 = _____%

Total Number Correct _____ /20 = _____%

LEVELS		
Independent	Instructional	Frustration
18–20	14–17	below 14
90–100%	70–85%	below 70%

Examiner Word Lists

Primer

	Identified Automatically	Identified
1. keep		
2. need		
3. going		
4. what		
5. children		
6. thing		
7. why		
8. again		
9. want		
10. animals		
11. sing		
12. went		
13. jump		
14. read		
15. said		
16. live		
17. there		
18. one		
19. great		
20. every		

Total Correct Automatic _____ /20 = _____%

Total Correct Identified _____ /20 = _____%

Total Number Correct _____ /20 = _____%

First

	Identified Automatically	Identified
1. bear		
2. father		
3. find		
4. sound		
5. friend		
6. song		
7. thought		
8. run		
9. enough		
10. brain		
11. air		
12. knew		
13. put		
14. heard		
15. afraid		
16. wind		
17. choose		
18. without		
19. move		
20. then		

Total Correct Automatic _____ /20 = _____%

Total Correct Identified _____ /20 = _____%

Total Number Correct _____ /20 = _____%

LEVELS		
Independent	Instructional	Frustration
18–20	14–17	below 14
90–100%	70–85%	below 70%

Examiner Word Lists

Second

	Identified Automatically	Identified
1. morning	————	————
2. tired	————	————
3. shiny	————	————
4. old	————	————
5. trade	————	————
6. promise	————	————
7. pieces	————	————
8. suit	————	————
9. push	————	————
10. though	————	————
11. begins	————	————
12. food	————	————
13. light	————	————
14. visit	————	————
15. clue	————	————
16. breathe	————	————
17. insects	————	————
18. weather	————	————
19. noticed	————	————
20. money	————	————

Total Correct Automatic ———— /20 = ————%

Total Correct Identified ———— /20 = ————%

Total Number Correct ———— /20 = ————%

Third

	Identified Automatically	Identified
1. lunch	————	————
2. celebrate	————	————
3. believe	————	————
4. confused	————	————
5. motion	————	————
6. rough	————	————
7. engines	————	————
8. tongue	————	————
9. crowded	————	————
10. wool	————	————
11. removed	————	————
12. curious	————	————
13. silver	————	————
14. electric	————	————
15. worried	————	————
16. enemies	————	————
17. glowed	————	————
18. clothing	————	————
19. interested	————	————
20. entrance	————	————

Total Correct Automatic ———— /20 = ————%

Total Correct Identified ———— /20 = ————%

Total Number Correct ———— /20 = ————%

Level 2

Level 3

LEVELS		
Independent	Instructional	Frustration
18–20	14–17	below 14
90–100%	70–85%	below 70%

Examiner Word Lists

Fourth

	Identified Automatically	Identified
1. sunlight	————	————
2. desert	————	————
3. crops	————	————
4. engine	————	————
5. favorite	————	————
6. adaptation	————	————
7. weather	————	————
8. pond	————	————
9. illustrated	————	————
10. ocean	————	————
11. pilot	————	————
12. fame	————	————
13. precious	————	————
14. settlers	————	————
15. guarded	————	————
16. passenger	————	————
17. memorize	————	————
18. environment	————	————
19. adventurer	————	————
20. invented	————	————

Total Correct Automatic ——— /20 = ———%

Total Correct Identified ——— /20 = ———%

Total Number Correct ——— /20 = ———%

Fifth

	Identified Automatically	Identified
1. attend	————	————
2. protest	————	————
3. movement	————	————
4. biography	————	————
5. attention	————	————
6. capture	————	————
7. oxygen	————	————
8. tales	————	————
9. creature	————	————
10. obstacles	————	————
11. divorced	————	————
12. registration	————	————
13. arrested	————	————
14. poison	————	————
15. material	————	————
16. bulletin	————	————
17. giant	————	————
18. fluent	————	————
19. pioneers	————	————
20. pouch	————	————

Total Correct Automatic ——— /20 = ———%

Total Correct Identified ——— /20 = ———%

Total Number Correct ——— /20 = ———%

LEVELS		
Independent	**Instructional**	**Frustration**
18–20	14–17	below 14
90–100%	70–85%	below 70%

Level 4

Level 5

Examiner Word Lists

Sixth

	Identified Automatically	Identified
1. sewed	_____	_____
2. controlled	_____	_____
3. championships	_____	_____
4. possessions	_____	_____
5. moisture	_____	_____
6. memories	_____	_____
7. abolish	_____	_____
8. pyramids	_____	_____
9. emerge	_____	_____
10. temperature	_____	_____
11. humidity	_____	_____
12. insistent	_____	_____
13. irrigated	_____	_____
14. thrived	_____	_____
15. slavery	_____	_____
16. evaporate	_____	_____
17. classified	_____	_____
18. preserved	_____	_____
19. fashioned	_____	_____
20. courageous	_____	_____

Total Correct Automatic	_____ /20 =	_____%
Total Correct Identified	_____ /20 =	_____%
Total Number Correct	_____ /20 =	_____%

Upper Middle School

	Identified Automatically	Identified
1. businesswoman	_____	_____
2. settlement	_____	_____
3. infrared	_____	_____
4. fusion	_____	_____
5. nebula	_____	_____
6. emulate	_____	_____
7. articulate	_____	_____
8. encyclopedia	_____	_____
9. persecution	_____	_____
10. inevitable	_____	_____
11. gravity	_____	_____
12. nuclear	_____	_____
13. assimilate	_____	_____
14. riffling	_____	_____
15. helium	_____	_____
16. migration	_____	_____
17. immigrants	_____	_____
18. miserable	_____	_____
19. berths	_____	_____
20. oppressed	_____	_____

Total Correct Automatic	_____ /20 =	_____%
Total Correct Identified	_____ /20 =	_____%
Total Number Correct	_____ /20 =	_____%

LEVELS		
Independent	**Instructional**	**Frustration**
18–20	14–17	below 14
90–100%	70–85%	below 70%

Examiner Word Lists

High School

		Identified Automatically	*Identified*
1.	armaments	————	————
2.	alliance	————	————
3.	enzyme	————	————
4.	hereditary	————	————
5.	escalation	————	————
6.	convoy	————	————
7.	opulence	————	————
8.	armistice	————	————
9.	idealism	————	————
10.	immunodeficiency	————	————
11.	mediated	————	————
12.	mandates	————	————
13.	infectious	————	————
14.	nucleic	————	————
15.	chromosome	————	————
16.	protestations	————	————
17.	disinfectant	————	————
18.	liberated	————	————
19.	chauffeur	————	————
20.	retrovirus	————	————

Total Correct Automatic ——— /20 = ———%

Total Correct Identified ——— /20 = ———%

Total Number Correct ——— /20 = ———%

LEVELS		
Independent	**Instructional**	**Frustration**
18–20	14–17	below 14
90–100%	70–85%	below 70%

Examiner Lists Reading by Analogy

Name _____ Date _____ Level _____

PP1

High-Frequency Words from the Word Lists	Correct	Low-Frequency Words	Correct
can		pan	
in		pin	
see		bee	
at		rat	

PP2

make		rake	
same		fame	
like		bike	
place		race	
play		bay	
look		book	

Primer

keep		peep	
need		seed	
thing		sing	
went		rent	
jump		bump	

First

sound		pound	
knew		chew	
brain		stain	
Total		Total	

I Can

I can jump. See me jump.

I can hop. See me hop.

I can run. See me run.

I can eat lunch. See me eat.

I can sleep. See me sleep.

I can dream. See me dream.

I See

I see a frog on a log.

I see an ant on a plant.

I see a bug on a rug.

I see a duck in a truck.

I see a pig doing a jig.

Just Like Mom

I can write.

Just like Mom.

I can read.

Just like Mom.

I can go to work.

Just like Mom.

I can work at home.

Just like Mom.

I can work with numbers.

Just like Mom.

I can do lots of things.

Just like Mom.

People at Work

Some people work at home.

Other people go to work.

Why do people work?

People work to make money.

People work at many things.

Some people write at work.

Other people read at work.

Some people make things at work.

Other people sell things at work.

People work together.

Lost and Found

I lost my cat.

Where was she?

I looked inside the house.

I looked under the bed.

I looked outside too.

I lost my dog.

Where was he?

I looked inside the house.

I looked under the bed.

I looked outside too.

I found my cat.

I found my dog.

Where were they?

They were in the same place.

They were under the table.

Spring and Fall

I like the spring.

When I can do many things.

I can play with my dog.

I can play with a frog.

I can play in the rain.

I can go see a train.

I like the fall.

I can do it all.

I can read a book.

I can help Mom cook.

I can ride my bike.

I can go on a hike.

In the spring and fall, there is much to do.

But what I like best is going to the zoo.

Level: Pre-Primer 1

Narrative

Concept Questions:

What does it mean to jump?

_____

_____

_____ (3-2-1-0)

What does it mean to hop?

_____

_____

_____ (3-2-1-0)

What does it mean to sleep?

_____

_____

_____ (3-2-1-0)

What does it mean to dream?

_____

_____

_____ (3-2-1-0)

Score: _____ /12 = _____ %

_____ FAM _____ UNFAM

Prediction:

_____

_____

"I Can"

I can jump. See me jump.

I can hop. See me hop.

I can run. See me run.

I can eat lunch. See me eat.

I can sleep. See me sleep.

I can dream. See me dream. (37 words)

Number of Total Miscues
(Total Accuracy): _____

Number of Meaning-Change Miscues
(Total Acceptability): _____

Total Accuracy		**Total Acceptability**	
0–1 miscue	_____ Independent	_____ 0–1 miscue	
2–4 miscues	_____ Instructional	_____ 2 miscues	
5+ miscues	_____ Frustration	_____ 3+ miscues	

Rate: 37 × 60 = 2,220/_____ seconds = _____ WPM

Correct WPM: (37 – _____ errors) × 60 =
_____ /_____ seconds = _____ CWPM

Retelling Scoring Sheet for "I Can"

____ I can jump.
____ See me jump.
____ I can hop.
____ See me hop.
____ I can run.
____ See me run.
____ I can eat lunch.
____ See me eat.
____ I can sleep.
____ See me sleep.
____ I can dream.
____ See me dream.

12 Ideas

Number of ideas recalled _____

Other ideas recalled, including inferences:

Level Pre-Primer 1

Questions for "I Can"

1. What can the girl at the beginning of the story do?
   Explicit: jump

2. What can another girl in the story do?
   Explicit: hop
   Note: if the student says "play hopscotch," count it as implicitly correct.

3. What can the group of children do?
   Explicit: run

4. What can the boy in the library do?
   Explicit: sleep

5. While the boy is sleeping, what can he do?
   Explicit: dream

Number Correct Explicit: _____

Number Correct Implicit: _____

Total: _____

_____ Independent: 5 correct

_____ Instructional: 4 correct

_____ Frustration: 0–3 correct

Level: Pre-Primer 1

Narrative

Concept Questions:

What is a frog?

_____

_____

_____ (3-2-1-0)

What is a bug?

_____

_____

_____ (3-2-1-0)

What is a pig?

_____

_____

_____ (3-2-1-0)

Score: _____ /9 = _____ %

_____ FAM _____ UNFAM

Prediction:

_____

_____

"I See"

I see a frog on a log.

I see an ant on a plant.

I see a bug on a rug.

I see a duck in a truck.

I see a pig doing a jig. (35 words)

Number of Total Miscues
(Total Accuracy): _____

Number of Meaning-Change Miscues
(Total Acceptability): _____

Total Accuracy		**Total Acceptability**	
0–1 miscue	_____ Independent	_____	0–1 miscue
2–3 miscues	_____ Instructional	_____	2 miscues
4+ miscues	_____ Frustration	_____	3+ miscues

Rate: $35 \times 60 = 2{,}100/$_____ seconds = _____ WPM

Correct WPM: $(35 - $_____ errors$) \times 60 =$
_____ / _____ seconds = _____ CWPM

Retelling Scoring Sheet for "I See"

_____ I see a frog
_____ on a log.
_____ I see an ant
_____ on a plant.
_____ I see a bug
_____ on a rug.
_____ I see a duck
_____ in a truck.
_____ I see a pig
_____ doing a jig.

10 ideas

Number of ideas recalled _____

Other ideas recalled, including inferences:

Questions for "I See"

1. Where was the frog?
   Explicit or Implicit from picture: on a log

2. Where was the ant?
   Explicit or Implicit from picture: on a plant

3. Where was the bug?
   Explicit or Implicit from picture: on a rug

4. Where was the duck?
   Explicit or Implicit from picture: in a truck

5. What was the pig doing?
   Explicit: a jig
   Note: if the student says "dancing" count it as a implicitly correct.

> Number Correct Explicit: ____
>
> Number Correct Implicit: ____
>
> **Total:** ____
>
> ____ Independent: 5 correct
>
> ____ Instructional: 4 correct
>
> ____ Frustration: 0–3 correct

Level: Pre-Primer 2

Narrative

Concept Questions:

What is a Mom?

_____

_____

_____ (3-2-1-0)

What does "working at home" mean to you?

_____

_____

_____ (3-2-1-0)

What does "going to work" mean to you?

_____

_____

_____ (3-2-1-0)

Score: _____ /9 = _____ %

_____ FAM _____ UNFAM

Prediction:

_____

_____

"Just Like Mom"

I can write.

Just like Mom.

I can read.

Just like Mom.

I can go to work.

Just like Mom.

I can work at home.

Just like Mom.

I can work with numbers.

Just like Mom.

I can do lots of things.

Just like Mom. (44 words)

Number of Total Miscues
(Total Accuracy): _____

Number of Meaning-Change Miscues
(Total Acceptability): _____

Total Accuracy		**Total Acceptability**
0–1 miscue	____ Independent	____ 0–1 miscue
2–3 miscues	____ Instructional	____ 2 miscues
5+ miscues	____ Frustration	____ 3+ miscues

Rate: $44 \times 60 = 2{,}640/$____ seconds = ____ WPM

Correct WPM: $(44 - $ ____ errors$) \times 60 =$

____ / ____ seconds = ____ CWPM

Retelling Scoring Sheet for "Just Like Mom"

___ I can write.
___ Just like Mom.
___ I can read.
___ Just like Mom.
___ I can go to work.
___ Just like Mom.
___ I can work
___ at home.
___ Just like Mom.
___ I can work
___ with numbers.
___ Just like Mom.
___ I can do lots
___ of things.

Level: Pre-Primer 2

_____ Just like Mom.

15 Ideas

Number of ideas recalled _____

Other ideas recalled, including inferences:

Questions for "Just Like Mom"

Note: If a question is answered with direct reference to pictures as opposed to text, score the answer as implicitly correct.

1. Name one thing the girl can do just like Mom.
   Explicit: write, read, go to work, work at home, or work with numbers
   Implicit: water the flowers, walk to work, or write numbers

2. Name another thing the girl can do just like Mom.
   Explicit: read, write, go to work, work at home, or work with numbers, depending on the answer above
   Implicit: same as #1

3. What can the girl work with just like Mom?
   Explicit: numbers
   Implicit: pencils, paper

4. Where can the girl work just like Mom?
   Explicit: at home or she can go to work
   Implicit: in the garden

5. Where is another place the girl can work just like Mom?
   Explicit: at home or at her workplace, depending on the answer above
   Implicit: same as #4

Number Correct Explicit: _____

Number Correct Implicit
 (from pictures): _____

Total: _____

_____ Independent: 5 correct

_____ Instructional: 4 correct

_____ Frustration: 0–3 correct

Level: Pre-Primer 2

Expository

> **Concept Questions:**
>
> Where do people work?
>
> _____
>
> _____
>
> _____ (3-2-1-0)
>
> Why do people work?
>
> _____
>
> _____
>
> _____ (3-2-1-0)
>
> What are different kinds of jobs?
>
> _____
>
> _____
>
> _____ (3-2-1-0)
>
> **Score:** _____ /9 = _____ %
>
> _____ FAM _____ UNFAM
>
> **Prediction:**
>
> _____
>
> _____

"People at Work"

Some people work at home.

Other people go to work.

Why do people work?

People work to make money.

People work at many things.

Some people write at work.

Other people read at work

Some people make things at work.

Other people sell things at work.

People work together. (49 words)

> Number of Total Miscues
> (Total Accuracy): _____
>
> Number of Meaning-Change Miscues
> (Total Acceptability): _____
>
> | **Total Accuracy** | | **Total Acceptability** |
> |---|---|---|
> | 0–1 miscue ____ | Independent | ____ 0–1 miscue |
> | 2–5 miscues ____ | Instructional | ____ 2 miscues |
> | 6+ miscues ____ | Frustration | ____ 3+ miscues |
>
> **Rate:** $49 \times 60 = 2{,}940/$____ seconds = ____ WPM
>
> **Correct WPM:** $(49 - $____ errors$) \times 60 =$
> ____ / ____ seconds = ____ CWPM

Retelling Scoring Sheet for "People at Work"

Details

___ Some people work

___ at home.

___ Other people go to work.

___ Why do people work?

___ People work to make money.

___ People work

___ at many things.

___ Some people write

___ at work.

___ Other people read

___ at work.

___ Some people make things

___ at work.

___ Other people sell things

___ at work.

___ People work

___ together.

17 Ideas

Number of ideas recalled _____

Level: Pre-Primer 2

Other ideas recalled, including inferences:

Questions for "People at Work"

Note: If a question is answered with direct reference to pictures as opposed to text, score the answer as implicitly correct.

1. Where do people work?
    Explicit: at home or they go to work

2. What is one thing that people do at work?
    Explicit: write, read, make things, or sell things
    Implicit: fix things

3. What is another thing that people do at work?
    Explicit: write, read, make things, or sell things, depending on answer above
    Implicit: fix things

4. What is another thing that people do at work?
    Explicit: write, read, make things, or sell things, depending on answers to previous questions
    Implicit: fix things

5. What is another thing that people do at work?
    Explicit: write, read, make things, or sell things, depending on answers to previous questions
    Implicit: fix things

Number Correct Explicit: _____

Number Correct Implicit
     (from pictures): _____

Total: _____

——— Independent: 5 correct

——— Instructional: 4 correct

——— Frustration: 0–3 correct

Level: Pre-Primer 3

Narrative

Concept Questions:

What does it mean when someone is lost?

_____

_____

_____ (3-2-1-0)

What does it mean when something is found?

_____

_____

_____ (3-2-1-0)

What does "looking for something" mean to you?

_____

_____

_____ (3-2-1-0)

Score: _____ /9 = _____ %

_____ FAM _____ UNFAM

Prediction:

_____

_____

"Lost and Found"

I lost my cat.

Where was she?

I looked inside the house.

I looked under the bed.

I looked outside too.

I lost my dog.

Where was he?

I looked inside the house.

I looked under the bed.

I looked outside too.

I found my cat.

I found my dog.

Where were they?

They were in the same place.

They were under the table. (64 words)

Number of Total Miscues
(Total Accuracy): _____

Number of Meaning-Change Miscues
(Total Acceptability): _____

Total Accuracy		Total Acceptability	
0–1 miscue	____ Independent	____	0–1 miscue
2–6 miscues	____ Instructional	____	2–3 miscues
7+ miscues	____ Frustration	____	4+ miscues

Rate: 64 × 60 = 3,840/____ seconds = ____ WPM

Correct WPM: (64 – ____ errors) × 60 =
____ /____ seconds = ____ CWPM

Retelling Scoring Sheet for "Lost and Found"

Events

____ I lost my cat.
____ Where was she?
____ I looked
____ inside the house.
____ I looked

Level: Pre-Primer 3

___ under the bed.

___ I looked

___ outside too.

___ I lost my dog.

___ Where was he?

___ I looked

___ inside the house.

___ I looked

___ under the bed.

___ I looked

___ outside too.

___ I found my cat.

___ I found my dog.

___ Where were they?

___ They were in the same place.

___ They were under the table.

21 Ideas

Number of ideas recalled _____

Other ideas recalled, including inferences:

Questions for "Lost and Found"

1. What did the person in the story lose?
   Explicit: cat or dog

2. What else did the person in the story lose?
   Explicit: cat or dog, depending on the answer above

3. Where did the person in the story look?
   Explicit: inside the house, under the bed, or outside

4. Where else did the person in the story look?
   Explicit: inside the house, under the bed, or outside, depending on the answer above

5. Where did the person find the dog and cat?
   Explicit: in the same place or under the table

Number Correct Explicit: ____

Total: ____

____ Independent: 5 correct

____ Instructional: 4 correct

____ Frustration: 0–3 correct

Level: Pre-Primer 3

Narrative

Concept Questions:

What does "spring" mean to you?

_____

_____

_____ (3-2-1-0)

What does "fall" mean to you??

_____

_____

_____ (3-2-1-0)

What does "doing something you like best" mean to you?

_____

_____

_____ (3-2-1-0)

Score: _____ /9 = _____ %

_____ FAM _____ UNFAM

Prediction:

_____

_____

"Spring and Fall"

I like the spring.

When I can do many things.

I can play with my dog.

I can play with a frog.

I can play in the rain.

I can go see a train.

I like the fall.

I can do it all.

I can read a book.

I can help Mom cook.

I can ride my bike.

I can go on a hike.

In the spring and fall, there is much to do.

But what I like best is going to the zoo. (84 words)

Number of Total Miscues
(Total Accuracy): _____

Number of Meaning-Change Miscues
(Total Acceptability): _____

Total Accuracy		**Total Acceptability**
0–2 miscues _____	Independent _____	0–2 miscues
3–8 miscues _____	Instructional _____	3–4 miscues
9+ miscues _____	Frustration _____	5+ miscues

Rate: $84 \times 60 = 5{,}040/$____ seconds = ____ WPM

Correct WPM: $(84 - $____ errors$) \times 60 = $

____ /____ seconds = ____ CWPM

Retelling Scoring Sheet for "Spring and Fall"

Details

___ I like the spring.
___ When I can do
___ many things.
___ I can play
___ with my dog.
___ I can play
___ with a frog.
___ I can play
___ in the rain.
___ I can go
___ see a train.
___ I like the fall.

Level: Pre-Primer 3

___ I can do it all.
___ I can read
___ a book.
___ I can help Mom
___ cook.
___ I can ride
___ my bike.
___ I can go
___ on a hike.
___ In the spring
___ and fall
___ there is much to do.
___ But what I like
___ best
___ is going
___ to the zoo.

28 Ideas

Number of ideas recalled _____

Other ideas recalled, including inferences:

Questions for "Spring and Fall"

1. What can the person in the story play with in the spring?
   Explicit: a dog or a frog

2. Name another thing the person can do in the spring.
   Explicit: play with a dog or frog (depending on above), or play in the rain, or go see a train

3. What can the person in the story ride on during the fall?
   Explicit: a bike

4. What can the person in the story help Mom do?
   Explicit: cook

5. What does the person like to do best?
   Explicit: go to the zoo

Number Correct Explicit: _____

Total: _____

_____ Independent: 5 correct

_____ Instructional: 4 correct

_____ Frustration: 0–3 correct

A Trip

It was a warm spring day.

The children were going on a trip.

The trip was to a farm.

The children wanted to see many animals.

They wanted to write down all they saw.

They were going to make a book for their class.

On the way to the farm the bus stopped moving.

The children thought their trip was over.

Then a man stopped his car.

He helped to fix the bus.

The bus started again.

The children said, "Yea!"

The children got to the farm.

They saw a pig.

They saw a hen and cows.

They liked petting the kittens.

They learned about milking cows.

They liked the trip to the farm.

They wanted to go again.

A Night in the City

It was a Saturday night in the city.

Ben and Ruth wanted something to do.

They heard a noise from outside.

They ran to their bedroom window.

They saw people in the street.

A man had a horn.

A woman had a guitar.

They were playing together.

Soon more people came.

They all started singing.

Ben had heard the songs before.

Their father had played CDs.

The songs were on them.

Ruth went to find their mother and father.

"Come and listen to the music," she said.

They all sat in the living room.

They listened to the music.

It went on for a long time.

Ben and Ruth fell asleep in the living room.

Mother and father carried them to bed.

It had been a great Saturday night.

Fox and Mouse

Fox wanted to plant a garden.

Mouse helped him.

They put the seeds in the ground.

They watered the seeds.

Then they waited.

One night Mouse went to the garden.

He dug up one of the seeds.

He wanted to see if it was growing.

The seed looked good to eat.

"It is only one seed," thought Mouse.

"Fox will not know who ate the seed."

The next night Mouse went to the garden again.

He dug up one seed and ate it.

He did this every night.

After a few weeks, all the seeds were gone.

"I wonder why the seeds didn't grow," said Fox.

Mouse didn't say a word.

So Fox planted more seeds.

And Mouse helped him.

The Pig Who Learned to Read

Once there was a pig.

His name was Pete.

He lived on a farm.

He was not like other pigs.

He was special.

He wanted to learn to read.

His father said, "But pigs can't read!"

"I don't care," said Pete.

"I want to read."

One day Pete went to a boy who lived on the farm.

"Teach me to read," he said.

The boy said, "But you're a pig. I don't know if I can.

But I'll do what my mother and father did with me."

Every night before bed, the boy read to the pig.

The pig loved the stories.

He liked one called "Pat the Bunny" best.

A week later Pete asked to take the book to the barn.

He looked at the words.

He thought about what the boy had said.

He did that every day.

One day he read a story to the boy.

He was so happy!

After that he read to the other animals every night.

The boy was happy too, because he'd taught his first
   pig to read.

Who Lives Near Lakes?

Many animals live near lakes.

Turtles sit on rocks.

They like to be in the sun.

You can see ducks near a lake.

There may be baby ducks.

The babies walk behind the mother duck.

There are fish in lakes.

You can see them when they jump out of the water.

People live near lakes too.

They like to see the animals.

Living and Not Living

Some things around us live.

Others are not living.

Things that live need air.

Things that live need food.

Things that live need water.

Things that live move and grow.

Animals are living things.

Plants are living things.

Is paper living?

No, but it comes from something living.

Paper comes from trees.

Is a wagon living?

No, it moves but it is not living.

Level: Primer

Narrative

Concept Questions:

What is a farm?

_____

_____

_____ (3-2-1-0)

What happens when a car or bus breaks down?

_____

_____

_____ (3-2-1-0)

What is a school trip?

_____

_____

_____ (3-2-1-0)

Score: _____ /9 = _____ %

_____ FAM _____ UNFAM

Prediction:

_____

_____

"A Trip"

It was a warm spring day. The <u>children</u> <u>were</u> <u>going</u> on a trip. The trip was to a farm. The <u>children</u> <u>wanted</u> to see many <u>animals</u>. <u>They</u> <u>wanted</u> to <u>write</u> down all <u>they</u> saw. <u>They</u> <u>were</u> <u>going</u> to <u>make</u> a book for their class. On the way to the farm the bus stopped moving. The <u>children</u> thought their trip was over. Then a man stopped his car. He <u>helped</u> to

fix the bus. The bus started <u>again</u>. The <u>children</u> <u>said</u>, "Yea!" The <u>children</u> got to the farm. <u>They</u> saw a pig. <u>They</u> saw a hen and cows. <u>They</u> <u>liked</u> petting the kittens. <u>They</u> learned about milking cows. <u>They</u> liked the trip to the farm. <u>They</u> <u>wanted</u> to go again. (119 words)

Number of Total Miscues
(Total Accuracy): _____

Number of Meaning-Change Miscues
(Total Acceptability): _____

Total Accuracy		**Total Acceptability**
0–2 miscues ____ Independent	____	0–2 miscues
3–12 miscues ____ Instructional	____	3–6 miscues
13+ miscues ____ Frustration	____	7+ miscues

Rate: $119 \times 60 = 7{,}140/$____ seconds = ____ WPM

Correct WPM: $(119 -$ ____ errors$) \times 60 =$
____ / ____ seconds = ____ CWPM

Retelling Scoring Sheet for "A Trip"

Setting/Background

____ The children were going on a trip
____ to a farm.

Goal

____ The children wanted to see animals
____ and write down all they saw.
____ They were going to make a book
____ for their class.

Events

____ On the way
____ to the farm
____ the bus broke down.
____ A man stopped his car.

Level: Primer

___ The man helped
___ to fix the bus.
___ The children got to the farm.
___ They saw a pig,
___ a hen,
___ and cows.
___ They liked
___ petting kittens.
___ They learned
___ about milking cows.

Resolution

___ They liked their trip
___ and wanted to go again.

22 Ideas

Number of ideas recalled _____

Other ideas recalled, including inferences:

Questions for "A Trip"

1. Where were the children going?
   Explicit: on a trip to a farm

2. What did they want to see?
   Explicit: many animals, or names of at least two types of animals

3. Who do you think went with the children on the trip?
   Implicit: their teacher. If the child says, "Bus driver," ask, "Who else went with them besides the bus driver?"

4. What happened on the way to the farm?
   Explicit: the bus stopped moving

5. What would have happened *to their trip* if the man hadn't stopped his car?
   Implicit: they wouldn't have gotten to the farm, they got to the farm late

6. What did the children learn at the farm?
   Explicit: about getting milk from cows. If the child says "About cows," say, "What about cows?"

Number Correct Explicit: ____

Number Correct Implicit: ____

Total: ____

___ Independent: 6 correct

___ Instructional: 4–5 correct

___ Frustration: 0–3 correct

Level: Primer

Narrative

Concept Questions:

What is a horn?

_____

_____

_____ (3-2-1-0)

What are CDs?

_____

_____

_____ (3-2-1-0)

Why do people sing together?

_____

_____

_____ (3-2-1-0)

Why happens when someone gets very tired?

_____

_____

_____ (3-2-1-0)

Score: _____ /12 = _____ %

_____ FAM _____ UNFAM

Prediction:

_____

_____

"A Night in the City"

It was a Saturday night in the city.

Ben and Ruth <u>wanted</u> something to do.

<u>They</u> heard a noise from outside.

<u>They</u> ran to their bedroom window.

<u>They</u> saw <u>people</u> in the street.

A man had a horn.

A woman had a guitar.

<u>They</u> <u>were</u> <u>playing</u> together.

Soon more <u>people</u> came.

<u>They</u> all started <u>singing</u>.

Ben had heard the songs before.

Their father had <u>played</u> CDs.

The songs <u>were</u> on them.

Ruth <u>went</u> to find their mother and father.

"Come and listen to the music," she <u>said</u>.

<u>They</u> all sat in the living room.

<u>They</u> listened to the music.

It <u>went</u> on for a long time.

Ben and Ruth fell asleep in the living room.

Mother and father carried them to bed.

It had been a <u>great</u> Saturday night.

(129 words)

Number of Total Miscues
(Total Accuracy): _____

Number of Meaning-Change Miscues
(Total Acceptability): _____

Total Accuracy		**Total Acceptability**
0–3 miscues ____ Independent	____ 0–3 miscues
4–13 miscues ____ Instructional	____ 4–6 miscues
14+ miscues ____ Frustration	____ 7+ miscues

Rate: 129 × 60 = 7,740/____ seconds = ____ WPM

Correct WPM: (129 – ____ errors) × 60
= ____ /____ seconds = ____ CWPM

Retelling Scoring Sheet for "A Night in the City"

Setting/Background

____ It was a Saturday night

____ in the city.

Level: Primer

Copyright © 2011 Pearson Education, Inc. Reproduction is permitted for classroom use only.

Goal

____ Ben
____ and Ruth wanted something to do.

Events

____ They heard a noise
____ from outside.
____ They ran
____ to their bedroom window.
____ They saw people
____ in the street.
____ A man had a horn.
____ A woman had a guitar.
____ They were playing together.
____ Soon more people came.
____ They all started singing.
____ Ben had heard the songs before.
____ Their father had played CDs.
____ The songs were on them.
____ Ruth went to find their mother
____ and father.
____ "Come
____ and listen to the music,"
____ she said.
____ They all sat
____ in the living room.
____ They listened to the music.
____ It went on
____ for a long time.

Resolution

____ Ben
____ and Ruth fell asleep
____ in the living room.
____ Mother
____ and father carried them
____ to bed.
____ It had been a great
____ Saturday night.

36 Ideas

Number of ideas recalled _____

Other ideas recalled, including inferences:

Questions for "A Night in the City"

1. What night was it?
   Explicit: Saturday

2. What did Ben and Ruth do when they heard a noise from outside?
   Explicit: ran to their bedroom window

3. What did they see outside their window?
   Explicit: people in the street; *or* a man with a horn; *or* a woman with a guitar

4. Why did the people in the street start singing together?
   Implicit: they liked the songs that were being played; *or* they knew the songs that were being played

5. What did Ruth do after she and her brother heard the music?
   Explicit: went to find their mother and father

6. Why did Ben and Ruth fall asleep?
   Implicit: the music went on a long time and they got tired; *or* it became late

Number Correct Explicit: ____

Number Correct Implicit: ____

Total: ____

____ Independent: 6 correct

____ Instructional: 4–5 correct

____ Frustration: 0–3 correct

Primer

Level: Primer

Narrative

Concept Questions:

What are seeds?

_____

_____

_____ (3-2-1-0)

What do gardens need to grow?

_____

_____

_____ (3-2-1-0)

What do mice eat?

_____

_____

_____ (3-2-1-0)

Score: _____ /9 = _____ %

_____ FAM _____ UNFAM

Prediction:

_____

_____

"Fox and Mouse"

Fox wanted to plant a garden.

Mouse helped him.

They put the seeds in the ground.

They watered the seeds.

Then they waited.

One night Mouse went to the garden.

He dug up one of the seeds.

He wanted to see if it was growing.

The seed looked good to eat.

"It is only one seed," thought Mouse.

"Fox will not know who ate the seed."

The next night Mouse went to the garden again.

He dug up one seed and ate it.

He did this every night.

After a few weeks all the seeds were gone.

"I wonder why the seeds didn't grow," said Fox.

Mouse didn't say a word.

So Fox planted more seeds.

And Mouse helped him. (122 words)

Number of Total Miscues
(Total Accuracy): _____

Number of Meaning-Change Miscues
(Total Acceptability): _____

Total Accuracy		**Total Acceptability**
0–3 miscues	____ Independent	____ 0–3 miscues
4–12 miscues	____ Instructional	____ 4–6 miscues
13+ miscues	____ Frustration	____ 7+ miscues

Rate: 122 × 60 = 7,320/____ seconds = ____ WPM

Correct WPM: (122 – ____ errors) × 60 =

____ /____ seconds = ____ CWPM

Retelling Scoring Sheet for "Fox and Mouse"

Setting/Background

___ Fox wanted to plant a garden.
___ Mouse helped him.
___ They put seeds
___ in the ground.
___ They watered the seeds.
___ Then they waited.

Level: Primer

Goal

____ One night
____ Mouse went to the garden.
____ He dug up one of the seeds.
____ He wanted to see
____ if it was growing.

Events

____ The seed looked good to eat.
____ "It is only one seed,"
____ thought Mouse.
____ "Fox will not know
____ who ate the seed."
____ The next night
____ Mouse went to the garden again.
____ He dug up one seed
____ and ate it.
____ He did this
____ every night.
____ After a few weeks
____ all the seeds were gone.

Resolution

____ "I wonder
____ why the seeds didn't grow?"
____ said Fox.
____ Mouse didn't say a word.
____ So Fox planted more seeds.
____ And Mouse helped him.

30 Ideas

Number of ideas recalled _____

Other ideas recalled, including inferences:

Questions for "Fox and Mouse"

1. What did Fox want to do?
   Explicit: to plant a garden

2. What did Fox and Mouse do?
   Explicit: put seeds in the ground *and* watered them. If child says only one part ask, "What else did they do?"

3. Why did Mouse dig up the first seed?
   Explicit: to see if it was growing

4. What did Mouse do with the first seed that he dug up?
   Explicit: ate it

5. Why didn't the garden grow?
   Implicit: because Mouse ate all the seeds in the garden

6. Why did Mouse help Fox plant the garden again?
   Implicit: because he had eaten all the seeds; *or* he felt bad; *or* he was Fox's friend; *or* so he can have more seeds to eat

Number Correct Explicit: ____

Number Correct Implicit: ____

Total: ____

____ Independent: 6 correct

____ Instructional: 4–5 correct

____ Frustration: 0–3 correct

Level: Primer

Narrative

Concept Questions:

What is doing something new?

_____

_____

_____ (3-2-1-0)

What is learning to read?

_____

_____

_____ (3-2-1-0)

What does it mean when people read stories to you?

_____

_____

_____ (3-2-1-0)

Score: _____ /9 = _____ %

_____ FAM _____ UNFAM

Prediction:

_____

_____

"The Pig Who Learned to Read"

Once there was a pig. His name was Pete. He lived on a farm. He was not like other pigs. He was special. He wanted to learn to read. His father said, "But pigs can't read!" "I don't care," said Pete. "I want to read."

One day Pete went to a boy who lived on the farm. "Teach me to read," he said. The boy said, "But you're a pig. I don't know if I can. But I'll do what my mother and father did with me." Every night before bed, the boy read to the pig. The pig loved the stories. He liked one called "Pat the Bunny" best. A week later Pete asked to take the book to the barn. He looked at the words. He thought about what the boy had said. He did that every day. One day he read a story to the boy. He was so happy! After that he read to the other animals every night. The boy was happy too, because he'd taught his first pig to read. (176 words)

Number of Total Miscues
(Total Accuracy): _____

Number of Meaning-Change Miscues
(Total Acceptability): _____

Total Accuracy		**Total Acceptability**
0–4 miscues	_____ Independent	_____ 0–4 miscues
5–18 miscues	_____ Instructional	_____ 5–9 miscues
19+ miscues	_____ Frustration	_____ 10+ miscues

Rate: $176 \times 60 = 10{,}560/$_____ seconds = _____ WPM

Correct WPM: $(176 -$ _____ errors$) \times 60 =$
_____ /_____ seconds = _____ CWPM

Retelling Scoring Sheet for "The Pig Who Learned to Read"

Setting/Background

___ There was a pig
___ named Pete.

Level: Primer

Primer

Goal

___ He wanted to learn
___ to read.
___ His father said,
___ "Pigs can't read."
___ Pete said,
___ "I don't care."

Events

___ He went to a boy
___ who lived on a farm.
___ He said,
___ "Teach me
___ to read."
___ The boy said,
___ "I'll do
___ what my mother
___ and father did."
___ Every night
___ before bed,
___ the boy read
___ to the pig.
___ The pig loved the stories.
___ Pete took the book
___ to the barn.
___ He looked at the words
___ every day.
___ One day
___ the pig read a story
___ to the boy.
___ He was so happy.

Resolution

___ He read
___ to the animals
___ every night.
___ The boy was happy.
___ He taught the pig
___ to read.

36 Ideas

Number of ideas recalled _____

Other ideas recalled, including inferences:

Questions for "The Pig Who Learned to Read"

1. Who was this story about?
   Explicit: Pete the pig

2. What did Pete want?
   Explicit: to learn to read

3. What did Pete do to get what he wanted?
   Explicit: he asked the boy who lived on the farm to teach him

4. Why was the boy not sure he could teach the pig to read?
   Implicit: because pigs didn't learn to read or because the boy had never taught anyone to read before

5. What did the boy do to teach Pete to read?
   Explicit: he read to him every night

6. What did the pig do in order to learn how to read?
   Implicit: he matched the words with what the boy had said. He did that every day.

Number Correct Explicit: ____

Number Correct Implicit: ____

Total: ____

___ Independent: 6 correct

___ Instructional: 4–5 correct

___ Frustration: 0–3 correct

Level: Primer

Expository

Concept Questions:

What animals live near lakes?

_____

_____

_____ (3-2-1-0)

When do you see turtles outside?

_____

_____

_____ (3-2-1-0)

Why do people live near lakes?

_____

_____

_____ (3-2-1-0)

Score: _____ /9 = _____ %

_____ FAM _____ UNFAM

Prediction:

_____

_____

"Who Lives Near Lakes?"

Many animals live lakes.

Turtles sit on rocks.

They like to be in the sun.

You can see ducks near a lake.

There may be baby ducks.

The babies walk behind the mother duck.

There are fish in lakes.

You can see them when they jump out of the water.

People live near lakes too.

They like to see the animals. (62 words)

Number of Total Miscues
(Total Accuracy): _____

Number of Meaning-Change Miscues
(Total Acceptability): _____

Total Accuracy			**Total Acceptability**
0–1 miscue	____	Independent	____ 0–1 miscue
2–6 miscues	____	Instructional	____ 2–3 miscues
7+ miscues	____	Frustration	____ 4+ miscues

Rate: 62 × 60 = 3,720/____ seconds = ____ WPM

Correct WPM: (62 – ____ errors) × 60 =

____ /____ seconds = ____ CWPM

Retelling Scoring Sheet for "Who Lives Near Lakes?"

Main Idea

___ Many animals live
___ near lakes.

Details

___ Turtles sit
___ on rocks.
___ They like to be in the sun.
___ You can see ducks
___ near a lake.
___ There may be baby ducks.
___ The babies walk
___ behind the mother duck.
___ There are fish
___ in lakes.
___ You can see them
___ when they jump
___ out of the water.
___ People live near lakes too.

Level: Primer

____ They like
____ to see the animals.

18 Ideas

Number of ideas recalled _____

Other ideas recalled, including inferences:

Questions for "Who Lives Near Lakes?"

1. What did the passage say turtles sit on?
   Explicit: rocks

2. When would turtles sit on rocks?
   Implicit: when it is sunny

3. Where do baby ducks walk?
   Explicit: behind the mother duck

4. What other animal besides a turtle and ducks does the passage talk about?
   Explicit: fish

5. When can you see fish?
   Explicit: when they jump out of the water

6. Why do people live near lakes?
   Implicit: they like to see animals

Number Correct Explicit: ____

Number Correct Implicit: ____

Total: ____

____ Independent: 6 correct

____ Instructional: 4–5 correct

____ Frustration: 0–3 correct

Level: Primer

Expository

Concept Questions:

What do plants need to grow?

_____

_____

_____ (3-2-1-0)

When do living things do?

_____

_____

_____ (3-2-1-0)

What are things that have never been alive?

_____

_____

_____ (3-2-1-0)

Score: _____ /9 = _____ %

_____ FAM _____ UNFAM

Prediction:

_____

_____

"Living and Not Living"

Some things around us live.

Others are not living.

Things that live need air.

Things that live need food.

Things that live need water.

Things that live move and grow.

Animals are living things.

Plants are living things.

Is paper living?

No, but it comes from something living.

Paper comes from trees.

Is a wagon living?

No, it moves but it is not living. (64 words)

Number of Total Miscues
(Total Accuracy): _____

Number of Meaning-Change Miscues
(Total Acceptability): _____

Total Accuracy		**Total Acceptability**
0–1 miscue _____ Independent		_____ 0–1 miscue
2–6 miscues _____ Instructional		_____ 2–3 miscues
7+ miscues _____ Frustration		_____ 4+ miscues

Rate: $64 \times 60 = 3{,}840/$ _____ seconds = _____ WPM

Correct WPM: $(64 -$ _____ errors$) \times 60 =$ _____ / _____ seconds = _____ CWPM

Retelling Scoring Sheet for "Living and Not Living"

Main Idea

_____ Some things live.
_____ Others are not living.

Details

_____ Things that live
_____ need air,
_____ food,
_____ and water.
_____ They move
_____ and grow.
_____ Animals are living.
_____ Plants are living.
_____ Paper is not living.
_____ It comes from something living.

Level: Primer

____ It comes from trees.

____ A wagon is not living.

14 Ideas

Number of ideas recalled _____

Other ideas recalled, including inferences:

Questions for "Living and Not Living"

1. Name two things that living things need.
   Explicit: air, food, water

2. What do living things do?
   Explicit: move and grow

3. What two things did your reading say were living things?
   Explicit: animals and plants

4. What causes a plant to die?
   Implicit: it doesn't have food or water or air

5. What living thing does paper come from?
   Explicit: trees

6. Why isn't a wagon that moves a living thing?
   Implicit: it does not grow

Number Correct Explicit: ____

Number Correct Implicit: ____

Total: ____

____ Independent: 6 correct

____ Instructional: 4–5 correct

____ Frustration: 0–3 correct

Mouse in a House

Once there was a mouse.

He lived in a wall of an old house.

Each night the mouse went to the kitchen.

He wanted to find something to eat.

The man who lived in the house heard the mouse.

He knew the mouse lived in the wall.

But he didn't mind.

Then one day the man decided to sell the house.

He loved the old house.

But it was too big.

He put an ad in the paper.

It said, "100-year-old house for sale.

Call 224-3414."

Many people called and wanted to visit the house.

Two people came on Sunday.

They walked up the old stairs.

When they got to the top, the mouse ran down the wall.

He ran up and down the inside of the wall.

Up and down.

The people heard the mouse.

They said, "We don't want the house."

The mouse was very happy.

He was afraid that new people would try to get rid of him.

Every time someone visited the house, the mouse would do the same thing.

He would run up and down the wall between the first and second floors.

Every time, the people left without buying the house.

Then a family came to see the house.

The house was just the right size for them.

When they walked up the stairs, the mouse ran up and down the wall.

They heard him and said, "Oh, you have a mouse.

We love the house so much we'll buy it, mouse and all."

The Surprise

Sam's birthday was in two days.

He was going to be seven years old.

He wanted a PlayStation game.

He also wanted a new bike.

But most of all he wanted a dog.

His father went to look for a present.

First, he went into the toy store.

He saw the PlayStation that Sam wanted.

But his father didn't have enough money.

Then he saw a red bike that Sam would love!

But that also cost too much.

He drove to the animal care center.

It was hard to choose just one dog.

All of them looked cute.

Finally he sat down outside of a cage.

A brown fuzzy puppy came up to him.

The puppy put his paw on the cage.

It seemed like he was saying, "Take me home!"

Sam's father thought, "Ok, little pup, I'll take you home."

He paid for the puppy and they put a HOLD note on his cage.

The next day Sam and his dad went for a ride.

His father drove to the animal care center.

Sam didn't understand why they were there.

When they walked in there was the brown fuzzy puppy.

The worker gave Sam the puppy and everyone sang, Happy Birthday.

It was the best birthday ever!

Marva Finds a Friend

One rainy day Marva heard a funny sound.

She looked out the window and saw a little gray cat with white feet.

It was wet and it looked hungry.

Marva went out and picked up the cat.

Then she brought it inside.

She and her mother took a soft towel and dried it.

Mother gave the cat some food.

And the cat ate it all up!

Marva said, "I will name this cat Boots. I will take care of it."

"I hope you don't belong to anyone," Marva said.

"Now, Marva, this cat may belong to somebody," her mother said. Marva felt sad.

She said to Boots, "But I want you to be *my* cat."

That night Marva's mother looked in the newspaper.

She saw an ad that read, "Lost. Gray cat with white feet. Call 376-2007."

Marva started to cry.

"But I want to keep Boots," she said.

"It's not right, Marva, we have to call," said her mother.

Marva knew her mother was right.

The next day a woman and a girl Marva's age came to the house.

When the girl saw Boots she cried, "That's my cat, Boots!"

"But I called her Boots too," Marva said.

The girl took Boots in her arms.

She thanked Marva and her mother for taking care of Boots.

Then she said, "I live on the next street.

Why don't you come over tomorrow and play with me and Boots?"

Marva was sad to give up Boots, but she was happy that she'd made a new friend.

Marva's mother now knew what to get Marva for her birthday!

The Bear and the Rabbit

Once there was a very big bear.

He lived in the woods.

He was sad because he didn't have anyone to play with.

He said to his father, "How can I find a friend?"

His father said, "By being you."

"But all the animals are afraid of me," said the bear.

"I can't even get near them."

But one day the bear was sitting by a river.

He was singing softly to himself.

A rabbit lived near the river.

He looked out of his hole when he heard the bear's song.

He thought, "Anyone who sings like that must be nice.

Maybe I don't need to be afraid of him.

It would be nice to have a friend."

The rabbit went and got his horn.

Very softly he began to play.

His music went well with the bear's song.

The bear looked around.

He couldn't see the rabbit.

Slowly, the rabbit walked up to the bear.

He kept playing and the bear kept singing.

They were both happy that they had found a friend.

And a bird joined in the song.

Air

Air is all around us.

But we can't see it.

How do we know it is there?

There are many ways.

We can see what air does.

Moving air is called wind.

Wind moves plants.

Wind moves dirt.

Strong winds can move heavy things.

Strong winds can even move a house.

We can weigh air.

We can weigh two balloons.

The one with a lot of air weighs more.

We can see what air does.

We can weigh air.

Then we know it is there.

The Brain and the Five Senses

All people have five senses.

People have eyes, ears, a nose, a mouth, and hands.

Each of the senses is part of the brain.

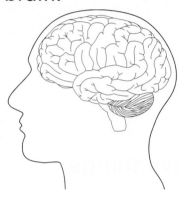

The brain makes the senses work.

People hear with their ears.

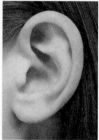

Ninell/Shutterstock

People see with their eyes.

They smell with their noses.

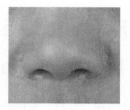

They taste with their mouths.

People touch things with their hands.

But, without the brain people would not see, hear, smell, taste, or touch.

The brain makes all our senses work.

Level: One

Narrative

Level 1

Concept Questions:

How do people feel about mice?

_____

_____

_____ (3-2-1-0)

What does "an old house for sale" mean to you?

_____

_____

_____ (3-2-1-0)

What does "a mouse inside a house" mean to you?

_____

_____

_____ (3-2-1-0)

Score: _____ /9 = _____ %

_____ FAM   _____ UNFAM

Prediction:

_____

_____

"Mouse in a House"

Once <u>there</u> was a mouse. He <u>lived</u> in a wall of an old house. Each night the mouse <u>went</u> to the kitchen. He <u>wanted</u> to <u>find</u> something to eat. The man who <u>lived</u> in the house <u>heard</u> the mouse. He <u>knew</u> the mouse <u>lived</u> in the wall. But he didn't mind.

<u>Then</u> <u>one</u> day the man decided to sell the house. He loved the old house. But it was too big. He <u>put</u> an ad in the paper. It <u>said</u>, "100-year-old house for sale. Call 224-3414." Many people called and <u>wanted</u> to visit the house. Two people came on Sunday. They walked up the old stairs. When they got to the top, the mouse ran down the wall. He ran up and down the inside of the wall. Up and down. The people <u>heard</u> the mouse. They <u>said</u>, "We don't <u>want</u> the house." The mouse was very happy. He was <u>afraid</u> that new people would try to get rid of him.

<u>Every</u> time someone visited the house, the mouse would do the same <u>thing</u>. He would <u>run</u> up and down the wall between the first and second floors. <u>Every</u> time, the people left <u>without</u> buying the house. <u>Then</u> a family came to see the house. The house was just the right size for them. When they walked up the stairs, the mouse ran up and down the wall. They <u>heard</u> him and <u>said</u>, "Oh, you have a mouse. We love the house so much we'll buy it, mouse and all." (250 words)

Level: One

Number of Total Miscues
(Total Accuracy): _____

Number of Meaning-Change Miscues
(Total Acceptability): _____

Total Accuracy		**Total Acceptability**
0–6 miscues ____ Independent		____ 0–6 miscues
7–26 miscues ____ Instructional		____ 7–13 miscues
27+ miscues ____ Frustration		____ 14+ miscues

Rate: 250 × 60 = 15,000/ ____ seconds = ____ WPM

Correct WPM: (250 – ____ errors) × 60 =
       ____ / ____ seconds = ____ CWPM

Retelling Scoring Sheet for "Mouse in a House"

Setting/Background

____ There was a mouse.
____ He lived
____ in a wall
____ of a house.
____ Each night
____ the mouse went
____ to the kitchen
____ to find something to eat.
____ The man who lived in the house
____ heard the mouse.
____ He knew
____ that the mouse lived
____ in the wall.
____ He didn't mind.

Goal

____ The man decided
____ to sell the house.
____ The mouse was afraid
____ that the people would try
____ to get rid of him.

Events

____ The man put an ad
____ in the paper.
____ It said,
____ Call 224-3414.
____ Two
____ people came
____ on Sunday.
____ They walked up the stairs.
____ The mouse ran up
____ and down.
____ The people heard the mouse.
____ They said,
____ "We don't want the house."
____ When someone visited the house,
____ the mouse ran up
____ and down.

Resolution

____ A family came
____ to see the house.
____ The house was right
____ for them.
____ They said
____ "You have a mouse.
____ We love the house.
____ We'll buy the house
____ mouse and all."

44 Ideas

Number of ideas recalled _____

Other ideas recalled, including inferences:

Questions for "Mouse in a House"

1. Where did the mouse live in the house?
   Explicit: in a wall

Level: One

2. What did the old man decide to do?
Explicit: sell the house

3. What did the mouse do when people came to visit the house?
Explicit: run up and down the inside of the walls

4. How many floors did the house have?
Implicit: two

5. Why didn't some people want to buy the house?
Implicit: they didn't want a mouse in their house

6. Why did the last family buy the house even though it had a mouse?
Explicit: it was the right size for them

Number Correct Explicit: _____

Number Correct Implicit: _____

Total: _____

_____ Independent: 6 correct

_____ Instructional: 4–5 correct

_____ Frustration: 0–3 correct

Level One

Narrative

Level 1

Concept Questions:

What is a puppy?

_____

_____

_____ (3-2-1-0)

What is an animal care center?

_____

_____

_____ (3-2-1-0)

Why wouldn't a child get everything he wanted for his birthday?

_____

_____

_____ (3-2-1-0)

Score: _____ /9 = _____ %

_____ FAM _____ UNFAM

Prediction:

_____

_____

"The Surprise"

Sam's birthday was in two days.

He was <u>going</u> to be seven years old.

He <u>wanted</u> a PlayStation game.

He also <u>wanted</u> a new bike.

But most of all he <u>wanted</u> a dog.

His <u>father</u> <u>went</u> to look for a present.

First, he <u>went</u> into the toy store.

He saw the PlayStation that Sam <u>wanted</u>.

But his <u>father</u> didn't have <u>enough</u> money.

<u>Then</u> he saw a red bike that Sam would love!

But that also cost too much.

He drove to the <u>animal</u> care center.

It was hard to <u>choose</u> just <u>one</u> dog.

All of them looked cute.

Finally he sat down outside of a cage.

A brown fuzzy puppy came up to him.

The puppy <u>put</u> his paw on the cage.

It seemed like he was saying, "Take me home!"

Sam's <u>father</u> <u>thought</u>, "Ok, little pup, I'll take you home."

He paid for the puppy and they <u>put</u> a HOLD note on his cage.

The next day Sam and his dad <u>went</u> for a ride.

His <u>father</u> drove to the animal care center.

Sam didn't understand <u>why</u> they were <u>there</u>.

When they walked in <u>there</u> was the brown fuzzy puppy.

The worker gave Sam the puppy and everyone sang, Happy Birthday.

It was the best birthday ever! (210 words)

Level One

Number of Total Miscues
(Total Accuracy): _____

Number of Meaning-Change Miscues
(Total Acceptability): _____

Total Accuracy		**Total Acceptability**
0–4 miscues	____ Independent	____ 0–4 miscues
5–21 miscues	____ Instructional	____ 5–10 miscues
22+ miscues	____ Frustration	____ 11+ miscues

Rate: $210 \times 60 = 12{,}600/$ ____ seconds = ____ WPM

Correct WPM: $(210 -$ ____ errors$) \times 60 =$
_____ /____ seconds = ____ CWPM

Retelling Scoring Sheet for "The Surprise"

Setting Background

____ Sam's birthday was
____ in two days.
____ He was going to be seven years old.

Goal

____ He wanted a PlayStation game.
____ He also wanted a new bike.
____ But most of all
____ he wanted a dog.

Events

____ His father went to look for a present.
____ First he went into the toy store.
____ He saw the PlayStation
____ that Sam wanted.
____ But his father didn't have enough money.
____ Then he saw a red bike
____ that Sam would love!
____ But that also cost too much.
____ He drove to the animal care center.
____ It was hard to choose
____ just one dog.

____ All of them looked cute.
____ Finally he sat down
____ outside of a cage.
____ A brown fuzzy
____ puppy came up to him.
____ The puppy put his paw
____ on the cage.
____ It seemed like he was saying,
____ Take me home.
____ Sam's father thought,
____ Ok, little pup,
____ I'll take you home.
____ He paid for the puppy
____ and they put a HOLD note
____ on his cage.

Resolution

____ The next day Sam
____ and his father went for a ride
____ His father drove
____ to the animal care center.
____ Sam didn't understand
____ why they were there.
____ When they walked in
____ there was the brown fuzzy puppy.
____ The worker gave Sam the puppy
____ and everyone sang, Happy Birthday.
____ It was the best birthday ever!

44 Ideas

Number of ideas recalled _____

Other ideas recalled, including inferences:

Questions for "The Surprise"

1. How old was Sam going to be on his birthday?
   Explicit: seven

Level One

2. Sam wanted many things for his birthday. What did he want <u>most</u>?
Explicit: a dog

3. What was Sam's father's problem?
Implicit: he didn't have enough money to buy some of the presents that Sam wanted

4. Where did Sam's father find the dog?
Explicit: at the animal care center

5. Why didn't Sam understand why he and his father went to the animal care center?
Implicit: because the present was a surprise; *or* he didn't know his father had been there before

6. What did the worker give Sam when he entered the center?
Explicit: a brown fuzzy puppy. *Note:* just "puppy" is acceptable.

Number Correct Explicit: _____

Number Correct Implicit: _____

Total: _____

_____ Independent: 6 correct

_____ Instructional: 4–5 correct

_____ Frustration: 3 or less correct

Level: One

Narrative

Concept Questions:

What is a newspaper advertisement?

_____

_____

_____ (3-2-1-0)

What do you do to take care of a pet?

_____

_____

_____ (3-2-1-0)

What should you do if you find something that belongs to someone else?

_____

_____

_____ (3-2-1-0)

Score: _____ /9 = _____ %

_____ FAM _____ UNFAM

Prediction:

_____

_____

"Marva Finds a Friend"

One rainy day Marva heard a funny sound. She looked out the window and saw a little gray cat with white feet. It was wet and it looked hungry. Marva went out and picked up the cat. Then she brought it inside. She and her mother took a soft towel and dried it. Mother gave the cat some food. And the cat ate it all up! Marva said, "I will name this cat Boots. I will take care of it." "I hope you don't belong to anyone," Marva said. "Now, Marva, this cat may belong to somebody," her mother said. Marva felt sad. She said to Boots, "But I want you to be *my* cat."

That night Marva's mother looked in the newspaper. She saw an ad that read, "Lost. Gray cat with white feet. Call 376-2007." Marva started to cry. "But I want to keep Boots," she said. "It's not right, Marva, we have to call," said her mother. Marva knew her mother was right.

The next day a woman and a girl Marva's age came to the house. When the girl saw Boots she cried, "That's my cat, Boots!" "But I called her Boots too," Marva said. The girl took Boots in her arms. She thanked Marva and her mother for taking care of Boots. Then she said, "I live on the next street. Why don't you come over tomorrow and play with me and Boots?" Marva was sad to give up Boots, but she was happy that she'd made a new friend. Marva's mother now knew what to get Marva for her birthday! (264 words)

Level: One

Number of Total Miscues
(Total Accuracy): _____

Number of Meaning-Change Miscues
(Total Acceptability): _____

Total Accuracy		Total Acceptability
0–6 miscues	____ Independent	____ 0–6 miscues
7–27 miscues	____ Instructional	____ 7–14 miscues
28+ miscues	____ Frustration	____ 15+ miscues

Rate: 264 × 60 = 15,840/ _____ seconds = _____ WPM

Correct WPM: (264 – _____ errors) × 60 =
_____ / _____ seconds = _____ CWPM

Retelling Scoring Sheet for "Marva Finds a Friend"

Setting/Background

____ One rainy day
____ Marva heard a sound
____ a funny sound.
____ She looked out
____ and saw a cat
____ a little cat
____ a gray cat
____ with white feet.
____ It was wet
____ and it looked hungry.
____ Marva picked up the cat.
____ She brought it inside.
____ Mother gave the cat some food.
____ And the cat ate it all up!

Goal

____ Marva said,
____ "I will name this cat Boots.
____ I will take care of it."
____ "This cat may belong to somebody,"
____ her mother said.
____ Marva felt sad.
____ "But I want you to be *my* cat."

Events

____ That night
____ Mother looked in the newspaper.
____ She saw an ad that read,
____ "Lost.
____ Gray cat
____ with white feet."
____ Marva started to cry.
____ "But I want to keep Boots."
____ "We have to call,"
____ said her mother.
____ The next day
____ a woman
____ and a girl came to the house.
____ The girl cried,
____ "That's my cat, Boots!"
____ The girl took Boots.
____ She thanked Marva
____ and her mother.

Resolution

____ The girl said,
____ "Why don't you come over
____ and play with Boots
____ and me?"
____ Marva was sad
____ to give up Boots,
____ but she was happy
____ that she'd made a new friend.
____ Marva's mother knew
____ what to get Marva
____ for her birthday.

50 Ideas

Number of ideas recalled _____

Other ideas recalled, including inferences:

Level: One

Questions for "Marva Finds a Friend"

1. What did Marva find outside her window?
   Explicit: a cat

2. What did Marva's mother do with the cat?
   Explicit: dried it with a towel; *or* gave it some food

3. What did Marva want to do with the cat?
   Explicit: keep it

4. What did Marva's mother do after she looked in the newspaper?
   Implicit: called the phone number listed in the paper

5. What happened the next day?
   Explicit: people that owned the cat came over and got the cat

6. How are Marva and the girl who owned the cat alike?
   Implicit: they both liked cats; *or* they both named the cat Boots

Number Correct Explicit: _____

Number Correct Implicit: _____

Total: _____

_____ Independent: 6 correct

_____ Instructional: 4–5 correct

_____ Frustration: 0–3 correct

Level 1

Narrative

Concept Questions:

What makes a friend?

_____

_____

_____ (3-2-1-0)

What is a bear?

_____

_____

_____ (3-2-1-0)

What does "being afraid of animals" mean to you?

_____

_____

_____ (3-2-1-0)

Score: _____ /9 = _____ %

_____ FAM· _____ UNFAM

Prediction:

_____

_____

"The Bear and the Rabbit"

Once there was a very big bear. He lived in the woods. He was sad because he didn't have anyone to play with. He said to his father, "How can I find a friend?" His father said, "By being you." "But all the animals are afraid of me," said the bear. "I can't even get near them."

But one day the bear was sitting by a river. He was singing softly to himself. A rabbit lived near the river. He looked out of his hole when he heard the bear's song. He thought, "Anyone who sings like that must be nice. Maybe I don't need to be afraid of him. It would be nice to have a friend." The rabbit went and got his horn. Very softly he began to play. His music went well with the bear's song. The bear looked around. He couldn't see the rabbit. Slowly, the rabbit walked up to the bear. He kept playing and the bear kept singing. They were both happy that they had found a friend. And a bird joined in the song. (181 words)

Number of Total Miscues
(Total Accuracy): _____

Number of Meaning-Change Miscues
(Total Acceptability): _____

Total Accuracy		**Total Acceptability**
0–4 miscues	____ Independent	____ 0–4 miscues
5–19 miscues	____ Instructional	____ 5–9 miscues
20+ miscues	____ Frustration	____ 10+ miscues

Rate: 181 × 60 = 10,860 / ____ seconds = ____ WPM

Correct WPM: (181 − ____ errors) × 60 =
____ /____ seconds = ____ CWPM

Retelling Scoring Sheet for "The Bear and the Rabbit"

Setting/Background

____ There was a bear
____ who was big.
____ He was sad
____ because he didn't have anyone
____ to play with.

Level: One

Goal

____ He asked his father

____ "How can I find a friend?"

Events

____ His father said,

____ "By being you."

____ "But all the animals are afraid of me,"

____ he said.

____ The bear was sitting

____ by the river.

____ He was singing

____ softly.

____ A rabbit lived there.

____ He looked out

____ of his hole

____ when he heard the song.

____ He thought

____ the bear was nice.

____ The rabbit went

____ and got his horn.

____ He began to play.

____ His music went well

____ with the bear's song.

____ The rabbit walked to the bear.

____ The bear kept singing.

Resolution

____ They were both happy

____ that they had found a friend.

____ A bird joined in.

31 Ideas

Number of ideas recalled _____

Other ideas recalled, including inferences:

Questions for "The Bear and the Rabbit"

1. Why was the bear sad at the beginning of the story?
   Explicit: because he didn't have anyone to play with

2. Why did the father think that the bear could find a friend just by being himself?
   Implicit: the bear was nice and being nice makes friends

3. What was the bear doing as he sat by a river?
   Explicit: singing

4. What did the rabbit think when he heard the bear singing?
   Explicit: that the bear must be nice; he doesn't have to be afraid of him; it would be nice to have a friend

5. What did the rabbit do?
   Explicit: went and got his horn; played his horn

6. Why did the bear and the rabbit become friends?
   Implicit: because of their love of music

Number Correct Explicit: ____

Number Correct Implicit: ____

   Total: ____

____ Independent: 6 correct

____ Instructional: 4–5 correct

____ Frustration: 0–3 correct

Level: One

Expository

Copyright © 2011 Pearson Education, Inc. Reproduction is permitted for classroom use only.

Concept Questions:

What is air?

_____

_____

_____ (3-2-1-0)

What can wind do?

_____

_____

_____ (3-2-1-0)

How do we know there is air?

_____

_____

_____ (3-2-1-0)

Score: _____ /9 = _____ %

_____ FAM   _____ UNFAM

Prediction:

_____

_____

Wind moves plants.

Wind moves dirt.

Strong winds can move heavy things.

Strong winds can even move a house.

We can weigh air.

We can weigh two balloons.

The one with a lot of air weighs more.

We can see what air does.

We can weigh air.

Then we know it is there. (85 words)

Number of Total Miscues
(Total Accuracy): _____

Number of Meaning-Change Miscues
(Total Acceptability): _____

Total Accuracy		Total Acceptability
0–2 miscues	____ Independent	____ 0–2 miscues
3–9 miscues	____ Instructional	____ 3–5 miscues
10+ miscues	____ Frustration	____ 6+ miscues

Rate: $85 \times 60 = 5{,}100$ / ____ seconds = ____ WPM

Correct WPM: $(85 -$ ____ errors$) \times 60 =$
                    ____ / ____ seconds = ____ CWPM

"Air"

Air is all around us.

But we can't see it.

How do we know it is there?

There are many ways.

We can see what air does.

Moving air is called wind.

Retelling Scoring Sheet for "Air"

Main Idea

___ Air is all around us.

___ But we can't see it.

___ How do we know it is there?

___ We can see

___ what air does.

Level: One

Details

____ Moving air
____ is called wind.
____ Wind moves plants.
____ Wind moves dirt.
____ Strong winds can move
____ heavy things.
____ Strong winds can move a house.

Main Idea

____ We can weigh air.

Details

____ We can weigh
____ two balloons.
____ The one with lots of air
____ weighs more.

Main Idea Restatement

____ We can see what air does.
____ We can weigh air.
____ Then we know it is there.

20 Ideas

Number of ideas recalled _____

Other ideas recalled, including inferences:

Questions for "Air"

1. How do we know air is there?
   Explicit: we can see what air does; *or* air moves things (reader can answer things, dirt, plants, or houses); *or* we can weigh air

2. How else do we know air is there?
   Explicit: any other of the above answers

3. What does air move?
   Explicit: plants or dirt or houses

4. What else does air move?
   Explicit: any other of the above answers

5. How do we know that wind could move a car?
   Implicit: it can move heavy things; *or* it can move a house

6. Why does a flat tire weigh less than a tire that is not flat?
   Implicit: the flat tire does not have as much air

Level 1

Number Correct Explicit: ____

Number Correct Implicit: ____

Total: ____

____ Independent: 6 correct

____ Instructional: 4–5 correct

____ Frustration: 0–3 correct

Level: One

Expository

Concept Questions:

What are our senses?

_____

_____

_____ (3-2-1-0)

What do we see with?

_____

_____

_____ (3-2-1-0)

What is the brain?

_____

_____

_____ (3-2-1-0)

Score: _____ /9 = _____ %

_____ FAM _____ UNFAM

Prediction:

_____

_____

"The Brain and the Five Senses"

All people have five senses.

People have eyes, ears, a nose, a mouth, and hands.

Each of the senses is part of the <u>brain</u>.

The <u>brain</u> makes the senses work.

People hear with their ears.

People see with their eyes.

They smell with their noses.

They taste with their mouths.

People touch <u>things</u> with their hands.

But, <u>without</u> the <u>brain</u> people would not see, hear, smell, taste, or touch.

The <u>brain</u> makes all our senses work. (76 words)

Number of Total Miscues
(Total Accuracy): _____

Number of Meaning-Change Miscues
(Total Acceptability): _____

Total Accuracy		**Total Acceptability**
0–1 miscues	____ Independent ____	0–1 miscues
2–7 miscues	____ Instructional ____	2–4 miscues
8+ miscues	____ Frustration ____	5+ miscues

Rate: 76 × 60 = 4,560 / ____ seconds = ____ WPM

Correct WPM: (76 − ____ errors) × 60 = ____ /____ seconds = ____ CWPM

Retelling Scoring Sheet for "The Brain and the Five Senses"

____ All people have five senses.
____ People have eyes,
____ ears,
____ a nose,
____ a mouth,
____ and hands.
____ Each of the senses is part
____ of the brain.
____ The brain makes
____ the senses work.
____ People hear
____ with their ears.
____ People see
____ with their eyes.
____ They smell

Level: One

____ with their noses.
____ They taste
____ with their mouths.
____ People touch things
____ with their hands.
____ But, without the brain
____ people would not see,
____ hear,
____ smell,
____ taste, or
____ touch.
____ The brain makes all
____ our senses work.

28 Ideas

Number of ideas recalled _____

Other ideas recalled, including summary statements and inferences:

Questions for "The Brain and the Five Senses"

1. Why is the brain important to the senses?
   Implicit: it makes the senses work

2. What do you use to taste things?
   Explicit: my mouth

3. Name one of the senses.
   Explicit: seeing, hearing, smelling, tasting, or touching

4. Name another one of the senses.
   Explicit: seeing, hearing, smelling, tasting, or touching (depending on what was said to #3.)

5. What would happen to the senses if the brain wasn't working right?
   Implicit: they wouldn't work right either

6. Name another one of the senses.
   Explicit: seeing, hearing, smelling, tasting, or touching (depending on what was said to #3 and #4)

Number Correct Explicit: _____

Number Correct Implicit: _____

Total: _____

_____ Independent: 6 correct

_____ Instructional: 4–5 correct

_____ Frustration: 0–3 correct

Level 1

What Can I Get for My Toy?

It was a Saturday morning. John looked at the toys in his room. They were all old and he wanted something new. John went to his mother. "All my toys are old," he said. "I want something new to play with." His mother looked at him, "John, we don't have the money to buy you anything new. You'll have to find a way to make something new." John went back to his room and looked around at the toys. There were many toys that were fun. But he had played with them so much that they weren't fun anymore. Then he had an idea. His friend Chris wanted a truck just like his red truck. And John wanted a car like the one Chris got for his birthday. Maybe they could trade. John ran down the street to Chris's house. "Hey, Chris, would you trade your car for my truck?" "Sure," said Chris, "I'll trade. Later we can trade something else. That way we'll always have something new to play with."

The Family's First Trip

Thomas lived in a small town with only 2,000 people. It was June 12th and Thomas was excited. His family was planning a trip to Atlanta to visit his aunt. Unlike his home town, Atlanta is a big city. Thomas had never traveled to a big city before. He had to decide what to bring. It was a two day car trip. So he needed to take along things to keep him busy in the car. He was reading a book and decided to bring it. But he realized that he couldn't read all the time in the car. If he read too much he would get dizzy. He had to think of something that wouldn't use his eyes. He decided to bring his CD player and favorite CDs.

Thomas knew that they would be going out to dinner. Another night they were going to a country music show. He brought long pants and a shirt for going out to dinner. But the music show would be outside. He brought a pair of shorts and a tee shirt for that. He had enough clothes, books, and CDs. What else did he need? He almost forgot his toothbrush and pajamas! He would have been embarrassed if he had forgotten them!

The first day of driving went quickly for Thomas as he read and listened to his CDs. His parents were looking for a hotel to stay in. Thomas and his sister begged their parents to find a place with a swimming pool. Luckily they had remembered to pack their swimming suits. Their parents found a small hotel with a heated pool. Thomas and his sister got in their suits and spent an hour in the pool before dinner. The first part of their trip was fun. They looked forward to seeing their aunt the next day.

The Lucky Cricket

Once upon a time there was a young girl by the name of Ling-Ling. She was playing in a garden one day and found a cricket. "Crickets are lucky," she said. "I will keep this cricket and it will bring me luck." Ling-Ling put the cricket in her pocket. The cricket heard Ling-Ling and said to himself, "I'm not lucky! How can I be lucky? I'm just a cricket."

Ling-Ling looked up at the sky. As she did, a lovely crane landed beside her. The crane looked at Ling-Ling for a long time before it nodded its head at her and flew away. "How lucky I am to have seen this beautiful crane," said Ling-Ling. "It must be because of my lucky cricket!" Again, the cricket heard Ling-Ling. "The crane did not come because of me. I am not lucky. Ling-Ling is wrong."

Then Ling-Ling walked onto a bridge. As she looked into the stream below, she saw a beautiful goldfish. She sat on the bridge to look at the fish more closely. The fish stopped swimming and looked into Ling-Ling's eyes. "What a beautiful fish," said Ling-Ling. "How lucky I am to have seen it. It must be because of my lucky cricket!" Again, the cricket heard her and thought, "The fish did not come to Ling-Ling because of me. I am not lucky. I want to get out of here."

Ling-Ling got up and saw a shiny stone in the water. "I will take that stone to my grandmother," thought Ling-Ling, and she reached to pick it up. Just then the cricket jumped out of her pocket and landed on her neck. Ling-Ling was surprised and pulled her hand back. As she looked down she saw a water snake coiled around the stone. "If I had picked up that stone, the snake would have bitten me," she said. "My lucky cricket saved me."

"I did save her!" said the cricket "If I hadn't jumped on her, she would have picked up that stone with the snake. Maybe I am lucky after all."

Father's New Game

It was a cold winter day. Too cold for Mary and Susan to go outside. They wanted something interesting to do. They went to their father and asked if he would take them to a movie. He said, "I'm sorry, girls. Someone is coming to see why the washer isn't working. If you'll play by yourselves for a while, I'll think of a new game for you. But you must promise to stay in your room until I call you." "Okay," said Mary and Susan.

Father wrote notes on pieces of paper and left them around the house. Each note gave a clue as to where to find the next note. Just as the person came to look at the washer, father called to them. "Mary, Susan, you can come out now!" Then he went into the basement.

Mary and Susan came out of their room. They didn't see anything to play with. They thought that their father had forgotten to think of a new game for them to play. Then Susan noticed a piece of paper on the floor. She picked it up and read it aloud. "I'm cold but I give off heat. I'm light when I'm open but dark when I'm closed. What am I? Open me and you'll find the next clue." The girls walked around their house thinking. They came into the kitchen and looked around. "That's it!" yelled Mary. "The refrigerator!" She opened the door and found the next clue taped to the inside of the door. The girls were off again in search of the next clue. After an hour they had found five clues. The person who had fixed the washer was just leaving as Susan found the last clue. It read, "Nice job, girls. Let's go to a movie!"

Whales and Fish

Whales and fish both live in the water, but they are different in many ways. Whales are large animals that live in the water. Even though whales live in the water, they must come to the top of the water to get air. When they come to the top of the water, whales breathe in air through a hole in the top of their heads. At the same time they blow out old air. Whales don't get air like fish. Fish take in air from the water.

Mother whales give birth to live whales. The baby whale must come to the top of the water right away for air. The baby drinks milk from its mother for about a year. Then it finds its own food. Fish have babies in a different way. Most mother fish lay eggs. The babies are born when the eggs hatch. Right after they are born, the baby fish must find their own food.

Whales and fish are alike in some ways too. Whales and fish have flippers on their sides. They also have fins on their tails. Flippers and fins help whales and fish swim. Fins move and push the water away.

Seasons

There are four seasons in a year. They are spring, summer, fall, and winter. Each season lasts about three months. Spring is the season when new life begins. The weather becomes warmer. Warm weather, rain, and light make plants grow. Some plants that looked dead during the winter grow again. Tulips are plants that come up every spring.

Summer begins on June 20th for people who live in the United States. June 20th is the longest day of the year for us. We have more sunlight that day than on any other day. Insects come out in summer. One bug that comes out in summer likes to bite. The bite hurts and it itches. Do you know what that bug is? It's the deerfly.

Summer ends and fall begins during September. In fall we continue to get less light from the sun. In the North, leaves begin to die. When they die they turn brown. Then they fall off. Nuts fall from trees. They are saved by squirrels to eat in the winter.

Winter begins just a few days before Christmas. December 21st is the shortest day of the year for us. We have less light that day than on any other day. In winter many animals have to live on food that they stored during the fall. There are no green plants for the animals to eat. Winter ends when spring begins on March 20th. The seasons keep changing. Plant life begins and ends each year.

Level: Two

Narrative

Concept Questions:

What does "new toys" mean to you?

_____

_____

_____ (3-2-1-0)

What does "toys you've had a long time" mean to you?

_____

_____

_____ (3-2-1-0)

What are reasons for trading toys?

_____

_____

_____ (3-2-1-0)

Score: _____ /9 = _____ %

_____ FAM   _____ UNFAM

Prediction:

_____

_____

"What Can I Get for My Toy?"

It was a Saturday <u>morning</u>. John looked at the toys in his room. They were all <u>old</u> and he wanted something new. John went to his mother. "All my toys are <u>old</u>," he said. "I want something new to play with." His mother looked at him, "John, we don't have the <u>money</u> to buy you anything new. You'll have to <u>find</u> a way to make something new." John went back to his room and looked around at the toys. There were many toys that were fun. But he had played with them so much that they weren't fun anymore. Then he had an idea. His friend Chris wanted a truck just like his red truck. And John wanted a car like the one Chris got for his birthday. Maybe they could <u>trade</u>. John ran down the street to Chris's house. "Hey, Chris, would you <u>trade</u> your car for my truck?" "Sure," said Chris. "I'll <u>trade</u>. Later we can <u>trade</u> something else. That way we'll always have something new to play with." (171 words)

Number of Total Miscues
(Total Accuracy): _____

Number of Meaning-Change Miscues
(Total Acceptability): _____

Total Accuracy		Total Acceptability
0–4 miscues	_____ Independent	_____ 0–1 miscues
5–18 miscues	_____ Instructional	_____ 5–9 miscues
19+ miscues	_____ Frustration	_____ 10+ miscues

Rate: 171 × 60 = 10,260 / _____ seconds = _____ WPM

Correct WPM: (171 − _____ errors) × 60 =

_____ / _____ seconds = _____ CWPM

Level: Two

Retelling Scoring Sheet for "What Can I Get for My Toy?"

Setting/Background

___ John looked at his toys.
___ They were old.

Goal

___ John wanted something
___ that was new.

Events

___ John went to his mother.
___ "My toys are old,"
___ he said.
___ "I want something
___ new
___ to play with."
___ His mother looked
___ at John.
___ "We don't have money
___ to buy something
___ new."
___ John had played with his toys
___ so much
___ that they weren't fun
___ anymore.
___ His friend
___ Chris wanted a truck
___ just like his truck
___ his red truck
___ and John wanted a car
___ like Chris's car.
___ Maybe they could trade.
___ John ran
___ down the street
___ to Chris's house.
___ "Would you trade your car
___ for my truck?"
___ "Sure,"
___ said Chris.

Resolution

___ "We can trade something else
___ later.
___ We'll always have something
___ new
___ to play with."

38 Ideas

Number of ideas recalled _____

Other ideas recalled, including inferences:

Questions for "What Can I Get for My Toy?"

1. At the beginning of the story, what did John tell his mother he wanted?
   Explicit: something new to play with

2. Why did John want a new toy to play with?
   Implicit: because he had played with his old toys so much they weren't interesting to him anymore; he got bored with them. *Note:* "Broken" is not acceptable—the story discusses John's boredom and indicates that his toys were desired by another child.

Level: Two

3. What did John's mother say when he asked her to buy something new for him?
Explicit: they didn't have the money to buy anything new; he'd have to make something new

4. What did John do to get what he wanted?
Explicit: he went to his friend's house and asked him to trade toys with him

5. Why was trading a good idea?
Implicit: the boys would always have something new to play with; boys had new toys without spending money

6. At the end of the story, what did his friend suggest that they do?
Explicit: trade again later

7. In the future what must both boys have for trading to make them both happy?
Implicit: toys that the other boy wanted

8. Why do you think that the boys will trade again?
Implicit: they will get bored with the toys they traded; they will want a new toy again

Number Correct Explicit: _____

Number Correct Implicit: _____

Total: _____

_____ Independent: 8 correct

_____ Instructional: 6–7 correct

_____ Frustration: 0–5 correct

Level: Two

Narrative

> **Concept Questions:**
>
> What does it mean to travel?
>
> _____
>
> _____
>
> _____ (3-2-1-0)
>
> What can children do to keep themselves busy on long rides in a car?
>
> _____
>
> _____
>
> _____ (3-2-1-0)
>
> What kinds of things should you pack if you are going on an overnight trip?
>
> _____
>
> _____
>
> _____ (3-2-1-0)
>
> How does the weather affect what you bring along on a trip?
>
> _____
>
> _____
>
> _____ (3-2-1-0)
>
> **Score:** _____ /12 = _____ %
>
> _____ FAM   _____ UNFAM
>
> **Prediction:**
>
> _____
>
> _____

"The Family's First Trip"

Thomas lived in a small town with only 2,000 people. It was June 12th and Thomas was excited. His family was planning a trip to Atlanta to <u>visit</u> his aunt.

Unlike his home town, Atlanta is a big city. Thomas had never traveled to a big city before. He had to decide what to bring. It was a two day car trip. So he needed to take along things to keep him busy in the car. He was reading a book and decided to bring it. But he realized that he couldn't read all the time in the car. If he read too much he would get dizzy. He had to think of something that wouldn't use his eyes. He decided to bring his CD player and favorite CDs.

Thomas <u>knew</u> that they would be going out to dinner. Another night they were going to a country music show. He brought long pants and a shirt for going out to dinner. But the music show would be outside. He brought a pair of shorts and a tee shirt for that. He had enough clothes, books, and CDs. What else did he need? He almost forgot his toothbrush and pajamas! He would have been embarrassed if he had forgotten them!

The first day of driving went quickly for Thomas as he read and listened to his CDs. His parents were looking for a hotel to stay in. Thomas and his sister begged their parents to <u>find</u> a place with a swimming pool. Luckily they had remembered to pack their swimming <u>suits</u>. Their parents found a small hotel with a heated pool. Thomas and his sister got in their <u>suits</u> and spent an hour in the pool before dinner. The first part of their trip was fun. They looked forward to seeing their aunt the next day. (304 words)

Level: Two

Number of Total Miscues
(Total Accuracy): _____

Number of Meaning-Change Miscues
(Total Acceptability): _____

Total Accuracy		Total Acceptability
0–6 miscues	_____ Independent	_____ 0–6 miscues
7–30 miscues	_____ Instructional	_____ 7–15 miscues
31+ miscues	_____ Frustration	_____ 16+ miscues

Rate: 304 × 60 = 18,240 / _____ seconds = _____ WPM

Correct WPM: (304 – _____ errors) × 60 =
_____ / _____ seconds = _____ CWPM

Retelling Scoring Sheet
for "The Family's First Trip"

Setting/Background

____ Thomas lived in a small town
____ with only 2,000 people.
____ It was June 12th.
____ and Thomas was excited.

Goal

____ His family was planning a trip
____ to Atlanta
____ to visit his aunt.
____ Atlanta is a big city.
____ Thomas had never traveled to a big city before.
____ He had to decide what to bring.
____ It was a two day car trip.
____ He needed to take along things to keep him busy
____ in the car.

Events

____ He was reading a book
____ and decided to bring it.
____ He couldn't read all the time.

____ He would get dizzy in the car.
____ He had to think of something
____ that wouldn't use his eyes.
____ He decided to bring his CD player
____ and favorite CDs.
____ They would be going out to dinner.
____ They were going to a country music show.
____ He brought long pants
____ and a shirt
____ for going out to dinner.
____ But the music show would be outside.
____ He brought a pair of shorts
____ and a tee shirt for that.
____ He almost forgot his toothbrush
____ and pajamas!
____ He would have been embarrassed
____ if he had forgotten them!
____ The first day of driving went quickly
____ as he read
____ and listened to his CDs.
____ His parents were looking for a hotel to stay in.
____ Thomas
____ and his sister begged their parents
____ to find a place with a swimming pool.
____ They had remembered
____ to pack their swimming suits.
____ Their parents found a small hotel
____ with a heated pool.
____ Thomas
____ and his sister got in their suits
____ and spent an hour
____ in the pool
____ before dinner.
____ The first part of their trip was fun.
____ They looked forward to seeing their aunt
____ the next day.

52 Ideas

Number of ideas recalled: _____

Other ideas recalled, including inferences:

Level 2

Level Two

Questions for "The Family's First Trip"

1. Who is the main character in this story?
   Explicit: Thomas

2. How does Thomas feel about the trip to Atlanta?
   Implicit: excited; concerned; worried

3. What was Thomas's problem?
   Implicit: to decide what to bring on the trip

4. What does Thomas decide to bring?
   Explicit: Book, CD player, and CDs

5. Why does Thomas decide to take his CDs along and not just books?
   Implicit: he gets dizzy if he uses his eyes too much

6. Why has Thomas decided to bring shorts and a tee shirt?
   Implicit: they are going to an *outdoor* country music show

7. Name two things that Thomas almost forgot to pack.
   Explicit: toothbrush and pajamas

8. Where do Thomas and his sister want to stay after the first day of driving?
   Explicit: a place with a swimming pool

Number Correct Explicit: _____

Number Correct Implicit: _____

Total: _____

_____ Independent: 7–8 correct

_____ Instructional: 6 correct

_____ Frustration: less than 6 correct

Level 2

Level: Two

Narrative

Concept Questions:

What does it mean if something is lucky?

_____

_____

_____ (3-2-1-0)

What is a cricket?

_____

_____

_____ (3-2-1-0)

What does "coiled" mean?

_____

_____

_____ (3-2-1-0)

How could a bird communicate with a person?

_____

_____

_____ (3-2-1-0)

Score: _____ /9 = _____ %

_____ FAM _____ UNFAM

Prediction:

_____

_____

"The Lucky Cricket"

Once upon a time there was a young girl by the name of Ling-Ling. She was playing in a garden one day and found a cricket. "Crickets are lucky," she said. "I will keep this cricket and it will bring me luck." Ling-Ling <u>put</u> the cricket in her pocket. The cricket <u>heard</u> Ling-Ling and said to himself, "I'm not lucky! How can I be lucky? I'm just a cricket."

Ling-Ling looked up at the sky. As she did, a lovely crane landed beside her. The crane looked at Ling-Ling for a long time before it nodded its head at her and flew away. "How lucky I am to have seen this beautiful crane," said Ling-Ling. "It must be because of my lucky cricket!" Again, the cricket <u>heard</u> Ling-Ling. "The crane did not come because of me. I am not lucky. Ling-Ling is wrong."

<u>Then</u> Ling-Ling walked onto a bridge. As she looked into the stream below, she saw a beautiful goldfish. She sat on the bridge to look at the fish more closely. The fish stopped swimming and looked into Ling-Ling's eyes. "What a beautiful fish," said Ling-Ling. "How lucky I am to have seen it. It must be because of my lucky cricket!" Again, the cricket <u>heard</u> her and <u>thought</u>, "The fish did not come to Ling-Ling because of me. I am not lucky. I want to get out of here."

Ling-Ling got up and saw a <u>shiny</u> stone in the water. "I will take that stone to my grandmother," <u>thought</u> Ling-Ling, and she reached to pick it up. Just <u>then</u> the cricket jumped out of her pocket and landed on her neck. Ling-Ling was surprised and

Level: Two

pulled her hand back. As she looked down, she saw a water snake coiled around the stone. "If I had picked up that stone, the snake would have bitten me," she said. "My lucky cricket saved me." "I did save her!" said the cricket. "If I hadn't jumped on her, she would have <u>picked</u> up that stone with the snake. Maybe I am lucky after all." (346 words)

Number of Total Miscues
(Total Accuracy): _____

Number of Meaning-Change Miscues
(Total Acceptability): _____

Total Accuracy		**Total Acceptability**
0–8 miscues	_____ Independent	_____ 0–8 miscues
9–36 miscues	_____ Instructional	_____ 9–17 miscues
37+ miscues	_____ Frustration	_____ 18+ miscues

Rate: 346 × 60 = 20,760 / _____ seconds = _____ WPM

Correct WPM: (346 – _____ errors) × 60 =
_____ / _____ seconds = _____ CWPM

Retelling Scoring Sheet for "The Lucky Cricket"

Setting/ Background

____ Once upon a time
____ there was a girl
____ by the name of Ling-Ling.
____ She was playing
____ and found a cricket.

Goal

____ "Crickets are lucky,"
____ she said.
____ "I will keep this cricket."

____ Ling-Ling put the cricket
____ in her pocket.
____ The cricket said to himself,
____ "I am not lucky."

Events

____ Ling-Ling looked at the sky.
____ A crane landed beside her.
____ The crane looked at Ling-Ling
____ for a long time
____ before it flew away.
____ "How lucky I am
____ to have seen this beautiful crane,"
____ said Ling-Ling.
____ "It must be because of my lucky cricket."
____ The cricket heard Ling-Ling.
____ "I am not lucky."
____ Ling-Ling walked onto a bridge.
____ She saw a goldfish.
____ The fish stopped swimming
____ and looked into Ling-Ling's eyes.
____ "What a beautiful fish,"
____ said Ling-Ling.
____ "How lucky I am to have seen it.
____ It must be because of my lucky cricket."
____ The cricket thought
____ "I'm not lucky.
____ I want to get out of here."
____ Ling-Ling saw a shiny stone
____ in the water.
____ She reached to pick it up.
____ The cricket jumped
____ out of her pocket
____ and landed on her neck.
____ Ling-Ling pulled her hand back.
____ She saw a snake
____ coiled around the stone.
____ "If I had picked up that stone,
____ the snake would have bitten me."
____ "My lucky cricket saved me."

Resolution

____ "I did save her!" said the cricket.
____ "If I hadn't jumped on her

Level: Two

_____ she would have picked up the stone

_____ with the snake.

_____ Maybe I am lucky

_____ after all."

52 Ideas

Number of ideas recalled _____

Other ideas recalled, including inferences:

Questions for "The Lucky Cricket "

1. Where did the story take place?
   Explicit: in a garden

2. At the beginning of the story, why did Ling-Ling keep the cricket she found?
   Explicit: because she thought it would bring her luck

3. Why did Ling-Ling think that the cricket was lucky after she'd seen the crane?
   Implicit: it looked at her for a long time; it nodded its head at her; it seemed to communicate with her; *or* she thought it came to her because of the cricket

4. Why did the cricket want to get away from Ling-Ling?
   Implicit: because he didn't think he was lucky

5. What did Ling-Ling see when she sat on the bridge?
   Explicit: a goldfish

6. Why did Ling-Ling want to pick up the shiny stone in the water?
   Explicit: she wanted to give it to her grandmother

7. How did the cricket surprise Ling-Ling when she reached to pick up the stone?
   Implicit: he jumped out of her pocket and landed on her neck

8. Why did the cricket decide at the end that he was lucky after all?
   Implicit: he thought that maybe he was lucky because he had saved her from picking up the snake

Number Correct Explicit: _____

Number Correct Implicit: _____

Total: _____

_____ Independent: 8 correct

_____ Instructional: 6–7 correct

_____ Frustration: 0–5 correct

Level: Two

Narrative

Concept Questions:

What is a repairman?

_____

_____

_____ (3-2-1-0)

What is a treasure hunt?

_____

_____

_____ (3-2-1-0)

What is it like inside a refrigerator?

_____

_____

_____ (3-2-1-0)

Score: _____ /9 = _____ %

_____ FAM   _____ UNFAM

Prediction:

_____

_____

"Father's New Game"

It was a cold winter day. Too cold for Mary and Susan to go outside. They wanted something interesting to do. They went to their father and asked if he would take them to a movie. He said, "I'm sorry, girls. Someone is coming to see why the washer isn't working. If you'll play by yourselves for a while,

I'll think of a new game for you. But you must promise to stay in your room until I call you." "Okay," said Mary and Susan.

Father wrote notes on pieces of paper and left them around the house. Each note gave a clue as to where to find the next note. Just as the person came to look at the washer, Father called to them. "Mary, Susan, you can come out now!" Then he went into the basement. Mary and Susan came out of their room. They didn't see anything to play with. They thought that their father had forgotten to think of a new game for them to play. Then Susan noticed a piece of paper on the floor. She picked it up and read it aloud. "I'm cold but I give off heat. I'm light when I'm open but dark when I'm closed. What am I? Open me and you'll find the next clue." The girls walked around their house thinking. They came into the kitchen and looked around. "That's it!" yelled Mary. "The refrigerator!" She opened the door and found the next clue taped to the inside of the door. The girls were off again in search for the next clue. After an hour they had found five clues. The person who had fixed the washer was just leaving as Susan found the last clue. It read, "Nice job, girls. Let's go to a movie!" (298 words)

Level: Two

Number of Total Miscues
(Total Accuracy): _____

Number of Meaning-Change Miscues
(Total Acceptability): _____

Total Accuracy		**Total Acceptability**
0–7 miscues	____ Independent	____ 0–8 miscues
8–31 miscues	____ Instructional	____ 8–16 miscues
32+ miscues	____ Frustration	____ 17+ miscues

Rate: 298 × 60 = 17,880 / _____ seconds = _____ WPM

Correct WPM: (298 − _____ errors) × 60 =
_____ / _____ seconds = _____ CWPM

Retelling Scoring Sheet for "Father's New Game"

Setting/Background

____ It was a cold day.
____ Too cold
____ for Mary
____ and Susan
____ to go outside.

Goal

____ They wanted something to do.

Events

____ They went to their father
____ and asked
____ if he would take them
____ to a movie.
____ He said,
____ "I'm sorry.
____ Someone is coming
____ to see
____ why the washer isn't working.
____ I'll think
____ of a game
____ a new game.

____ But you stay
____ in your room
____ until I call you."
____ Father wrote notes
____ on pieces
____ of paper
____ and left them
____ around the house.
____ Each note gave a clue
____ where to find the next note.
____ Father called to them,
____ "You can come out now."
____ Mary
____ and Susan came out
____ of their room.
____ Susan noticed a piece
____ of paper.
____ She read it.
____ They found the next clue
____ in the refrigerator.
____ They found clues
____ five clues.
____ The person who fixed the washer
____ was leaving
____ as Susan found the last clue.

Resolution

____ The last clue
____ read,
____ "Nice job,
____ girls.
____ Let's go
____ to a movie."

49 Ideas

Number of ideas recalled _____

Other ideas recalled, including inferences:

Level: Two

Questions for "Father's New Game"

1. What kind of day was it?
   Explicit: very cold; winter

2. What did Mary and Susan want?
   Explicit: to go to a movie

3. Why couldn't their father take them to the movie when they asked to go?
   Implicit: their father needed to stay home to wait for someone to come to repair the washer

4. What did their father write in the notes he left them?
   Explicit: clues

5. Why did Mary and Susan think their father had forgotten to think up a new game?
   Implicit: when they came out of their room, they didn't see anything; their dad wasn't there

6. Where did the first clue lead them?
   Explicit: to the refrigerator; if student says, "To the kitchen," ask, "Where in the kitchen?"

7. How did they know it was the refrigerator?
   Implicit: any of the clues—it was cold, but gave off heat; I'm light when I'm opened but dark when I'm closed

8. Why could they go to the movie when they found the last clue?
   Implicit: because the washer was fixed so their father could leave the house; *or* because the note said so

Number Correct Explicit: _____

Number Correct Implicit: _____

Total: _____

_____ Independent: 8 correct

_____ Instructional: 6–7 correct

_____ Frustration: 0–5 correct

Level 2

Level: Two

Expository

Concept Questions:

How do whales breathe?

_____

_____

_____ (3-2-1-0)

What does "baby animals staying with their mother" mean to you?

_____

_____

_____ (3-2-1-0)

How are baby fish born?

_____

_____

_____ (3-2-1-0)

Score: _____ /9 = _____ %

_____ FAM _____ UNFAM

Prediction:

_____

_____

"Whales and Fish"

Whales and fish both live in the water, but they are different in many ways. Whales are large animals that live in the water. Even though whales live in the water, they must come to the top of the water to get air. When they come to the top of the water, whales breathe in air through a hole in the top of their heads. At the same time they blow out old air. Whales don't get air like fish. Fish take in air from the water.

Mother whales give birth to live whales. The baby whale must come to the top of the water right away for air. The baby drinks milk from its mother for about a year. Then it finds its own food. Fish have babies in a different way. Most mother fish lay eggs. The babies are born when the eggs hatch. Right after they are born, the baby fish must find their own food.

Whales and fish are alike in some ways too. Whales and fish have flippers on their sides. They also have fins on their tails. Flippers and fins help whales and fish swim. Fins move and push the water away. (197 words)

Number of Total Miscues
(Total Accuracy): _____

Number of Meaning-Change Miscues
(Total Acceptability): _____

Total Accuracy		**Total Acceptability**
0–4 miscues	____ Independent	____ 0–4 miscues
5–20 miscues	____ Instructional	____ 5–10 miscues
21+ miscues	____ Frustration	____ 11+ miscues

Rate: 197 × 60 = 11,820 / ____ seconds = ____ WPM

Correct WPM: (197 – ____ errors) × 60 =
____ / ____ seconds = ____ CWPM

Level: Two

Retelling Scoring Sheet for "Whales and Fish"

Main Idea

___ Whales
___ and fish both live
___ in the water
___ but they are different
___ in many ways.

Details

___ Whales are large
___ animals.
___ They must come
___ to the top
___ of the water
___ to get air.
___ Whales breathe
___ in air
___ through a hole
___ in the top
___ of their heads.
___ At the same time,
___ they blow out
___ old air.
___ Fish take in air
___ from the water.
___ Mother whales give birth
___ to live whales.
___ The baby whale comes
___ to the top
___ of the water
___ right away
___ for air.
___ The baby drinks milk
___ from its mother
___ for about a year.
___ Most mother fish lay eggs.
___ The babies are born
___ when the eggs hatch.
___ Right after they are born,
___ the baby fish must find their own food.

Main Idea

___ Whales
___ and fish are alike
___ in some ways too.

Details

___ Whales
___ and fish have flippers
___ on their sides.
___ They have fins
___ on their tails.
___ Flippers
___ and fins help whales
___ and fish swim.
___ Fins move
___ and push the water away.

49 Ideas

Number of ideas recalled _____

Other ideas recalled, including inferences:

Questions for "Whales and Fish"

1. What is this passage mainly about?
   Implicit: how whales and fish are alike and different

2. According to the passage, how are whales and fish different?
   Explicit: whales breathe air and fish take in air from the water; whales give birth to live babies and fish lay eggs; baby whales get food from their mother, and baby fish have to get it for themselves

Level 2

Level: Two

3. According to the passage, name another way that whales and fish are different.
Explicit: any other of the above answers

4. What part of the whale is like our nose?
Implicit: the air hole or the hole in the whale's head

5. Why does a baby whale stay with its mother for a year?
Implicit: it gets food from its mother

6. What part of whales and fish are alike?
Explicit: fins or flippers

7. Where are fins found on fish and whales?
Explicit: on the tail

8. Why might a mother fish not know her baby?
Implicit: the mother does not see the babies when they are born; *or* the babies hatch from eggs

---

Number Correct Explicit: _____

Number Correct Implicit: _____

Total: _____

_____ Independent: 8 correct

_____ Instructional: 6–7 correct

_____ Frustration: 0–5 correct

Level: Two

Expository

Level 2

Concept Questions:

What do flowers need to grow?

_____

_____

_____ (3-2-1-0)

What does "forest animals in the winter" mean to you?

_____

_____

_____ (3-2-1-0)

What does "changing seasons" mean to you?

_____

_____

_____ (3-2-1-0)

Score: _____ /9 = _____ %

_____ FAM   _____ UNFAM

Prediction:

_____

_____

"Seasons"

There are four seasons in a year. They are spring, summer, fall, and winter. Each season lasts about three months. Spring is the season when new life begins. The weather becomes warmer. Warm weather, rain, and light make plants grow. Some plants that looked dead during the winter grow again. Tulips are plants that come up every spring.

Summer begins on June 20th for people who live in the United States. June 20th is the longest day of the year for us. We have more sunlight that day than on any other day. Insects come out in summer. One bug that comes out in summer likes to bite. The bite hurts and it itches. Do you know what that bug is? It's the deerfly.

Summer ends and fall begins during September. In fall we continue to get less light from the sun. In the North, leaves begin to die. When they die they turn brown. Then they fall off. Nuts fall from trees. They are saved by squirrels to eat in the winter.

Winter begins just a few days before Christmas. December 21st is the shortest day of the year for us. We have less light that day than on any other day. In winter many animals have to live on food that they stored during the fall. There are no green plants for the animals to eat. Winter ends when spring begins on March 20th. The seasons keep changing. Plant life begins and ends each year. (247 words)

Level: Two

Number of Total Miscues
(Total Accuracy): _____

Number of Meaning-Change Miscues
(Total Acceptability): _____

Total Accuracy		**Total Acceptability**
0–6 miscues	_____ Independent	_____ 0–6 miscues
7–25 miscues	_____ Instructional	_____ 7–13 miscues
26+ miscues	_____ Frustration	_____ 14+ miscues

Rate: 247 × 60 = 14,820 / _____ seconds = _____ WPM

Correct WPM: (247 – _____ errors) × 60 =
_____ / _____ seconds = _____ CWPM

Retelling Scoring Sheet for "Seasons"

Main Idea

____ There are seasons
____ four seasons
____ in a year.

Details

____ They are spring,
____ summer,
____ fall,
____ and winter.

Main Idea

____ Spring is the season
____ when new life begins.

Details

____ The weather becomes warmer.
____ Rain
____ and light make plants grow.
____ Tulips come up
____ every spring.

Main Idea

____ Summer begins
____ on June 20th.

Details

____ June 20th is the longest day
____ of the year.
____ Insects come out
____ in the summer.
____ One bug likes to bite.
____ It's the deerfly.

Main Idea

____ Fall begins
____ during September.

Details

____ We continue to get less light
____ from the sun
____ in the fall.
____ Leaves begin to die.
____ They turn brown.
____ Then they fall off.
____ Nuts are saved
____ by squirrels
____ to eat
____ in the winter.

Main Idea

____ Winter begins
____ a few days
____ before Christmas.

Details

____ December 21st is the shortest day
____ of the year.
____ Animals have to live on food
____ that they stored
____ during the fall.

42 Ideas

Number of ideas recalled _____

Other ideas recalled, including inferences:

Level: Two

Copyright © 2011 Pearson Education, Inc. Reproduction is permitted for classroom use only.

Questions for "Seasons"

1. How long does each season usually last?
   Explicit: three months

2. What are the conditions needed for flowers to come up in spring?
   Implicit: warm weather, rain, or light

3. Which day has more sunlight than any other?
   Explicit: June 20th

4. According to your reading, what insect's bite makes you itch?
   Explicit: deerfly

5. How do you know that fall is coming even if the weather is warm?
   Explicit: there is less daylight; *or* the leaves turn brown

6. Why do leaves die in the fall even when the weather is warm?
   Implicit: there is less light

7. About when in September does fall begin?
   Implicit: around September 20th

8. Why do squirrels save nuts for eating in winter?
   Implicit: Food is scarce; *or* there is less food available in the winter

Number Correct Explicit: _____

Number Correct Implicit: _____

Total: _____

_____ Independent: 8 correct

_____ Instructional: 6–7 correct

_____ Frustration: 0–5 correct

Level 2

The Trip to the Zoo

The day was bright and sunny. Carlos and Maria jumped out of bed and dressed in a hurry. They didn't want to be late for school today. It was a special day because their classes were going to the zoo. When they got to school, all of the children were waiting outside to get on the bus. When everyone was there, the second and third graders got on the bus and rode to the zoo. On the bus, the children talked about the zoo animals that they liked the best. Joe and Carlos wanted to see the lion, king of the beasts. Maria and Angela wanted to see the chimps. Maria thought they acted a lot like people.

When they got to the zoo, their teachers divided the children into four groups. One teacher, Mr. Lopez, told them if anyone got lost to go to the ice cream stand. Everyone would meet there at noon. Maria went with the group to the monkey house, where she spent a long time watching the chimps groom each other. She wrote down all the ways that the chimps acted like people. Her notes would help her write a good report of what she liked best at the zoo.

Carlos went with the group to the lion house. He watched the cats pace in front of the glass. Carlos was watching a lion so carefully that he didn't see his group leave. Finally, he noticed that it was very quiet in the lion house. He turned around and didn't see anyone. At first he was worried. Then he remembered what Mr. Lopez had said. He traced his way back to the entrance and found a map. He followed the map to the ice cream stand, just as everyone was meeting there for lunch. Joe smiled and said, "We thought that the lion had you for lunch!"

A Special Birthday for Rosa

Today was the day Rosa had eagerly been waiting for, her birthday! She was very happy but she also felt sad. This would be the first birthday that she would celebrate without all her family around her. The company that Rosa's father worked for had given him a wonderful promotion. But this meant that Rosa, her parents, and her little brother, Jose, had to move to another state. Rosa liked her new home and friends. But, she really wanted to celebrate her birthday with her grandparents, aunts, uncles, and cousins all around her.

They had sent presents but it wouldn't be the same if she couldn't thank them in person. They wouldn't be there to watch her blow out all the candles. And what kind of a birthday would it be without listening to her grandparents' stories about growing up in Italy and Cuba? Also, four people could never sing as loudly or joyfully as her whole family could sing together!

That night, Mama made Rosa's favorite meal. Afterwards, there was a beautiful cake. Mother, Father, and Jose sang "Happy Birthday" while the eight candles glowed. Rosa made a wish, took a deep breath, and blew out all the candles. "I know I won't get what I wished for," she said to herself, "but I'm going to wish for it anyway."

Then it was time for the presents. Rosa's father gave her the first present. It was a DVD. "I think we should play it right now before you open any more presents," her father said. He put the DVD into the player. Suddenly, there on the television screen was the rest of Rosa's family smiling and waving and wishing her a happy birthday. One by one, each person on the DVD asked Rosa to open the present they had sent. Her father put the DVD on pause while Rosa did this. Then they explained why they had chosen that gift especially for Rosa. After all the presents were unwrapped, her family sang some favorite songs and Rosa, her mother, father, and Jose joined in.

Then, Rosa's grandfather spoke to her. "Rosa, this is a new story, one you have never heard before. I am going to tell it to you as a special birthday gift. It is about my first birthday in this country when I was very lonely for my friends and family. It is about how I met your grandmother." When Grandfather was finished, he and Grandmother blew Rosa a kiss and the DVD was finished.

Rosa felt wonderful. It was almost like having her family in the room with her. Rosa hugged her parents and her little brother. "I didn't think I would get my wish but I did," she said. That night, when Mama and Papa came to say goodnight to Rosa, they found her in bed, already asleep, with the DVD next to her. It had been the best birthday ever.

The Friend

Once upon a time there was a boy named Mark. Mark loved to go to the ocean and play his flute. One day he was playing his flute when a school of dolphins swam by. They leaped in the air every 30 seconds. Mark could almost predict when they would leap again. He watched them for a long time because he was so interested in their play. That day he decided that he wanted to learn more about dolphins. Mark went to the library.

The next weekend he took a boat and rowed out about as far as he had seen the dolphins before. He started playing his flute, trying to mimic the pulsed sounds he had heard on tapes of dolphin sounds. He had learned that they make two kinds of pulsed sounds. One kind is called sonar and is used to locate dolphins and objects. The other kind of sound is a burst pulse that tells the emotional state of the dolphin. Mark was trying to mimic sonar. Soon, about 400 yards away, he saw the roll of the dolphins. The boat bounced in the waves as the dolphins came closer. They seemed to be curious about the sounds coming from the boat. Suddenly, the boat tipped sharply and Mark fell out. Somehow he held on to his flute. Mark was a good swimmer, but he was too far from land to swim. The only thing to do was to try to mimic the sound of a dolphin in trouble. Maybe then the dolphins would help him to land. Kicking strongly, he kept himself up above the water. He blew high, burst pulse sounds. Just when he was about to go under water, he felt a push against his leg. Again and again a dolphin pushed him. She managed to keep his face above water as she gently pushed him to shore. Mark couldn't believe what was happening. He got safely to shore, although the boat was never seen again. As he sat on the beach, still shaking from fear, he realized that he had reached his goal. He had surely learned a lot about dolphins that day!

A New Friend from Europe

Mrs. Wagner was reading a story to her 5th grade class. While Joseph listened carefully, he also watched the new boy. Ivan looked sad and confused and Joseph could understand why. Mrs. Wagner had introduced Ivan to the class about a week ago. Ivan was from a country in Europe. It had a very long name that Joseph found hard to pronounce. Ivan's parents were both dead and he had spent most of his life in an orphanage. Then Mr. and Mrs. Mayer adopted him and brought him to America. Mrs. Wagner explained that Ivan did not speak English but she was sure he would learn it very soon. No wonder Ivan looked sad and confused. Joseph would feel that way if he could not understand the story that Mrs. Wagner was reading.

Joseph wanted to make friends with Ivan but he didn't know how to do this if Ivan could not understand English. That night, Joseph asked his parents what he should do. Father thought a bit and then he answered, "You know, Joseph, words are not the only way to communicate with people. You can let Ivan know you want to be friends by the look on your face and the gestures you make. You can share things with Ivan such as a special treat from your lunch or perhaps a toy."

Joseph thought about this when he went to bed. Before he fell asleep, he had a plan. Joseph loved trains. He had played with toy trains since he was a baby. He had his own model train set and he had many books about trains. The next morning, Joseph chose his favorite book. It had beautifully colored pictures of trains from the first steam to the sleek modern diesel engines of today. Joseph also liked to draw trains and he tucked one of his pictures between the pages of the book.

After lunch, Joseph walked toward Ivan who, as usual, was sitting alone on the playground. When Ivan looked up, Joseph smiled. He sat down next to Ivan, pointed to himself, and said "I'm Joseph." Then he took the train book out of his backpack. He placed it on Ivan's knees and slowly began to turn the pages. Ivan seemed very interested and once, he put his hand over Joseph's to stop him from turning the page. Ivan looked for a long time at a picture of a silver streamliner crossing a bridge over a deep ravine. When he came to Joseph's drawing, he pointed at Joseph. His whole expression indicated that he was asking if Joseph drew the picture. Joseph nodded and Ivan smiled.

The next day, it was raining heavily. Joseph knew that the class would spend recess indoors. So he added something new to his backpack. When lunch was over, Joseph walked over to Ivan who seemed glad to see him. Joseph took out his drawing tablet and his set of colored pencils. Then he opened the train book to the picture of the streamliner and began to draw the engine. Ivan watched closely. After a bit, Joseph handed the tablet to Ivan and held out the pencils. Ivan paused for a little. Then he took a pencil and continued the drawing. The boys worked together to draw and color the silver streamliner. When they were finished, Joseph made a sharp forward motion with his arm and said "Whoosh!" to indicate that the train went fast. Ivan made the same motion. "It goes fast," said Joseph. "Fast," Ivan repeated and both boys laughed.

Cats: Lions and Tigers in Your House

House cats, lions, and tigers are part of the same family. When animals are part of the same family, they are alike in many ways. House cats are like lions and tigers in many ways, too. When kittens are first born, they drink milk from their mothers. Lions and tigers drink milk from their mothers, too. When kittens are born, they have claws, just like big cats. Claws are used by lions, tigers, and kittens to help them keep away enemies. As kittens get bigger, they learn to hunt from their mother. House cats hunt in the same way that lions and tigers do. They hide and lie very still. When the animal they are hunting comes close, they jump on it and grab it by the back of the neck. Cats kill other animals by shaking them and breaking their necks.

Lions, tigers, and house cats show when they are afraid in the same ways, too. Their fur puffs up, making them look bigger. They hiss and spit, too. Those are their ways of saying, "I'm afraid, don't come closer."

A cat's tongue has many uses. Because it is rough with little bumps on it, it can be used as a spoon. A cat drinks milk by lapping it. Because of the bumps, the milk stays on the tongue until the cat can swallow it. If you feel the top of a cat's tongue, it is rough. This makes the tongue good for brushing the cat's hair. Lions and tigers clean themselves with their tongues just like house cats do.

Where Do People Live?

People live in different places. Some people live in a city. Others live in the country. Still other people live in between the city and the country. They live in suburbs. Why do people live in these different places?

People live in the city to be near their jobs. Cities have lots of factories, schools, and offices. People work in these buildings. If people don't want to drive a long way to their jobs, they live in the city. There are many other things to do in the city. Cities have museums and zoos. They also have many movie theaters.

People live in the country to be close to their jobs, too. Many people who live in the country are farmers. They plant crops on their land. They may sell their crops or may use them to feed the animals that live on the farm. Farmers raise cows, pigs, and chickens. The main food that these animals eat is grain. There are other things to do in the country. You can find a river to fish in or take walks in the woods. The life in the country is quiet.

People live in between the country and the city. They live in suburbs. Some people think that people who live in the suburbs have the best of both worlds. They live close to their jobs in the city. The suburbs are quieter than the city. They often have many movie theaters, too. It doesn't take as long to go to either the city or the country. The suburbs are more crowded than the country but less crowded than the city. Where people live depends upon what they like most.

Wool: From Sheep to You

Do you have a sweater? Do you know what it is made from? One fiber used to make sweaters is wool. Do you know where wool comes from? It comes from a sheep. However, many things must be done before the wool on a sheep can be woven or knitted to make clothing for you.

First, the wool must be removed from the sheep. People shear the wool off the sheep with electric clippers somewhat like a barber uses when he gives haircuts. Like our hair, the sheep's wool will grow back again. Most sheep are shorn only once a year. After the wool is removed, it must be washed very carefully to get out all the dirt. When the locks of wool dry, they are combed or carded to make all the fibers lie in the same direction. It is somewhat like combing or brushing your hair. Then the wool is formed into fine strands. These can be spun to make yarn. The yarn is knitted or woven into fabric. The fabric is made into clothing.

Yarn can also be used to knit sweaters by hand. Sweaters made from wool are very warm. They help keep you warm even when they are damp. Just think, the sweater you wear on a winter day may once have been on a sheep.

Level: Three

Narrative

> **Concept Questions:**
>
> What is a class trip?
>
> _____
>
> _____
>
> _____ (3-2-1-0)
>
> When does "taking notes" mean to you?
>
> _____
>
> _____
>
> _____ (3-2-1-0)
>
> What does "being by yourself" mean to you?
>
> _____
>
> _____
>
> _____ (3-2-1-0)
>
> Why do people use maps?
>
> _____
>
> _____
>
> _____ (3-2-1-0)
>
> **Score:** _____ /12= _____ %
>
> _____ FAM _____ UNFAM
>
> **Prediction:**
>
> _____
>
> _____

"The Trip to the Zoo"

The day was bright and sunny. Carlos and Maria jumped out of bed and dressed in a hurry. They didn't want to be late for school today. It was a spe-cial day because their classes were going to the zoo. When they got to school, all of the children were waiting outside to get on the bus. When everyone was there, the second and third graders got on the bus and rode to the zoo. On the bus, the children talked about the zoo animals that they liked the best. Joe and Carlos wanted to see the lion, king of the beasts. Maria and Angela wanted to see the chimps. Maria thought they acted a lot like people.

When they got to the zoo, their teachers divided the children into four groups. One teacher, Mr. Lopez, told them if anyone got lost to go to the ice cream stand. Everyone would meet there at noon. Maria went with the group to the monkey house, where she spent a long time watching the chimps groom each other. She wrote down all the ways that the chimps acted like people. Her notes would help her write a good report of what she liked best at the zoo.

Carlos went with the group to the lion house. He watched the cats pace in front of the glass. Carlos was watching a lion so carefully that he didn't see his group leave. Finally, he <u>noticed</u> that it was very quiet in the lion house. He turned around and didn't see anyone. At first he was <u>worried</u>. Then he remembered what Mr. Lopez had said. He traced his way back to the <u>entrance</u> and found a map. He followed the map to the ice cream stand, just as

Level: Three

everyone was meeting there for <u>lunch</u>. Joe smiled and said, "We thought that the lion had you for <u>lunch</u>!" (312 words)

Number of Total Miscues
(Total Accuracy): _____

Number of Meaning-Change Miscues
(Total Acceptability): _____

Total Accuracy		Total Acceptability
0–7 miscues ____ Independent	____	0–8 miscues
8–32 miscues ____ Instructional	____	8–17 miscues
33+ miscues ____ Frustration	____	18+ miscues

Rate: 312 × 60 = 18,720/____ seconds = ____ WPM

Correct WPM: (312 – ____ errors) × 60 =
　　　　　　　　____ /____ seconds = ____ CWPM

Retelling Scoring Sheet for "The Trip to the Zoo"

Setting/Background

____ Carlos
____ and Maria jumped
____ out of bed.
____ They didn't want
____ to be late
____ for school.
____ Their classes were going
____ to the zoo.
____ The second
____ and third graders
____ got on the bus
____ and rode
____ to the zoo.
____ They talked
____ about the animals
____ they liked best.

Goal

____ Carlos wanted
____ to see the lion.
____ Maria wanted
____ to see the chimps.

Events

____ Their teacher told them
____ their teacher, Mr. Lopez
____ if anyone got lost
____ to go
____ to the ice cream stand
____ where everyone would meet
____ at noon.
____ Maria went
____ to the monkey house.
____ She wrote down all the ways
____ that chimps acted like people.
____ Her notes would help her
____ write a report.
____ Carlos went
____ to the lion house.

Problem

____ Carlos was watching a lion
____ so carefully
____ he didn't see his group
____ leave.
____ He noticed
____ that it was quiet.
____ He turned around
____ and didn't see anyone.
____ He remembered
____ what Mr. Lopez said.
____ He traced his way
____ to the entrance
____ and found a map.
____ He followed the map
____ to the ice cream stand.

Resolution

____ Everyone was there
____ for lunch.

Level 3

Level: Three

____ They thought
____ the lion had Carlos
____ for lunch.

55 Ideas

Number of ideas recalled _____

Other ideas recalled, including inferences:

Questions for "The Trip to the Zoo"

1. Why was it a special day for Carlos and Maria?
   Explicit: their classes were going to the zoo

2. What grades were Carlos and Maria in?
   Implicit: second and third

3. What animal did Carlos want to see?
   Explicit: lions

4. Why was Maria watching the chimps so carefully?
   Implicit: so she could write a report for school

5. How did Carlos get separated from his group?
   Explicit: he was watching the lions so carefully he didn't see his group leave

6. What made Carlos realize that his classmates had left the lion house?
   Implicit: it was quiet; he didn't hear any talking; *or* he turned around and no one was there

7. Where did Carlos find the map?
   Explicit: at the zoo entrance

8. Why did Carlos go to get a map from the zoo entrance?
   Implicit: to help him find his way to the ice cream stand

Without Look-Backs

Number Correct Explicit: ____

Number Correct Implicit: ____

Total: ____

____ Independent: 8 correct

____ Instructional: 6–7 correct

____ Frustration: 0–5 correct

With Look-Backs

Number Correct Explicit: ____

Number Correct Implicit: ____

Total: ____

____ Independent: 8 correct

____ Instructional: 6–7 correct

____ Frustration: 0–5 correct

Level 3

Level: Three

Narrative

Concept Questions:

What does "celebration" mean?

_____

_____

_____ (3-2-1-0)

What does it mean for you to miss someone?

_____

_____

_____ (3-2-1-0)

If you are sad, how can someone cheer you up?

_____

_____

_____ (3-2-1-0)

How many candles are on a birthday cake?

_____

_____

_____ (3-2-1-0)

Score: _____ /12= _____ %

_____ FAM _____ UNFAM

Prediction:

_____

_____

"A Special Birthday for Rosa"

Today was the day Rosa had eagerly been waiting for, her birthday! She was very happy but she also felt sad. This would be the first birthday that she would <u>celebrate</u> without all her family around her. The company that Rosa's father worked for had given him a wonderful promotion. But this meant that Rosa, her parents, and her little brother, Jose, had to move to another state. Rosa liked her new home and friends. But, she really wanted to <u>celebrate</u> her birthday with her grandparents, aunts, uncles, and cousins all around her.

They had sent presents but it wouldn't be the same if she couldn't thank them in person. They wouldn't be there to watch her blow out all the candles. And what kind of a birthday would it be without listening to her grandparents' stories about growing up in Italy and Cuba? Also, four people could never sing as loudly or joyfully as her whole family could sing together!

That night, Mama made Rosa's favorite meal. Afterwards, there was a beautiful cake. Mother, Father, and Jose sang "Happy Birthday" while the eight candles <u>glowed</u>. Rosa made a wish, took a deep breath, and blew out all the candles. "I know I won't get what I wished for," she said to herself, "but I'm going to wish for it anyway."

Then it was time for the presents. Rosa's father gave her the first present. It was a DVD. "I think we should play it right now before you open any more presents," her father said. He put the DVD into the

Level: Three

player. Suddenly, there on the television screen was the rest of Rosa's family smiling and waving and wishing her a happy birthday. One by one, each person on the DVD asked Rosa to open the present they had sent. Her father put the DVD on pause while Rosa did this. Then they explained why they had chosen that gift especially for Rosa. After all the presents were unwrapped, her family sang some favorite songs and Rosa, her mother, father, and Jose joined in.

Then, Rosa's grandfather spoke to her. "Rosa, this is a new story, one you have never heard before. I am going to tell it to you as a special birthday gift. It is about my first birthday in this country when I was very lonely for my friends and family. It is about how I met your grandmother." When Grandfather was finished, he and Grandmother blew Rosa a kiss and the DVD was finished.

Rosa felt wonderful. It was almost like having her family in the room with her. Rosa hugged her parents and her little brother. "I didn't think I would get my wish but I did," she said. That night, when Mama and Papa came to say goodnight to Rosa, they found her in bed, already asleep, with the DVD next to her. It had been the best birthday ever. (487 words)

Number of Total Miscues
(Total Accuracy): _____

Number of Meaning-Change Miscues
(Total Acceptability): _____

Total Accuracy		**Total Acceptability**
0–12 miscues ____ Independent	____	0–12 miscues
13–51 miscues ____ Instructional	____	13–24 miscues
52+ miscues ____ Frustration	____	25+ miscues

Rate: 487 × 60 = 29,220/____ seconds = ____ WPM

Correct WPM: (487 – ____ errors) × 60 =
____ /____ seconds = ____ CWPM

Retelling Scoring Sheet for "A Special Birthday for Rosa"

Setting/Background
____ Today was Rosa's birthday.
____ She was happy
____ but she also felt sad.
____ This would be the first birthday
____ she would celebrate
____ without all her family
____ around her.
____ Her father had been given a promotion.
____ Rosa,
____ her parents,
____ and her brother had to move
____ to another state.

Goal
____ Rosa wanted to celebrate her birthday
____ with her grandparents,
____ aunts,
____ uncles,
____ and cousins around her.
____ They had sent presents
____ but she couldn't thank them in person.

Level 3

Level: Three

___ They wouldn't watch her blow out candles.
___ She couldn't listen to stories
___ her grandparents' stories
___ about growing up
___ in Italy
___ and Cuba.
___ They wouldn't sing together.

Events

___ Mama made Rosa's favorite meal.
___ Mother,
___ Father,
___ and Jose sang "Happy Birthday."
___ Rosa made a wish.
___ "I know I won't get it,"
___ she said to herself,
___ "but I'm going to wish for it anyway."
___ She blew out all the candles.
___ Rosa's father gave her the first present.
___ It was a DVD.
___ He put the DVD into the player.
___ On the television screen
___ was the rest of Rosa's family
___ smiling
___ and waving
___ and wishing her a happy birthday.
___ Each person asked Rosa
___ to open the present they sent.
___ They explained
___ why they chose that gift for Rosa.
___ Her family sang favorite songs
___ and Rosa,
___ her mother,
___ her father,
___ and Jose joined in.
___ Grandfather spoke to Rosa.
___ "This is a new story,
___ one you have never heard before.
___ I am going to tell it
___ as a special birthday gift.
___ It's about my first birthday
___ in this country
___ when I was very lonely.
___ It is about how I met your grandmother."
___ When Grandfather was finished,

___ he
___ and Grandmother blew Rosa a kiss.
___ The DVD was finished.

Resolution

___ Rosa felt wonderful.
___ "I didn't think I would get my wish
___ but I did,"
___ she said.
___ When Mama
___ and Papa came to say goodnight,
___ they found Rosa asleep
___ with the DVD next to her.
___ It had been the best birthday ever.

74 Ideas

Number of ideas recalled _____

Other ideas recalled, including inferences:

Questions for "A Special Birthday for Rosa"

1. The story took place on what day?
   Explicit: Rosa's birthday

2. At the beginning of the story what was Rosa's problem?
   Implicit: she would not be celebrating her birthday with her whole family

Level 3

Level: Three

3. How old was Rosa on this birthday?
   Implicit: eight

4. What did Rosa wish for before she blew out the candles?
   Implicit: that she would be able to spend her birthday with her whole family

5. What was on the DVD?
   Explicit: the rest of Rosa's family wishing her a happy birthday

6. What special birthday gift did her grandfather give her?
   Explicit: he told her a story about when he came to the United States and how he met her grandmother

7. How did the DVD help to solve Rosa's problem?
   Implicit: it brought her family to her; *or* it helped her miss the family less

8. At the end of the story where was the DVD?
   Explicit: in bed beside Rosa

Without Look-Backs

Number Correct Explicit: _____

Number Correct Implicit: _____

Total: _____

_____ Independent: 8 correct

_____ Instructional: 6–7 correct

_____ Frustration: 0–5 correct

With Look-Backs

Number Correct Explicit: _____

Number Correct Implicit: _____

Total: _____

_____ Independent: 8 correct

_____ Instructional: 6–7 correct

_____ Frustration: 0–5 correct

Level 3

Level: Three

Narrative

Concept Questions:

Why do people go to libraries?

_____

_____

_____ (3-2-1-0)

What does "getting animals to come to you" mean to you?

_____

_____

_____ (3-2-1-0)

What can waves do?

_____

_____

_____ (3-2-1-0)

What sounds does a dolphin make?

_____

_____

_____ (3-2-1-0)

Score: _____ /12= _____ %

_____ FAM _____ UNFAM

Prediction:

_____

_____

"The Friend"

Once upon a time there was a boy named Mark. Mark loved to go to the ocean and play his flute. One day he was playing his flute when a school of dolphins swam by. They leaped in the air every 30 seconds. Mark could almost predict when they would leap again. He watched them for a long time because he was so <u>interested</u> in their play. That day he decided that he wanted to learn more about dolphins. Mark went to the library.

The next weekend he took a boat and rowed out about as far as he had seen the dolphins before. He started playing his flute, trying to mimic the pulsed sounds he had heard on tapes of dolphin sounds. He had learned that they make two kinds of pulsed sounds. One kind is called sonar and is used to locate dolphins and objects. The other kind of sound is a burst pulse that tells the emotional state of the dolphin. Mark was trying to mimic sonar. Soon, about 400 yards away, he saw the roll of the dolphins. The boat bounced in the waves as the dolphins came closer. They seemed to be <u>curious</u> about the sounds coming from the boat. Suddenly, the boat tipped sharply and Mark fell out. Somehow he held on to his flute. Mark was a good swimmer, but he was too far from land to swim. The only thing to do was to try to mimic the sound of a dolphin in trouble. Maybe then the dolphins would help him to land. Kicking strongly, he kept himself up above the water. He blew high, burst pulse sounds. Just when he was about to go under water, he felt a <u>push</u> against his leg. Again and again a dol-

Level: Three

phin <u>pushed</u> him. She managed to keep his face above water as she gently <u>pushed</u> him to shore. Mark couldn't <u>believe</u> what was happening. He got safely to shore, although the boat was never seen again. As he sat on the beach, still shaking from fear, he realized that he had reached his goal. He had surely learned a lot about dolphins that day! (357 words)

Number of Total Miscues
(Total Accuracy): _____

Number of Meaning-Change Miscues
(Total Acceptability): _____

Total Accuracy			**Total Acceptability**
0–8 miscues	____ Independent	____	0–8 miscues
9–37 miscues	____ Instructional	____	9–19 miscues
38+ miscues	____ Frustration	____	20+ miscues

Rate: 357 × 60 = 21,420/____ seconds = ____ WPM

Correct WPM: (357 – ____ errors) × 60 =
____ /____ seconds = ____ CWPM

Retelling Scoring Sheet for "The Friend"

Setting/Background
____ There was a boy
____ named Mark.
____ Mark loved
____ to go
____ to the ocean
____ and play his flute.
____ A school
____ of dolphins swam by.

____ They leaped
____ every 30 seconds.

Goal
____ Mark wanted
____ to learn more
____ about dolphins.

Events
____ Mark went to the library.
____ He took a boat
____ and rowed out
____ where he had seen the dolphins.
____ He played his flute
____ to mimic sounds
____ pulsed sounds
____ of dolphins.
____ One sound is sonar
____ and is used to locate things.
____ Another kind is a pulse
____ burst pulse
____ that tells the emotional state
____ of the dolphin.
____ Mark saw the roll
____ of the dolphins.
____ The boat bounced
____ in the waves
____ as the dolphins came closer.
____ The boat tipped.
____ Mark fell out.
____ He held on to his flute.
____ Mark was a good swimmer
____ but he was too far
____ from land.
____ He tried
____ to mimic the sound
____ of the dolphin
____ in trouble
____ so the dolphin would help him.
____ Kicking
____ strongly
____ he kept himself
____ above water.
____ He blew sounds.

Level: Three

___ A dolphin pushed him
___ to shore.

Resolution

___ He got safely
___ to shore.
___ He realized
___ he had learned a lot
___ about dolphins.

55 Ideas

Number of ideas recalled _____

Other ideas recalled, including inferences:

Questions for "The Friend"

1. What instrument did Mark play?
   Explicit: the flute

2. Where did Mark go to learn more about dolphins?
   Explicit: the library

3. How did Mark learn about the dolphin sounds?
   Implicit: he read about them; *or* he listened to tapes. If the student says, "He went to the library," ask, "How did that help him learn about dolphins?"

4. What two kinds of sounds do dolphins make?
   Explicit: sonar, or sounds to locate objects, and burst pulse, or sounds to indicate emotions

5. Why was Mark trying to mimic sonar?
   Implicit: to see if the dolphins would come to him

6. Why did the boat tip over?
   Implicit: the dolphins came close enough to cause waves

7. What did Mark do to save himself?
   Implicit: he tried to make a burst pulse sound like a dolphin in trouble, hoping a dolphin would come to help him. If the student says, "He kicked strongly," ask, "What other thing did Mark do?"

8. How did Mark get to shore?
   Explicit: a dolphin pushed him to shore

Without Look-Backs

Number Correct Explicit: _____

Number Correct Implicit: _____

Total: _____

_____ Independent: 8 correct

_____ Instructional: 6–7 correct

_____ Frustration: 0–5 correct

With Look-Backs

Number Correct Explicit: _____

Number Correct Implicit: _____

Total: _____

_____ Independent: 8 correct

_____ Instructional: 6–7 correct

_____ Frustration: 0–5 correct

Level 3

Level: Three

Concept Questions:

What does it mean to be adopted?

_____

_____

_____ (3-2-1-0)

What does it mean to communicate with another person?

_____

_____

_____ (3-2-1-0)

What is a gesture?

_____

_____

_____ (3-2-1-0)

What is a streamliner?

_____

_____

_____ (3-2-1-0)

Score: _____ /12= _____ %

_____ FAM _____ UNFAM

Prediction:

_____

_____

"A New Friend from Europe"

Mrs. Wagner was reading a story to her 5th grade class. While Joseph listened carefully, he also watched the new boy. Ivan looked sad and <u>confused</u> and Joseph could understand why. Mrs. Wagner had introduced Ivan to the class about a week ago.

Ivan was from a country in Europe. It had a very long name that Joseph found hard to pronounce. Ivan's parents were both dead and he had spent most of his life in an orphanage. Then Mr. and Mrs. Mayer adopted him and brought him to America. Mrs. Wagner explained that Ivan did not speak English but she was sure he would learn it very soon. No wonder Ivan looked sad and <u>confused</u>. Joseph would feel that way if he could not understand the story that Mrs. Wagner was reading.

Joseph wanted to make friends with Ivan but he didn't know how to do this if Ivan could not understand English. That night, Joseph asked his parents what he should do. Father thought a bit and then he answered, "You know, Joseph, words are not the only way to communicate with people. You can let Ivan know you want to be friends by the look on your face and the gestures you make. You can share things with Ivan such as a special treat from your <u>lunch</u> or perhaps a toy."

Joseph thought about this when he went to bed. Before he fell asleep, he had a plan. Joseph loved trains. He had played with toy trains since he was a baby. He had his own model train set and he had many books about trains. The next <u>morning</u>, Joseph chose his favorite book. It had beautifully colored pictures of trains from the first steam <u>engines</u> to the sleek modern diesel <u>engines</u> of today. Joseph also

Level 3

Level: Three

liked to draw trains and he tucked one of his pictures between the pages of the book.

After lunch, Joseph walked toward Ivan who, as usual, was sitting alone on the playground. When Ivan looked up, Joseph smiled. He sat down next to Ivan, pointed to himself, and said "I'm Joseph." Then he took the train book out of his backpack. He placed it on Ivan's knees and slowly began to turn the pages. Ivan seemed very interested and once, he put his hand over Joseph's to stop him from turning the page. Ivan looked for a long time at a picture of a silver streamliner crossing a bridge over a deep ravine. When he came to Joseph's drawing, he pointed at Joseph. His whole expression indicated that he was asking if Joseph drew the picture. Joseph nodded and Ivan smiled.

The next day, it was raining heavily. Joseph knew that the class would spend recess indoors. So he added something new to his backpack. When lunch was over, Joseph walked over to Ivan who seemed glad to see him. Joseph took out his drawing tablet and his set of colored pencils. Then he opened the train book to the picture of the streamliner and began to draw the engine. Ivan watched closely. After a bit, Joseph handed the tablet to Ivan and held out the pencils. Ivan paused for a little. Then he took a pencil and continued the drawing. The boys worked together to draw and color the silver streamliner. When they were finished, Joseph

made a sharp forward motion with his arm and said "Whoosh!" to indicate that the train went fast. Ivan made the same motion. "It goes fast," said Joseph. "Fast," Ivan repeated and both boys laughed. (591 words)

Number of Total Miscues
(Total Accuracy): _____

Number of Meaning-Change Miscues
(Total Acceptability): _____

Total Accuracy		Total Acceptability
0–14 miscues ____ Independent	____	0–14 miscues
15–59 miscues ____ Instructional	____	15–30 miscues
60+ miscues ____ Frustration	____	31+ miscues

Rate: 591 × 60 = 35,460/____ seconds = ____ WPM

Correct WPM: (591 – ____ errors) × 60 =
____ /____ seconds = ____ CWPM

Retelling Scoring Sheet for "A New Friend from Europe"

Setting/Background

____ Mrs. Wagner was reading a story
____ to her 5th grade class.
____ While Joseph listened carefully,
____ he also watched the new boy.
____ Ivan looked sad and confused.
____ And Joseph could understand why.
____ Mrs. Wagner had introduced Ivan to the class about a week ago.
____ Ivan was from a country in Europe.
____ It had a very long name
____ that Joseph found hard to pronounce.
____ Ivan's parents were both dead
____ and he had spent most of his life in an orphanage.

Level 3

Level: Three

____ Then Mr. and Mrs. Mayer adopted him
____ and brought him to America.
____ Mrs. Wagner explained
____ that Ivan did not speak English
____ but she was sure
____ he would learn it very soon.
____ No wonder Ivan looked sad and confused.
____ Joseph would feel that way
____ if he could not understand the story
____ that Mrs. Wagner was reading.

Goal

____ Joseph wanted to make friends with Ivan
____ but he didn't know how to do this
____ if Ivan could not understand English.

Events

____ That night, Joseph asked his parents
____ what he should do.
____ Father thought a bit
____ and then he answered,
____ "You know, Joseph, words are not the only way to communicate with people.
____ You can let Ivan know you want to be friends
____ by the look on your face
____ and the gestures you make.
____ You can share things with Ivan
____ such as a special treat from your lunch
____ or perhaps a toy."
____ Joseph thought about this
____ when he went to bed.
____ Before he fell asleep,
____ he had a plan.
____ Joseph loved trains.
____ He had played with toy trains since he was a baby.
____ He had his own model train set
____ and he had many books about trains.
____ The next morning, Joseph chose his favorite book.
____ It had beautifully colored pictures of trains
____ from the first steam engines
____ to the sleek modern diesel engines of today.
____ Joseph also liked to draw trains
____ and he tucked one of his pictures

____ between the pages of the book.
____ After lunch, Joseph walked toward Ivan
____ who was sitting alone on the playground.
____ When Ivan looked up,
____ Joseph smiled.
____ He sat down next to Ivan,
____ pointed to himself
____ and said "I'm Joseph."
____ Then he took the train book out of his backpack.
____ He placed it on Ivan's knees
____ and slowly began to turn the pages.
____ Ivan seemed very interested
____ and once, he put his hand over Joseph's
____ to stop him from turning the page.
____ Ivan looked for a long time at a picture of a silver streamliner
____ When he came to Joseph's drawing,
____ he pointed at Joseph.
____ His whole expression indicated
____ that he was asking if Joseph drew the picture.
____ Joseph nodded
____ and Ivan smiled.

Resolution

____ The next day, it was raining heavily.
____ the class would spend recess indoors.
____ So he added something new to his backpack.
____ When lunch was over,
____ Joseph walked over to Ivan
____ who seemed glad to see him.
____ Joseph took out his drawing tablet
____ and his set of colored pencils.
____ Then he opened the train book to the picture of the streamliner
____ and began to draw the engine.
____ Ivan watched closely.
____ After a bit, Joseph handed the tablet to Ivan
____ and held out the pencils.
____ Ivan took a pencil
____ and continued the drawing.
____ The boys worked together to draw
____ and color the silver streamliner.
____ When they were finished,
____ Joseph made a motion with his arm

Level: Three

___ and said "Whoosh!"
___ to indicate that the train went fast.
___ Ivan made the same motion.
___ "It goes fast," said Joseph.
___ "Fast," Ivan repeated
___ and both boys laughed.

96 Ideas

Number of ideas recalled _____

Other ideas recalled, including inferences:

Questions for "A New Friend from Europe"

1. What was one of the reasons why Ivan might have looked sad?
   Implicit: he had moved to a new country; *or* he didn't know anyone; *or* his parents were dead; *or* he was raised in an orphanage; *or* he didn't understand what the teacher was saying

2. What did Joseph want?
   Explicit: to be friends with Ivan

3. Why was it difficult for Joseph to become friends with Ivan?
   Explicit: Ivan didn't speak English

4. How did Joseph's father help his son solve his problem?
   Implicit: he gave him suggestions about how to communicate with Ivan

5. What did Joseph bring to school the first time to show Ivan?
   Explicit: book of trains *or* his drawing of a train

6. How do we know that Ivan was interested in becoming friends with Joseph?
   Implicit: his facial expressions changed; *or* he smiled at Joseph

7. What did Joseph begin to draw at recess the second day?
   Explicit: the streamliner

8. What did Joseph do at the end of the story to help Ivan learn English?
   Implicit: he said "whoosh" and used gestures, then said the word "fast," which Ivan repeated

Number Correct Explicit: ____

Number Correct Implicit: ____

Total: ____

____ Independent: 7–8 items

____ Instructional: 6 items

____ Frustration: 5 or few items

Level 3

Level: Three

Expository

Concept Questions:

What is the cat family?

_____

_____

_____ (3-2-1-0)

How do cats protect themselves?

_____

_____

_____ (3-2-1-0)

What does a cat's tongue look like?

_____

_____

_____ (3-2-1-0)

What are cat sounds?

_____ (3-2-1-0)

_____

_____

Score: _____ /12= _____ %

_____ FAM _____ UNFAM

Prediction:

_____

_____

"Cats: Lions and Tigers in Your House"

House cats, lions, and tigers are part of the same family. When animals are part of the same family, they are alike in many ways. House cats are like lions and tigers in many ways, too. When kittens are first born, they drink milk from their mothers. Lions and tigers drink milk from their mothers, too. When kittens are born, they have claws just like big cats. Claws are used by lions, tigers, and kittens to help them keep away <u>enemies</u>. As kittens get bigger, they learn to hunt from their mother. House cats hunt in the same way that lions and tigers do. They hide and lie very still. When the animal they are hunting comes close, they jump on it and grab it by the back of the neck. Cats kill other animals by shaking them and breaking their necks.

Lions, tigers, and house cats show when they are afraid in the same ways, too. Their fur puffs up, making them look bigger. They hiss and spit, too. Those are their ways of saying, "I'm afraid, don't come closer."

A cat's <u>tongue</u> has many uses. Because it is <u>rough</u> with little bumps on it, it can be used as a spoon. A cat drinks milk by lapping it. Because of the bumps, the milk stays on the <u>tongue</u> until the cat can swallow it. If you feel the top of a cat's <u>tongue</u>, it is <u>rough</u>. This makes the tongue good for brushing the cat's hair. Lions and tigers clean themselves with their <u>tongues</u> just like house cats do. (261 words)

Level: Three

Number of Total Miscues
(Total Accuracy): _____

Number of Meaning-Change Miscues
(Total Acceptability): _____

Total Accuracy		**Total Acceptability**
0–6 miscues	____ Independent	____ 0–6 miscues
7–27 miscues	____ Instructional	____ 7–14 miscues
28+ miscues	____ Frustration	____ 15+ miscues

Rate: 261 × 60 = 15,660/____ seconds = ____ WPM

Correct WPM: (261 − ____ errors) × 60 =
____ /____ seconds = ____ CWPM

Retelling Scoring Sheet for "Cats: Lions and Tigers in Your House"

Main Idea

___ Cats,
___ lions,
___ and tigers
___ are part of the same family.
___ They are alike
___ in many ways.

Details

___ When kittens are first born,
___ they drink milk
___ from their mothers.
___ Lions
___ and tigers
___ drink milk
___ from their mothers.
___ Kittens have claws.
___ Lions,
___ tigers,
___ and kittens use claws
___ to keep away enemies.
___ Cats hunt
___ in the same way

___ that lions
___ and tigers do.
___ They jump on the animal
___ and grab it
___ by the neck.
___ Cats kill animals
___ by breaking their necks.
___ When lions,
___ tigers,
___ and cats are afraid,
___ their fur puffs up.
___ They hiss
___ and spit.
___ Because a cat's tongue is rough
___ with bumps,
___ it can be used
___ as a spoon.
___ A cat drinks milk
___ by lapping it.
___ Because of the bumps,
___ the milk stays
___ on the tongue
___ until the cat can swallow it.
___ Lions
___ and tigers clean themselves
___ with their tongues
___ just like cats.

47 Ideas

Number of ideas recalled _____

Other ideas recalled, including inferences:

Questions for "Cats: Lions and Tigers in Your House"

1. What is this passage mostly about?
   Implicit: that cats, lions, and tigers are alike in many ways

Level 3

Level: Three

2. How are lions, tigers, and cats alike?
Explicit: any one of the ways presented in the story: milk from their mothers as babies; they have claws; the way they hunt; the way they show fear; *or* the uses of their tongues

3. What is another way that lions, tigers, and cats are alike?
Explicit: any other of the above responses

4. What is still another way that lions, tigers, and cats are alike?
Explicit: any other of the above responses

5. What does a cat do when it is scared or trapped in a corner?
Implicit: it would hiss, spit, or puff up

6. Why is it important for cats to have claws when they're born?
Implicit: for protection from their enemies

7. Why is the top of a cat's tongue rough?
Implicit: because of the bumps on it; *or* so it can drink

8. Why doesn't milk fall off a cat's tongue?
Explicit: because of the bumps that make cups on the tongue

Without Look-Backs

Number Correct Explicit: _____

Number Correct Implicit: _____

Total: _____

_____ Independent: 8 correct

_____ Instructional: 6–7 correct

_____ Frustration: 0–5 correct

With Look-Backs

Number Correct Explicit: _____

Number Correct Implicit: _____

Total: _____

_____ Independent: 8 correct

_____ Instructional: 6–7 correct

_____ Frustration: 0–5 correct

Level 3

Level: Three

Expository

> **Concept Questions:**
>
> What does "getting to work" mean to you?
>
> _____
>
> _____
>
> _____ (3-2-1-0)
>
> What does "life in the country" mean to you?
>
> _____
>
> _____
>
> _____ (3-2-1-0)
>
> What do farm animals eat?
>
> _____
>
> _____
>
> _____ (3-2-1-0)
>
> What does "living in the suburbs" mean to you?
>
> _____
>
> _____
>
> _____ (3-2-1-0)
>
> **Score:** _____ /12= _____ %
>
> _____ FAM _____ UNFAM
>
> **Prediction:**
>
> _____
>
> _____

"Where Do People Live?"

People live in different places. Some people live in a city. Others live in the country. Still other people live in between the city and the country. They live in suburbs. Why do people live in these different places?

People live in the city to be near their jobs. Cities have lots of factories, schools, and offices. People work in these buildings. If people don't want to drive a long way to their jobs, they live in the city. There are many other things to do in the city. Cities have museums and zoos. They also have many movie theaters.

People live in the country to be close to their jobs, too. Many people who live in the country are farmers. They plant crops on their land. They may sell their crops or may use them to feed the animals that live on the farm. Farmers raise cows, pigs, and chickens. The main <u>food</u> that these animals eat is grain. There are other things to do in the country. You can find a river to fish in or take walks in the woods. The life in the country is quiet.

People live in between the country and the city. They live in suburbs. Some people think that people who live in the suburbs have the best of both worlds. They live close to their jobs in the city. The suburbs are quieter than the city. They often have many movie theaters, too. It doesn't take as long to go to either the city or the country. The suburbs are more <u>crowded</u> than the country but less <u>crowded</u> than the city. Where people live depends upon what they like most. (279 words)

Level: Three

Number of Total Miscues
(Total Accuracy): _____

Number of Meaning-Change Miscues
(Total Acceptability): _____

Total Accuracy		**Total Acceptability**
0–6 miscues	____ Independent	____ 0–6 miscues
7–28 miscues	____ Instructional	____ 7–14 miscues
29+ miscues	____ Frustration	____ 15+ miscues

Rate: $279 \times 60 = 16{,}740/$____ seconds = ____ WPM

Correct WPM: $(279 - $____ errors$) \times 60 =$
____ / ____ seconds = ____ CWPM

Retelling Scoring Sheet for "Where Do People Live?"

Main Idea

___ People live
___ in different places.

Details

___ Some people live
___ in the city.
___ Others live
___ in the country.
___ Others live
___ in the suburbs.

Main Idea

___ People live
___ in the city
___ to be near their jobs.

Details

___ Cities have factories,
___ schools,
___ and offices.
___ People work
___ in these buildings.
___ There are many things
___ to do in the city.

___ Cities have museums
___ and zoos.
___ They have theaters
___ movie theaters.

Main Idea

___ People live
___ in the country
___ to be close to their jobs.

Details

___ Many people are farmers.
___ They plant crops.
___ Farmers raise cows,
___ pigs,
___ and chickens.
___ The food that these animals eat
___ is grain.
___ There are other things
___ to do in the country.
___ You can find a river
___ to fish in
___ or take walks
___ in the woods.
___ The life in the country
___ is quiet.

Main Idea

___ Some people think
___ that people who live in the suburbs
___ have the best of both worlds.

Details

___ They live close to their jobs
___ in the city.
___ The suburbs are quieter
___ than the city.
___ The suburbs are more crowded
___ than the country
___ but less crowded
___ than the city.

51 Ideas

Number of ideas recalled _____

Other ideas recalled, including inferences:

Level 3

Level: Three

Questions for "Where Do People Live?"

1. What is this passage mostly about?
   Implicit: why people live where they do

2. Why do people live in the city?
   Explicit: to be near their jobs

3. Why do people want to live close to their jobs?
   Implicit: so they don't have to drive far to work; *or* so they don't have to get up so early to go to work

4. Why would someone who isn't a farmer like to live in the country?
   Implicit: they like the quiet life; they like to fish or take walks; *or* they don't like noise, crowds, etc.

5. What is one thing that the passage says you can do in the country besides farm?
   Explicit: take walks; *or* fish

6. What crop would be planted by farmers who raise animals?
   Implicit: grain

7. How do the city and suburbs differ?
   Explicit: the suburbs are less crowded than the city or quieter

8. According to the passage, why do people choose different places to live?
   Explicit: it depends on what they like most

Without Look-Backs

Number Correct Explicit: _____

Number Correct Implicit: _____

Total: _____

_____ Independent: 8 correct

_____ Instructional: 6–7 correct

_____ Frustration: 0–5 correct

With Look-Backs

Number Correct Explicit: _____

Number Correct Implicit: _____

Total: _____

_____ Independent: 8 correct

_____ Instructional: 6–7 correct

_____ Frustration: 0–5 correct

Level: Three

Expository

Concept Questions:

What are sheep used for?

_____

_____

_____ (3-2-1-0)

What is wool used for?

_____

_____

_____ (3-2-1-0)

What is yarn used for?

_____

_____

_____ (3-2-1-0)

Why do people get haircuts?

_____

_____

_____ (3-2-1-0)

Score: _____ /12= _____ %

_____ FAM _____ UNFAM

Prediction:

_____

_____

_____

"Wool: From Sheep to You"

Do you have a sweater? Do you know what it is made from? One fiber used to make sweaters is wool. Do you know where wool comes from? It comes from a sheep. However, many things must be done before the wool on a sheep can be woven or knitted to make clothing for you.

First, the wool must be removed from the sheep. People shear the wool off the sheep with electric clippers somewhat like a barber uses when he gives haircuts. Like our hair, the sheep's wool will grow back again. Most sheep are shorn only once a year. After the wool is removed, it must be washed very carefully to get out all the dirt. When the locks of wool dry, they are combed or carded to make all the fibers lie in the same direction. It is somewhat like combing or brushing your hair. Then the wool is formed into fine strands. These can be spun to make yarn. The yarn is knitted or woven into fabric. The fabric is made into clothing.

Yarn can also be used to knit sweaters by hand. Sweaters made from wool are very warm. They help keep you warm even when they are damp. Just think, the sweater you wear on a winter day may once have been on a sheep. (221 words)

Level 3

Level: Three

Copyright © 2011 Pearson Education, Inc. Reproduction is permitted for classroom use only.

Number of Total Miscues
(Total Accuracy): _____

Number of Meaning-Change Miscues
(Total Acceptability): _____

Total Accuracy		**Total Acceptability**
0–5 miscues	____ Independent	____ 0–5 miscues
6–23 miscues	____ Instructional	____ 6–12 miscues
24+ miscues	____ Frustration	____ 13+ miscues

Rate: 221 × 60 = 13,260/____ seconds = ____ WPM

Correct WPM: (221 – ____ errors) × 60 =
_____ /____ seconds = ____ CWPM

Retelling Scoring Sheet for "Wool: From Sheep to You"

Main Idea

____ Many things have to be done
____ before wool can be woven
____ or knitted
____ to make clothing.

Details

____ Wool is a fiber
____ used to make sweaters.
____ It comes from a sheep.
____ The wool must be removed
____ from the sheep.
____ People shear the wool
____ off the sheep
____ with clippers
____ electric clippers
____ like a barber uses.
____ The wool will grow back again.
____ Most sheep are shorn
____ once a year.
____ After the wool is removed,
____ it must be washed
____ very carefully
____ to get out the dirt.

____ When the locks are dry,
____ they are combed
____ to make the fibers
____ lie in the same direction.
____ It is like combing
____ or brushing
____ your hair.
____ Then the wool is formed
____ into strands.
____ These can be spun
____ to make yarn.
____ The yarn is knitted
____ or woven into fabric.
____ The fabric is made
____ into clothing
____ and knitted
____ into sweaters.
____ Sweaters made
____ from wool
____ are very warm
____ even when they are damp.

42 Ideas

Number of ideas recalled _____

Other ideas recalled, including inferences:

Questions for "Wool: From Sheep to You"

1. What is this passage mainly about?
   Implicit: how wool is made; *or* what you do to wool in order to use it

2. What is the first step in the making of wool?
   Explicit: cutting it off the sheep

Level: Three

3. What do people use to cut wool off sheep?
   Explicit: electric clippers; electric scissors; electric shears (*electric* must be in the answer)

4. Why can sheep give wool for many years?
   Implicit: because it grows back after it is cut off

5. What is done to the wool after it is washed and dried?
   Explicit: it is combed

6. What happens to wool fibers after they are combed?
   Explicit: the fibers lie in the same direction

7. What two different things can people do with the wool yarn?
   Implicit: knit; weave into fabric; make into clothing

8. Why would it be good to wear a wool sweater out in the snow?
   Implicit: it will keep you warm even when it's damp. *Note:* If the student omits the idea of dampness and says only, "It will keep you warm," ask, "Why would it be especially warm in the snow?"

Without Look-Backs

Number Correct Explicit: _____

Number Correct Implicit: _____

Total: _____

_____ Independent: 8 correct

_____ Instructional: 6–7 correct

_____ Frustration: 0–5 correct

With Look-Backs

Number Correct Explicit: _____

Number Correct Implicit: _____

Total: _____

_____ Independent: 8 correct

_____ Instructional: 6–7 correct

_____ Frustration: 0–5 correct

Level 3

Johnny Appleseed

John Chapman was born in 1774 and grew up in Massachusetts. He became a farmer and learned how to grow different kinds of crops and trees. John especially liked to grow and eat apples. Many people were moving west at that time. They were heading for Ohio and Pennsylvania. John knew that apples were a good food for settlers to have. Apple trees were strong and easy to grow. Apples could be eaten raw and they could be cooked in many ways. They could also be dried for later use. So in 1797, John decided to go west. He wanted to plant apple trees for people who would build their new homes there.

John first gathered bags of apple seeds. He got many of his seeds from farmers who squeezed apples to make a drink called cider. Then, in the spring, he left for the western frontier. He planted seeds as he went along. Also, he gave them to people who knew how valuable apple trees were.

John walked many miles in all kinds of weather. He had to cross dangerous rivers and find his way through strange forests. Often he was hungry, cold, and wet. Sometimes he had to hide from unfriendly Indians. His clothes became ragged and torn. He used a sack for a shirt, and he cut out holes for the arms. He wore no shoes. But he never gave up. He guarded his precious seeds and carefully planted them where they had the best chance of growing into strong trees.

John's fame spread. He was nicknamed Johnny Appleseed. New settlers welcomed him and gratefully accepted a gift of apple seeds. Many legends grew up about Johnny Appleseed that were not always true. However, one thing is true. Thanks to Johnny Appleseed, apple trees now grow in parts of America where they once never did.

From *America's History* by Armbruster et al., copyright © 1986 by Schoolhouse Press. Reprinted by permission of Pearson Education, Inc.

Amelia Earhart

Amelia Earhart was an adventurer and a pioneer in the field of flying. She did things no other woman had ever done before.

During World War I, Earhart worked as a nurse. She cared for pilots who had been hurt in the war. Earhart listened to what they said about flying. She watched planes take off and land. She knew that she, too, must fly.

In 1928, Earhart was the first woman to cross the Atlantic in a plane. But someone else flew the plane. Earhart wanted to be more than just a passenger. She wanted to fly a plane across the ocean herself. For four years, Earhart trained to be a pilot. Then, in 1932, she flew alone across the Atlantic to Ireland. The trip took over fourteen hours.

Flying may seem easy today. However, Earhart faced many dangers. Airplanes had just been invented. They were much smaller than our planes today. Mechanical problems happened quite often. There were also no computers to help her. Flying across the ocean was as frightening as sailing across it had been years before. Earhart knew the dangers she faced. However, she said, "I want to do it because I want to do it. Women must try to do things as men have tried. When they fail, their failure must be a challenge to others."

Earhart planned to fly around the world. She flew more than twenty thousand miles. Then, her plane disappeared somewhere over the huge Pacific Ocean. People searched for a long time. Finally they gave up. Earhart and her plane were never found.

From *Scott, Foresman Social Studies, Grade 4: Regions of Our Country and Our World,* copyright © 1983 by Scott, Foresman and Co. Adapted by permission of Pearson Education, Inc.

Tomie dePaola

Tomie dePaola has illustrated over 200 books. He has also authored over 100 of those he has illustrated. Tomie was born in 1934 in Connecticut, one of four children. Tomie's mother read to him as a young boy, and encouraged his early interest in art. His father loved to take pictures and there are many home movies of the dePaola family. Tomie knew what he wanted to do when he grew up by the time he was five years old. One day he came home from kindergarten and told his mother he was "going to draw pictures for books, sing and dance on stage, and paint all the scenery."

In elementary school he was gifted in his ability to learn songs after hearing them only once and to memorize poems. But, he had a terrible time memorizing math facts. He told his second grade teacher he was not going to be an "arithmeticer." He was going to be an artist. He thought writing numbers on paper was a waste of good paper that could be used to draw pictures. In fourth grade Tomie sent a drawing to Walt Disney and was excited to get an answer. Mr. Disney suggested that Tomie "continue to practice."

One of his favorite childhood memories was the building of his family's new home at 26 Fairmont Avenue. As the house was being built he found a lot of blank walls to draw on. He drew pictures of his family with chalk. Think how he felt when the walls were painted! At night he drew pictures on his sheets until his mother stopped him.

Tomie's writings show the complex feelings of children in a world of grown-ups. One of his major gifts as a writer is to use his childhood memories to remind adults what they were like as children. And more importantly, his books help children see themselves grow to face the adult world. Examples from his childhood include *The Art Lesson,* a book about an understanding teacher, and *The Baby Sister,* a book about the arrival of a new baby to the family.

Early Railroads

Railroads began as rails laid down in a road. The rails were made of wood topped with iron. Horses pulled carts running along the rails. The rails were smoother than the roads so the horses could pull the carts faster than they could pull wagons over roads.

Then Peter Cooper got a better idea. Why not develop a steam engine, or locomotive, to pull the carts? He believed a steam engine would be able to pull heavier loads faster than horses could.

In 1830, Cooper built a steam-powered engine. It was small and weighed barely a ton. Because of its small size, it became known as the Tom Thumb, who was a tiny hero in old English stories. Cooper wanted to let people know about his new machine so he advertised a race between the Tom Thumb and a gray horse.

On an August day that year, the locomotive and the gray horse lined up side by side. Cooper stood at the controls of the Tom Thumb. The race began. At first the horse pulled ahead. Then the train picked up speed and soon it was neck and neck with the horse. Then Tom Thumb pulled ahead and a great cheer went up.

But suddenly a safety valve in the engine broke. The locomotive slowed and then fell behind the horse. Although Tom Thumb lost the race, steam engines would soon take over from horses.

Over the next 20 years, railroads replaced canals as the easiest and cheapest way to travel. By 1840, the United States had about 3,000 miles of railroad tracks. This was almost twice as much as Europe. A person could travel about 90 miles by railroad in just a few hours. Such a trip took a day and a half by horse-drawn wagon.

From *Scott Foresman Social Studies: The United States, Pupil Edition, Grade 5.* Copyright © 2003 Pearson Education, Inc. or its affiliates. Adapted by permission. All Rights Reserved.

The Busy Beaver

Have you ever heard someone say "busy as a beaver"? Beavers are very busy animals and they are master builders. This furry animal spends its life working and building. As soon as a beaver leaves its family, it has much work to do.

First, the beaver must build a dam. It uses sticks, leaves, and mud to block a stream. The beaver uses its two front teeth to get the sticks. The animal uses its large flat tail to pack mud into place. A pond forms behind the dam. The beaver spends most of its life near this pond.

In the middle of the beaver's pond is a large mound. This mound of mud and twigs is the beaver's lodge or house. The beaver's family is safe in the lodge because it is well hidden. The doorway to the lodge is under the water. After the lodge is built, the beaver still cannot rest. More trees must be cut down to be used as food for the coming winter. Sometimes there will be no more trees around the pond. Then the beaver has to find trees elsewhere. These trees will have to be carried to the pond. The beaver might build canals leading deep into the forest.

All this work changes the land. As trees are cut down, birds, squirrels, and other animals may have to find new homes. Animals that feed on trees lose their food supply. The pond behind the dam floods part of the ground. Animals that used to live there have to move. However, the new environment becomes a home for different kinds of birds, fish, and plants. All this happens because of the very busy beaver.

Plant Structures for Survival

Plants and animals live in many different environments—hot, cold, wet, dry. But no matter where they live, all living things have basic needs that must be met. Any structure or behavior that helps a living thing meet those needs and survive in its environment is called an adaptation.

Plants need sunlight to live and grow. Many plants have special adaptations for getting sunlight. Vines climb up the sides of taller plants or objects where there is more sunlight. Water lilies have large, round leaves called pads that can take in more sunlight than small leaves. The giant water lily pads are so big that you could stand on them without sinking!

Plants also need water. In cold climates, water is frozen in ice and snow for part of the year. Plants that live in these areas have adaptations to help them conserve water. Because trees and other plants lose water through their leaves, some trees lose their leaves before the weather gets cold. Pine trees, such as Christmas trees, do not lose their leaves. However, their leaves are very thin and have a waxy covering that helps keep the trees from losing water. This adaptation helps pine trees survive during the cold winter months.

Plants that grow in very dry places have special adaptations for getting and storing water. The cactus plant lives in the desert where it doesn't rain very often. A cactus has long, shallow roots that cover a large area. When it rains, the roots can absorb a great deal of water very quickly. The cactus stores the extra water. Its thick, waxy covering is an adaptation that helps keep moisture inside the plant.

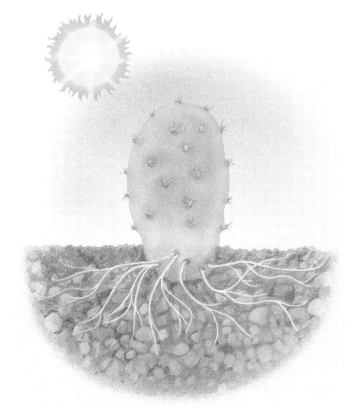

Level: Four

Narrative

Concept Questions:

Who was Johnny Appleseed?

_____

_____

_____ (3-2-1-0)

Why do people plant fruit trees in certain places?

_____

_____

_____ (3-2-1-0)

Why do people plant apple trees?

_____

_____

_____ (3-2-1-0)

What does "making apple cider" mean to you?

_____

_____

_____ (3-2-1-0)

Score: _____ /12= _____ %

_____ FAM _____ UNFAM

Prediction:

_____

_____

"Johnny Appleseed"

John Chapman was born in 1774 and grew up in Massachusetts. He became a farmer and learned how to grow different kinds of <u>crops</u> and trees. John especially liked to grow and eat apples. Many peo- ple were moving west at that time. They were head- ing for Ohio and Pennsylvania. John knew that ap- ples were a good food for <u>settlers</u> to have. Apple trees were strong and easy to grow. Apples could be eaten raw and they could be cooked in many ways. They could also be dried for later use. So in 1797, John decided to go west. He wanted to plant apple trees for people who would build their new homes there.

John first gathered bags of apple seeds. He got many of his seeds from farmers who squeezed ap- ples to make a drink called cider. Then, in the spring, he left for the western frontier. He planted seeds as he went along. Also, he gave them to peo- ple who knew how valuable apple trees were.

John walked many miles in all kinds of <u>weather</u>. He had to cross dangerous rivers and find his way through strange forests. Often he was hungry, cold, and wet. Sometimes he had to hide from unfriendly Indians. His clothes became ragged and torn. He used a sack for a shirt, and he cut out holes for the arms. He wore no shoes. But he never gave up. He <u>guarded</u> his <u>precious</u> seeds and carefully planted them where they had the best chance of growing into strong trees.

John's <u>fame</u> spread. He was nicknamed Johnny Appleseed. New <u>settlers</u> welcomed him and grate- fully accepted a gift of apple seeds. Many legends grew up about Johnny Appleseed that were not al-

Level: Four

ways true. However, one thing is true. Thanks to Johnny Appleseed, apple trees now grow in parts of America where they once never did. (308 words)

From *America's History* by Armbruster, et al., copyright © 1986 by Schoolhouse Press. Reprinted by permission of Pearson Education, Inc.

Number of Total Miscues
(Total Accuracy): _____

Number of Meaning-Change Miscues
(Total Acceptability): _____

Total Accuracy		**Total Acceptability**	
0–7 miscues	____ Independent	____	0–8 miscues
8–32 miscues	____ Instructional	____	8–16 miscues
33+ miscues	____ Frustration	____	17+ miscues

Rate: 308 × 60 = 18,480/____ seconds = ____ WPM

Correct WPM: (308 – ____ errors) × 60 =
____ /____ seconds = ____ CWPM

Retelling Scoring Sheet for "Johnny Appleseed"

Setting/Background

____ John Chapman was born
____ in 1774.
____ He became a farmer
____ and grew crops.
____ John liked
____ to grow
____ and eat apples.
____ People were moving west.
____ Apples were a good food
____ for settlers to have.

Goal

____ John decided
____ to go west.

____ He wanted
____ to plant apple trees.

Events

____ John got many seeds
____ from farmers
____ who squeezed apples
____ to make a drink
____ called cider.
____ He left
____ for the frontier.
____ He planted seeds
____ as he went along.
____ He gave them away.
____ John walked miles.
____ He crossed rivers
____ and went through forests.
____ He was hungry
____ and wet.
____ He had to hide
____ from Indians
____ unfriendly Indians.
____ His clothes were torn.
____ He used a sack
____ for a shirt
____ and he cut out holes
____ for the arms.
____ He wore no shoes.

Resolution

____ John's fame spread.
____ He was nicknamed
____ Johnny Appleseed.
____ Settlers accepted seeds
____ gratefully.
____ Thanks to Johnny Appleseed,
____ apple trees grow
____ in many parts
____ of America.

47 Ideas

Number of ideas recalled _____

Other ideas recalled, including inferences:

Level: Four

Questions for "Johnny Appleseed"

1. What was John Chapman's main goal?
   Implicit: to plant apple trees across the country

2. Why did John choose apples to plant instead of some other fruit?
   Implicit: the trees were easy to grow; the fruit could be used in a lot of ways; *or* he especially liked apples

3. Where did John get most of his seeds?
   Explicit: from farmers or from people who made cider

4. Why would John be able to get so many seeds from cider makers?
   Implicit: cider is a drink and you don't drink seeds; *or* apples have a lot of seeds and you don't use seeds in cider

5. How do we know that John cared about planting apple trees?
   Implicit: he suffered hardships; *or* he guarded the apple seeds carefully

6. How did John get to the many places he visited?
   Explicit: he walked

7. Name one hardship John suffered.
   Explicit: being hungry, cold, wet, lost, in danger from unfriendly Indians

8. Why should we thank Johnny Appleseed?
   Explicit: apple trees now grow in parts of America where they once never did

---

Without Look-Backs

Number Correct Explicit: _____

Number Correct Implicit: _____

Total: _____

_____ Independent: 8 correct

_____ Instructional: 6–7 correct

_____ Frustration: 0–5 correct

With Look-Backs

Number Correct Explicit: _____

Number Correct Implicit: _____

Total: _____

_____ Independent: 8 correct

_____ Instructional: 6–7 correct

_____ Frustration: 0–5 correct

Level: Four

Narrative

Concept Questions:

Who was Amelia Earhart?

_____

_____

_____ (3-2-1-0)

What are the dangers of flying a small plane?

_____

_____

_____ (3-2-1-0)

What is an adventurer?

_____

_____

_____ (3-2-1-0)

What are women's rights?

_____

_____

_____ (3-2-1-0)

Score: _____ /12= _____ %

_____ FAM _____ UNFAM

Prediction:

_____

_____

"Amelia Earhart"

Amelia Earhart was an <u>adventurer</u> and a pioneer in the field of flying. She did things no other woman had ever done before.

During World War I, Earhart worked as a nurse. She cared for <u>pilots</u> who had been hurt in the war. Earhart listened to what they said about flying. She watched planes take off and land. She knew that she, too, must fly.

In 1928, Earhart was the first woman to cross the Atlantic in a plane. But someone else flew the plane. Earhart wanted to be more than just a <u>passenger</u>. She wanted to fly a plane across the <u>ocean</u> herself. For four years, Earhart trained to be a <u>pilot</u>. Then, in 1932, she flew alone across the Atlantic to Ireland. The trip took over fourteen hours.

Flying may seem easy today. However, Earhart faced many dangers. Airplanes had just been <u>in-vented</u>. They were much smaller than our planes today. Mechanical problems happened quite often. There were also no computers to help her. Flying across the <u>ocean</u> was as frightening as sailing across it had been years before. Earhart knew the dangers she faced. However, she said, "I want to do it because I want to do it. Women must try to do things as men have tried. When they fail, their failure must be a challenge to others."

Earhart planned to fly around the world. She flew more than twenty thousand miles. Then, her plane disappeared somewhere over the huge Pacific <u>Ocean</u>. People searched for a long time. Finally they

Level: Four

gave up. Earhart and her plane were never found.

(263 words)

Number of Total Miscues
(Total Accuracy): _____

Number of Meaning-Change Miscues
(Total Acceptability): _____

Total Accuracy			Total Acceptability
0–6 miscues	____ Independent	____	0–6 miscues
7–27 miscues	____ Instructional	____	7–14 miscues
28+ miscues	____ Frustration	____	15+ miscues

Rate: $263 \times 60 = 15,780/$____ seconds = ____ WPM

Correct WPM: $(263 - $____ errors$) \times 60 = $
                     ____ /____ seconds = ____ CWPM

Retelling Scoring Sheet for "Amelia Earhart"

Setting/Background

____ Amelia Earhart was an adventurer.
____ During World War I
____ she was a nurse.
____ She cared for pilots
____ who had been hurt.
____ Earhart watched planes
____ take off
____ and land.

Goal

____ She knew
____ that she must fly.
____ Earhart was the first woman
____ to cross
____ the Atlantic

____ in a plane.
____ Someone else flew the plane.
____ Earhart wanted to be more
____ than a passenger.
____ She wanted
____ to fly a plane
____ across the ocean.

Events

____ Earhart trained
____ to be a pilot.
____ In 1932
____ she flew
____ alone
____ across the Atlantic
____ to Ireland.
____ Earhart faced dangers.
____ Airplanes were smaller.
____ Problems happened often.
____ There were no computers.
____ Earhart said
____ women must try
____ to do things
____ as men have tried.
____ Earhart planned
____ to fly
____ around the world.

Resolution

____ Her plane disappeared
____ over the ocean
____ the Pacific Ocean.
____ People searched
____ for a long time.
____ They gave up.
____ Earhart
____ and her plane were
____ never found.

47 Ideas

Number of ideas recalled _____

Other ideas recalled, including inferences:

Level: Four

Questions for "Amelia Earhart"

1. What was Amelia Earhart's main goal?
   Implicit: to fly; *or* to do things that were challenging

2. What was Amelia Earhart doing in a plane when she first crossed the Atlantic?
   Explicit: she was a passenger

3. How long did it take Amelia Earhart when she flew alone across the Atlantic?
   Explicit: over fourteen hours

4. Why would flying *alone* across the Atlantic be an especially dangerous thing to do?
   Implicit: it was a long trip; there was no one to help with problems; *or* there was no one to help her stay awake or give her a break

5. What was one of the dangers of flying in those early days?
   Explicit: small planes; mechanical problems; *or* no computers

6. How do we know Amelia Earhart believed in equal rights for women?
   Implicit: she said women should try to do things just as men have tried

7. What was Amelia Earhart trying to do when her plane disappeared?
   Explicit: fly around the world

8. Why do you think her plane was never found?
   Implicit: probably sank in the ocean; ocean was so big; *or* plane was very small

---

Without Look-Backs

Number Correct Explicit: _____

Number Correct Implicit: _____

Total: _____

_____ Independent: 8 correct

_____ Instructional: 6–7 correct

_____ Frustration: 0–5 correct

With Look-Backs

Number Correct Explicit: _____

Number Correct Implicit: _____

Total: _____

_____ Independent: 8 correct

_____ Instructional: 6–7 correct

_____ Frustration: 0–5 correct

Level 4

Level: Four

Narrative

Copyright © 2011 Pearson Education, Inc. Reproduction is permitted for classroom use only.

Concept Questions:

Who was Tomie dePaola?

_____

_____

_____ (3-2-1-0)

What is an illustrator?

_____

_____

_____ (3-2-1-0)

What does it mean to be gifted?

_____

_____

_____ (3-2-1-0)

Where do writers get their ideas?

_____

_____

_____ (3-2-1-0)

Score: _____ /12= _____ %

_____ FAM _____ UNFAM

Prediction:

_____

_____

"Tomie dePaola"

Tomie dePaola has <u>illustrated</u> over 200 books. He has also authored over 100 of those he has <u>illustrated</u>. Tomie was born in 1934 in Connecticut, one of four children. Tomie's mother read to him as a young boy, and encouraged his early interest in art. His father loved to take pictures and there are many home movies of the dePaola family. Tomie knew what he wanted to do when he grew up by the time he was five years old. One day he came home from kindergarten and told his mother he was "going to draw pictures for books, sing and dance on stage, and paint all the scenery."

In elementary school he was gifted in his ability to learn songs after hearing them only once and to <u>memorize</u> poems. But, he had a terrible time memorizing math facts. He told his second grade teacher he was not going to be an "arithmetic-er." He was going to be an artist. He thought writing numbers on paper was a waste of good paper that could be used to draw pictures. In fourth grade Tomie sent a drawing to Walt Disney and was excited to get an answer. Mr. Disney suggested that Tomie "continue to practice."

One of his <u>favorite</u> childhood memories was the building of his family's new home at 26 Fairmont Avenue. As the house was being built he found a lot of blank walls to draw on. He drew pictures of his family with chalk. Think how he felt when the walls were painted! At night he drew pictures on his sheets until his mother stopped him.

Tomie's writings show the complex feelings of children in a world of grown-ups. One of his major gifts as a writer is to use his childhood memories to

Level: Four

remind adults what they were like as children. And more importantly, his books help children see themselves grow to face the adult world. Examples from his childhood include *The Art Lesson,* a book about an understanding teacher, and *The Baby Sister,* a book about the arrival of a new baby to the family. (349 words)

Number of Miscues
(Total Accuracy): _____

Number of Meaning-Change Miscues
(Total Acceptability): _____

Total Accuracy			Total Acceptability
0–8 miscues	____ Independent	____	0–8 miscues
9–36 miscues	____ Instructional	____	9–19 miscues
37+ miscues	____ Frustration	____	20+ miscues

Rate: 349 × 60 = 20,940/____ seconds = ____ WPM

Correct WPM: (349 – ____ errors) × 60 =
____ /____ seconds = ____ CWPM

Retelling Scoring Sheet for "Tomie dePaola"

Setting/Background

____ Tomie dePaola has illustrated books
____ over 200 books.
____ He has authored over 100.
____ Tomie's mother read to him
____ as a young boy
____ and encouraged
____ his interest in art.
____ His father loved
____ to take pictures
____ and there are many movies
____ of the family.

Goal

____ Tomie knew what he wanted to do
____ when he grew up
____ by the time he was five years old.
____ One day he came home
____ from kindergarten
____ and told his mother
____ he was going to draw pictures for books,
____ sing
____ and dance on stage,
____ and paint the scenery.

Events

____ He was gifted
____ in his ability to learn songs
____ after hearing them once
____ and to memorize poems.
____ But he had a terrible time
____ memorizing math facts.
____ He told his teacher
____ he was not going to be an arithmetic-er.
____ He was going to be an artist.
____ He thought writing numbers
____ on paper
____ was a waste of paper
____ that could be used to draw pictures.
____ In fourth grade,
____ Tomie sent a drawing to Walt Disney
____ and was excited
____ to get an answer.
____ Mr. Disney suggested
____ that Tomie continue to practice.
____ One of his favorite memories
____ was the building
____ of his family's new home.
____ As the house was being built
____ he found a lot
____ of blank walls to draw on.
____ He drew pictures of his family
____ with chalk.
____ At night
____ he drew pictures
____ on his sheets
____ until his mother stopped him.

Level: Four

Resolution

___ Tomie's writings show the feelings
___ of children
___ in a world of grown-ups.
___ One of his major gifts
___ is to use his childhood memories
___ to remind adults
___ what they were like as children.
___ His books help children
___ see themselves grow
___ to face the adult world.
___ Examples include
___ *The Art Lesson,*
___ about an understanding teacher,
___ and *The Baby Sitter,*
___ about the arrival
___ of a new baby.

68 Ideas

Number of ideas recalled _____

Other ideas recalled, including inferences:

Questions for "Tomie dePaola"

1. Who is Tomie dePaola?
   Explicit: an author and illustrator of children's books (either is acceptable)

2. What did Tomie tell his mother one day after kindergarten?
   Explicit: that he wanted to draw pictures for books; *or* sing and dance on stage; *or* paint all the scenery (The student must provide 2 of the 3 answers above. If the student says, "He wanted to be an artist," ask, "what specific things did he tell his mother he wanted to do?")

3. In second grade, what could Tomie memorize well?
   Explicit: songs; *or* poems

4. What did Walt Disney tell Tomie to do?
   Explicit: practice

5. What examples in the story tell us that Tomie would draw on anything?
   Implicit: he drew on the walls of his new home when it was being built; *or* he drew on his sheets

6. How did Tomie's artist abilities get him into trouble?
   Implicit: he got in trouble with his mother for drawing on his sheets

7. Why might adults like Tomie's books?
   Implicit: they remind adults what they were like as children

8. What ideas in the story tell us why Tomie wrote the book, *The Art Lesson?*
   Implicit: Tomie was an artist; *or* he loved drawing; *or* he had an understanding teacher

---

Without Look-Backs

Number Correct Explicit: _____

Number Correct Implicit: _____

Total: _____

_____ Independent: 8 correct

_____ Instructional: 6–7 correct

_____ Frustration: 0–5 correct

With Look-Backs

Number Correct Explicit: _____

Number Correct Implicit: _____

Total: _____

_____ Independent: 8 correct

_____ Instructional: 6–7 correct

_____ Frustration: 0–5 correct

Level 4

Level: Four

Expository

Concept Questions:

What are railroads?

_____

_____

_____ (3-2-1-0)

What is steam?

_____

_____

_____ (3-2-1-0)

Why do people run races?

_____

_____

_____ (3-2-1-0)

What is travel?

_____

_____

_____ (3-2-1-0)

Score: _____ /12= _____ %

_____ FAM _____ UNFAM

Prediction:

_____

_____

"Early Railroads"

Railroads began as rails laid down in a road. The rails were made of wood topped with iron. Horses pulled carts running along the rails. The rails were smoother than the roads so the horses could pull the carts faster than they could pull wagons over roads.

Then Peter Cooper got a better idea. Why not develop a steam engine, or locomotive, to pull the carts? He believed a steam engine would be able to pull heavier loads faster than horses could.

In 1830, Cooper built a steam-powered engine. It was small and weighed barely a ton. Because of its small size, it became known as the Tom Thumb, who was a tiny hero in old English stories. Cooper wanted to let people know about his new machine so he advertised a race between the Tom Thumb and a gray horse.

On an August day that year, the locomotive and the gray horse lined up side by side. Cooper stood at the controls of the Tom Thumb. The race began. At first the horse pulled ahead. Then the train picked up speed and soon it was neck and neck with the horse. Then Tom Thumb pulled ahead and a great cheer went up.

But suddenly a safety valve in the engine broke. The locomotive slowed and then fell behind the horse. Although Tom Thumb lost the race, steam engines would soon take over from horses.

Over the next 20 years, railroads replaced canals as the easiest and cheapest way to travel. By 1840, the United States had about 3,000 miles of railroad tracks. This was almost twice as much as

Level: Four

Europe. A person could travel about 90 miles by railroad in just a few hours. Such a trip took a day and a half by horse-drawn wagon. (297 words)

Number of Total Miscues
(Total Accuracy): _____

Number of Meaning-Change Miscues
(Total Acceptability): _____

Total Accuracy		Total Acceptability
0–7 miscues	____ Independent	____ 0–7 miscues
8–31 miscues	____ Instructional	____ 8–16 miscues
32+ miscues	____ Frustration	____ 17+ miscues

Rate: 297 × 60 = 17,820/____ seconds = ____ WPM

Correct WPM: (297 − ____ errors) × 60 =
____ /____ seconds = ____ CWPM

Retelling Scoring Sheet for "Early Railroads"

Main Idea

____ Railroads began as rails
____ laid down in a road.

Details

____ The rails were wood
____ topped with iron.
____ Horses pulled carts
____ running along the rails.
____ The rails were smoother
____ than the roads
____ so the horses could pull the carts
____ faster.

Main Idea

____ Peter Cooper got an idea.

Details

____ Why not develop a steam engine,
____ or locomotive,
____ to pull the carts?
____ He believed
____ an engine would be able to pull heavier loads
____ faster
____ than horses could.

Main Idea

____ In 1830,
____ Cooper built a steam engine.

Details

____ It was small.
____ Because of its size,
____ it became known as the Tom Thumb.
____ Tom Thumb was a tiny hero
____ in old stories.

Main Idea

____ Cooper wanted people to know
____ about his machine
____ so he advertised a race
____ between the Tom Thumb
____ and a horse.

Details

____ On an August day,
____ the locomotive
____ and the horse lined up.
____ The race began.
____ At first,
____ the horse pulled ahead.
____ Then the train picked up speed.
____ Soon it was neck and neck.
____ Then Tom Thumb pulled ahead
____ and a cheer went up.
____ But a valve broke.
____ The locomotive slowed
____ and fell behind the horse.

Main Idea

____ Although Tom Thumb lost the race,
____ engines would take over from horses.

Level: Four

Details

____ Over the next 20 years,
____ railroads replaced canals
____ as the easiest
____ and cheapest way to travel.
____ By 1840,
____ the United States had 3,000 miles
____ of tracks.
____ A person could travel 90 miles
____ by railroad
____ in a few hours.
____ Such a trip took a day and a half
____ by wagon.

57 Ideas

Number of ideas recalled _____

Other ideas recalled, including inferences:

Questions for "Early Railroads"

1. What is this passage mainly about?
   Implicit: a race between the first steam engine and a horse; *or* how the steam engine replaced the horse in hauling things and people

2. Why did Peter Cooper build a steam engine?
   Implicit: it could pull heavier loads and go faster than horses (If the students says, "to make money," ask, "Why would it make money?")

3. Why was the first steam engine called Tom Thumb?
   Explicit: it was small and Tom Thumb was small

4. Why did Cooper set up the race between Tom Thumb and the horse?
   Explicit: to let people know about the engine

5. How do you know that people who watched the race wanted Tom Thumb to win?
   Implicit: they cheered when Tom Thumb pulled ahead

6. Even though the horse won the race, why could you say that Tom Thumb really won?
   Implicit: because steam engines later replaced horses

7. Why did the horse win the race?
   Explicit: a part of the locomotive's engine broke

8. By 1840, what country had more miles of railroad track?
   Explicit: United States

Without Look-Backs

Number Correct Explicit: _____

Number Correct Implicit: _____

Total: _____

____ Independent: 8 correct

____ Instructional: 6–7 correct

____ Frustration: 0–5 correct

With Look-Backs

Number Correct Explicit: _____

Number Correct Implicit: _____

Total: _____

____ Independent: 8 correct

____ Instructional: 6–7 correct

____ Frustration: 0–5 correct

Level 4

Level: Four

Expository

Copyright © 2011 Pearson Education, Inc. Reproduction is permitted for classroom use only.

Concept Questions:

What is a beaver?

_____

_____

_____ (3-2-1-0)

What are dams built by beavers?

_____

_____

_____ (3-2-1-0)

What are problems caused by beavers?

_____

_____

_____ (3-2-1-0)

How do beavers protect their young?

_____

_____

_____ (3-2-1-0)

Score: _____ /12= _____ %

_____ FAM _____ UNFAM

Prediction:

_____

_____)

"The Busy Beaver"

Have you ever heard someone say "busy as a beaver"? Beavers are very busy animals and they are master builders. This furry animal spends its life working and building. As soon as a beaver leaves its family, it has much work to do.

First, the beaver must build a dam. It uses sticks, leaves, and mud to block a stream. The beaver uses its two front teeth to get the sticks. The animal uses its large flat tail to pack mud into place. A pond forms behind the dam. The beaver spends most of its life near this pond.

In the middle of the beaver's pond is a large mound. This mound of mud and twigs is the beaver's lodge or house. The beaver's family is safe in the lodge because it is well hidden. The doorway to the lodge is under the water. After the lodge is built, the beaver still cannot rest. More trees must be cut down to be used as food for the coming winter. Sometimes there will be no more trees around the pond. Then the beaver has to find trees elsewhere. These trees will have to be carried to the pond. The beaver might build canals leading deep into the forest.

All this work changes the land. As trees are cut down, birds, squirrels, and other animals may have to find new homes. Animals that feed on trees lose their food supply. The pond behind the dam floods part of the ground. Animals that used to live there have to move. However, the new environment becomes a home for different kinds of birds, fish, and plants. All this happens because of the very busy beaver. (281 words)

From *Scott Foresman Science, Pupil Edition, Grade 4,* by Cohen et al. Copyright © 1984 by Pearson Education, Inc. or its affiliates. Adapted by permission. All Rights Reserved.

Level 4

Level: Four

Number of Total Miscues
(Total Accuracy): _____

Number of Meaning-Change Miscues
(Total Acceptability): _____

Total Accuracy			Total Acceptability
0–7 miscues	_____ Independent	_____	0–7 miscues
8–29 miscues	_____ Instructional	_____	8–15 miscues
30+ miscues	_____ Frustration	_____	16+ miscues

Rate: 281 × 60 = 16,860/_____ seconds = _____ WPM

Correct WPM: (281 – _____ errors) × 60 =
_____ /_____ seconds = _____ CWPM

Retelling Scoring Sheet for "The Busy Beaver"

Main Idea

____ Have you heard
____ "busy as a beaver"?
____ Beavers are animals
____ busy animals
____ and builders
____ master builders.

Details

____ As soon as a beaver leaves its family,
____ it has much work to do.
____ The beaver builds a dam.
____ It uses sticks,
____ leaves,
____ and mud
____ to block a stream.
____ The beaver uses its teeth
____ its front teeth
____ to get sticks.
____ The animal uses its tail
____ to pack mud.
____ A pond forms
____ behind the dam.

____ The beaver spends its life
____ near the pond.
____ The beaver's home is a mound
____ in the pond.
____ The family is safe
____ because the lodge is well hidden.
____ The doorway
____ to the lodge
____ is under the water.
____ Trees are cut down
____ to be used as food
____ for the winter.
____ Sometimes there will be no trees
____ around the pond.
____ The beaver has to find trees
____ and carry them
____ to the pond.
____ The beaver might build canals.

Main Idea

____ This changes the land.

Details

____ As trees are cut,
____ birds,
____ squirrels,
____ and animals have to find new homes.
____ Animals lose their food supply.
____ The pond floods the land.
____ Animals have to move.
____ A new environment becomes home
____ for different birds
____ and fish.

49 Ideas

Number of ideas recalled _____

Other ideas recalled, including inferences:

Level 4

Level: Four

Copyright © 2011 Pearson Education, Inc. Reproduction is permitted for classroom use only.

Questions for "The Busy Beaver"

1. What is the passage mainly about?
   Implicit: how a beaver keeps busy; *or* what a beaver does

2. According to the passage, what are the beaver's front teeth used for?
   Explicit: to get the sticks

3. Describe the beaver's tail.
   Explicit: large and flat

4. Why does the beaver build a dam?
   Implicit: to make a pond; *or* to make a place for his lodge

5. What is the beaver's lodge or house made of?
   Explicit: mud and sticks

6. Why is the doorway to the beaver's house under the water?
   Implicit: it is safer and more hidden; *or* so enemies can't get in

7. What does the beaver eat during the winter?
   Explicit: trees

8. Why might some people dislike beavers?
   Implicit: they change the land by flooding; they drive out animals; *or* they cut down too many trees

---

Without Look-Backs

Number Correct Explicit: _____

Number Correct Implicit: _____

   Total: _____

   _____ Independent: 8 correct

   _____ Instructional: 6–7 correct

   _____ Frustration: 0–5 correct

With Look-Backs

Number Correct Explicit: _____

Number Correct Implicit: _____

   Total: _____

   _____ Independent: 8 correct

   _____ Instructional: 6–7 correct

   _____ Frustration: 0–5 correct

Level 4

Level: Four

Expository

Concept Questions:

What does "survive" mean?

_____

_____

_____ (3-2-1-0)

What does "environment" mean?

_____

_____

_____ (3-2-1-0)

What does "adapt" mean?

_____

_____

_____ (3-2-1-0)

What do plants need to live?

_____

_____

_____ (3-2-1-0)

Score: _____ /12 = _____ %

_____ FAM _____ UNFAM

Prediction:

_____

_____

"Plant Structures for Survival"

Plants and animals live in many different environments—hot, cold, wet, dry. But no matter where they live, all living things have basic needs that must be met. Any structure or behavior that helps a living thing meet those needs and survive in its environment is called an adaptation.

Plants need sunlight to live and grow. Many plants have special adaptations for getting sunlight. Vines climb up the sides of taller plants or objects where there is more sunlight. Water lilies have large, round leaves called pads that can take in more sunlight than small leaves. The giant water lily pads are so big that you could stand on them without sinking!

Plants also need water. In cold climates, water is frozen in ice and snow for part of the year. Plants that live in these areas have adaptations to help them conserve water. Because trees and other plants lose water through their leaves, some trees lose their leaves before the weather gets cold. Pine trees, such as Christmas trees, do not lose their leaves. However, their leaves are very thin and have a waxy covering that helps keep the trees from losing water. This adaptation helps pine trees survive during the cold winter months.

Plants that grow in very dry places have special adaptations for getting and storing water. The cactus plant lives in the desert where it doesn't rain very often. A cactus has long, shallow roots that cover a large area. When it rains, the roots can absorb a great deal of water very quickly. The cactus

Level: Four

stores the extra water. Its thick, waxy covering is an adaptation that helps keep moisture inside the plant. (278 words)

Number of Total Miscues
(Total Accuracy): _____

Number of Meaning-Change Miscues
(Total Acceptability): _____

Total Accuracy		**Total Acceptability**
0–6 miscues	____ Independent	____ 0–6 miscues
7–29 miscues	____ Instructional	____ 7–15 miscues
30+ miscues	____ Frustration	____ 16+ miscues

Rate: 278 × 60 = 16,680/____ seconds = ____ WPM

Correct WPM: (278 – ____ errors) × 60 =
____ /____ seconds = ____ CWPM

Retelling Scoring Sheet for "Plant Structures for Survival"

Main Idea

____ Plants
____ and animals live in different environments.

Details

____ No matter where they live,
____ all have needs.
____ A structure
____ or behavior that helps them
____ meet those needs
____ and survive in an environment
____ is called an adaptation.

Main Idea

____ Plants need sunlight
____ to live

____ and grow.

Details

____ Plants have adaptations
____ for getting sunlight.
____ Vines climb up
____ where there is more sunlight.
____ Water lilies have leaves
____ large leaves
____ called pads
____ that can take in more sunlight.
____ The giant pads are so big
____ you could stand on them
____ without sinking.

Main Idea

____ Plants also need water.

Details

____ In cold climates,
____ water is frozen.
____ Plants have adaptations
____ to conserve water.
____ Because plants lose water
____ through their leaves,
____ trees lose their leaves
____ before the weather gets cold.
____ Pine trees do not lose their leaves
____ trees such as Christmas trees.
____ Their leaves are very thin
____ and have a waxy covering
____ that helps keep the trees
____ from losing water.
____ This adaptation helps pine trees survive
____ during the winter.

Main Idea

____ Plants in very dry areas
____ have adaptations
____ for getting and storing water.

Details

____ The cactus lives in the desert
____ where it doesn't rain.
____ A cactus has roots

Level: Four

___ long roots
___ shallow roots
___ that cover a large area.
___ The roots can absorb a great deal of water
___ very quickly.
___ The cactus stores extra water.
___ Its covering is an adaptation
___ thick covering
___ waxy covering
___ that helps keep moisture
___ inside the plant.

57 Ideas

Number of ideas recalled _____

Other ideas recalled, including inferences:

Questions for "Plant Structures for Survival"

1. What was the most important idea in what you read?
   Implicit: that plants develop structures to help them live (survive) in certain climates

2. What is adaptation?
   Explicit: any structures; *or* behavior that helps a living thing to survive in its environment

3. What is one example of how a plant adapts to get more sunlight?
   Explicit: a vine grows up a tall plant to get more sunlight; *or* lily pads grow very large to capture sunlight

4. Why do some trees lose their leaves before the weather gets cold?
   Explicit: to prevent the tree from losing water through their leaves

5. Why don't pine trees lose water through their leaves?
   Implicit: their leaves are very thin *and* are protected by a waxy substance

6. Describe the root system of a cactus.
   Explicit: long; *or* shallow

7. How is the root system of a cactus an example of adaptation to the desert?
   Implicit: the roots can absorb the small amounts of rain that fall in the desert

8. How are a cactus and a pine tree alike?
   Implicit: a waxy substance that prevents loss of water covers them both

Without Look-Backs

Number Correct Explicit: ____

Number Correct Implicit: ____

Total: ____

____ Independent: 8 correct

____ Instructional: 6–7 correct

____ Frustration: 0–5 correct

With Look-Backs

Number Correct Explicit: ____

Number Correct Implicit: ____

Total: ____

____ Independent: 8 correct

____ Instructional: 6–7 correct

____ Frustration: 0–5 correct

Level 4

Martin Luther King, Jr.

When Martin Luther King, Jr., was a boy, many laws would not allow black people to go to the same places as whites. Some people thought blacks were not as good as whites. Black children could not attend some schools, and certain restaurants had signs that said "whites only." Blacks could not sit in the front of a bus and, if a bus got crowded, they had to give up their seat to a white person. King did not agree with laws like these, for he believed that all people are equal. He did not think that skin color should keep people apart. Laws separating blacks and whites were unjust, and King decided to protest such laws.

Many people organized to help him. King said that they must protest in a peaceful way. King told his followers to "meet hate with love." In Montgomery, Alabama, Rosa Parks, a black woman, was arrested and fined for not giving up her seat to a white man on a bus. King led the movement to protest this action. Thousands of people refused to ride the buses. The bus companies began to lose money. In time the law was changed. King traveled to many cities. He talked to the people and led them in peaceful marches.

More and more people heard about King's peaceful protests and joined him. King led a march to our center of government, Washington, D.C., to ask that the unjust laws be changed. Finally, the United States Supreme Court agreed with King. The laws separating blacks and whites were changed. King was given the Nobel Peace Prize for his work. Today people still admire King because he fought for justice in a peaceful way. January 15 was named as a national holiday in honor of Martin Luther King, Jr.

From *Holt Social Studies,* edited by JoAnn Cangemi, copyright © 1983 by Holt, Rinehart, and Winston, Inc. Reproduced by permission of Houghton Mifflin Harcourt Publishing Company. This material may not be reproduced in any form or by any means without the prior written permission of the publisher.

Margaret Mead

Margaret Mead had always been interested in the ways of life of people from other lands. When Mead went to college, she took a class in anthropology. This is the study of how different people live. Mead decided to make this her career. She wanted to study primitive people before modern ways of living destroyed their culture.

Mead realized that living with a people is the only effective way to learn about them. She chose a village in Samoa to investigate. Several islands make up Samoa, which is in the Pacific Ocean. Mead worked hard to prepare for Samoa. She studied languages like the Samoan language. She read everything she could about the Samoan people. She read about their food and how they built their homes. She read about their ceremonies, their past history, and their taboos. But she wanted to learn much more.

Finally Mead arrived in Samoa. At first life was difficult for her. She was alone. She was not fluent in the Samoan language. She lived in a house with no walls and no electricity or gas. It had no running water and no bathroom. One day she said to herself, "I can't go on" in Samoan. Then she thought that maybe she could continue after all. Mead became fluent in the Samoan language, and the people soon regarded her as one of the village. She listened to their talk, their jokes, and their gossip. They told her their problems. Mead felt that being a woman assisted her in learning more about the lives of these people. Instead of having to go on hunts with the men, Mead stayed with the women. She observed the children play and learned how food was prepared. She made efforts to get the older people to recount tales of the past.

Mead learned many things from the Samoan people. She always took notes and kept careful records. These notes were used to write her first book, which was called *Coming of Age in Samoa*. It made her famous. Mead spent the rest of her life studying and writing about primitive ways of life that no longer exist today.

From *Our People* by Nelle Diederick et al. Copyright © 1979 by Ginn and Company. Adapted by permission of Pearson Education, Inc. All Rights Reserved.

Patricia McKissack

Patricia McKissack is the author of biographies of famous African Americans and of several picture books. Two of her most widely known picture books are *Mirandy and Brother Wind* and *Flossie and the Fox*. Patricia was the oldest of three children whose family moved to St. Louis, Missouri, when she was very young. Her parents divorced when she was ten, and her mother moved to Nashville to be close to her parents. Her grandparents in Nashville were very important in Patricia's life. They gave her a lot of love and attention, particularly her grandfather, who, she says, "spoiled her rotten." Her grandfather was a great storyteller, and he would always include Patricia's or her siblings' names in his stories. He told a story of a girl named Pat who could outsmart foxes, and we all know that foxes are smart. This story forms the foundation of Patricia's famous book, *Flossie and the Fox*. His many stories are the inspiration for many of her picture books.

Patricia began to see herself as an author in third grade. She wrote a poem, and her teacher put it on the bulletin board and said she liked it. It was thrilling to have other people read and respond to something she had written. She was forever scribbling ideas and thoughts down for future reference, and she realized early that she wanted to be a writer. But she was told black people couldn't do that. "Girl, you better take something you can do. You'd better be a teacher." Despite this advice, reading and writing remained an important part of her life. She kept a journal, and always kept a diary. She spent a lot of time in the Nashville Public Library because it was one public place that was open to blacks. Every week she checked out three books, the maximum allowed. The minute she was done, she went back for more. Fairy tales and myths were her favorite, but she was troubled because she never saw people who looked like her in the stories. She searched the libraries for books with African American characters and found them in books of nonfiction. She began reading biographies of people like Mary McLeod Bethune, and her search led her to the poetry of Langston Hughes. She even searched the encyclopedia for pictures of African Americans.

In college Patricia majored in English and Education. Again she was steered toward getting a teaching certificate "so you can have something to do when you graduate." When she taught eighth grade, she was bothered by the lack of material for African American children. She loved the poetry of Paul Laurence Dunbar that her mother had read to her, so she wrote her first biography of Dunbar. Since then she has continued to write biographies of important African Americans such as Frederick Douglass, W. E. B. Du Bois, Martin Luther King, and Jesse Jackson. She is committed to writing strong, accurate, and appealing stories about African Americans to improve the self-esteem of African American children and encourage all children to have an open mind toward cultures different from their own.

Farming on the Great Plains

In the 1800s, the Great Plains was a vast region of dry grasslands. People did not think it would ever make good farmland. As a result, the Great Plains attracted very few pioneers.

The United States government decided to try to encourage people to move to the Great Plains. In 1862, Congress passed the Homestead Act. This act offered free land to pioneers willing to start new farms. If you were a man over the age of 21, a woman whose husband had died, or the head of a family, you could claim 160 acres of land. You had to pay a small registration fee, usually about $10. You also had to farm your land and live on it for five years. Then the land was yours. Settlers who claimed land through this law were called homesteaders.

It was not easy to establish a farm on the Great Plains. The grasses, or sod, had thick tangled roots. The roots reached several inches down into the soil. Before planting crops, farmers had to dig through this sod. Great Plains farmers soon became known as sodbusters.

After ripping up the sod, most homesteaders used it to build houses. There were few trees or rocks so sod was a useful building material. Houses built from blocks of sod stayed cool in the summer. They were warm in the winter and were fireproof. Unfortunately for the homesteaders, the sod walls were often home to bugs, mice, and snakes.

The homesteaders faced many obstacles such as harsh weather conditions and deadly natural disasters. Spring often brought tornadoes, hailstorms, and flooding. Summers could mean scorching heat and frequent droughts. In fall, the prairie grass dried and settlers had to watch for prairie fires. Winter brought bitter cold along with ice storms and blizzards.

Farmers also faced the dreaded grasshopper. In the mid-1870s, millions of grasshoppers swarmed across the Great Plains. They darkened the sky and covered the ground in layers up to six inches high. The insects ate everything in their path, crops, grass, even fences and axe handles.

From *Scott Foresman Social Studies: The United States: Pupil Edition, Grade 5.* Copyright © 2003 by Pearson Education, Inc. or its affiliates. Adapted by permission. All Rights Reserved.

The Octopus

Some people think of the octopus as a giant creature. They have seen this in science fiction movies. They think the octopus is a mean creature who attacks people and other animals. The octopus is really a shy animal. It is usually quite small.

The octopus has eight arms. Its name tells us this because "octo" means eight. The octopus uses its arms to walk on the ocean floor. Its arms are also used to capture crabs. Crabs are its favorite food. The octopus bites into the crab with its strong beak. This sends poison into the crab's body.

The octopus protects itself in three ways. First, when frightened, the octopus can push water from its body in a powerful stream. This action pushes the octopus forward very rapidly. This allows it to escape.

Second, the body of the octopus has a special sac or pouch that holds a dark, ink-like fluid. When an enemy comes close, the octopus squirts some of this fluid. It then swims away. All that the predator sees is a dark cloud in the water where the octopus was. Meanwhile, the octopus has escaped.

Finally, the octopus's body changes color when the octopus is excited or frightened. Suppose an octopus sees a crab. Patches of pink, purple, or blue will appear on the octopus's skin. Suppose the octopus sees an enemy. The octopus will completely change color. Then it seems to disappear into the background of its hiding place. It is hard for the predator to find the octopus.

From *Scott Foresman Science, Pupil Edition, Grade 5,* by Cohen et al. Copyright © 1984 by Pearson Education, Inc. or its affiliates. Adapted by permission. All Rights Reserved.

How Does Your Body Take in Oxygen?

Preparing Air for Your Lungs

About one-fifth of the air that you breathe in is a gas called oxygen. Your cells must have oxygen to do their work. Without oxygen, cells will die— some within 3–5 minutes. When you breathe in, your respiratory system brings air containing oxygen into your body. The cells in your body use the oxygen, and as they work, the cells produce carbon dioxide. This gas leaves your body as waste when you breathe out.

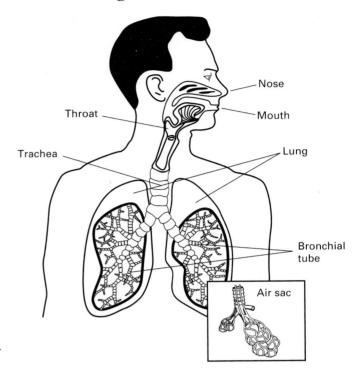

The respiratory system includes your nose, your lungs, and the tubes that connect them. Air enters the body through the nose, which has the job of getting the air ready for the lungs. If air is very cold, dry, or dirty it could damage your lungs. Your nose warms, moistens, and cleans the air that you breathe in. The blood supply and mucus in your nose keeps it warm and moist. The hairs in your nose capture the dust from the air.

After the air is warmed, moistened, and cleaned it goes to the throat and down the trachea, or windpipe. The trachea divides into two bronchial tubes, each of which goes into a lung.

Inside the Lung

Inside the lungs, the bronchial tubes divide into smaller and smaller tubes. Look at the picture above to help you visualize this description. The smallest tubes lead to clusters of tiny pouches called air sacs. A net of tiny blood vessels surrounds each air sac. Inhaled air, which is rich in oxygen, enters the air sacs. At this moment, the blood in the vessels around the air sacs contains a lot of carbon dioxide, which the blood has picked up from body cells. That blood contains little oxygen. An air exchange quickly takes place. Oxygen passes from the air sacs into the blood vessels. The blood now has oxygen to deliver to body cells. At the same time that oxygen passes out of the air sacs, carbon dioxide passes from the blood vessels into the air sacs. The carbon dioxide leaves your body when you exhale.

From *Scott Foresman Science, Teacher Edition, Grade 5.* Copyright © 2000 by Pearson Education, Inc. or its affiliates. Reprinted by permission. All Rights Reserved.

Level: Five

Narrative

Concept Questions:

Who was Martin Luther King?

_____

_____

_____ (3-2-1-0)

What is racism?

_____

_____

_____ (3-2-1-0)

What is Washington, D.C.?

_____

_____

_____ (3-2-1-0)

What does "equal rights for blacks" mean to you?

_____

_____

_____ (3-2-1-0)

Score: _____ /12 = _____ %

_____ FAM _____ UNFAM

Prediction:

_____

_____

"Martin Luther King, Jr."

When Martin Luther King, Jr., was a boy, many laws would not allow black people to go to the same places as whites. Some people thought blacks were not as good as whites. Black children could not attend some schools, and certain restaurants had signs that said "whites only." Blacks could not sit in the front of a bus and, if a bus got crowded, they had to give up their seat to a white person. King did not agree with laws like these, for he believed that all people are equal. He did not think that skin color should keep people apart. Laws separating blacks and whites were unjust, and King decided to protest such laws.

Many people organized to help him. King said that they must protest in a peaceful way. King told his followers to "meet hate with love." In Montgomery, Alabama, Rosa Parks, a black woman, was arrested and fined for not giving up her seat to a white man on a bus. King led the movement to protest this action. Thousands of people refused to ride the buses. The bus companies began to lose money. In time the law was changed. King traveled to many cities. He talked to the people and led them in peaceful marches.

More and more people heard about King's peaceful protests and joined him. King led a march to our center of government, Washington, D.C., to ask that the unjust laws be changed. Finally, the United States Supreme Court agreed with King. The laws separating blacks and whites were changed. King was given the Nobel Peace Prize for his work.

Level 5

Level: Five

Today people still admire King because he fought for justice in a peaceful way. January 15 was named as a national holiday in honor of Martin Luther King, Jr. (297 words)

Number of Total Miscues
(Total Accuracy): _____

Number of Meaning-Change Miscues
(Total Acceptability): _____

Total Accuracy		**Total Acceptability**
0–7 miscues	____ Independent	____ 0–7 miscues
8–31 miscues	____ Instructional	____ 8–16 miscues
32+ miscues	____ Frustration	____ 17+ miscues

Rate: 297 × 60 = 17,820/ ____ seconds = ____ WPM

Correct WPM: (297 – ____ errors) × 60 =
_____ /____ seconds = ____ CWPM

Retelling Scoring Sheet for "Martin Luther King, Jr."

Setting/Background

___ When Martin Luther King, Jr., was a boy,
___ laws would not allow blacks
___ to go to the same places
___ as whites.
___ People thought
___ blacks weren't as good
___ as whites.
___ Black children could not attend some schools.
___ Certain restaurants had signs
___ that said

___ "whites only."
___ Blacks could not sit
___ in front
___ of a bus.
___ If the bus got crowded,
___ they had to give up their seat
___ to a white.

Goal

___ King did not agree
___ with these laws.
___ He believed
___ that all people are equal.
___ He decided
___ to protest these laws.

Events

___ King said
___ they must protest
___ in a peaceful way.
___ In Alabama,
___ Rosa Parks was arrested
___ for not giving up her seat
___ to a white man.
___ King led a movement
___ to protest this action.
___ Thousands refused
___ to ride the buses.
___ The bus company lost money.
___ The law was changed.
___ King led a march
___ to our center of government,
___ Washington, D.C.,
___ to ask
___ that the laws be changed
___ the unjust laws.

Resolution

___ The Supreme Court agreed.
___ The laws were changed
___ laws separating blacks and whites.
___ King was given a prize
___ the Nobel Peace Prize
___ for his work.

Level: Five

___ People still admire King.
___ January 15 was named
___ as a holiday
___ a national holiday
___ in honor of King.

53 Ideas

Number of ideas recalled _____

Other ideas recalled, including references:

Questions for "Martin Luther King, Jr."

1. What was Martin Luther King's main goal?
   Implicit: he wanted equality for black people

2. Why had people made laws separating blacks and whites?
   Implicit: they thought blacks were not as good as whites

3. In some cities, what did blacks have to do on a crowded bus?
   Explicit: give up their seat to a white person

4. Why was Rosa Parks arrested?
   Explicit: she refused to give up her seat

5. What did many people do to protest Rosa Parks's arrest?
   Explicit: they refused to ride the buses

6. What happened when people refused to ride the buses?
   Implicit: the law was changed. If the student says, "The bus companies lost money," ask "What happened because of that?"

7. Why was Washington, D.C., an important place to protest unjust laws?
   Implicit: it is where the president and government officials are, so they would see the protest

8. Name one way in which Martin Luther King was honored for his work.
   Explicit: the Nobel Peace Prize; *or* the national holiday

Without Look-Backs

Number Correct Explicit: _____

Number Correct Implicit: _____

Total: _____

_____ Independent: 8 correct

_____ Instructional: 6–7 correct

_____ Frustration: 0–5 correct

With Look-Backs

Number Correct Explicit: _____

Number Correct Implicit: _____

Total: _____

_____ Independent: 8 correct

_____ Instructional: 6–7 correct

_____ Frustration: 0–5 correct

Level 5

Level: Five

Narrative

Concept Questions:

Who was Margaret Mead?

_____

_____

_____ (3-2-1-0)

How do we learn about different people?

_____

_____

_____ (3-2-1-0)

What are primitive people?

_____

_____

_____ (3-2-1-0)

What are problems learning a new language?

_____

_____

_____ (3-2-1-0)

Score: _____ /12 = _____ %

_____ FAM _____ UNFAM

Prediction:

_____

_____

"Margaret Mead"

Margaret Mead had always been interested in the ways of life of people from other lands. When Mead went to college, she took a class in anthropol-ogy. This is the study of how different people live. Mead decided to make this her career. She wanted to study primitive people before modern ways of living destroyed their culture.

Mead realized that living with a people is the only effective way to learn about them. She chose a village in Samoa to investigate. Several islands make up Samoa, which is in the Pacific <u>Ocean</u>. Mead worked hard to prepare for Samoa. She studied lan-guages like the Samoan language. She read every-thing she could about the Samoan people. She read about their food and how they built their homes. She read about their ceremonies, their past history, and their taboos. But she wanted to learn much more.

Finally Mead arrived in Samoa. At first life was difficult for her. She was alone. She was not <u>fluent</u> in the Samoan language. She lived in a house with no walls and no electricity or gas. It had no running water and no bathroom. One day she said to her-self, "I can't go on" in Samoan. Then she thought that maybe she could continue after all. Mead be-came <u>fluent</u> in the Samoan language, and the people soon regarded her as one of the village. She listened to their talk, their jokes, and their gossip. They told her their problems. Mead felt that being a woman assisted her in learning more about the lives of these people. Instead of having to go on hunts with the men, Mead stayed with the women. She observed

Level: Five

the children play and learned how food was pre-pared. She made efforts to get the older people to recount <u>tales</u> of the past.

Mead learned many things from the Samoan people. She always took notes and kept careful re-cords. These notes were used to write her first book, which was called *Coming of Age in Samoa*. It made her famous. Mead spent the rest of her life studying and writing about primitive ways of life that no lon-ger exist today. (357 words)

Number of Total Miscues
(Total Accuracy): _____

Number of Meaning-Change Miscues
(Total Acceptability): _____

Total Accuracy		**Total Acceptability**
0–8 miscues	____ Independent	____ 0–8 miscues
9–37 miscues	____ Instructional	____ 9–19 miscues
38+ miscues	____ Frustration	____ 20+ miscues

Rate: 357 × 60 = 21,420/ _____ seconds = _____ WPM

Correct WPM: (357 – _____ errors) × 60 =

_____ /_____ seconds = _____ CWPM

Retelling Scoring Sheet for "Margaret Mead"

Background/Setting

____ When Margaret Mead went to college,
____ she took a class
____ in anthropology.
____ She decided to make this her career.

Goal

____ She wanted to study people
____ primitive people.
____ She chose a village
____ in Samoa
____ to investigate.
____ Islands make up Samoa,
____ which is in the Pacific Ocean.

Events

____ Margaret Mead studied languages
____ like the Samoan language.
____ She read everything she could
____ about the Samoan people.
____ She read
____ about their food
____ and how they built their homes.
____ She arrived in Samoa.
____ Life was difficult.
____ She lived
____ in a house
____ with no walls
____ with no electricity.
____ She said,
____ "I can't go on"
____ in Samoan.
____ Then she thought
____ that she could continue.
____ The people regarded her
____ as one of the village.
____ She listened
____ to their jokes,
____ their gossip.
____ Instead of having to go
____ on hunts
____ with the men,
____ Margaret Mead stayed
____ with the women.
____ She observed the children
____ play
____ and learned
____ how food was prepared.

Level: Five

Resolutions

____ She wrote a book
____ called *Coming of Age in Samoa*.
____ It made her famous.

46 Ideas

Number of ideas recalled _____

Other ideas recalled, including inferences:

Questions for "Margaret Mead"

1. What was Margaret Mead's main goal?
   Implicit: to study primitive people

2. What people did Margaret Mead choose to investigate?
   Explicit: people in Samoa

3. Name one thing Margaret Mead read about to prepare her for Samoa.
   Explicit: homes; food; ceremonies; *or* Samoa's history; taboos; *or* the Samoan language

4. Give one reason why life in Samoa was difficult at first.
   Explicit: she was alone; there were no walls, electricity, running water, or bathroom; *or* she was not fluent in the language

5. What made Margaret Mead decide she would be able to stay in Samoa?
   Implicit: when she talked to herself in Samoan and realized she knew the language

6. Why was Margaret Mead able to learn a lot about the family life of the Samoans?
   Implicit: she stayed with the women and children; *or* the women and children talked to her

7. Why did Margaret Mead want to hear the stories of the Samoans' past?
   Implicit: she wanted to learn as much about them as she could

8. What did Margaret Mead do with the notes and records she kept?
   Explicit: she wrote a book

Without Look-Backs

Number Correct Explicit: ____
Number Correct Implicit: ____
   Total: ____
   ____ Independent: 8 correct
   ____ Instructional: 6–7 correct
   ____ Frustration: 0–5 correct

With Look-Backs

Number Correct Explicit: ____
Number Correct Implicit: ____
   Total: ____
   ____ Independent: 8 correct
   ____ Instructional: 6–7 correct
   ____ Frustration: 0–5 correct

Level 5

Level: Five

Narrative

Concept Questions:

Who is Patricia McKissack?

_____

_____

_____ (3-2-1-0)

What is a biography?

_____

_____

_____ (3-2-1-0)

What does it mean to inspire someone?

_____

_____

_____ (3-2-1-0)

What are nonfiction books?

_____

_____

_____ (3-2-1-0)

Score: _____ /12 = _____ %

_____ FAM _____ UNFAM

Prediction:

_____

_____

"Patricia McKissack"

Patricia McKissack is the author of biographies of famous African Americans and of several picture books. Two of her most widely known picture books are *Mirandy and Brother Wind* and *Flossie and the Fox*. Patricia was the oldest of three children whose family moved to St. Louis, Missouri, when she was very young. Her parents <u>divorced</u> when she was ten, and her mother moved to Nashville to be close to her parents. Her grandparents in Nashville were very important in Patricia's life. They gave her a lot of love and <u>attention</u>, particularly her grandfather, who, she says, "spoiled her rotten." Her grandfather was a great storyteller, and he would always include Patricia's or her siblings' names in his stories. He told a story of a girl named Pat who could outsmart foxes, and we all know that foxes are smart. This story forms the foundation of Patricia's famous book, *Flossie and the Fox*. His many stories are the inspiration for many of her picture books.

Patricia began to see herself as an author in third grade. She wrote a poem, and her teacher put it on the <u>bulletin</u> board and said she liked it. It was thrilling to have other people read and respond to something she had written. She was forever scribbling ideas and thoughts down for future reference, and she realized early that she wanted to be a writer. But she was told black people couldn't do that. "Girl, you better take something you can do. You'd better be a teacher." Despite this advice, reading and writing remained an important part of her life. She kept a journal, and always kept a diary. She spent a lot of time in the Nashville Public Library because it

Level 5

Level: Five

was one public place that was open to blacks. Every week she checked out three books, the maximum allowed. The minute she was done, she went back for more. Fairy <u>tales</u> and myths were her <u>favorite</u>, but she was troubled because she never saw people who looked like her in the stories. She searched the libraries for books with African American characters and found them in books of nonfiction. She began reading biographies of people like Mary McLeod Bethune, and her search led her to the poetry of Langston Hughes. She even searched the encyclopedia for pictures of African Americans.

In college Patricia majored in English and Education. Again she was steered toward getting a teaching certificate "so you can have something to do when you graduate." When she taught eighth grade, she was bothered by the lack of <u>material</u> for African American children. She loved the poetry of Paul Laurence Dunbar that her mother had read to her, so she wrote her first <u>biography</u> of Dunbar. Since then she has continued to write biographies of important African Americans such as Frederick Douglass, W. E. B. Du Bois, Martin Luther King, and Jesse Jackson. She is committed to writing strong, accurate, and appealing stories about African Americans to improve the self-esteem of African American children and encourage all children to have an open mind toward cultures different from their own. (516 words)

Number of Total Miscues
(Total Accuracy): _____

Number of Meaning-Change Miscues
(Total Acceptability): _____

Total Accuracy		**Total Acceptability**
0–12 miscues ____ Independent	____	0–12 miscues
13–54 miscues ____ Instructional	____	13–28 miscues
55+ miscues ____ Frustration	____	29+ miscues

Rate: 516 × 60 = 30,960/ _____ seconds = _____ WPM

Correct WPM: (516 – _____ errors) × 60 =
_____ /_____ seconds = _____ CWPM

Retelling Scoring Sheet for "Patricia McKissack"

Setting/Background

____ Patricia McKissack is the author
____ of biographies
____ of famous African Americans
____ and of picture books.
____ Two of her most widely known
____ are *Mirandy and Brother Wind*
____ and *Flossie and the Fox.*
____ Patricia was the oldest
____ of three children
____ whose family moved
____ to St. Louis, Missouri,
____ when she was very young.
____ Her parents divorced
____ when she was ten
____ and her mother moved to Nashville
____ to be close to her parents.
____ Her grandparents were very important
____ in Patricia's life,
____ particularly her grandfather
____ who "spoiled her rotten."
____ Her grandfather was a storyteller,
____ and he would always include names
____ Patricia's name

Level 5

Level: Five

____ or her siblings' names
____ in his stories.
____ His stories are the inspiration
____ for many books.

Goal

____ Patricia began to see herself as an author
____ in third grade.

Events

____ She wrote a poem
____ and her teacher put it on the bulletin board
____ and said she liked it.
____ It was thrilling to have people read
____ something she had written.
____ She was forever scribbling ideas
____ for reference.

Goal

____ She wanted to be a writer

Events

____ But she was told
____ black people couldn't do that.
____ "You'd better be a teacher."
____ Reading
____ and writing remained a part
____ an important part
____ of her life.
____ She kept a journal
____ and always kept a diary.
____ She spent a lot of time
____ in the Public Library
____ because it was one place
____ that was open to blacks.
____ Every week
____ she checked out three books,
____ the maximum allowed.
____ The minute she was done,
____ she went back for more.
____ She was troubled
____ because she never saw people who looked like her
____ in the stories.

Goal

____ She searched the libraries for books
____ with African American characters

Events

____ She found them
____ in nonfiction.
____ She began reading biographies.
____ She even searched the encyclopedia
____ for pictures of African Americans.
____ In college Patricia majored in English
____ and Education.
____ She was steered toward getting a teaching certificate.
____ When she taught eighth grade,
____ she was bothered by the lack of material
____ for African American children.

Resolution

____ She loved the poetry of Paul Laurence Dunbar
____ so she wrote her first biography
____ of Dunbar.
____ She has continued to write biographies
____ of important African Americans
____ such as Frederick Douglass,
____ W. E. B. Du Bois,
____ Martin Luther King,
____ and Jesse Jackson.

Goal

____ She is committed to writing stories
____ strong stories
____ accurate stories
____ and appealing stories
____ about African Americans
____ to improve the self-esteem
____ of African American children
____ and encourage all children
____ to have an open mind
____ toward different cultures.

90 Ideas

Number of ideas recalled _____

Other ideas recalled, including summary statements and inferences:

Level 5

Level: Five

Questions for "Patricia McKissack"

1. Who is Patricia McKissack?
   Explicit: an author of biographies and picture books. If the student says, "an author," ask, "What kinds of books does she write?" Either type of book is acceptable.

2. Who was the most influential in developing Patricia's love of story?
   Implicit: her grandfather

3. How did Patricia's third grade teacher encourage her writing?
   Explicit: she liked a poem Patricia had written and put it on the bulletin board. (Both ideas must be included.)

4. Why did some people tell Patricia to be a teacher rather than an author?
   Implicit: they told her blacks couldn't become authors; *or* they told her she should "do something she could do"

5. How do we know that Patricia was determined to be an author?
   Implicit: reading and writing remained important to her (despite the advice to become a teacher); she went to the library a lot and kept reading; *or* she kept a journal and a diary

6. Why did Patricia decide to write biographies of African American people?
   Explicit: she found few books in the library on African Americans; *or* when she taught eighth grade there were few books written about African Americans

7. Name two persons that Patricia McKissack has written biographies about.
   Explicit: Paul Laurence Dunbar, Martin Luther King, W. E. B. Du Bois, Frederick Douglass, or Jesse Jackson

8. How do we know that Patricia McKissack would want children who are *not* African American to read her books?
   Implicit: by reading her books children would learn about other cultures; *or* she wants all children to have an open mind toward cultures different from their own.

Without Look-Backs

Number Correct Explicit: _____

Number Correct Implicit: _____

Total: _____

_____ Independent: 8 correct

_____ Instructional: 6–7 correct

_____ Frustration: 0–5 correct

With Look-Backs

Number Correct Explicit: _____

Number Correct Implicit: _____

Total: _____

_____ Independent: 8 correct

_____ Instructional: 6–7 correct

_____ Frustration: 0–5 correct

Level 5

Level: Five

Expository

Concept Questions:

What are the Great Plains?

_____

_____

_____ (3-2-1-0)

What is a homesteader?

_____

_____

_____ (3-2-1-0)

What is sod?

_____

_____

_____ (3-2-1-0)

What is a natural disaster?

_____

_____

_____ (3-2-1-0)

Score: _____ /12 = _____ %

_____ FAM _____ UNFAM

Prediction:

_____

_____

"Farming on the Great Plains"

In the 1800s, the Great Plains was a vast region of dry grasslands. People did not think it would ever make good farmland. As a result, the Great Plains attracted very few <u>pioneers</u>.

The United States government decided to try to encourage people to move to the Great Plains. In 1862, Congress passed the Homestead Act. This act offered free land to <u>pioneers</u> willing to start new farms. If you were a man over the age of 21, a woman whose husband had died, or the head of a family, you could claim 160 acres of land. You had to pay a small <u>registration</u> fee, usually about $10. You also had to farm your land and live on it for five years. Then the land was yours. <u>Settlers</u> who claimed land through this law were called homesteaders.

It was not easy to establish a farm on the Great Plains. The grasses, or sod, had thick tangled roots. The roots reached several inches down into the soil. Before planting <u>crops</u>, farmers had to dig through this sod. Great Plains farmers soon became known as sodbusters.

After ripping up the sod, most homesteaders used it to build houses. There were few trees or rocks so sod was a useful building <u>material</u>. Houses built from blocks of sod stayed cool in the summer. They were warm in the winter and were fireproof. Unfortunately for the homesteaders, the sod walls were often home to bugs, mice, and snakes.

The homesteaders faced many <u>obstacles</u> such as harsh <u>weather</u> conditions and deadly natural disasters. Spring often brought tornadoes, hailstorms, and flooding. Summers could mean scorching heat and frequent droughts. In fall, the prairie grass dried

Level: Five

and <u>settlers</u> had to watch for prairie fires. Winter brought bitter cold along with ice storms and blizzards.

Farmers also faced the dreaded grasshopper. In the mid-1870s, millions of grasshoppers swarmed across the Great Plains. They darkened the sky and covered the ground in layers up to six inches high. The insects ate everything in their path, <u>crops</u>, grass, even fences and axe handles. (344 words)

From *Scott Foresman Social Studies: The United States, Pupil Edition, Grade 5.* Copyright © 2003 by Pearson Education, Inc. or its affiliates. Adapted by permission. All Rights Reserved.

Number of Total Miscues
(Total Accuracy): _____

Number of Meaning-Change Miscues
(Total Acceptability): _____

Total Accuracy		**Total Acceptability**
0–8 miscues	____ Independent	____ 0–8 miscues
9–36 miscues	____ Instructional	____ 9–18 miscues
37+ miscues	____ Frustration	____ 19+ miscues

Rate: 344 × 60 = 20,640/ _____ seconds = _____ WPM

Correct WPM: (344 – _____ errors) × 60 =
_____ /_____ seconds = _____ CWPM

Retelling Scoring Sheet for "Farming on the Great Plains"

Main Idea
____ In the 1800s,
____ the Great Plains was a region
____ of grasslands
____ dry grasslands.

Details
____ People did not think
____ it would make good farmland.
____ The Great Plains attracted very few pioneers.

Main Idea
____ The government decided to encourage people
____ to move to the Great Plains.

Details
____ In 1862,
____ Congress passed the Homestead Act.
____ This act offered free land
____ to pioneers.
____ If you were a man
____ over the age of 21,
____ a woman whose husband had died,
____ or the head of a family,
____ you could claim land
____ 160 acres of land.
____ You had to pay a fee
____ a registration fee
____ of about $10.
____ You also had to farm your land
____ and live on it
____ for five years.
____ Then the land was yours.
____ Settlers were called homesteaders.

Main Idea
____ It was not easy to farm
____ on the Great Plains.

Details
____ The grasses had roots
____ tangled roots
____ several inches down
____ into the soil.
____ Before planting crops,
____ farmers had to dig
____ through this sod.
____ They became known as sodbusters.

Main Idea
____ Homesteaders used sod to build houses.

Farming on the Great Plains   303

Level: Five

Details

___ Houses stayed cool

___ in the summer.

___ They were warm

___ in the winter

___ and were fireproof.

___ The walls were often home

___ to bugs,

___ mice,

___ and snakes.

Main Idea

___ The homesteaders faced many obstacles

___ such as weather

___ harsh weather

___ and disasters

___ natural disasters.

Details

___ Spring often brought tornadoes,

___ hailstorms,

___ and flooding.

___ Summers could mean heat

___ scorching heat

___ and droughts.

___ In fall,

___ the grass dried

___ and settlers had to watch

___ for fires.

___ Winter brought cold

___ bitter cold

___ along with ice storms

___ and blizzards.

Main Idea

___ Farmers also faced the grasshopper.

Details

___ In the mid-1870s,

___ millions

___ of grasshoppers swarmed

___ across the Great Plains.

___ They darkened the sky

___ and covered the ground

___ in layers six inches high.

___ The insects ate everything

___ in their path,

___ crops,

___ grass,

___ even fences,

___ and axe

___ handles.

81 Ideas

Number of ideas recalled _____

Other ideas recalled, including inferences:

Questions for "Farming on the Great Plains"

1. What is this passage mainly about?
   Implicit: the difficulties of farming on the Great Plains

2. Why did the Homestead Act attract pioneers to the Great Plains?
   Implicit: it offered free land

Level: Five

3. How long did farmers have to live on the land before it became theirs?
Explicit: five years

4. Why did Great Plains farmers become known as sodbusters?
Implicit: they had to dig up or bust the sod before they could plant crops

5. Give one reason why sod was a good material for building houses.
Explicit: warmth in winter; coolness in summer; fireproof; *or* few rocks or trees available

6. Name one obstacle that homesteaders faced in the spring.
Explicit: tornadoes; hailstorms; *or* floods

7. What obstacle did homesteaders face in the fall?
Explicit: prairie fires

8. Why would the grasshoppers cause a lot of hardship to the farmers?
Implicit: they ate crops and tools

Without Look-Backs

Number Correct Explicit: _____

Number Correct Implicit: _____

Total: _____

_____ Independent: 8 correct

_____ Instructional: 6–7 correct

_____ Frustration: 0–5 correct

With Look-Backs

Number Correct Explicit: _____

Number Correct Implicit: _____

Total: _____

_____ Independent: 8 correct

_____ Instructional: 6–7 correct

_____ Frustration: 0–5 correct

Level 5

Level: Five

Expository

Concept Questions:

What is an octopus?

_____

_____

_____ (3-2-1-0)

Why does an animal attack another animal?

_____

_____

_____ (3-2-1-0)

What are animal defenses?

_____

_____

_____ (3-2-1-0)

What is animal camouflage?

_____

_____

_____ (3-2-1-0)

Score: _____ /12 = _____ %

_____ FAM _____ UNFAM

Prediction:

_____

_____

"The Octopus"

Some people think of the octopus as a giant creature. They have seen this in science fiction movies. They think the octopus is a mean creature who attacks people and other animals. The octopus is really a shy animal. It is usually quite small.

The octopus has eight arms. Its name tells us this because "octo" means eight. The octopus uses its arms to walk on the ocean floor. Its arms are also used to capture crabs. Crabs are its favorite food. The octopus bites into the crab with its strong beak. This sends poison into the crab's body.

The octopus protects itself in three ways. First, when frightened, the octopus can push water from its body in a powerful stream. This action pushes the octopus forward very rapidly. This allows it to escape.

Second, the body of the octopus has a special sac or pouch that holds a dark, ink-like fluid. When an enemy comes close, the octopus squirts some of this fluid. It then swims away. All that the predator sees is a dark cloud in the water where the octopus was. Meanwhile, the octopus has escaped.

Finally, the octopus's body changes color when the octopus is excited or frightened. Suppose an octopus sees a crab. Patches of pink, purple, or blue will appear on the octopus's skin. Suppose the octopus sees an enemy. The octopus will completely change color. Then it seems to disappear into the background of its hiding place. It is hard for the predator to find the octopus. (254 words)

Level 5

Level: Five

Number of Total Miscues
(Total Accuracy): _____

Number of Meaning-Change Miscues
(Total Acceptability): _____

Total Accuracy		Total Acceptability
0–6 miscues	____ Independent	____ 0–6 miscues
7–26 miscues	____ Instructional	____ 7–13 miscues
27+ miscues	____ Frustration	____ 14+ miscues

Rate: 254 × 60 = 15,240/ ____ seconds = ____ WPM

Correct WPM: (254 – ____ errors) × 60 =
____ /____ seconds = ____ CWPM

Retelling Scoring Sheet for "The Octopus"

Main Idea

____ Some people think
____ the octopus is a giant creature
____ and a mean creature.
____ They have seen this
____ in movies
____ science fiction movies.
____ The octopus is shy
____ and small.

Details

____ The octopus has eight arms.
____ Octo means "eight."
____ It uses its arms
____ to walk
____ and capture crabs.
____ Crabs are its food
____ its favorite food.
____ The octopus bites
____ into the crab.
____ This sends poison
____ into the crab's body.
____ The octopus protects itself
____ in three ways.
____ First,

____ when frightened,
____ the octopus can push water
____ from its body.
____ This action pushes the octopus
____ forward
____ very rapidly.
____ This allows it
____ to escape.
____ Second,
____ the octopus has a sac
____ that holds a liquid
____ an ink-like liquid.
____ When an enemy comes close,
____ the octopus squirts fluid.
____ It swims away.
____ The predator sees a cloud
____ a dark cloud.
____ The octopus has escaped.
____ Finally,
____ the octopus changes color
____ when it is excited
____ or scared.
____ Suppose the octopus sees a crab.
____ Pink patches,
____ purple patches,
____ or blue patches
____ appear.
____ If the octopus sees an enemy,
____ the octopus will change color
____ completely.
____ It seems to disappear
____ into the background.

54 Ideas

Number of ideas recalled _____

Other ideas recalled, including inferences:

Questions for "The Octopus"

1. What is this passage mainly about?
   Implicit: what the octopus is like; *or* how it behaves

Level: Five

2. What is the favorite food of the octopus?
Explicit: crabs

3. How does the octopus move forward very rapidly when it is frightened?
Explicit: it pushes water from its body

4. What does the ink-like fluid do to the water?
Explicit: it changes it into a dark cloud

5. What is one color that an octopus can change to?
Explicit: pink; purple; *or* blue

6. Why doesn't an octopus completely change color when it sees a crab?
Implicit: it is excited, not frightened

7. What color does an octopus probably become when it sees an enemy?
Implicit: a dark blue or brown or black; *or* it camouflages itself with the background

8. Why might the shy octopus attack another creature?
Implicit: for food

Without Look-Backs

Number Correct Explicit: _____

Number Correct Implicit: _____

Total: _____

_____ Independent: 8 correct

_____ Instructional: 6–7 correct

_____ Frustration: 0–5 correct

With Look-Backs

Number Correct Explicit: _____

Number Correct Implicit: _____

Total: _____

_____ Independent: 8 correct

_____ Instructional: 6–7 correct

_____ Frustration: 0–5 correct

Level 5

Level: Five

Expository

Concept Questions:

What does the word "moist" mean?

_____

_____

_____ (3-2-1-0)

Why does your body need oxygen?

_____

_____

_____ (3-2-1-0)

Why is it important to breathe through your nose?

_____

_____

_____ (3-2-1-0)

How does the air that you breathe get into your bloodstream?

_____

_____

_____ (3-2-1-0)

Score: _____ /12 = _____ %

_____ FAM _____ UNFAM

Prediction:

_____

_____

"How Does Your Body Take in Oxygen?"

Preparing Air for Your Lungs

About one-fifth of the air that you breathe in is a gas called <u>oxygen</u>. Your cells must have <u>oxygen</u> to do their work. Without <u>oxygen</u>, cells will die—some within 3–5 minutes. When you breathe in, your respiratory system brings air containing <u>oxygen</u> into your body. The cells in your body use the <u>oxygen</u>, and as they work, the cells produce carbon dioxide. This gas leaves your body as waste when you breathe out.

The respiratory system includes your nose, your lungs, and the tubes that connect them. Air enters the body through the nose, which has the job of getting the air ready for the lungs. If air is very cold, dry, or dirty it could damage your lungs. Your nose warms, moistens, and cleans the air that you breathe in. The blood supply and mucus in your nose keeps it warm and moist. The hairs in your nose <u>capture</u> the dust from the air.

After the air is warmed, moistened, and cleaned it goes to the throat and down the trachea, or windpipe. The trachea divides into two bronchial tubes, each of which goes into a lung.

Inside the Lung

Inside the lungs, the bronchial tubes divide into smaller and smaller tubes. Look at the picture above

Level 5

Level: Five

to help you <u>visualize</u> this description. The smallest tubes lead to clusters of tiny <u>pouches</u> called air sacs. A net of tiny blood vessels surrounds each air sac. Inhaled air, which is rich in <u>oxygen</u> enters the air sacs. At this moment, the blood in the vessels around the air sacs contains a lot of carbon dioxide, which the blood has picked up from body cells. That blood contains little <u>oxygen</u>. An air exchange quickly takes place. <u>Oxygen</u> passes from the air sacs into the blood vessels. The blood now has <u>oxygen</u> to deliver to body cells. At the same time that <u>oxygen</u> passes out of the air sacs, carbon dioxide passes from the blood vessels into the air sacs. The carbon dioxide leaves your body when you exhale.

(343 words)

Number of Total Miscues
(Total Accuracy): _____

Number of Meaning-Change Miscues
(Total Acceptability): _____

Total Accuracy

Total Acceptability

0–8 miscues _____ Independent _____ 0–8 miscues

9–36 miscues _____ Instructional _____ 9–18 miscues

37+ miscues _____ Frustration _____ 19+ miscues

Rate: 343 × 60 = 20,580/ _____ seconds = _____ WPM

Correct WPM: (343 – _____ errors) × 60 =
_____ / _____ seconds = _____ CWPM

Retelling Scoring Sheet for "How Does Your Body Take in Oxygen?"

Main Idea

____ Your cells must have oxygen
____ to do their work.

Details

____ About one-fifth
____ of the air you breathe
____ is oxygen.
____ Without oxygen,
____ cells will die
____ within minutes
____ within 3–5 minutes.
____ When you breathe in,
____ your system brings air or oxygen
____ to your respiratory system
____ into your body.
____ The cells use the oxygen,
____ and produce carbon dioxide.
____ This gas leaves your body
____ when you breathe out.

Main Idea

____ Your respiratory system includes your nose,
____ your lungs,
____ and the tubes
____ that connect them.

Details

____ Air enters the body
____ through the nose.
____ The nose gets the air ready
____ for your lungs.
____ If air is very cold,
____ dry,
____ or dirty,
____ it could damage your lungs.
____ Your nose warms,
____ moistens,
____ and cleans the air.
____ The blood supply
____ and mucus keeps it warm
____ and moist.

Level 5

Level: Five

____ The hairs capture the dust
____ from the air.

Main Idea

____ After the air is warmed,
____ moistened,
____ and cleaned,
____ it goes to the throat
____ and down the trachea,
____ or windpipe.

Details

____ The trachea divides into tubes,
____ two tubes
____ bronchial tubes
____ each of which goes into a lung.
____ Inside the lungs,
____ the tubes divide
____ into smaller tubes.
____ The tubes lead to clusters
____ of pouches
____ of tiny pouches
____ called air sacs.
____ A net surrounds each air sac
____ a net of vessels
____ of tiny vessels
____ of blood vessels.

Main Idea

____ Air enters the air sacs
____ air rich in oxygen.

Details

____ Blood vessels contain carbon dioxide
____ vessels around the air sacs
____ blood from cells.
____ The blood contains little oxygen.
____ An exchange takes place.
____ Oxygen passes from the air sacs
____ into the vessels.
____ The blood now has oxygen
____ to deliver to cells.
____ Carbon dioxide passes
____ from the blood vessels
____ into the air sacs.

____ The carbon dioxide leaves your body
____ when you exhale.

74 Ideas

Number of ideas recalled _____

Other ideas recalled, including summary statements and inferences:

Questions for "How Does Your Body Take in Oxygen?"

1. What is *one* of the main ideas of what you have read thus far?
   Implicit: that oxygen is needed by cells; *or* that the air is cleaned and moistened by your nose before it enters the lungs; *or* how air is exchanged inside your lungs.

2. Why do your cells need oxygen?
   Explicit: to do their work; they need it to live

3. When the cells use the oxygen, what other gas do they make?
   Explicit: carbon dioxide

Level: Five

4. How is the air that you breathe cleaned *and* moistened?
   Explicit: nose hairs clean it, and blood supply *and/or* mucous warms and moistens it.

5. Why can't you hold your breath for 20 minutes?
   Implicit: your body would force you to breathe to keep your cells alive.

6. Explain how air goes from your nose to your lungs.
   Explicit: it goes to your throat and down the windpipe or trachea through the bronchial tubes to the lungs. (If the student omits "throat" the answer is still correct, but the student must describe the air going down the windpipe or trachea and through the bronchial tubes.)

7. Why are there two bronchial tubes?
   Implicit: because there are two lungs and so a tube is connected to each one

8. Why is it important that tiny blood vessels surround each air sac?
   Implicit: so that the oxygen can enter the bloodstream and carbon dioxide can be released from the blood into the lungs to exhale; *or* so the air exchange (carbon dioxide for oxygen) can take place.

Without Look-Backs

Number Correct Explicit: _____

Number Correct Implicit: _____

   Total: _____

   _____ Independent: 8 correct

   _____ Instructional: 6–7 correct

   _____ Frustration: 0–5 correct

With Look-Backs

Number Correct Explicit: _____

Number Correct Implicit: _____

   Total: _____

   _____ Independent: 8 correct

   _____ Instructional: 6–7 correct

   _____ Frustration: 0–5 correct

Level 5

The Mining Boom (Modeling Passage for Think-Alouds)

The mining boom in the western United States had begun with the California Gold Rush of 1849. When the Gold Rush ended, miners looked for new opportunities. The merest rumor of gold sent them racing east in search of new strikes. **STOP**

Gold and Silver Strikes

In 1859, two young prospectors struck gold in the Sierra Nevada Mountains. Suddenly, another miner, Henry Comstock, appeared. "The land is mine," he cried and demanded to be made a partner. From then on, Comstock boasted about "his" mine. The strike became known as the Comstock Lode. A lode is a rich vein of gold or silver. **STOP**

Comstock and his partners often complained about the heavy blue sand that was mixed in with the gold. It clogged the devices used for separating the gold and made the gold hard to reach. When the Mexican miners took the "danged blue stuff" to an expert in California, tests showed it was loaded with silver. Comstock had stumbled onto one of the richest silver mines in the world. **STOP**

Miners moved into many other areas of the West. Some found valuable ore in Montana and Idaho. Others struck it rich in Colorado. In the 1870s, miners discovered gold in the Black Hills of South Dakota. In the late 1890s, thousands rushed north to Alaska after major gold strikes were made there. **STOP**

Boom Towns and Ghost Towns

Towns sprang up near all the major mining sites. First, miners built a tent city near the diggings. Then, thousands of people came to supply the miners' needs. Traders brought mule teams loaded with tools, food, and clothing. Merchants hauled in wagonloads of supplies and set up stores. **STOP**

Soon, wood-frame houses, hotels, restaurants, and stores replaced the tents. For example, it took less than a year for the mining camp at the Comstock Lode to become the boom town of Virginia City, Nevada. **STOP**

Many boom towns lasted for only a few years. When the gold or silver was gone, miners moved away. Without miners for customers, businesses often had to close. In this way, a boom town could quickly go bust and turn into a ghost town. Still, some boom towns survived and prospered even after the mines shut down. In these towns, miners stayed and found new ways to make a living. **STOP**

The surge of miners into the West created problems. Mines and towns polluted clear mountain streams. Miners cut down forests to get wood for buildings. Few miners got rich quickly. Much of the gold and silver lay deep underground. It could be reached only with costly machinery. Eventually, most mining in the West was taken over by large companies that could afford to buy the equipment. **STOP**

From *The American Nation* by James West Davidson, Pedro Castillo, and Michael B. Stoff. Copyright © 2002 Pearson Education, Inc., or its affiliates. Adapted by permission. All Rights Reserved.

Pele

Pele was born in the South American country of Brazil. He lived in a small village and his family was very poor. But Pele had a dream. He wanted to become a professional soccer player. He could not afford a soccer ball so he fashioned one. He took an old sock, stuffed it with newspapers, and sewed it together with string. It was a poor substitute, but it was better than nothing. Pele and his friends formed their own team. They did not have enough money to purchase shoes, but that did not stop them. They played barefoot and became known as the "barefoot team."

Pele and his friends saved their money, and eventually the team was able to get a regular ball and shoes. Pele discovered that the ball could be better controlled when he wore shoes. Pele and his team practiced continuously. They soon began playing older and more established teams from the big cities. The team began to win most of its games. Pele was the star of the team. People thought this was amazing because he was only eleven years old!

Pele's skill at soccer came to the attention of influential people, and when he was fifteen, he was signed by the Santos team. Pele led the Santos team to many championships. He also led the Brazilian national team to three world championships. Pele also holds many records and has scored over twelve hundred goals in his career as a professional player.

Pele decided to retire in 1974. Then he changed his mind and came to the United States, where he joined the New York Cosmos. Soccer had not been very popular in the United States up to this point, but Pele's presence had a dramatic effect. Crowds at games doubled and tripled as people came to see the famous and exciting Pele. Games began to be shown on television. Soccer gained in popularity and many children in the United States began to play soccer. Soccer is now one of the most popular sports in the United States, due in part to the dream of a young boy in Brazil.

Abraham Lincoln

When Abraham Lincoln was nineteen years old, he visited the city of New Orleans. He saw things he would never forget. He saw black people being sold in slave markets. They were chained together and treated like animals. Lincoln watched little children being sold to strangers and taken away from their parents. Lincoln was heartbroken and these memories stayed with him for the rest of his life. Although slavery was allowed in many states of the Union, Lincoln believed that it was wrong and he was not afraid to say so.

In 1858, Lincoln ran for the United States Senate against Stephen Douglas. There was much talk about slavery. Should the owning of slaves be allowed in new states that were just coming into the Union? Douglas said that the decision to own slaves was up to each individual person. Lincoln said that slavery must not be allowed to spread because it was wrong. But he knew that it would not be easy to end slavery in those states that had allowed it for so many years. Lincoln believed it was important to keep the United States strong. He felt that slavery weakened the country. In one speech, he said the country could not last half slave and half free. He said, "A house divided against itself cannot stand." Lincoln lost the election to the Senate, but he became well known for his views. In 1860 he ran for president of the United States.

The slave states opposed Lincoln as president. They did not want to abolish slavery. They threatened to leave the Union if Lincoln was elected. When he became president, the slave states carried out their threat. A terrible war broke out between the northern and southern states. At times, members of the same family were fighting against one another.

In 1863, Lincoln gave an order called the Emancipation Proclamation, which ended slavery. The war finally ended two years later. The southern states once more became part of the Union, but slavery was no longer allowed. No more would little children be torn from their parents and sold to strangers. Abraham Lincoln had achieved his goal.

The Early Life of Lois Lowry

Lois Lowry, author of two Newbery Award–winning books, *Number the Stars* (1990) and *The Giver* (1994), was born in Hawaii in 1937. Like many authors she uses childhood events and her feelings about them as ideas for her books. Because her father was an army dentist, the family moved often, rarely settling in one place for more than a few years. Perhaps because of the many moves and Lois's shy personality, making friends was difficult, and Lois became very close with her older sister, Helen.

By the time she was 3 years old Lois could read, and books became a central part of her life. Already a keen observer of the world around her, books fed her active imagination. Lois's mother fostered the love of books by reading to the children frequently. When Lois was 9 and her sister, Helen, was 12, their mother read *The Yearling* to them. The life of one of the characters, Jody, made Lois want to be a boy. She wanted a life like Jody's, to be poor, living in a swamp, having animals as friends. Jody was only one of the characters who filled Lois's life with adventure. Her love of books drew her to the public library. When she was 10 years old, she found a book called *A Tree Grows in Brooklyn.* The title piqued her curiosity and she decided to check it out. The librarian told her it was not a book for children, but Lois was insistent. Before Lois arrived home the librarian had called to warn her mother that Lois had checked out a book that was not suitable for children. Her mother was polite but not concerned. She had read the book herself and recalled nothing that would harm her 10-year-old daughter. Lois loved the book and wanted to be like Francie, making a better life for herself through grit and determination. Lois was drawn to characters with lives of adventure, and given the right opportunity Lois would explore the world herself.

After World War II Lois's father was stationed in Japan. Lois, her mother, sister, and younger brother, Jon, joined him there in 1948. The family lived in an American enclave where all the houses were American style, all the neighbors American, and the little community had their own movie-theater, church, library, and elementary school. Lois didn't understand why they lived in this enclave with the excitement of Tokyo all around them. At 11 years of age, Lois often sneaked out of the American area to explore the city of Tokyo. She still remembers the smells: fish and charcoal; and the sounds: music, shouting, and the clatter of wooden wheels. But most of all she remembers children her own age dressed in dark blue school uniforms. Although she saw the children frequently, she never spoke to them. They must have found her curious, a light-haired girl riding her bicycle alone in the city. Through her journeys she came face to face with the tragedy of war. She found families whose homes had been destroyed living in packing boxes. The images of Tokyo, like all the other experiences of her early life, remain with her to emerge in her stories.

Lois began writing for young people in the mid-1970s at the suggestion of an editor of a publishing company. She has been writing for young people ever since. Her goal as a writer for young people is to help her readers cope with the difficulties of being young in a world that doesn't always respect youth.

The Lifeline of the Nile

The Nile River is the longest river in the world. It begins in East Africa and flows northward into Egypt. Surrounded by hot, sandy deserts, the Nile brought life to the people who lived by it. In ancient Egypt, the Nile irrigated land that stretched about five miles on both sides of the river. This is where Egyptian civilization began and agriculture thrived.

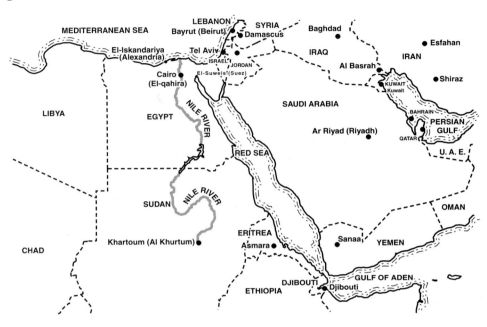

The Nile overflowed because of heavy rains in east Africa. People living near the Nile planted seeds after the floods and harvested in late summer. They called this area "black land" because the land was very fertile. Wheat and barley were the most important crops in ancient Egypt. Papyrus was another valuable crop. The Egyptians used its stems to make paper. The papermaking process involved cutting thin strips from the plant's stem and pressing them together. When the pressed strips dried, they produced a smooth surface. Papyrus became widely used for record keeping.

The Nile was also a means of transporting goods; however, the geography of the Nile caused some roadblocks for travelers. Six cataracts or waterfalls break up the flow of the Nile. The cataracts made it impossible to sail south to East Africa without taking a boat out of the water and carrying it. Because the river moves from south to north, a boat also needed sails to move it.

The Nile gave the Egyptians many gifts but it also caused problems. Although the Nile did flood regularly, it did not always do so in the same way. Sometimes heavy rains caused too much water to overflow. Crops were destroyed and people lost their lives. Other times, the Nile did not flood enough and crops could not grow. When this happened, Egyptians used the food they stored from surplus harvests.

Building Pyramids

Ancient Egyptian kings are best known for the huge structures they built called pyramids. These large stone buildings served as houses or tombs for the dead. The Egyptians believed that kings, or pharaohs, remained gods even after death, and that pyramids were their palaces. Kings were buried with their possessions. The Egyptians thought that kings took their possessions with them to the afterlife or the life that continued after death. **STOP**

Because the afterlife was more important than life on earth, the Egyptians took great care in preparing kings for burial. They believed the bodies of the pharaohs needed to be preserved. They used a process called mummification. **STOP** Mummification took 70 days. First, the Egyptians removed all organs except the heart from the body. Then they rubbed oils and perfumes over the body. Next, they wrapped the body in linen bandages. Finally, the mummy, or preserved body, was placed in a coffin and put into a tomb. **STOP**

Archaeologists and historians estimate that some pyramids took about 20 years to build and that slave labor was not used. When the Nile River was flooding, farmers could not work in their fields. They were then available to work on a pyramid. **STOP** Perhaps as many as 20,000 workers cut more than two million blocks of heavy stone from cliffs to the south. Then they dragged the stones with rope to ramps that led to the building site.

Building the tombs was important but many people died because the work was difficult and dangerous. Workers labored eight hours every day for ten days in a row. Then they received one day of rest. **STOP** They were paid with food. The pharaohs counted on the tomb builders to be both committed and courageous. Because no one knew how long the pharaoh would live, they had to work quickly and accurately. **STOP**

Temperature and Humidity

When you go outside the air temperature is often the first weather condition that you notice. In the summer, if the sun has been out the air usually feels warm. On hot days the air temperature can be above 90°. If there are clouds the air often feels cooler because the clouds have blocked some of the heat from the sun's rays. The air is cooler at very high altitudes because the air is less dense and the warm ground is too far away to affect air temperature. Also, there are fewer molecules to absorb the sun's energy.

Humidity is moisture in the air in the form of a gas called water vapor. This water vapor comes from oceans, lakes, rainfall, and other sources from which water evaporates into the air.

Sometimes the air has more water vapor than at other times. The amount of water vapor that the air can hold depends largely on the air temperature. The warmer the air temperature, the more water vapor it can hold.

Meteorologists refer to relative humidity when reporting how much water vapor is in the air. Relative humidity is a ratio that compares the amount of water vapor in the air to the largest amount of moisture the air can hold at that temperature. A 65% relative humidity means the air is holding 65% of the water vapor it can hold at that temperature.

Once the air has reached 100 percent relative humidity, it can't hold any more water vapor. When this happens water vapor condenses, or changes from a gas to a liquid. The temperature at which water vapor condenses is called a dew point. Water droplets form on a plant when the night air cools and reaches its dew point.

Clouds and Precipitation

Clouds are mostly water. To understand how clouds form, remember how changes in temperature affect humidity. **STOP** Think of a clear spring day when the sun warms the ground, which in turn warms the air. Warm air holds a certain amount of water, and warm air rises. Eventually, the warm air cools when it joins the cooler air away from the ground. At the cooler temperature the air cannot hold as much water vapor. As the water vapor separates from the air, it connects with dust and microscopic particles of salt to form tiny drops of water. They are so small and light that they float in the air. Collections of millions of these droplets form clouds. **STOP**

As clouds move in the wind and evaporate, they may take on different shapes. Clouds may be classified into a few basic kinds with a few different shapes. **STOP** The types of clouds are classified according to their height above the ground. And the names of clouds give a clue to their appearance. For example, low clouds that are close to the ground are usually thick, even sheets. The term *strato* means "sheetlike," so the low sheetlike clouds are called stratus clouds. You can see these clouds in the first photo.

Middle-level clouds may appear in groups in an otherwise blue sky. *Cumulo* means "pile or heap," so these middle-level groups of clouds are a type of cumulus cloud. These are pictured in the second photo below.

High clouds that are wispy with curled edges across a background of blue sky are called cirrus clouds because *cirro* means "curl." The third photo is a good example of cirrus clouds. **STOP** Finally, there are clouds that build upon each other into very high vertical clouds. Because they occur in heaps, they are a type of cumulus cloud, but because they often result in thunderstorms they are called cumulonimbus because *nimbo* means "rain." **STOP**

Clouds are associated with rain and snow. Most rain that occurs in the United States begins as snow. Ice crystals that are high in the cirrus clouds grow when more and more water vapor condenses on them. **STOP** Eventually, they become so heavy that the crystals start to fall. When ice crystals fall through clouds, they may collide and combine with other ice crystals or water droplets. When the crystals become too heavy to float in the air, they drop as precipitation. **STOP**

If all the bands of air that the crystals fall through are cold, then the precipitation reaches the ground as snow. If the ice crystals fall far enough through warm air, they reach the ground as rain.

Sometimes if a band of cold air is near the ground, the rain becomes colder and freezes when it hits the ground. This is freezing rain that becomes ice on the ground, making walking and driving dangerous. **STOP**

Hail is formed when ice crystals are thrown up and down within a cumulonimbus cloud. Water collects on the crystal as it falls through the cloud and freezes on the crystal as it rises higher in the cloud. The hailstone grows larger in this way until it becomes too heavy to float and then falls to the ground. **STOP**

Examiner Copy Think-Aloud Protocol

Instructions for Modeling Thinking Aloud: Have you ever heard the term *thinking aloud?* When people read, they usually think about what they are reading. Sometimes they think to themselves and other times they think aloud. I'm going to show you how to think aloud by reading this text and when I come to the stop marks, I will tell you what I am thinking. After I have shown you how to do it, I will ask you to do it on the next material that you read.

Read aloud the next two sections while the student follows along in his or her copy of the text. Read what is written in italics. And make it sound like you are really thinking aloud.

The Mining Boom

The mining boom in the western United States had begun with the California Gold Rush of 1849. When the Gold Rush ended, miners looked for new opportunities. The merest rumor of gold sent them racing east in search of new strikes. **STOP** *I saw a movie about the Gold Rush and how people fought each other over a tiny patch of land if they thought there was gold on it. A lot of people died and most of them never really found any gold. (Reporting prior knowledge)*

Gold and Silver Strikes

In 1859, two young prospectors struck gold in the Sierra Nevada Mountains. Suddenly, another miner, Henry Comstock, appeared. "The land is mine," he cried and demanded to be made a partner. From then on, Comstock boasted about "his" mine. The strike became known as the Comstock Lode. A lode is a rich vein of gold or silver. **STOP** *I wonder why the two miners just let him butt in like that and take over. Did they ask for any proof that the land was his? (Question that indicates understanding)*

Comstock and his partners often complained about the heavy blue sand that was mixed in with the gold. It clogged the devices used for separating the gold and made the gold hard to reach. When the Mexican miners took the "danged blue stuff" to an expert in California, tests showed it was loaded with silver. Comstock had stumbled onto one of the richest silver mines in the world. **STOP** *Comstock wasn't much of a miner not to have checked the blue stuff himself. He was certainly very lucky but it doesn't seem really fair that he should make all the money when it was the Mexicans who found out what the blue sand was. (Making new meaning)*

Now ask the student whether he or she would rather read silently to each STOP signal or have you continue to read orally. Do what the student prefers and continue to the end of the selection.

Miners moved into many other areas of the West. Some found valuable ore in Montana and Idaho. Others struck it rich in Colorado. In the 1870s, miners discovered gold in the Black Hills of South Dakota. In the late 1890s, thousands rushed north to Alaska after major gold strikes were made

Level: Six

there. **STOP** *This is just telling where they found ore in different states other than California such as Alaska and Montana. (Paraphrasing/summarizing)*

Boom Towns and Ghost Towns

Towns sprang up near all the major mining sites. First, miners built a tent city near the diggings. Then, thousands of people came to supply the miners' needs. Traders brought mule teams loaded with tools, food, and clothing. Merchants hauled in wagonloads of supplies and set up stores. **STOP** *This makes a lot of sense. You go where the business is. If I were living then, I probably wouldn't have wanted to be a miner but I wouldn't mind being a shopkeeper. It was probably an easier job. (Identifying personally)*

Soon, wood-frame houses, hotels, restaurants, and stores replaced the tents. For example, it took less than a year for the mining camp at the Comstock Lode to become the boom town of Virginia City, Nevada. **STOP** *I just figured it out. They were called boom towns because business was booming there. I never thought of it that way before. (Noting understanding)*

Many boom towns lasted for only a few years. When the gold or silver was gone, miners moved away. Without miners for customers, businesses often had to close. In this way, a boom town could quickly go bust and turn into a ghost town. Still, some boom towns survived and prospered even after the mines shut down. In these towns, miners stayed and found new ways to make a living. **STOP** *They probably became farmers or raised cattle. Maybe they made stuff like furniture, wagons, or guns. The ones who stayed had to be pretty clever to survive. (Making new meaning)*

The surge of miners into the West created problems. Mines and towns polluted clear mountain streams. Miners cut down forests to get wood for buildings. Few miners got rich quickly. Much of the gold and silver lay deep underground. It could be reached only with costly machinery. Eventually, most mining in the West was taken over by large companies that could afford to buy the equipment. **STOP** *This doesn't make a lot of sense to me. How did they know it was underground if it was so deep? (Noting lack of understanding)*

Level 6

Narrative

Concept Questions:

Who is Pele?

_____

_____

_____ (3-2-1-0)

What is soccer?

_____

_____

_____ (3-2-1-0)

What are professional athletes?

_____

_____

_____ (3-2-1-0)

Why do some sports become popular?

_____

_____

_____ (3-2-1-0)

Score: _____ /12 = _____ %

_____ FAM _____ UNFAM

Prediction:

_____

_____

"Pele"

Pele was born in the South American country of Brazil. He lived in a small village and his family was very poor. But Pele had a dream. He wanted to be-come a professional soccer player. He could not af-ford a soccer ball so he <u>fashioned</u> one. He took an old sock, stuffed it with newspapers, and <u>sewed</u> it together with string. It was a poor substitute, but it was better than nothing. Pele and his friends formed their own team. They did not have enough money to purchase shoes, but that did not stop them. They played barefoot and became known as the "barefoot team."

Pele and his friends saved their money, and eventually the team was able to get a regular ball and shoes. Pele discovered that the ball could be better <u>controlled</u> when he wore shoes. Pele and his team practiced continuously. They soon began play-ing older and more established teams from the big cities. The team began to win most of its games. Pele was the star of the team. People thought this was amazing because he was only eleven years old!

Pele's skill at soccer came to the <u>attention</u> of in-fluential people, and when he was fifteen, he was signed by the Santos team. Pele led the Santos team to many <u>championships</u>. He also led the Brazilian national team to three world <u>championships</u>. Pele also holds many records and has scored over twelve hundred goals in his career as a professional player.

Pele decided to retire in 1974. Then he changed his mind and came to the United States, where he joined the New York Cosmos. Soccer had not been very popular in the United States up to this point,

Level: Six

but Pele's presence had a dramatic effect. Crowds at games doubled and tripled as people came to see the famous and exciting Pele. Games began to be shown on television. Soccer gained in popularity and many children in the United States began to play soccer. Soccer is now one of the most popular sports in the United States, due in part to the dream of a young boy in Brazil. (354 words)

From *Holt Social Studies*, edited by JoAnn Cangemi, copyright © 1983 by Holt, Rinehart, and Winston, Inc. Reproduced by permission of Houghton Mifflin Harcourt Publishing Company. This material may not be reproduced in any form or by any means without the prior written permission of the publisher.

Number of Total Miscues
(Total Accuracy): _____

Number of Meaning-Change Miscues
(Total Acceptability): _____

Total Accuracy		Total Acceptability
0–8 miscues	____ Independent	____ 0–8 miscues
9–36 miscues	____ Instructional	____ 9–19 miscues
37+ miscues	____ Frustration	____ 20+ miscues

Rate: 354 × 60 = 21,240/ ____ seconds = ____ WPM

Correct WPM: (354 – ____ errors) × 60 =
____ /____ seconds = ____ CWPM

Retelling Scoring Sheet for "Pele"

Setting/Background

____ Pele was born
____ in Brazil.
____ Pele's family was poor.

Goal

____ Pele had a dream.
____ He wanted

____ to become a soccer player
____ a professional player.

Events

____ He could not afford a ball.
____ He fashioned a ball.
____ He took a sock
____ and stuffed it
____ with newspapers
____ and sewed it together
____ with string.
____ Pele
____ and his friends formed a team
____ their own team.
____ They did not have enough money
____ to purchase shoes.
____ They played barefoot
____ and became known
____ as the "barefoot team."
____ Pele
____ and his friends saved their money,
____ and eventually
____ the team was able
____ to get a ball
____ a regular ball
____ and shoes.
____ Pele discovered
____ that the ball could be controlled
____ better
____ when he wore shoes.
____ They began
____ to play teams
____ from big cities
____ and to win games
____ most of their games.
____ Pele was the star.
____ He was only eleven.
____ He was signed
____ by the Santos team.

Resolution

____ Pele led the team
____ to championships.
____ He led the team
____ the Brazilian team

Level: Six

___ to championships
___ world championships.
___ Pele held many records.
___ Pele decided
___ to retire
___ in 1974.
___ Then he changed his mind
___ and came to the United States,
___ where he joined the Cosmos
___ the New York Cosmos.
___ Pele's presence had an effect.
___ Crowds doubled
___ and tripled
___ and people came
___ to see Pele.
___ Soccer gained
___ in popularity.
___ Soccer is now one
___ of the most popular sports
___ in the United States.

66 Ideas

Number of ideas recalled _____

Other ideas recalled, including inferences:

Questions for "Pele"

1. What was Pele's main goal?
   Implicit: to become a professional soccer player

2. What did Pele use to make a soccer ball?
   Explicit: an old sock, string, and newspaper

3. What was Pele's team called when they had no shoes?
   Explicit: the barefoot team

4. Why did the purchase of shoes affect the number of games won by Pele's team?
   Implicit: they played better because they could control the ball more effectively

5. Why was it amazing that Pele became a star at the age of eleven?
   Implicit: he was very young to be playing so well against older and more established teams from the big cities

6. How old was Pele when he was signed by a professional soccer team?
   Explicit: fifteen

7. What American team did Pele join?
   Explicit: New York Cosmos

8. How did Pele's presence help to make soccer popular in the United States?
   Implicit: people came to see Pele and grew to like the game itself

Without Look-Backs

Number Correct Explicit: _____
Number Correct Implicit: _____
        Total: _____
        _____ Independent: 8 correct
        _____ Instructional: 6–7 correct
        _____ Frustration: 0–5 correct

With Look-Backs

Number Correct Explicit: _____
Number Correct Implicit: _____
        Total: _____
        _____ Independent: 8 correct
        _____ Instructional: 6–7 correct
        _____ Frustration: 0–5 correct

Level: Six

Narrative

Concept Questions:

Who was Abraham Lincoln?

_____

_____

_____ (3-2-1-0)

What are the evils of slavery?

_____

_____

_____ (3-2-1-0)

Why was the Civil War fought?

_____

_____

_____ (3-2-1-0)

What were the results of the Civil War?

_____

_____

_____ (3-2-1-0)

Score: _____ /12 = _____ %

_____ FAM _____ UNFAM

Prediction:

_____

_____

"Abraham Lincoln"

When Abraham Lincoln was nineteen years old, he visited the city of New Orleans. He saw things he would never forget. He saw black people being sold in slave markets. They were chained together and treated like animals. Lincoln watched little children being sold to strangers and taken away from their parents. Lincoln was heartbroken and these memories stayed with him for the rest of his life. Although slavery was allowed in many states of the Union, Lincoln believed that it was wrong and he was not afraid to say so.

In 1858, Lincoln ran for the United States Senate against Stephen Douglas. There was much talk about slavery. Should the owning of slaves be allowed in new states that were just coming into the Union? Douglas said that the decision to own slaves was up to each individual person. Lincoln said that slavery must not be allowed to spread because it was wrong. But he knew that it would not be easy to end slavery in those states that had allowed it for so many years. Lincoln believed that it was important to keep the United States strong. He felt that slavery weakened the country. In one speech, he said the country could not last half slave and half free. He said, "A house divided against itself cannot stand." Lincoln lost the election to the Senate, but he became well known for his views. In 1860 he ran for president of the United States.

The slave states opposed Lincoln as president. They did not want to abolish slavery. They threatened to leave the Union if Lincoln was elected. When he became president, the slave states carried out their threat. A terrible war broke out between the northern and southern states. At times, members of the same family were fighting against one another.

In 1863, Lincoln gave an order called the Emancipation Proclamation, which ended slavery. The war finally ended two years later. The southern states once more became part of the Union, but slavery was no longer allowed. No more would little children be torn from their parents and sold to strangers. Abraham Lincoln had achieved his goal. (358 words)

Number of Total Miscues
(Total Accuracy): _____

Number of Meaning-Change Miscues
(Total Acceptability): _____

Total Accuracy		**Total Acceptability**
0–8 miscues	_____ Independent	_____ 0–8 miscues
9–37 miscues	_____ Instructional	_____ 9–19 miscues
38+ miscues	_____ Frustration	_____ 20+ miscues

Rate: 358 × 60 = 21,480/ _____ seconds = _____ WPM

Correct WPM: (358 – _____ errors) × 60 =
_____ / _____ seconds = _____ CWPM

Retelling Scoring Sheet for "Abraham Lincoln"

Setting/Background

___ When Abraham Lincoln was nineteen,
___ he visited the city
___ of New Orleans.
___ He saw things
___ he would never forget.

___ He saw black people
___ being sold
___ in slave markets.
___ They were chained together
___ and treated like animals.
___ Lincoln watched children
___ being sold
___ to strangers
___ and taken away
___ from their parents.

Goal

___ Lincoln believed
___ that slavery was wrong.
___ He was not afraid
___ to say so.

Events

___ Lincoln ran
___ for the Senate
___ against Stephen Douglas.
___ Lincoln said
___ that slavery must not spread.
___ He felt
___ that slavery weakened the country.
___ Lincoln lost the election
___ to the Senate.
___ He ran
___ for president.
___ The slave states opposed Lincoln.
___ They did not want
___ to abolish slavery.
___ They threatened
___ to leave the union
___ if Lincoln was elected.
___ When Lincoln became president,
___ a war broke out
___ a war between the states.

Resolution

___ Lincoln gave an order
___ called the Emancipation Proclamation,
___ which ended slavery.
___ The war ended.
___ The southern states became part

Level: Six

____ of the Union
____ but slavery was not allowed.
____ Abraham Lincoln had achieved his goal.

47 Ideas

Number of ideas recalled _____

Other ideas recalled, including inferences:

Questions for "Abraham Lincoln"

1. What was Abraham Lincoln's main goal?
   Implicit: to end slavery in the United States

2. Name one thing that Abraham Lincoln saw in the slave markets of New Orleans.
   Explicit: blacks chained together; blacks treated like animals; blacks being sold; children being separated from parents; *or* children being sold to strangers

3. How did the sights of the slave market influence Abraham Lincoln's later life?
   Implicit: he was against slavery and fought to end it; *or* it made him sick and he wanted to stop it

4. What office did Abraham Lincoln run for against Douglas?
   Explicit: he ran for the U.S. Senate

5. What did the southern states threaten to do if Abraham Lincoln was elected president?
   Explicit: leave the Union

6. Why did the southern states oppose Abraham Lincoln as president?
   Implicit: he was against slavery and he would fight to end it in their states

7. How did Abraham Lincoln's prediction, "A house divided against itself cannot stand," come true?
   Implicit: the war between the states broke out

8. What did the Emancipation Proclamation do?
   Explicit: it ended slavery

Without Look-Backs

Number Correct Explicit: _____
Number Correct Implicit: _____
   Total: _____
   _____ Independent: 8 correct
   _____ Instructional: 6–7 correct
   _____ Frustration: 0–5 correct

With Look-Backs

Number Correct Explicit: _____
Number Correct Implicit: _____
   Total: _____
   _____ Independent: 8 correct
   _____ Instructional: 6–7 correct
   _____ Frustration: 0–5 correct

Level 6

Level: Six

Narrative

> **Concept Questions:**
>
> Who is Lois Lowry?
>
> _____
>
> _____
>
> _____ (3-2-1-0)
>
> What does "imagination" mean?
>
> _____
>
> _____
>
> _____ (3-2-1-0)
>
> What does it mean to have a shy personality?
>
> _____
>
> _____
>
> _____ (3-2-1-0)
>
> What does "emerge" mean?
>
> _____
>
> _____
>
> _____ (3-2-1-0)
>
> **Score:** _____ /12 = _____ %
>
> _____ FAM _____ UNFAM
>
> **Prediction:**
>
> _____
>
> _____

"The Early Life of Lois Lowry"

Lois Lowry, author of two Newbery Award–winning books, *Number the Stars* (1990) and *The Giver* (1994), was born in Hawaii in 1937. Like many authors she uses childhood events and her feelings about them as ideas for her books. Because her father was an army dentist, the family moved often, rarely settling in one place for more than a few years. Perhaps because of the many moves and Lois's shy personality, making friends was difficult, and Lois became very close with her older sister, Helen.

By the time she was 3 years old Lois could read, and books became a central part of her life. Already a keen observer of the world around her, books fed her active imagination. Lois's mother fostered the love of books by reading to the children frequently. When Lois was 9 and her sister, Helen, was 12, their mother read *The Yearling* to them. The life of one of the characters, Jody, made Lois want to be a boy. She wanted a life like Jody's, to be poor, living in a swamp, having animals as friends. Jody was only one of the characters who filled Lois's life with adventure. Her love of books drew her to the public library. When she was 10 years old, she found a book called *A Tree Grows in Brooklyn*. The title piqued her curiosity and she decided to check it out. The librarian told her it was not a book for children, but Lois was <u>insistent</u>. Before Lois arrived home the librarian had called to warn her mother that Lois had checked out a book that was not suitable for children. Her mother was polite but not concerned. She had read the book herself and

Level: Six

recalled nothing that would harm her 10-year-old daughter. Lois loved the book and wanted to be like Francie, making a better life for herself through grit and determination. Lois was drawn to characters with lives of adventure, and given the right opportunity Lois would explore the world herself.

After World War II Lois's father was stationed in Japan. Lois, her mother, sister, and younger brother, Jon, joined him there in 1948. The family lived in an American enclave where all the houses were American style, all the neighbors American, and the little community had their own movie-theater, church, library, and elementary school. Lois didn't understand why they lived in this enclave with the excitement of Tokyo all around them. At 11 years of age, Lois often sneaked out of the American area to explore the city of Tokyo. She still remembers the smells: fish and charcoal; and the sounds: music, shouting, and the clatter of wooden wheels. But most of all she remembers children her own age dressed in dark blue school uniforms. Although she saw the children frequently, she never spoke to them. They must have found her curious, a light-haired girl riding her bicycle alone in the city. Through her journeys she came face to face with the tragedy of war. She found families whose homes had been destroyed living in packing boxes. The images of Tokyo, like all the other experiences of her early life, remain with her to <u>emerge</u> in her stories.

Lois began writing for young people in the mid-1970s at the suggestion of an editor of a publishing company. She has been writing for young people ever since. Her goal as a writer for young people is to help her readers cope with the difficulties of being young in a world that doesn't always respect youth. (591 words)

Number of Total Miscues
(Total Accuracy): _____

Number of Meaning-Change Miscues
(Total Acceptability): _____

Total Accuracy		**Total Acceptability**
0–14 miscues ____ Independent	____	0–14 miscues
15–62 miscues ____ Instructional	____	15–32 miscues
63+ miscues ____ Frustration	____	33+ miscues

Rate: 591 × 60 = 35,460/ _____ seconds = _____ WPM

Correct WPM: (591 – _____ errors) × 60 = _____ /_____ seconds = _____ CWPM

Retelling Scoring Sheet for "The Early Life of Lois Lowry"

Setting/Background
____ Lois Lowry was born in Hawaii.
____ Lois Lowry is the author of books
____ two books
____ award–winning books,
____ *Number the Stars*
____ and *The Giver.*

Goal
____ She uses childhood events
____ and her feelings about them
____ as ideas for her books.

Level: Six

Events

____ Because her father was a dentist,

____ an Army dentist

____ the family moved often

____ rarely settling in one place

____ for more than a few years.

____ Because of the moves

____ and Lois's shy personality,

____ making friends was difficult

____ and Lois became close with her sister,

____ her older sister,

____ Helen.

____ By the time she was 3 years old,

____ Lois could read.

Goal

____ Books became a central part

____ of her life.

Events

____ A keen observer

____ of the world,

____ books fed her imagination.

____ Lois's mother fostered the love of books

____ by reading to the children frequently.

____ Their mother read *The Yearling* to them.

Goal

____ The book made Lois want to be a boy.

____ She wanted a life like Jody's,

____ to be poor,

____ living in a swamp,

____ and having animals as friends.

Events

____ Her love of books drew her

____ to the public library.

____ When she was 10 years old,

____ she found a book

____ called *A Tree Grows in Brooklyn*.

Goal

____ The title piqued her curiosity

____ and she decided to check it out.

Events

____ The librarian told her

____ it was not a book for children,

____ but Lois was insistent.

____ Before Lois arrived home,

____ the librarian had called

____ to warn her mother.

____ Her mother was polite

____ but not concerned.

____ She had read the book herself

____ and recalled nothing

____ that would harm her daughter.

____ Lois loved the book.

Goals

____ Lois wanted to be like Francie,

____ making a better life

____ through grit

____ and determination.

____ Lois was drawn to characters

____ with lives of adventure,

____ and given the opportunity

____ Lois would explore the world.

Events

____ After World War II,

____ Lois's father was stationed in Japan.

____ Lois,

____ her mother,

____ sister,

____ and brother joined him there.

____ The family lived in an enclave

____ an American enclave

____ where the houses were in an American style

____ and all the neighbors were American.

____ The community had a movie theater,

____ church,

____ library,

____ and school.

____ Lois didn't understand

____ why they lived there

____ with the excitement of Tokyo

____ around them.

Level: Six

Goal

____ Lois often sneaked out
____ to explore Tokyo.

Events

____ She still remembers the smells
____ of fish
____ and charcoal
____ and the sounds of
____ music,
____ shouting,
____ and the clatter of wheels.
____ She remembers the children
____ dressed in uniforms
____ dark uniforms
____ blue uniforms
____ school uniforms.
____ She never spoke to them.
____ They must have found her curious,
____ riding her bicycle
____ alone.
____ She came face to face
____ with the tragedy of war.
____ She found families
____ whose homes had been destroyed
____ living in boxes
____ in packing boxes.
____ The images of Tokyo remain,
____ like all other early experiences,
____ to emerge in her stories.

Resolution

____ Lois began writing
____ for young people
____ in the mid-1970s
____ at the suggestion of an editor
____ of a publishing company.
____ She has been writing
____ for young people
____ ever since.

Goal

____ Her goal is to help readers
____ cope with the difficulties

____ of being young
____ in a world
____ that doesn't always respect youth.

120 Ideas

Number of ideas recalled _____

Other ideas recalled, including summary statements and inferences:

Questions for "The Early Life of Lois Lowry"

1. Who is Lois Lowry?
   Explicit: author of books for young people. If the student says only, "An author," ask, "Who does she write for?" or "What kind of author?"

2. According to the story, where does Lois Lowry get the ideas for her books?
   Explicit: from things that happened to her as a child and how she felt about them

3. How did the fact that Lois learned to read very young affect her childhood?
   Implicit: books fed her imagination; *or* they became a central part of her life

Level: Six

4. Why didn't Lois's mother get upset when Lois checked out *A Tree Grows in Brooklyn* from the library?
Explicit: her mother had read it and didn't see anything in it that would harm Lois

5. How might Lois's understanding of the main characters in *The Yearling* and *A Tree Grows in Brooklyn* have affected her behavior in Japan?
Implicit: she wanted to have adventures like the characters, so she sneaked out of the American enclave to have adventures

6. What does Lois remember about Tokyo?
Explicit: its smells: fish and charcoal; its sounds: music, shouting, and the clatter of wooden wheels; *or* children her age dressed in dark blue school uniforms. One example of each sound or smell must be provided. If the student says, "Its sounds and smells," ask, "Can you name one smell and one sound?"

7. Why didn't Lois speak to the Japanese school children her age?
Implicit: she was shy; *or* she didn't speak their language

8. Why does Lois write about the difficulties of being young?
Implicit: to help them cope with similar problems; *or* because she had problems when she was young. If the student just names a problem, such as being shy or having to move a lot, ask, "Why would this influence Lois to write about the difficulties of young people?"

Without Look-Backs

Number Correct Explicit: _____

Number Correct Implicit: _____

Total: _____

_____ Independent: 8 correct

_____ Instructional: 6–7 correct

_____ Frustration: 0–5 correct

With Look-Backs

Number Correct Explicit: _____

Number Correct Implicit: _____

Total: _____

_____ Independent: 8 correct

_____ Instructional: 6–7 correct

_____ Frustration: 0–5 correct

Level 6

Level: Six

Expository

Concept Questions:

What happens when there is a flood?

_____

_____

_____ (3-2-1-0)

What does it mean if something thrives?

_____

_____

_____ (3-2-1-0)

What is meant by fertile land?

_____

_____

_____ (3-2-1-0)

What is a harvest?

_____

_____

_____ (3-2-1-0)

Score: _____ /12 = _____ %

_____ FAM _____ UNFAM

Prediction:

_____

_____

"The Lifeline of the Nile"

The Nile River is the longest river in the world. It begins in East Africa and flows northward into Egypt. Surrounded by hot, sandy deserts, the Nile brought life to the people who lived by it. In ancient Egypt, the Nile irrigated land that stretched about five miles on both sides of the river. This is where Egyptian civilization began and agriculture thrived.

The Nile overflowed because of heavy rains in east Africa. People living near the Nile planted seeds after the floods and harvested in late summer. They called this area "black land" because the land was very fertile. Wheat and barley were the most important crops in ancient Egypt. Papyrus was another valuable crop. The Egyptians used its stems to make paper. The papermaking process involved cutting thin strips from the plant's stem and pressing them together. When the pressed strips dried, they produced a smooth surface. Papyrus became widely used for record keeping.

The Nile was also a means of transporting goods; however, the geography of the Nile caused some roadblocks for travelers. Six cataracts or waterfalls break up the flow of the Nile. The cataracts made it impossible to sail south to East Africa without taking a boat out of the water and carrying it. Because the river moves from south to north, a boat also needed sails to move it.

The Nile gave the Egyptians many gifts but it also caused problems. Although the Nile did flood regularly, it did not always do so in the same way. Sometimes heavy rains caused too much water to

Level: Six

overflow. Crops were destroyed and people lost their lives. Other times, the Nile did not flood enough and crops could not grow. When this happened, Egyptians used the food they stored from surplus harvests. (295 words)

Number of Total Miscues
(Total Accuracy): _____

Number of Meaning-Change Miscues
(Total Acceptability): _____

Total Accuracy		**Total Acceptability**
0–7 miscues	____ Independent	____ 0–7 miscues
8–30 miscues	____ Instructional	____ 8–16 miscues
31+ miscues	____ Frustration	____ 17+ miscues

Rate: 295 × 60 = 17,700/ _____ seconds = _____ WPM

Correct WPM: (295 – ____ errors) × 60 =
_____ /_____ seconds = _____ CWPM

Retelling Scoring Sheet for "The Lifeline of the Nile"

Main Idea

____ The Nile River brought life to people
____ in Egypt.

Details

____ The Nile begins in East Africa
____ and flows north
____ into Egypt.
____ The Nile irrigated land
____ for five miles

____ on both sides of the river.
____ Agriculture thrived.

Main Idea

____ They called the area "black land"
____ because the land was very fertile.

Details

____ The Nile overflowed
____ because of heavy rains
____ in East Africa.
____ People planted seeds
____ after the floods
____ and harvested
____ in summer.
____ Wheat
____ and barley were important crops.
____ Papyrus was a valuable crop.
____ The Egyptians used its stems
____ to make paper.
____ Papyrus was used for record keeping.

Main Idea

____ The Nile was a means of transporting goods.

Details

____ The geography caused roadblocks.
____ Cataracts,
____ or waterfalls, break up the flow
____ of the Nile.
____ The cataracts made it impossible
____ to sail south
____ to east Africa
____ without taking a boat
____ out of the water.
____ Because the river moves from south
____ to north,
____ a boat needed sails
____ to move it.

Main Idea

____ The Nile gave gifts
____ to the Egyptians
____ but it also caused problems.

Level: Six

Details

___ Although the Nile did flood
___ regularly,
___ it did not always do so
___ in the same way.
___ Sometimes rains caused too much water
___ to overflow.
___ Crops were destroyed
___ and people lost their lives.
___ Other times,
___ the Nile did not flood enough
___ and crops could not grow.
___ When this happened,
___ Egyptians used the food
___ they stored
___ from surplus harvests.

56 Ideas

Number of ideas recalled _____

Other ideas recalled, including summary statements and inferences:

Questions for "The Lifeline of the Nile"

1. What is this passage mainly about?
   Implicit: the importance of the Nile River to ancient Egypt; *or* how the Nile helped Egypt

2. Why did the Nile River overflow?
   Explicit: because of heavy rains in east Africa

3. Name one important crop that the Egyptians grew.
   Explicit: wheat; barley; *or* papyrus

4. How do we know the ancient Egyptians were a literate people—that is, they could read and write?
   Implicit: papyrus was an important crop that they used to make paper

5. Why did the Egyptians store surplus food?
   Implicit: in case the Nile did not flood enough and crops were poor

6. What is another word for waterfall?
   Explicit: cataract

7. In what direction did the Nile flow?
   Explicit: from south to north

8. Why would a boat need a sail to travel to the south?
   Implicit: you would be going against the current

Without Look-Backs

Number Correct Explicit: _____

Number Correct Implicit: _____

   Total: _____

   _____ Independent: 8 correct

   _____ Instructional: 6–7 correct

   _____ Frustration: 0–5 correct

With Look-Backs

Number Correct Explicit: _____

Number Correct Implicit: _____

   Total: _____

   _____ Independent: 8 correct

   _____ Instructional: 6–7 correct

   _____ Frustration: 0–5 correct

Level 6

Level: Six

Expository

Concept Questions:

What are pyramids?

_____

_____

_____ (3-2-1-0)

What is a pharaoh?

_____

_____

_____ (3-2-1-0)

What is a mummy?

_____

_____

_____ (3-2-1-0)

What is an archaeologist?

_____

_____

_____ (3-2-1-0)

Score: _____ /12 = _____ %

_____ FAM _____ UNFAM

Prediction:

_____

_____

"Building Pyramids"

Ancient Egyptian kings are best known for the huge structures they built called <u>pyramids</u>. These large stone buildings served as houses or tombs for the dead. The Egyptians believed that kings, or pharaohs, remained gods even after death, and that <u>pyramids</u> were their palaces. Kings were buried with their <u>possessions</u>. The Egyptians thought that kings took their <u>possessions</u> with them to the afterlife or the life that continued after death. **STOP**

_____

_____

_____

_____

_____

Because the afterlife was more important than life on earth, the Egyptians took great care in preparing kings for burial. They believed the bodies of the pharaohs needed to be <u>preserved</u>. They used a process called mummification. **STOP**

_____

_____

_____

_____

_____

Mummification took 70 days. First, the Egyptians removed all organs except the heart from the body. Then they rubbed oils and perfumes over the body. Next, they wrapped the body in linen bandages. Finally, the mummy, or <u>preserved</u> body, was placed in a coffin and put into a tomb. **STOP**

Level 6

Level: Six

_____

_____

_____

_____

_____

Archaeologists and historians estimate that some pyramids took about 20 years to build and that slave labor was not used. When the Nile River was flooding, farmers could not work in their fields. They were then available to work on a pyramid. **STOP**

_____

_____

_____

_____

Perhaps as many as 20,000 workers cut more than two million blocks of heavy stone from cliffs to the south. Then they dragged the stones with rope to ramps that led to the building site.

Building the tombs was important but many people died because the work was difficult and dangerous. Workers labored eight hours every day for ten days in a row. Then they received one day of rest. **STOP**

_____

_____

_____

_____

_____

They were paid with food. The pharaohs counted on the tomb builders to be both committed and courageous. Because no one knew how long the pharaoh would live, they had to work quickly and accurately. **STOP**

_____

_____

_____

_____

_____

(303 words)

_____

From _Scott Foresman Social Studies: The World, Grade 6._ Copyright © 2003 Pearson Education, Inc. or its affiliates. Adapted by permission. All Rights Reserved.

Number of Miscues
(Total Accuracy): _____

Number of Meaning-Change Miscues
(Total Acceptability): _____

Total Accuracy		Total Acceptability
0–7 miscues	____ Independent	____ 0–7 miscues
8–32 miscues	____ Instructional	____ 8–16 miscues
33+ miscues	____ Frustration	____ 17+ miscues

Rate: (If you used this passage as a think-aloud passage, you cannot compute rate):

$303 \times 60 = 18,180/$ ____ seconds = ____ WPM

Correct WPM: $(303 -$ ____ errors$) \times 60 =$
____ / ____ seconds = ____ CWPM

Level: Six

Retelling Scoring Sheet for "Building Pyramids"

Main Idea

____ Egyptian kings built pyramids.

Details

____ These buildings served as houses
____ or tombs
____ for the dead.
____ The Egyptians believed
____ that kings
____ or pharaohs remained gods
____ after death.
____ Pyramids were their palaces.
____ Kings were buried
____ with their possessions.
____ The Egyptians thought
____ that kings took their possessions
____ with them
____ to the afterlife.

Main Idea

____ Because the afterlife was important,
____ the Egyptians took care
____ great care
____ in preparing kings
____ for burial.

Details

____ They preserved the bodies
____ of the pharaohs.
____ They used a process
____ called mummification.
____ Mummification took 70 days.
____ The Egyptians removed all organs
____ except the heart
____ from the body.
____ They rubbed oils
____ and perfumes
____ over the body.
____ They wrapped the body
____ in bandages
____ linen bandages.

____ The mummy was placed
____ in a coffin
____ and put into a tomb.

Main Idea

____ Archaeologists estimate
____ that pyramids took 20 years
____ to build
____ and that slave labor was not used.

Details

____ When the Nile River was flooding,
____ farmers could not work in their fields.
____ They worked on a pyramid.
____ As many as 20,000 workers
____ cut blocks
____ of stone
____ heavy stone
____ and dragged them
____ to the site.

Main Idea

____ The work was difficult
____ and dangerous.

Details

____ People died.
____ Workers labored eight hours
____ every day
____ for ten days.
____ Then they received one day
____ of rest.
____ They were paid
____ with food.
____ Because no one knew
____ how long the pharaoh would live,
____ they had to work quickly
____ and accurately.

64 Ideas

Number of ideas recalled _____

Other ideas recalled, including summary statements and inferences:

Level 6

Level: Six

Questions for "Building Pyramids"

1. What is this passage mainly about?
   Implicit: why and how pyramids were built; *or* ancient Egyptian burial practices

2. What was the purpose of pyramids?
   Explicit: they served as houses or tombs for the dead; *or* they were the dead pharaoh's palace

3. Why were pharaohs buried with their possessions?
   Explicit: the Egyptians thought the pharaoh took his possessions with him to the afterlife

4. Why did the ancient Egyptians believe the body of the pharaoh should be preserved?
   Implicit: the pharaoh would need the body in the afterlife

5. What organ did the ancient Egyptians leave in the dead pharaoh's body?
   Explicit: the heart

6. Name one step in the process of mummification.
   Explicit: remove the organs; rub the body with oils and perfumes; *or* wrap the body in linen

7. Why did it take so long to build a pyramid?
   Implicit: pyramids were very large, workers did not have modern tools; *or* workers could only work when they were not farming

8. Why was building a pyramid considered to be important work?
   Implicit: they were preparing for the pharaoh's afterlife; *or* they were working for a god

---

Without Look-Backs

Number Correct Explicit: _____

Number Correct Implicit: _____

Total: _____

_____ Independent: 8 correct

_____ Instructional: 6–7 correct

_____ Frustration: 0–5 correct

With Look-Backs

Number Correct Explicit: _____

Number Correct Implicit: _____

Total: _____

_____ Independent: 8 correct

_____ Instructional: 6–7 correct

_____ Frustration: 0–5 correct

Think-Aloud Summary

Think-Aloud Statements That Indicate Understanding

Paraphrasing/Summarizing _____

Making New Meaning _____

Questioning That Indicates Understanding _____

Noting Understanding _____

Reporting Prior Knowledge _____

Identifying Personally _____

Think-Aloud Statements That Indicate Lack of Understanding

Questioning That Indicates Lack of Understanding _____

Noting Lack of Understanding _____

Level 6

Level: Six

Expository

Concept Questions:

How is air temperature and air density related?

_____

_____

_____ (3-2-1-0)

What is water vapor?

_____

_____

_____ (3-2-1-0)

What is humidity?

_____

_____

_____ (3-2-1-0)

What is a ratio?

_____

_____

_____ (3-2-1-0)

Score: _____ /12 = _____ %

_____ FAM _____ UNFAM

Prediction:

_____

_____

"Temperature and Humidity"

When you go outside the air temperature is often the first weather condition that you notice. In the summer, if the sun has been out the air usually feels warm. On hot days the air temperature can be above 90°. If there are clouds the air often feels cooler because the clouds have blocked some of the heat from the sun's rays. The air is cooler at very high altitudes because the air is less dense and the warm ground is too far away to affect air temperature. Also, there are fewer molecules to absorb the sun's energy.

Humidity is moisture in the air in the form of a gas called water vapor. This water vapor comes from oceans, lakes, rainfall, and other sources from which water evaporates into the air.

Sometimes the air has more water vapor than at other times. The amount of water vapor that the air can hold depends largely on the air temperature. The warmer the air temperature the more water vapor it can hold.

Meteorologists refer to relative humidity when reporting how much water vapor is in the air. Relative humidity is a ratio that compares the amount of water vapor in the air to the largest amount of moisture the air can hold at that temperature. A 65% relative humidity means the air is holding 65% of the water vapor it can hold at that temperature.

Once the air has reached 100 percent relative humidity, it can't hold any more water vapor. When this happens water vapor condenses, or changes from a gas to a liquid. The temperature at which water vapor condenses is called a dew point. Water

Level: Six

droplets form on a plant when the night air cools and reaches its dew point. (291 words)

Number of Total Miscues
(Total Accuracy): _____

Number of Meaning-Change Miscues
(Total Acceptability): _____

Total Accuracy			**Total Acceptability**
0–7 miscues	_____ Independent	_____	0–7 miscues
8–30 miscues	_____ Instructional	_____	8–16 miscues
31+ miscues	_____ Frustration	_____	17+ miscues

Rate: 291 × 60 = 17,460/ _____ seconds = _____ WPM

Correct WPM: (291 – _____ errors) × 60 =
_____ / _____ seconds = _____ CWPM

Retelling Scoring Sheet for "Temperature and Humidity"

Main Idea

___ When you go outside
___ the air temperature is the first condition
___ that you notice.

Details

___ In the summer,
___ if the sun has been out
___ the air feels warm.
___ On hot days
___ the temperature can be above 90°.
___ If there are clouds
___ the air feels cooler
___ because the clouds have blocked the heat
___ from the sun.
___ The air is cooler
___ at high altitudes
___ because the air is less dense
___ and the ground is too far away

___ the warm ground
___ to affect the temperature.
___ There are fewer molecules
___ to absorb the energy
___ of the sun.

Main Idea

___ Humidity is moisture
___ in the air.

Details

___ It is in the form of a gas
___ called water vapor.
___ This comes from oceans,
___ lakes,
___ rainfall,
___ and sources from which water evaporates
___ into the air.

Main Idea

___ Sometimes the air has more water vapor
___ than at other times.

Details

___ The amount that the air can hold depends
___ on the air temperature.
___ The warmer the air temperature,
___ the more water vapor it can hold.

Main Idea

___ Meteorologists refer to relative humidity
___ when reporting
___ how much water vapor is in the air.

Details

___ Relative humidity is a ratio
___ that compares the amount of water vapor
___ in the air
___ to the largest amount
___ of moisture
___ the air can hold
___ at that temperature.
___ A 65% relative humidity means
___ the air is holding 65%
___ of the water vapor
___ it can hold.

Level: Six

Main Idea

____ Once the air has reached 100% relative humidity

____ it can't hold any more water vapor.

Details

____ Water vapor condenses

____ or changes from a gas

____ to a liquid.

____ The temperature at which water vapor condenses

____ is called the dew point.

____ Water droplets form

____ on a plant

____ when the air is cooled

____ the night air

____ and reaches its dew point.

62 Ideas

Number of ideas recalled _____

Other ideas recalled, including summary statements and inferences:

Questions for "Temperature and Humidity"

1. What is this section mostly about?
   Implicit: how temperature and humidity are related

2. What is humidity?
   Explicit: moisture in the air or water vapor in the air

3. Why does it feel more humid when the humidity is high in warm weather rather than in cold weather?
   Implicit: warmer air can hold more water vapor than cooler air

4. What is relative humidity?
   Explicit: the ratio of the amount of water vapor in the air relative to the maximum amount the air could hold at that temperature

5. If the temperature increases and the amount of water vapor in the air stayed the same, what would happen to the relative humidity, and why?
   Implicit: it would decrease because warm air can hold more humidity, so the amount of water vapor stays the same but it is a lower percent of the maximum the warm air can hold.

6. What happens when the air can't hold any more water vapor?
   Explicit: the vapor changes to a liquid

7. What is dew point?
   Explicit: the temperature at which water vapor turns to liquid

8. Why do we find the grass wet in the morning even when it hasn't rained?
   Implicit: the temperature of the air decreased overnight. Either of the following answers are correct: the water vapor reached 100% (or its maximum) and turned to a liquid; *or* dew formed when the water vapor hit 100%.

Without Look-Backs

Number Correct Explicit: ____

Number Correct Implicit: ____

Total: ____

____ Independent: 8 correct

____ Instructional: 6–7 correct

____ Frustration: 0–5 correct

With Look-Backs

Number Correct Explicit: ____

Number Correct Implicit: ____

Total: ____

____ Independent: 8 correct

____ Instructional: 6–7 correct

____ Frustration: 0–5 correct

Level 6

Level: Six

Expository

Concept Questions:

What is precipitation?

_____

_____

_____ (3-2-1-0)

How do clouds form?

_____

_____

_____ (3-2-1-0)

What is the relationship between the temperature of air and its movement?

_____

_____

_____ (3-2-1-0)

Score: _____ /12 = _____ %

_____ FAM _____ UNFAM

Prediction:

_____

_____

"Clouds and Precipitation"

Clouds are mostly water. To understand how clouds form, remember how changes in <u>temperature</u> affect <u>humidity</u>. **STOP**

_____

_____

_____

_____

_____

_____

Think of a clear spring day when the sun warms the ground, which in turn warms the air. Warm air holds a certain amount of water, and warm air rises. Eventually, the warm air cools when it joins the cooler air away from the ground. At the cooler <u>temperature</u> the air cannot hold as much water vapor. As the water vapor separates from the air, it connects with dust and microscopic particles of salt to form tiny drops of water. They are so small and light that they float in the air. Collections of millions of these droplets form clouds. **STOP**

_____

_____

_____

_____

_____

As clouds move in the wind and <u>evaporate</u>, they may take on different shapes. Clouds may be <u>classified</u> into a few basic kinds with a few different shapes. **STOP**

Level: Six

_____

_____

_____

_____

_____

The types of clouds are <u>classified</u> according to their height above the ground. And the names of clouds give a clue to their appearance. For example, low clouds that are close to the ground are usually thick, even sheets. The term _strato_ means "sheetlike," so the low sheetlike clouds are called stratus clouds. You can see these clouds in the first photo.

Middle-level clouds may appear in groups in an otherwise blue sky. _Cumulo_ means "pile or heap," so these middle-level groups of clouds are a type of cumulus cloud. These are pictured in the second photo below.

High clouds that are wispy with curled edges across a background of blue sky are called cirrus clouds because _cirro_ means "curl." The third photo is a good example of cirrus clouds. **STOP**

_____

_____

_____

_____

_____

Finally, there are clouds that build upon each other into very high vertical clouds. Because they occur in heaps, they are a type of cumulus cloud, but because they often result in thunderstorms they are called cumulonimbus, because _nimbo_ means "rain." **STOP**

_____

_____

_____

_____

_____

Clouds are associated with rain and snow. Most rain that occurs in the United States begins as snow. Ice crystals that are high in the cirrus clouds grow when more and more water vapor condenses on them. **STOP**

_____

_____

_____

_____

_____

Eventually, they become so heavy that the crystals start to fall. When ice crystals fall through clouds, they may collide and combine with other ice crystals or water droplets. When the crystals become

Level 6

Level: Six

too heavy to float in the air, they drop as precipitation. **STOP**

_____

_____

_____

_____

_____

If all the bands of air that the crystals fall through are cold, then the precipitation reaches the ground as snow. If the ice crystals fall far enough through warm air, they reach the ground as rain.

Sometimes if a band of cold air is near the ground, the rain becomes colder and freezes when it hits the ground. This is freezing rain that becomes ice on the ground, making walking and driving dangerous. **STOP**

_____

_____

_____

_____

_____

Hail is formed when ice crystals are thrown up and down within a cumulonimbus cloud. Water collects on the crystal as it falls through the cloud and freezes on the crystal as it rises higher in the cloud. The hailstone grows larger in this way until it becomes too heavy to float and then falls to the ground. **STOP**

_____

_____

_____

_____

(528 words)

_____

From _Scott Foresman Science, Teacher Edition, Grade 6._ Copyright © 2000 Pearson Education, Inc. or its affiliates. Reprinted by permission. All Rights Reserved.

Number of Total Miscues
(Total Accuracy): _____

Number of Meaning-Change Miscues
(Total Acceptability): _____

Total Accuracy		**Total Acceptability**
0–11 miscues	_____ Independent	_____ 0–11 miscues
12–54 miscues	_____ Instructional	_____ 12–29 miscues
55+ miscues	_____ Frustration	_____ 30+ miscues

Rate: (If you used this passage as a think-aloud passage, you cannot compute rate):

$528 \times 60 = 31{,}680/$ _____ seconds = _____ WPM

Correct WPM: $(528 -$ _____ errors$) \times 60 =$
_____ / _____ seconds = _____ CWPM

Retelling Scoring Sheet for "Clouds and Precipitation"

Main Idea

_____ Clouds are mostly water.

Details

_____ Changes in temperature affect humidity.
_____ The sun warms the ground
_____ which warms the air.

Level 6

Level: Six

____ Warm air holds water
____ and the air rises.
____ The air cools
____ when it joins cooler air.
____ At a cooler temperature
____ the air cannot hold water vapor.
____ The water vapor separates
____ and connects with dust,
____ and particles of salt
____ to form drops
____ of water.
____ They are so small
____ and light
____ that they float.
____ These droplets form clouds
____ millions of these droplets.

Main Idea

____ Clouds may be classified
____ into a few kinds
____ with different shapes.

Details

____ As clouds move
____ and evaporate,
____ they take on shapes.
____ They are classified according to height
____ above the ground.
____ The names give a clue
____ to their appearance.
____ Low clouds close to the ground
____ are sheets
____ thick sheets
____ even sheets.
____ *Strato* means "sheetlike,"
____ so they are called stratus clouds.
____ Middle-level clouds appear in groups.
____ *Cumulo* means "pile
____ or heap,"
____ so these clouds are cumulus clouds.
____ Clouds that are wispy
____ high clouds
____ with curled edges
____ are called cirrus clouds

____ because *cirro* means "curl."
____ Clouds build upon each other
____ into very high clouds
____ vertical clouds.
____ They are a type of cumulus cloud,
____ but because they often result in thunder-storms
____ they are called cumulonimbus
____ because *nimbo* means "rain."

Main Idea

____ Clouds are associated with rain
____ and snow.

Details

____ Most rain begins as snow.
____ Ice crystals grow
____ crystals in cirrus clouds
____ when water vapor condenses on them.
____ They become so heavy
____ that the crystals fall.
____ They may combine with other crystals
____ or water droplets.
____ When the crystals become too heavy
____ to float,
____ they drop
____ as precipitation.
____ If the air is cold,
____ then the precipitation is snow.
____ If the air is warm,
____ the precipitation is rain.
____ If cold air is near the ground,
____ the rain freezes
____ when it hits the ground.
____ This becomes ice,
____ making walking
____ and driving dangerous.
____ Hail is formed
____ when ice crystals are thrown up and down
____ within a cloud.
____ Water collects on the crystal
____ as it falls
____ and freezes
____ on the crystal

Level: Six

___ as it rises higher.
___ The hailstone grows larger
___ until it becomes too heavy
___ to float
___ and then falls
___ to the ground.

89 Ideas

Number of ideas recalled _____

Other ideas recalled including summary statements and inferences

Questions for "Clouds and Precipitation"

1. What is this section mostly about?
   Implicit: how clouds and precipitation are related

2. Name one thing needed for clouds to form.
   Explicit: water vapor; *or* dust

3. How are clouds classified?
   Explicit: according to height from the ground

4. Why are clouds named as they are?
   Implicit: because part of their name describes how they look (in Latin)

5. What does a stratus cloud look like?
   Explicit: a sheet

Level: Six

6. What can you predict about the weather if the clouds are cumulonimbus?
   Explicit: a thunderstorm is likely

> Without Look-Backs
>
> Number Correct Explicit: ____
>
> Number Correct Implicit: ____
>
> **Total:** ____
>
> ____ Independent: 8 correct
>
> ____ Instructional: 6–7 correct
>
> ____ Frustration: 0–5 correct
>
> With Look-Backs
>
> Number Correct Explicit: ____
>
> Number Correct Implicit: ____
>
> **Total:** ____
>
> ____ Independent: 8 correct
>
> ____ Instructional: 6–7 correct
>
> ____ Frustration: 0–5 correct

7. What can you conclude about the atmosphere above the ground when it snows?
   Implicit: that all of [the bands of] the air above the ground is/are cold

8. What happened to an ice crystal that resulted in a golf-ball sized hailstone?
   Implicit: it was thrown up and down a lot in a cloud that contained a lot of water

> **Think-Aloud Summary**
>
> **Think-Aloud Statements That Indicate Understanding**
>
> Paraphrasing/Summarizing ____
>
> Making New Meaning ____
>
> Questioning That Indicates Understanding ____
>
> Noting Understanding ____
>
> Reporting Prior Knowledge ____
>
> Identifying Personally ____
>
> **Think-Aloud Statements That Indicate Lack of Understanding**
>
> Questioning That Indicates Lack of Understanding ____
>
> Noting Lack of Understanding ____

Level 6

Biddy Mason

Sometimes it seemed they would never stop traveling. First there had been the long trip to Utah. All day Biddy had walked along behind the wagons, tending the cattle. For months they walked, getting farther and farther from Mississippi. It was a hard trip, especially for her children. But what could Biddy do? She was born a slave. She was a slave today. Her master told her to walk across the plains and she did it.

They had stayed in Utah only one year. Then word came of a new settlement in southern California. Robert Smith decided to go. Again the wagons were packed. Again they began the long days of walking.

Biddy had plenty of time for thinking along the way. What she mostly thought about was freedom. As a child she had never known a black person who wasn't a slave. Oh, she heard about them, about the ones who escaped to the North. But it was so hard to imagine!

Then came the trip west. Things were different here. She had seen families, *black families,* traveling west with their own wagons! Just think of it! They planned to find their own land, start their own farms, or find work in the towns. Biddy had thought about them for days.

Biddy looked down at her bare feet. They were tired and sore and covered with dust. "These feet walked every mile from Mississippi," she thought. "And they remembered every step. They have walked for Mr. Smith and his family. They have walked after his crops and his wagons and his cattle. But someday these feet are going to walk for me. Someday these feet will walk me to freedom. I'm sure of it."

A few days later, the tired travelers arrived at San Bernardino, California. It was a lovely place. It was their new home.

There were many reasons to enjoy living in California in 1852. The climate was pleasant. The land was good. The air was fresh and warm. Cities were booming. Everywhere there was a sense of promise and excitement.

The most important thing for Biddy was the promise of freedom. She had heard people talking. The new state of California did not permit slavery, they said. By law, all people here were free. Biddy looked again at her dusty traveling feet. "Soon," she said to herself, "soon."

Three years passed. Life was pretty good, but Mr. Smith must have loved traveling. Even this beautiful settlement could not hold him. He decided to move again, this time to Texas. The wagons were loaded and made ready to go.

Biddy knew she had to act. As soon as the wagons left San Bernardino, she began looking for an opportunity. She found one. Somehow she sent word to the sheriff in Los Angeles. He stopped the wagons before they left California.

"I hear you have slaves in your party," said the sheriff. "I suppose you know that's against the law. Is it true?" Biddy came forward. In all her life this was the first time she had ever spoken to a white sheriff. Still her voice was strong. "It is true," she said. "Mr. Smith is taking us to Texas and we don't want to go."

That statement led to the most important slavery trial in southern California. Biddy spoke to the judge, and her words were strong and clear: "I want to stay in California. I want to be free."

The judge sided with Biddy. He scolded Mr. Smith for breaking the law. He gave all the slaves their freedom.

Biddy gathered up her children and said, "We are moving once more, but it won't be very far. We are going to Los Angeles, and this time," she said looking at her tired feet, "I am walking for me!"

She started her new life by taking as her full name Biddy Mason. She went to work as a nurse and a housekeeper. Before long she had saved enough money to buy a house. Soon she bought other property too. Biddy Mason was a good businesswoman. She became one of the wealthiest blacks in Los Angeles.

She shared that wealth with others. She gave land to build schools and hospitals and nursing homes. She supported the education of black children and helped people in need. Biddy Mason had come a long way from that slave's cabin in Mississippi. She still remembered the walking. And she made sure she helped others along their way.

From *Black Heroes of the Wild West* by Ruth Pelz (pp. 31–35, Sixth Printing 2003), copyright © 1990 by Open Hand Publishing, Inc. Reprinted by permission of Open Hand Publishing, LLC (www.openhand.com).

Malcolm X

It was because of my letters that I happened to stumble upon starting to acquire some kind of homemade education.

I became increasingly frustrated at not being able to express what I wanted to convey in letters that I wrote, especially those to Mr. Elijah Muhammad. In the street, I had been the most articulate hustler out there. I had commanded attention when I said something. But now, trying to write simple English, I not only wasn't articulate, I wasn't even functional. How would I sound writing in slang, the way I would *say* it, something such as, "Look, daddy, let me pull your coat about a cat, Elijah Muhammad."

Many who today hear me somewhere in person, or on television, or those who read something I've said, will think I went to school far beyond the eighth grade. This impression is due entirely to my prison studies.

It had really begun back in the Charlestown Prison, when Bimbi first made me feel envy of his stock of knowledge. Bimbi had always taken charge of any conversation he was in, and I had tried to emulate him. But every book I picked up had few sentences which didn't contain anywhere from one to nearly all of the words that might as well have been in Chinese. When I just skipped those words, of course, I really ended up with little idea of what the book said. So I had come to the Norfolk Prison Colony still going through only book-reading motions. Pretty soon, I would have quit even these motions, unless I had received the motivation that I did.

I saw that the best thing I could do was get hold of a dictionary to study, to learn some words. I was lucky enough to reason also that I should try to improve my penmanship. It was sad. I couldn't even write in a straight line. It was both ideas together that moved me to request a dictionary along with some tablets and pencils from the Norfolk Prison Colony school.

I spent two days just riffling uncertainly through the dictionary's pages. I'd never realized so many words existed! I didn't know *which* words I needed to learn. Finally, just to start some kind of action, I began copying.

In my slow, painstaking, ragged handwriting, I copied into my tablet everything printed on that first page, down to the punctuation marks.

I believe it took me a day. Then, aloud, I read back to myself everything I'd written on the tablet. Over and over, aloud, to myself, I read my own handwriting.

I woke up the next morning, thinking about those words, immensely proud to realize that not only had I written so much at one time, but I'd written words that I never knew were in the world. Moreover, with a little effort, I also could remember what many of these words meant. I reviewed the words whose meanings I didn't remember. Funny thing, from the dictionary first page right now, that "aardvark" springs to my mind. The dictionary had a picture of it, a long-tailed, long-eared, burrowing African mammal, which lives off termites caught by sticking out its tongue as an anteater does for ants.

I was so fascinated that I went on. I copied the dictionary's next page. And the same experience came when I studied that. With every succeeding page, I also learned of people and places and events from history. Actually, the dictionary is like a miniature encyclopedia. Finally, the dictionary's A section had filled a whole tablet—and I went on to the B's. That was the way I started copying what eventually became the entire dictionary. It went a lot faster after so much practice helped me to pick up handwriting speed. Between what I wrote in my tablet, and writing letters, during the rest of my time in prison I would guess I wrote a million words.

I suppose it was inevitable that as my word-base broadened, I could for the first time pick up a book and read and now begin to understand what the book was saying. Anyone who has read a great deal can imagine the new world that opened. Let me tell you something: from then until I left that prison, in every free moment I had, if I was not reading in the library, I was reading on my bunk. You couldn't have gotten me out of books with a wedge. Between Mr. Muhammad's teachings, my correspondence, my visitors, usually Ella and Reginald, and my reading of books, months passed without my even thinking about being imprisoned. In fact, up to then, I never had been so truly free in my life.

Immigration—Part 1

Reasons for Immigration

Between 1866 and 1915, more than a million immigrants poured into the United States. Both push and pull factors played a part in this vast migration. Push factors are conditions that drive people from their homes. Pull factors are conditions that attract immigrants to a new area.

Push Factors

Many immigrants were small farmers or landless farm workers. As European populations grew, land for farming became scarce. Small farms could barely support the families who worked them. In some areas, new farm machines replaced farm workers.

Another factor was political and religious persecution that pushed many people to leave their homes. In the late 1800s, the Russian government supported pogroms or organized attacks on Jewish villages. "Every night," recalled a Jewish girl who fled Russia, "they were chasing after us, to kill everyone." Millions of Jews fled Russia and eastern Europe to settle in the American cities.

Persecution was also a push factor for Armenian immigrants. The Armenians lived in the Ottoman Empire (present-day Turkey). Between the 1890s and the 1920s, the Ottoman government killed a million or more Armenians. Many fled, eventually settling in California and elsewhere in the United States.

War and hardship were other push factors. In 1913, a civil war raged in Mexico and this caused thousands of Mexicans to cross the border into the American Southwest. Poverty and hardship in China drove many Chinese to make new homes across the Pacific. After gold was discovered in California, thousands of Chinese poured into California attracted, like so many others, by tales of "mountains of gold."

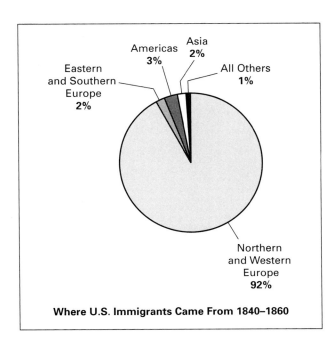

Where U.S. Immigrants Came From 1840–1860

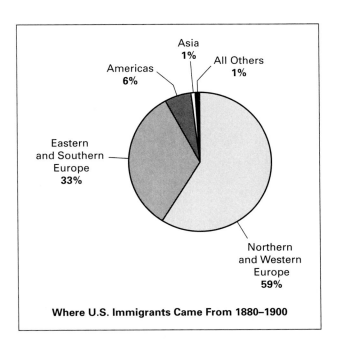

Where U.S. Immigrants Came From 1880–1900

Pull Factors

The promise of freedom and hopes for a better life attracted poor and oppressed people from Europe, Asia, and Latin America. Often one bold family member—usually a young single male—set off for the United States. Before long, he would write home with news of the rich land across the ocean or across the border. Once settled, he would send for family members to join him.

Once settled, the newcomers helped pull neighbors from the old country to the United States. In the 1800s, one out of every ten Greeks left their homes for the United States. Thousands of Italians, Poles, and eastern European Jews also sailed to America. Jobs were another pull factor. American factories needed workers and factory owners sent agents to Europe and Asia to hire workers at low wages. Steamship companies competed to offer low fares for the ocean crossing and railroads posted notices in Europe advertising cheap land in the American west.

From *The American Nation* by James West Davidson, Pedro Castillo, and Michael B. Stoff. Copyright © 2002 Pearson Education, Inc., or its affiliates. Adapted by permission. All Rights Reserved.

The Long Voyage

Leaving home required great courage. The voyage across the Atlantic or Pacific was often miserable. Most immigrants could afford only the cheapest berths. Ship owners jammed up to 2,000 people in steerage, as the airless rooms below decks were called. On the return voyage, cattle and cargo filled these same spaces. In such close quarters, diseases spread rapidly. **STOP**

For most European immigrants the voyage ended in New York City. There, after 1886, they saw the giant Statue of Liberty in the harbor. The statue was a gift from France to the United States. The Statue of Liberty became a symbol of the hope and freedom offered by the United States. **STOP**

Adjusting to the New Land

Many immigrants had heard stories that the streets in the United States were paved with gold. Once in the United States, the newcomers had to adjust their dreams to reality. They immediately set out to find work. European peasants living on the land had little need for money, but it took cash to survive in the United States. Through friends, relatives, labor contractors, and employment agencies, the new arrivals found jobs. **STOP**

Most immigrants stayed in the cities where they landed. The slums of the cities soon became packed with poor immigrants. By 1900, one such neighborhood on the lower east side of New York had become the most crowded place in the world. **STOP**

Ethnic Neighborhoods

Immigrants adjusted to their new lives by settling in neighborhoods with their own ethnic group. An ethnic group is a group of people who share a common culture. Across the United States, cities were patchworks of Italian, Irish, Polish, Hungarian, German, Jewish, and Chinese neighborhoods. Within these ethnic neighborhoods, newcomers spoke their own language and celebrated special holidays with food prepared as in the old country. **STOP**

Becoming Americans

Often newcomers were torn between the old traditions and American ways. Still, many struggled to learn the language of their new nation. Learning English was an important step toward becoming a citizen. The process of becoming part of another culture is called assimilation. Many Americans opposed the increase in immigration. They felt the newcomers would not assimilate because their languages, religions, and customs were too different. However, they were wrong. **STOP**

Children assimilated more quickly than their parents. They learned English in school and then helped their families learn to speak it. Because children wanted to be seen as American, they often gave up customs their parents honored. They played American games and dressed in American-style clothes. **STOP**

Life Cycles of Stars—Part 1

Stars have life cycles, just like humans. In fact, a star is born, changes, and then dies. In contrast to the human life cycle that lasts about 75 years, the life cycle of a typical star is measured in billions of years.

Every star in the sky is at a different stage in its life cycle. Some stars are relatively young, while others are near the end of their existence. The sun is about halfway through its 10-billion-year-long life cycle.

Birth of a Star

The space between stars is not entirely empty. In some places, there are great clouds of gas and dust. Each of these clouds is a nebula. A nebula is where stars are born.

The element hydrogen makes up most of a nebula. Helium and a sprinkling of dust are also present. The particles in a nebula are spread very thin. In fact, the particles are a million times less dense than the particles in the air you breathe. However, since nebulae are very large, they contain enormous amounts of matter.

Gravity causes matter to be attracted to other matter. Therefore, as a nebula travels though space, it collects more dust and gas. The clouds become packed tighter and tighter, as gravity pulls it all together. Whenever matter is packed in this way, it heats up. An especially dense part of the nebula may form a hot, spinning ball of matter. Such a ball of hot matter is called a protostar.

A protostar doesn't yet shine by ordinary light, but it does give off infrared energy. Scientists identify protostars within nebulae using infrared telescopes. A protostar eventually becomes hot enough for nuclear fusion to take place in its core. When nuclear fusion produces great amounts of energy, a star comes to life.

Low-Mass Star

Stars begin their life cycle with different masses. A star's mass determines how long its life cycle will last and how it will die. Stars with a mass less than five times that of the sun are called low-mass stars. Most stars are in this group.

A low-mass star begins its life cycle as a main-sequence star. Over a period of billions of years, its supply of hydrogen is slowly changed by nuclear fusion into helium. During this time, the star changes very little.

From *Science Insights: Exploring Earth and Space* by M. DeSpezio, M. Linner-Luebe, M. Lisowski, B. Sparks, and G. Skoog. Copyright © 2002 by Addison Wesley Longman. Adapted by permission of Pearson Education, Inc. All Rights Reserved.

Life Cycles of Stars—Part 2

Red Giant Stage

As the hydrogen in the core of a low-mass star is used up, the core starts to collapse. The core of the star becomes denser and hotter. The increased temperature causes another kind of nuclear reaction. Helium is converted to carbon. This nuclear reaction gives off great amounts of energy, causing the star to expand. It becomes a red giant. **STOP** The red giant stage in a star's life is relatively short. The sun will be a main-sequence star for a total of 10 billion years. But the sun will be a red giant for only about 500 million years. **STOP**

Dwarf Stage

Eventually, most of the helium in a red giant's core is changed into carbon. Nuclear fusion slows. The star cools, and gravity makes it collapse inward. The matter making up the star is squeezed together very tightly, and the star becomes a white dwarf. **STOP** A typical white dwarf is about the size of Earth. But its matter is far denser than any matter on Earth. Eventually, the star becomes a burned-out black chunk of very dense matter that gives off no visible light. Then it is called a black dwarf. **STOP**

Life of a High-Mass Star

Stars more than six times as massive as the sun have a very different life cycle than low-mass stars. A high-mass star uses up its hydrogen at a much faster rate. After only about 50 to 100 million years, a high-mass star has no hydrogen left. At this time, the core collapses and the outer layers expand greatly. The star becomes a super giant. **STOP** Eventually, the core of the super giant can no longer stand the pressure of the outside layers of the star. The outside layers crash in very suddenly, causing a tremendous explosion that gives off an extraordinary amount of light. Great shells of gases fly off the star. The star becomes a supernova. A supernova explosion is the most violent event known to happen in the universe. **STOP**

Stellar Evolution

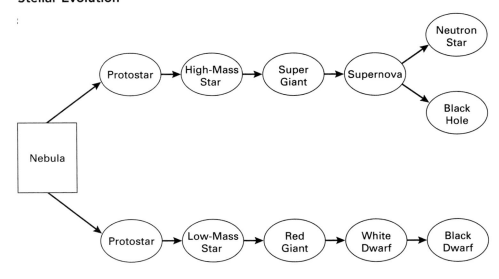

After a supernova explodes, only the tiny core of the star remains. This core, made up of neutrons, is called a neutron star. Neutron stars are extremely dense. Astronomers hypothesize that after a massive star undergoes a supernova explosion, it may also become a black hole. A black hole is so dense and its gravity is so strong that nothing can escape from it, not even light. Do black holes really exist? So far, scientists have no real proof. Black holes do not release light so they can't be observed directly. **STOP**

From *Science Insights: Exploring Earth and Space* by M. DeSpezio, M. Linner-Luebe, M. Lisowski, B. Sparks, and G. Skoog. Copyright © 2002 by Addison Wesley Longman. Adapted by permission of Pearson Education, Inc. All Rights Reserved.

Level: Upper Middle School

Literature

Concept Questions:

What is a biography?

_____

_____

_____ (3-2-1-0)

What is slavery?

_____

_____

_____ (3-2-1-0)

What does it mean to be courageous?

_____

_____

_____ (3-2-1-0)

What is a settlement?

_____

_____

_____ (3-2-1-0)

Score: _____ /12 = _____ %

_____ FAM _____ UNFAM

Prediction:

_____

_____

"Biddy Mason"

Sometimes it seemed they would never stop traveling. First there had been the long trip to Utah. All day Biddy had walked along behind the wagons, tending the cattle. For months they walked, getting farther and farther from Mississippi. It was a hard trip, especially for her children. But what could Biddy do? She was born a slave. She was a slave to-day. Her master told her to walk across the plains and she did it.

They had stayed in Utah only one year. Then word came of a new settlement in southern California. Robert Smith decided to go. Again the wagons were packed. Again they began the long days of walking.

Biddy had plenty of time for thinking along the way. What she mostly thought about was freedom. As a child she had never known a black person who wasn't a slave. Oh, she heard about them, about the ones who escaped to the North. But it was so hard to imagine!

Then came the trip west. Things were different here. She had seen families, *black families*, traveling west with their own wagons! Just think of it! They planned to find their own land, start their own farms, or find work in the towns. Biddy had thought about them for days.

Biddy looked down at her bare feet. They were tired and sore and covered with dust. "These feet walked every mile from Mississippi," she thought. "And they remembered every step. They have walked for Mr. Smith and his family. They have walked after his crops and his wagons and his cattle. But someday these feet are going to walk for me. Someday these feet will walk me to freedom. I'm sure of it."

A few days later, the tired travelers arrived at San Bernardino, California. It was a lovely place. It was their new home.

There were many reasons to enjoy living in California in 1852. The climate was pleasant. The land was good. The air was fresh and warm. Cities were booming. Everywhere there was a sense of promise and excitement.

The most important thing for Biddy was the promise of freedom. She had heard people talking. The new state of California did not permit slavery, they said. By law, all people here were free. Biddy looked again at her dusty traveling feet. "Soon," she said to herself, "soon."

Three years passed. Life was pretty good, but Mr. Smith must have loved traveling. Even this beautiful settlement could not hold him. He decided to move again, this time to Texas. The wagons were loaded and made ready to go.

Biddy knew she had to act. As soon as the wagons left San Bernardino, she began looking for an opportunity. She found one. Somehow she sent word to the sheriff in Los Angeles. He stopped the wagons before they left California.

"I hear you have slaves in your party," said the sheriff. "I suppose you know that's against the law. Is it true?" Biddy came forward. In all her life this was the first time she had ever spoken to a white sheriff. Still her voice was strong. "It is true," she said. "Mr. Smith is taking us to Texas and we don't want to go."

That statement led to the most important slavery trial in southern California. Biddy spoke to the judge, and her words were strong and clear: "I want to stay in California. I want to be free."

The judge sided with Biddy. He scolded Mr. Smith for breaking the law. He gave all the slaves their freedom.

Biddy gathered up her children and said, "We are moving once more, but it won't be very far. We are going to Los Angeles, and this time," she said looking at her tired feet, "I am walking for me!"

She started her new life by taking as her full name Biddy Mason. She went to work as a nurse and a housekeeper. Before long she had saved enough money to buy a house. Soon she bought other property too. Biddy Mason was a good businesswoman. She became one of the wealthiest blacks in Los Angeles.

She shared that wealth with others. She gave land to build schools and hospitals and nursing homes. She supported the education of black

Level: Upper Middle School

children and helped people in need. Biddy Mason had come a long way from that slave's cabin in Mississippi. She still remembered the walking. And she made sure she helped others along their way. (745 words)

From *Black Heroes of the Wild West* by Ruth Pelz (pp. 31–35, Sixth Printing 2003), copyright © 1990 by Open Hand Publishing, Inc. Reprinted by permission of Open Hand Publishing, LLC (www.openhand.com).

Number of Total Miscues
(Total Accuracy): _____

Number of Meaning-Change Miscues
(Total Acceptability): _____

Total Accuracy			**Total Acceptability**
0–18 miscue	____ Independent	____	0–18 miscue
19–78 miscues	____ Instructional	____	19–40 miscues
79+ miscues	____ Frustration	____	41+ miscues

Rate: 745 × 60 = 44,700/____ seconds = ____ WPM

Correct WPM: (745 – ____ errors) × 60 =
____ /____ seconds = ____ CWPM

Retelling Scoring Sheet for "Biddy Mason"

Setting/Background

____ Biddy walked
____ behind the wagons.
____ She was a slave.
____ Her master told her to walk
____ and she did it.
____ Word came
____ of a settlement
____ in California.
____ Robert Smith decided to go.

Goal

____ Biddy thought about freedom.
____ She had never known a black person
____ who wasn't a slave.
____ On the trip west,
____ she saw black families
____ traveling west
____ planning to find land
____ and start farms.
____ Her feet were tired.
____ "They have walked for Mr. Smith,
____ but someday
____ they are going to walk for me
____ to freedom!"

Events

____ They arrived in California.
____ Biddy heard people talking.
____ California did not permit slavery.
____ Mr. Smith decided to move again.
____ The wagons were packed.

Goal

____ Biddy knew
____ she had to act.
____ She sent word
____ to the sheriff
____ in Los Angeles.

Events

____ He stopped the wagons.
____ "I hear you have slaves.
____ Is it true?"
____ Biddy came forward.
____ Her voice was strong.
____ "It is true.
____ We don't want to go."
____ Her statement led to a trial.
____ Biddy spoke to the judge.
____ "I want to stay in California."
____ The judge sided with Biddy.
____ He scolded Mr. Smith
____ for breaking the law.
____ The judge gave the slaves

Level: Upper Middle School

____ their freedom.

____ Biddy gathered her children.

____ "We are moving

____ to Los Angeles.

____ I am walking for me."

Resolution

____ She went to work

____ as a nurse

____ and housekeeper.

____ She saved money.

____ She bought property.

____ She was a good businesswoman.

____ She became one of the wealthiest blacks.

____ She shared her wealth.

____ She gave land for schools

____ and hospitals

____ and nursing homes.

____ She helped people

____ in need.

64 Ideas

Number of ideas recalled _____

Other ideas recalled, including summary statements and inferences:

Questions for "Biddy Mason"

1. What is this selection mainly about?
   Implicit: how a slave gained freedom

2. What did Biddy think about while she was walking from state to state?
   Explicit: freedom

3. What did Biddy see on the trip west that was different from anything she had ever seen before?
   Explicit: black families traveling west with their own wagons and planning to start their own farms

4. What was special about California in the 1850s?
   Explicit: California did not permit slavery *and* one of the following: the climate was good, cities were booming, there was a sense of promise and excitement

5. Why did Biddy need to act quickly when Mr. Smith decided to move to Texas?
   Implicit: when they left California, she would lose her chance of being freed

Level: Upper Middle School

6. What two events happened when the Los Angeles sheriff stopped Mr. Smith's wagons?
   Explicit: the sheriff asked if there were slaves *and* Biddy spoke up saying she didn't want to go to Texas

7. What was the outcome of the trial?
   Explicit: the slaves were freed

8. What did Biddy mean when she told her children that they were going to Los Angeles but that this time her feet were walking for her?
   Implicit: she was walking as a free person going where she wanted to go

9. Give two examples of Biddy's behavior that indicate that she was a courageous person.
   Implicit: she took risks such as speaking up to the sheriff; *or* she told the judge she wanted to stay in California; *or* she became a successful businesswoman

10. Why do you think the author chose to write a biography of Biddy Mason?
    Implicit: because Biddy went from slavery to success; *or* she helped others in need; *or* her life could be an inspiration to others

Without Look-Backs

Number Correct Explicit: _____

Number Correct Implicit: _____

Total: _____

_____ Independent: 9–10 correct

_____ Instructional: 7–8 correct

_____ Frustration: 0–6 correct

With Look-Backs

Number Correct Explicit: _____

Number Correct Implicit: _____

Total: _____

_____ Independent: 9–10 correct

_____ Instructional: 7–8 correct

_____ Frustration: 0–6 correct

Level: Upper Middle School

Literature

Concept Questions:

What is an autobiography?

_____

_____

_____ (3-2-1-0)

Who was Malcolm X?

_____

_____

_____ (3-2-1-0)

What does the word "articulate" mean?

_____

_____

_____ (3-2-1-0)

What does it mean to emulate someone?

_____

_____

_____ (3-2-1-0)

Score: _____ /12 = _____ %

_____ FAM _____ UNFAM

Prediction:

_____

_____

"Malcolm X"

It was because of my letters that I happened to stumble upon starting to acquire some kind of homemade education.

I became increasingly frustrated at not being able to express what I wanted to convey in letters that I wrote, especially those to Mr. Elijah Muhammad. In the street, I had been the most articulate hustler out there. I had commanded attention when I said something. But now, trying to write simple English, I not only wasn't articulate, I wasn't even functional. How would I sound writing in slang, the way I would *say* it, something such as, "Look, daddy, let me pull your coat about a cat, Elijah Muhammad."

Many who today hear me somewhere in person, or on television, or those who read something I've said, will think I went to school far beyond the eighth grade. This impression is due entirely to my prison studies.

It had really begun back in the Charlestown Prison, when Bimbi first made me feel envy of his stock of knowledge. Bimbi had always taken charge of any conversation he was in, and I had tried to emulate him. But every book I picked up had few sentences which didn't contain anywhere from one to nearly all of the words that might as well have been in Chinese. When I just skipped those words, of course, I really ended up with little idea of what the book said. So I had come to the Norfolk Prison Colony still going through only book-reading motions. Pretty soon, I would have quit even these motions, unless I had received the motivation that I did.

Level: Upper Middle School

I saw that the best thing I could do was get hold of a dictionary to study, to learn some words. I was lucky enough to reason also that I should try to improve my penmanship. It was sad. I couldn't even write in a straight line. It was both ideas together that moved me to request a dictionary along with some tablets and pencils from the Norfolk Prison Colony school.

I spent two days just <u>riffling</u> uncertainly through the dictionary's pages. I'd never realized so many words existed! I didn't know *which* words I needed to learn. Finally, just to start some kind of action, I began copying.

In my slow, painstaking, ragged handwriting, I copied into my tablet everything printed on that first page, down to the punctuation marks.

I believe it took me a day. Then, aloud, I read back to myself everything I'd written on the tablet. Over and over, aloud, to myself, I read my own handwriting.

I woke up the next morning, thinking about those words, immensely proud to realize that not only had I written so much at one time, but I'd written words that I never knew were in the world. Moreover, with a little effort, I also could remember what many of these words meant. I reviewed the words whose meanings I didn't remember. Funny thing, from the dictionary first page right now, that "aardvark" springs to my mind. The dictionary had a picture of it, a long-tailed, long-eared, burrowing African mammal, which lives off termites caught by sticking out its tongue as an anteater does for ants.

I was so fascinated that I went on. I copied the dictionary's next page. And the same experience came when I studied that. With every succeeding page, I also learned of people and places and events from history. Actually, the dictionary is like a miniature <u>encyclopedia</u>. Finally, the dictionary's A section had filled a whole tablet—and I went on to the B's. That was the way I started copying what eventually became the entire dictionary. It went a lot faster after so much practice helped me to pick up handwriting speed. Between what I wrote in my tablet, and writing letters, during the rest of my time in prison I would guess I wrote a million words.

I suppose it was <u>inevitable</u> that as my word-base broadened, I could for the first time pick up a book and read and now begin to understand what the book was saying. Anyone who has read a great deal can imagine the new world that opened. Let me tell you something: from then until I left that prison, in every free moment I had, if I was not reading in the library, I was reading on my bunk. You couldn't have gotten me out of books with a wedge. Between Mr. Muhammad's teachings, my correspondence, my visitors, usually Ella and Reginald, and my reading of books, months passed without my even thinking about being imprisoned. In fact, up to then, I never had been so truly free in my life. (786 words)

_____

From _The Autobiography of Malcolm X_ by Malcolm X and Alex Haley, copyright © 1964 by Alex Haley and Malcolm X. Copyright © 1965 by Alex Haley and Betty Shabazz. Used by permission of Random House, Inc.

Number of Total Miscues
(Total Accuracy): _____

Number of Meaning-Change Miscues
(Total Acceptability): _____

Total Accuracy		**Total Acceptability**
0–19 miscue	____ Independent	____ 0–19 miscue
20–82 miscues	____ Instructional	____ 20–43 miscues
83+ miscues	____ Frustration	____ 44+ miscues

Rate: 786 × 60 = 47,160/____ seconds = ____ WPM

Correct WPM: (786 – ____ errors) × 60 =
____ /____ seconds = ____ CWPM

Retelling Scoring Sheet for "Malcolm X"

Goal

____ I became frustrated
____ at not being able to express myself
____ in letters.
____ I had been a hustler
____ a most articulate hustler.
____ But trying to write English,
____ I wasn't functional.
____ Today
____ people think I went to school
____ beyond eighth grade.
____ This impression is due to my prison studies.

Setting/Background

____ It began in prison
____ where Bimbi made me envious

____ of his knowledge.
____ He took charge of conversation.
____ I tried to emulate him.
____ I had little idea
____ of what a book said.

Events

____ I got hold of a dictionary
____ to study some words.
____ I reasoned
____ that I should improve my penmanship.
____ I couldn't write in a straight line.
____ I requested a dictionary
____ along with tablets
____ and pencils.
____ I spent two days
____ riffling through the pages.
____ I never realized
____ that so many words existed.
____ I began copying
____ in my slow handwriting.
____ I copied the first page.
____ It took me a day.
____ I read back to myself
____ everything I'd written
____ over and over.
____ I woke up the next morning
____ immensely proud.
____ I could remember
____ what the words meant.
____ I reviewed the words
____ whose meanings I didn't remember.
____ I copied the next page.
____ With every page,
____ I learned of people,
____ places,
____ and events.
____ I copied the entire dictionary.
____ It went a lot faster
____ after practice helped me
____ pick up handwriting speed.
____ Between what I wrote
____ and writing letters
____ I wrote a million words.

Level: Upper Middle School

Resolution

___ As my word-base broadened,
___ I could pick up a book
___ and understand it.
___ From then until I left prison,
___ I spent every free moment
___ reading.
___ I had never been so free
___ in my life.

63 Ideas

Number of ideas recalled _____

Other ideas recalled, including summary statements and inferences:

Questions for "Malcolm X"

1. What was this selection mostly about?
   Implicit: how Malcolm X got an education in prison by reading; *or* how Malcolm X improved his reading and writing by studying in prison

2. How did Malcolm X describe his early writing abilities?
   Explicit: he couldn't express what he wanted to say; *or* the writing wasn't even functional

3. Why did Malcolm X decide he should learn to write better?
   Explicit: he couldn't express his ideas clearly in writing, especially in letters to Elijah Muhammad

4. Before he went to prison, what was the highest grade of formal schooling that Malcolm X had completed?
   Implicit: eighth grade

5. Before Malcolm X improved his reading skills, what did he do when he was reading and came to words that he didn't know?
   Explicit: he skipped them

Level: Upper Middle School

6. How did Malcolm X begin his informal, prison-based education?
   Explicit: by reading and copying the dictionary

7. What evidence do we have that Malcolm X was highly motivated to improve his vocabulary?
   Implicit: he copied the entire first page of the dictionary and read it over and over; *or* he copied the entire dictionary

8. In addition to the meanings of many words, what else improved as Malcolm X copied the dictionary?
   Explicit: his knowledge of people, places, and events from history; *or* his handwriting speed

9. What kept Malcolm X motivated to continue his study of the dictionary?
   Implicit: he was proud when he had copied the first page and learned many new words; he could remember many of the words he had copied; *or* he could read with understanding

10. Why did Malcolm X say, "I never had been so truly free in my life" even though he was in prison at the time?
    Implicit: because he was learning so much; *or* he loved reading

---

Without Look-Backs

Number Correct Explicit: ____

Number Correct Implicit: ____

Total: ____

____ Independent: 9–10 correct

____ Instructional: 7–8 correct

____ Frustration: 0–6 correct

With Look-Backs

Number Correct Explicit: ____

Number Correct Implicit: ____

Total: ____

____ Independent: 9–10 correct

____ Instructional: 7–8 correct

____ Frustration: 0–6 correct

This passage and associated materials do not appear on the *QRI-5* DVD due to copyright restrictions.

Level: Upper Middle School

Expository

Concept Questions:

What is an immigrant?

_____

_____

_____ (3-2-1-0)

What do we mean by persecution?

_____

_____

_____ (3-2-1-0)

What do we mean by hardship?

_____

_____

_____ (3-2-1-0)

What is oppression?

_____

_____

_____ (3-2-1-0)

Score: _____ /12= _____ %

_____ FAM _____ UNFAM

Prediction:

_____

_____

"Immigration—Part 1"

Reasons for Immigration

Between 1866 and 1915, more than a million immigrants poured into the United States. Both push and pull factors played a part in this vast migration. Push factors are conditions that drive people from their homes. Pull factors are conditions that attract immigrants to a new area.

Push Factors

Many immigrants were small farmers or landless farm workers. As European populations grew, land for farming became scarce. Small farms could barely support the families who worked them. In some areas, new farm machines replaced farm workers.

Another factor was political and religious persecution that pushed many people to leave their homes. In the late 1800s, the Russian government supported pogroms or organized attacks on Jewish villages. "Every night," recalled a Jewish girl who fled Russia, "they were chasing after us, to kill everyone." Millions of Jews fled Russia and eastern Europe to settle in the American cities.

Persecution was also a push factor for Armenian immigrants. The Armenians lived in the Ottoman Empire (present-day Turkey). Between the 1890s and the 1920s, the Ottoman government killed a million or more Armenians. Many fled, eventually settling in California and elsewhere in the United States.

War and hardship were other push factors. In 1913, a civil war raged in Mexico and this caused thousands of Mexicans to cross the border into the American Southwest. Poverty and hardship in China

Level: Upper Middle School

drove many Chinese to make new homes across the Pacific. After gold was discovered in California, thousands of Chinese poured into California attracted, like so many others, by tales of "mountains of gold."

Pull Factors

The promise of freedom and hopes for a better life attracted poor and <u>oppressed</u> people from Europe, Asia, and Latin America. Often one bold family member—usually a young single male—set off for the United States. Before long, he would write home with news of the rich land across the ocean or across the border. Once settled, he would send for family members to join him.

Once settled, the newcomers helped pull neighbors from the old country to the United States. In the 1800s, one out of every ten Greeks left their homes for the United States. Thousands of Italians, Poles, and eastern European Jews also sailed to America. Jobs were another pull factor. American factories needed workers and factory owners sent agents to Europe and Asia to hire workers at low wages. Steamship companies competed to offer low fares for the ocean crossing and railroads posted notices in Europe advertising cheap land in the American west. (423 words)

From *The American Nation* by James West Davidson, Pedro Castillo, and Michael B. Stoff. Copyright © 2002 Pearson Education, Inc., or its affiliates. Adapted by permission. All Rights Reserved.

Number of Total Miscues
(Total Accuracy): _____

Number of Meaning-Change Miscues
(Total Acceptability): _____

Total Accuracy		**Total Acceptability**
0–10 miscue	____ Independent	____ 0–10 miscue
11–44 miscues	____ Instructional	____ 11–23 miscues
45+ miscues	____ Frustration	____ 24+ miscues

Rate: $423 \times 60 = 25{,}380/$____ seconds = ____ WPM

____ WPM – ____ errors = ____ CWPM

Correct WPM: $(423 -$ ____ errors$) \times 60 =$
____ /____ seconds = ____ CWPM

Retelling Scoring Sheet for "Immigration—Part 1"

Main Idea

____ More than a million
____ immigrants poured into the United States.

Details

____ Push factors
____ and pull factors played a part.
____ Push factors drive people from their homes.
____ Pull factors are conditions that attract immigrants.

Main Idea

____ A push factor was scarce land.

Details

____ Many immigrants were farmers.
____ Small farms could not support them.
____ Machines replaced farm workers.

Main Idea

____ Religious
____ and political persecution were push factors.

Level: Upper Middle School

Details

____ The government supported pogroms or attacks

____ the Russian government

____ on Jewish villages.

____ Millions of Jews fled Russia

____ and eastern Europe.

Main Idea

____ Persecution was a push factor

____ for Armenians.

Details

____ The Ottoman government killed Armenians

____ a million or more Armenians.

____ Many fled.

Main Idea

____ War

____ and hardship were push factors.

Details

____ War raged in Mexico

____ and Mexicans crossed the border

____ thousands of Mexicans.

____ Poverty and hardship drove Chinese

____ many Chinese

____ across the Pacific.

____ After gold was discovered,

____ thousands poured into California

____ attracted by tales

____ of "mountains of gold."

Main Idea

____ The promise of freedom

____ and hopes for a better life attracted people.

Details

____ It attracted poor people

____ and oppressed people

____ from Europe,

____ Asia,

____ and Latin America.

____ A bold

____ family member set off—

____ usually a male

____ a young male

____ a single male.

____ He would write home

____ with news

____ of the rich land.

____ Once settled,

____ he would send

____ for family members.

Main Idea

____ Newcomers helped pull neighbors

____ from the old country.

Details

____ One out of every ten Greeks

____ left their homes.

____ Thousands of Italians,

____ Poles,

____ and eastern European Jews

____ sailed to America.

Main Idea

____ Jobs were another pull factor.

Details

____ American factories needed workers.

____ Owners sent agents

____ to hire workers

____ at low wages.

____ Steamship companies offered low fares

____ and railroads posted notices

____ advertising cheap land.

68 Ideas

Number of ideas recalled _____

Other ideas recalled, including summary statements and inferences:

Level: Upper Middle School

Upper Middle School

Questions for "Immigration—Part 1"

1. What is this passage mostly about?
   Implicit: reasons why immigrants came to America

2. Why did farmers leave Europe and come to America?
   Explicit: land became scarce or farms could not support families

3. Why would growing populations result in scarce farming land?
   Implicit: more land would be needed for cities and places for people to live

4. Name two push factors affecting immigration.
   Explicit: scarce land; persecution; war; *or* hardship

5. What push factor caused Mexicans to cross the border into America?
   Explicit: civil war in their country

6. Why was a young single male usually the first family member to immigrate?
   Implicit: he was not burdened by a family; *or* he could get a job easier than a woman or an older man; *or* he might be more adventurous or courageous

Level: Upper Middle School

7. Give two examples of pull factors that affected immigration.
   Explicit: promise of freedom; promise of a better life; a family member who immigrated; a neighbor who immigrated; *or* jobs

8. Why would having a neighbor in America be a pull factor?
   Implicit: the immigrant would know someone in America; the neighbor could help the immigrant get settled; *or* the neighbor might convince the immigrant that it was a good idea to come to America

9. Why did factory owners send agents to Europe to hire workers?
   Explicit: they needed workers; *or* they could hire immigrants for low wages

10. Why would railroads advertise cheap land in the American west?
    Implicit: the immigrants would have to travel on the railroads to get to the west

---

Without Look-Backs

Number Correct Explicit: _____

Number Correct Implicit: _____

Total: _____

_____ Independent: 9–10 correct

_____ Instructional: 7–8 correct

_____ Frustration: 0–6 correct

With Look-Backs

Number Correct Explicit: _____

Number Correct Implicit: _____

Total: _____

_____ Independent: 9–10 correct

_____ Instructional: 7–8 correct

_____ Frustration: 0–6 correct

Upper Middle School

Social Studies

Concept Questions:

What is a symbol?

_____

_____

_____ (3-2-1-0)

What is the difference between a dream and reality?

_____

_____

_____ (3-2-1-0)

What do we mean by culture?

_____

_____

_____ (3-2-1-0)

Why might it be difficult to move to another country?

_____

_____

_____ (3-2-1-0)

Score: _____ /12 = _____ %

_____ FAM _____ UNFAM

Prediction:

_____

_____

"Immigration—Part 2"

The Long Voyage

Leaving home required great courage. The voyage across the Atlantic or Pacific was often miserable.

Most immigrants could afford only the cheapest berths. Ship owners jammed up to 2,000 people in steerage, as the airless rooms below decks were called. On the return voyage, cattle and cargo filled these same spaces. In such close quarters, diseases spread rapidly. **STOP**

_____

_____

_____

_____

For most European immigrants the voyage ended in New York City. There, after 1886, they saw the giant Statue of Liberty in the harbor. The statue was a gift from France to the United States. The Statue of Liberty became a symbol of the hope and freedom offered by the United States. **STOP**

_____

_____

_____

_____

Adjusting to the New Land

Many immigrants had heard stories that the streets in the United States were paved with gold. Once in the United States, the newcomers had to adjust their dreams to reality. They immediately set out to find work. European peasants living on the

Level: Upper Middle School

land had little need for money, but it took cash to survive in the United States. Through friends, relatives, labor contractors, and employment agencies, the new arrivals found jobs. **STOP**

_____
_____
_____
_____
_____

Most immigrants stayed in the cities where they landed. The slums of the cities soon became packed with poor immigrants. By 1900, one such neighborhood on the lower east side of New York had become the most crowded place in the world. **STOP**

_____
_____
_____
_____
_____

Ethnic Neighborhoods

Immigrants adjusted to their new lives by settling in neighborhoods with their own ethnic group. An ethnic group is a group of people who share a common culture. Across the United States, cities were patchworks of Italian, Irish, Polish, Hungarian, German, Jewish, and Chinese neighborhoods. Within these ethnic neighborhoods, newcomers spoke their own language and celebrated special

holidays with food prepared as in the old country. **STOP**

_____
_____
_____
_____
_____

Becoming Americans

Often newcomers were torn between the old traditions and American ways. Still, many struggled to learn the language of their new nation. Learning English was an important step toward becoming a citizen. The process of becoming part of another culture is called assimilation. Many Americans opposed the increase in immigration. They felt the newcomers would not assimilate because their languages, religions, and customs were too different. However, they were wrong. **STOP**

_____
_____
_____
_____
_____

Children assimilated more quickly than their parents. They learned English in school and then helped their families learn to speak it. Because children wanted to be seen as American, they often gave up customs their parents honored. They played

Level: Upper Middle School

American games and dressed in American-style clothes. **STOP**

_____

_____

_____

_____

_____

(417 words)

_____

From *The American Nation* by James West Davidson, Pedro Castillo, and Michael B. Stoff. Copyright © 2002 Pearson Education, Inc., or its affiliates. Adapted by permission. All Rights Reserved.

Number of Total Miscues
(Total Accuracy): _____

Number of Meaning-Change Miscues
(Total Acceptability): _____

Total Accuracy		**Total Acceptability**	
0–10 miscue	____ Independent	____	0–10 miscue
11–43 miscues	____ Instructional	____	11–22 miscues
44+ miscues	____ Frustration		23+ miscues

Rate (If you used this passage as a think-aloud passage, you cannot compute rate): 417 × 60 = 25,020/____ seconds = ____ WPM

Correct WPM: (417 – ____ errors) × 60 =
____ /____ seconds = ____ CWPM

Retelling Scoring Sheet for "Immigration—Part 2"

Main Idea

___ Leaving home required courage.
___ great courage.

Details

___ The voyage was miserable.
___ Most immigrants could only afford the cheapest berths.

___ Ship owners jammed people
___ up to 2,000 people
___ in steerage,
___ the airless rooms
___ below decks.
___ On the return voyage,
___ cattle and cargo filled these spaces.
___ In such close quarters
___ diseases spread rapidly.

Main Idea

___ For most European immigrants
___ the voyage ended in New York City.

Details

___ They saw the Statue of Liberty.
___ The statue was a gift from France.
___ The Statue of Liberty became a symbol
___ of hope.

Main Idea

___ Once in the United States,
___ the newcomers had to adjust their dreams
___ to reality.

Details

___ Immigrants had heard
___ that streets were paved with gold
___ streets in the United States.
___ They set out to find work.
___ It took cash
___ to survive.
___ Through friends
___ and relatives
___ they found jobs.

Main Idea

___ Most immigrants stayed in the cities
___ where they landed.

Details

___ The slums became packed
___ with poor immigrants.
___ One neighborhood became the most crowded place

Level: Upper Middle School

____ in the world
____ neighborhood on the lower east side
____ of New York.

Main Idea

____ Immigrants adjusted by settling in neighborhoods
____ with their own ethnic group.

Details

____ Cities were patchworks
____ of Italian,
____ Irish,
____ Polish,
____ Hungarian,
____ German,
____ Jewish,
____ and Chinese neighborhoods.
____ Newcomers spoke their own language
____ and celebrated holidays.

Main Idea

____ Many struggled to learn English.

Details

____ Learning English was an important step
____ toward becoming a citizen.
____ Becoming part of another culture
____ is called assimilation.
____ Many Americans opposed immigration.
____ They felt the newcomers would not assimilate.
____ They were wrong.

Main Idea

____ Children assimilated more quickly.

Details

____ They learned English
____ in school
____ and helped their families learn it.
____ Because children wanted to be seen as American,
____ they often gave up customs
____ their parents honored.

____ They played American games
____ and dressed
____ in American clothes.

69 Ideas

Number of ideas recalled _____

Other ideas recalled, including summary statements and inferences:

Questions for "Immigration—Part 2"

1. What is this passage mainly about?
   Implicit: How immigrants came to America and how they settled and adjusted

2. Give one reason why ocean voyages were so difficult.
   Explicit: immigrants could only afford the cheapest berths; they were too crowded; there was not much air; *or* disease spread rapidly

3. Why did disease spread so fast on the ocean voyages?
   Implicit: immigrants were too crowded; there was no good air; *or* cattle filled the spaces on the return voyage

4. What was one way in which the immigrants found jobs?
   Explicit: Through friends, relatives, labor contractors, *or* employment agencies

Level: Upper Middle School

5. Why was cash so important to an immigrant?
   Implicit: they needed it for food, clothing, and rent

6. Why did immigrants stay in the crowded slums?
   Implicit: they were too poor to move; *or* they were with their own ethnic group

7. What is assimilation?
   Explicit: the process of becoming part of another culture

8. Name one element of a common culture that is mentioned in the passage.
   Explicit: language; holidays; *or* food

9. Why did some Americans oppose immigration?
   Explicit: they did not feel that the immigrants would be able to assimilate; *or* they thought the immigrants were too different

10. What might cause disagreements between immigrant children and their parents?
    Implicit: children giving up honored customs; children wanting to act like Americans; *or* children acting different from their parents

---

Without Look-Backs

Number Correct Explicit: _____

Number Correct Implicit: _____

Total: _____

_____ Independent: 9–10 correct

_____ Instructional: 7–8 correct

_____ Frustration: 0–6 correct

With Look-Backs

Number Correct Explicit: _____

Number Correct Implicit: _____

Total: _____

_____ Independent: 9–10 correct

_____ Instructional: 7–8 correct

_____ Frustration: 0–6 correct

Think-Aloud Summary

Think-Aloud Statements That Indicate Understanding

Paraphrasing/Summarizing _____

Making New Meaning _____

Questioning That Indicates Understanding _____

Noting Understanding _____

Reporting Prior Knowledge _____

Identifying Personally _____

Think-Aloud Statements That Indicate Lack of Understanding

Questioning That Indicates Lack of Understanding _____

Noting Lack of Understanding _____

Level: Upper Middle School

Science

Concept Questions:

What are stars made of?

_____

_____

_____ (3-2-1-0)

What is gravity?

_____

_____

_____ (3-2-1-0)

What is mass?

_____

_____

_____ (3-2-1-0)

What do nuclear reactions produce?

_____

_____

_____ (3-2-1-0)

Score: _____ /12 = _____ %

_____ FAM _____ UNFAM

Prediction:

_____

_____

"Life Cycles of Stars—Part 1"

Stars have life cycles, just like humans. In fact, a star is born, changes and then dies. In contrast to the human life cycle that lasts about 75 years, the life cycle of a typical star is measured in billions of years.

Every star in the sky is at a different stage in its life cycle. Some stars are relatively young, while others are near the end of their existence. The sun is about halfway through its 10-billion-year-long life cycle.

Birth of a Star

The space between stars is not entirely empty. In some places, there are great clouds of gas and dust. Each of these clouds is a nebula. A nebula is where stars are born.

The element hydrogen makes up most of a nebula. Helium and a sprinkling of dust are also present. The particles in a nebula are spread very thin. In fact, the particles are a million times less dense than the particles in the air you breathe. However, since nebulae are very large, they contain enormous amounts of matter.

Gravity causes matter to be attracted to other matter. Therefore, as a nebula travels though space, it collects more dust and gas. The clouds become packed tighter and tighter, as gravity pulls it all together. Whenever matter is packed in this way, it heats up. An especially dense part of the nebula may form a hot, spinning ball of matter. Such a ball of hot matter is called a protostar.

A protostar doesn't yet shine by ordinary light, but it does give off infrared energy. Scientists identify protostars within nebulae using infrared telescopes. A protostar eventually becomes hot enough

Level: Upper Middle School

for <u>nuclear</u> <u>fusion</u> to take place in its core. When <u>nuclear fusion</u> produces great amounts of energy, a star comes to life.

Low-Mass Star

Stars begin their life cycle with different masses. A star's mass determines how long its life cycle will last and how it will die. Stars with a mass less than five times that of the sun are called low-mass stars. Most stars are in this group.

A low-mass star begins its life cycle as a main-sequence star. Over a period of billions of years, its supply of hydrogen is slowly changed by <u>nuclear</u> <u>fusion</u> into <u>helium</u>. During this time, the star changes very little. (382 words)

From *Science Insights: Exploring Earth and Space* by M. DeSpezio, M. Linner-Luebe, M. Lisowski, B. Sparks, and G. Skoog. Copyright © 2002 by Addison Wesley Longman. Adapted by permission of Pearson Education, Inc. All Rights Reserved.

Number of Total Miscues
(Total Accuracy): _____

Number of Meaning-Change Miscues
(Total Acceptability): _____

Total Accuracy		**Total Acceptability**
0–9 miscue	____ Independent	____ 0–9 miscue
10–40 miscues	____ Instructional	____ 10–21 miscues
41+ miscues	____ Frustration	____ 22+ miscues

Rate: 382 × 60 = 22,920/____ seconds = ____ WPM

Correct WPM: (382 – ____ errors) × 60 =
____ /____ seconds = ____ CWPM

Retelling Scoring Sheet for "Life Cycles of Stars—Part 1"

Main Idea

____ Stars have life cycles.

Details

____ A star is born,
____ changes,
____ and then dies.
____ The life cycle is measured
____ in billions of years.
____ Every star is at a different stage.
____ Some stars are young
____ while others are near the end of their existence.
____ The sun is about halfway through its cycle
____ of 10 billion years.

Main Idea

____ A nebula is where stars are born.

Details

____ The space between stars is not empty.
____ There are clouds
____ of gas
____ and dust.
____ Each is a nebula.
____ Hydrogen makes up most of a nebula.
____ Helium is also present.
____ The particles are spread very thin.
____ They are less dense
____ a million times less dense
____ than the particles in the air.
____ Since nebulae are very large,
____ they contain enormous amounts
____ of matter.

Main Idea

____ Gravity causes matter to be attracted to matter.

Details

____ As a nebula travels though space,
____ it collects more dust

Level: Upper Middle School

____ and gas.
____ The clouds become packed tighter
____ as gravity pulls it together.
____ It heats up.
____ A part of the nebula may form a ball
____ a dense part
____ a hot ball
____ a spinning ball
____ a ball of matter
____ called a protostar.

Main Idea

____ A protostar doesn't shine
____ but it gives off energy
____ infrared energy.

Details

____ Scientists identify protostars
____ with infrared telescopes.
____ A protostar becomes hot enough
____ for fusion to take place
____ nuclear fusion.
____ When nuclear fusion produces energy,
____ great amounts of energy,
____ a star comes to life.

Main Idea

____ Stars begin their cycle
____ with different masses.

Details

____ A star's mass determines
____ how long its cycle will last
____ and how it will die.
____ Stars with a mass less than five times
____ that of the sun
____ are low-mass stars.
____ Most stars are in this group.

Main Idea

____ A low-mass star begins its cycle
____ as a main-sequence star.

Details

____ Over billions of years,
____ its supply of hydrogen is changed
____ slowly changed
____ into helium
____ by nuclear fusion.
____ During this time
____ the star changes very little.

68 Ideas

Number of ideas recalled _____

Other ideas recalled, including summary statements and inferences:

Questions for "Life Cycles of Stars—Part 1"

1. What is this passage mainly about?
   Implicit: how stars are born

2. How long is the life cycle of the sun?
   Explicit: 10 billion years

3. What is a nebula?
   Explicit: a cloud of gas and dust

Level: Upper Middle School

4. Why do nebulae collect more dust and gas as they move through space?
Implicit: gravity causes dust to be attracted to other dust

5. What is a protostar?
Explicit: a dense hot part of the nebula

6. If a protostar doesn't give off light, how do scientists know it exists?
Implicit: it gives off infrared energy which can be detected using infrared telescopes

7. What is the final action that causes a protostar to become a star?
Implicit: the core becomes so hot that nuclear fusion occurs and produces great amounts of energy

8. What determines how long a star will live?
Explicit: its mass

9. Why is gravity crucial to the birth of a star?
Implicit: gravity packs matter which causes it to heat up and become a protostar

10. In a low-mass star, what does hydrogen change into?
Explicit: helium

Without Look-Backs

Number Correct Explicit: _____

Number Correct Implicit: _____

Total: _____

_____ Independent: 9–10 correct

_____ Instructional: 7–8 correct

_____ Frustration: 0–6 correct

With Look-Backs

Number Correct Explicit: _____

Number Correct Implicit: _____

Total: _____

_____ Independent: 9–10 correct

_____ Instructional: 7–8 correct

_____ Frustration: 0–6 correct

Level: Upper Middle School

Science

Concept Questions:

How do stars change over time?

_____

_____

_____ (3-2-1-0)

What is a supernova?

_____

_____

_____ (3-2-1-0)

What is density?

_____

_____

_____ (3-2-1-0)

What is a black hole?

_____

_____

_____ (3-2-1-0)

Score: _____ /12 = _____ %

_____ FAM _____ UNFAM

Prediction:

_____

_____

"Life Cycles of Stars—Part 2"

Red Giant Stage

As the hydrogen in the core of a low-mass star is used up, the core starts to collapse. The core of the star becomes denser and hotter. The increased temperature causes another kind of nuclear reaction. Helium is converted to carbon. This nuclear reaction gives off great amounts of energy, causing the star to expand. It becomes a red giant. **STOP**

_____

_____

_____

_____

The red giant stage in a star's life is relatively short. The sun will be a main-sequence star for a total of 10 billion years. But the sun will be a red giant for only about 500 million years. **STOP**

_____

_____

_____

_____

Dwarf Stage

Eventually, most of the helium in a red giant's core is changed into carbon. Nuclear fusion slows. The star cools, and gravity makes it collapse inward. The matter making up the star is squeezed together very tightly, and the star becomes a white dwarf. **STOP**

_____

_____

_____

_____

_____

Level: Upper Middle School

A typical white dwarf is about the size of Earth. But its matter is far denser than any matter on Earth. Eventually, the star becomes a burned-out black chunk of very dense matter that gives off no visible light. Then it is called a black dwarf. **STOP**

_____

_____

_____

_____

Life of a High-Mass Star

Stars more than six times as massive as the sun have a very different life cycle than low-mass stars. A high-mass star uses up its hydrogen at a much faster rate. After only about 50 to 100 million years, a high-mass star has no hydrogen left. At this time, the core collapses and the outer layers expand greatly. The star becomes a super giant. **STOP**

_____

_____

_____

_____

Eventually, the core of the super giant can no longer stand the pressure of the outside layers of the star. The outside layers crash in very suddenly, causing a tremendous explosion that gives off an extraordinary amount of light. Great shells of gases fly off the star. The star becomes a supernova. A supernova explosion is the most violent event known to happen in the universe. **STOP**

_____

_____

_____

After a supernova explodes, only the tiny core of the star remains. This core, made up of neutrons, is called a neutron star. Neutron stars are extremely dense. Astronomers hypothesize that after a massive star undergoes a supernova explosion, it may also become a black hole. A black hole is so dense and its gravity is so strong that nothing can escape from it, not even light. Do black holes really exist? So far, scientists have no real proof. Black holes do not release light so they can't be observed directly. **STOP**

_____

_____

_____

_____

_____

(421 words)

_____

From *Science Insights: Exploring Earth and Space* by M. DeSpezio, M. Linner-Luebe, M. Lisowski, B. Sparks, and G. Skoog. Copyright © 2002 by Addison Wesley Longman. Adapted by permission of Pearson Education, Inc. All Rights Reserved.

Level: Upper Middle School

Number of Total Miscues
(Total Accuracy): _____

Number of Meaning-Change Miscues
(Total Acceptability): _____

Total Accuracy		**Total Acceptability**	
0–10 miscue	____ Independent	____	0–10 miscue
11–44 miscues	____ Instructional	____	11–23 miscues
45+ miscues	____ Frustration	____	24+ miscues

Rate: (If you used this passage as a think-aloud passage, you cannot compute rate): 421 × 60 = 25,260/____ seconds = ____ WPM

Correct WPM: (421 – ____ errors) × 60 =
____ /____ seconds = ____ CWPM

Retelling Scoring Sheet for "Life Cycles of Stars—Part 2"

Main Idea

____ The star becomes a red giant.

Details

____ As the hydrogen is used up
____ in a low-mass star
____ the core starts to collapse.
____ The core becomes denser
____ and hotter.
____ The temperature causes a nuclear reaction.
____ Helium is converted to carbon.
____ The reaction gives off great amounts
____ of energy.
____ A red giant stage is short.
____ The sun will be a red giant
____ for about 500 million years.

Main Idea

____ The star enters the dwarf stage.

Details

____ Helium changes into carbon
____ helium in the core.
____ The star cools
____ and gravity makes it collapse.
____ The matter is squeezed together.
____ It becomes a white dwarf.
____ A dwarf is about the size of Earth
____ but its matter is denser
____ than any matter on Earth.
____ The star becomes a chunk of matter
____ a burned-out chunk
____ a black chunk
____ that gives off no light.
____ Then it is called a black dwarf.

Main Idea

____ High-mass stars have a different life cycle.

Details

____ It uses up its hydrogen
____ at a fast rate.
____ After 50 to 100 million years,
____ it has no hydrogen left.
____ The core collapses
____ and the layers expand
____ the outer layers.
____ The star becomes a super giant.
____ The core can no longer stand the pressure
____ of the outer layers.
____ The layers crash in,
____ causing an explosion
____ a tremendous explosion
____ that gives off light
____ an extraordinary amount of light.
____ Shells fly off the star
____ shells of gases.
____ The star becomes a supernova.
____ A supernova explosion is the most violent event
____ in the universe.

Level: Upper Middle School

Main Idea

____ After a supernova explodes,
____ only the core remains.

Details

____ This core is called a neutron star.
____ It is made up of neutrons.
____ Neutron stars are dense
____ extremely dense.
____ After a star undergoes a supernova,
____ it may become a black hole.
____ A black hole is so dense
____ and its gravity is so strong
____ that nothing can escape from it,
____ not even light.
____ Scientists have no real proof.
____ Black holes do not release light
____ so they can't be observed directly.

64 Ideas

Number of ideas recalled _____

Other ideas recalled, including summary statements and inferences:

Questions for "Life Cycles of Stars—Part 2"

1. What is this passage mainly about?
   Implicit: stages in a star's life

2. What causes all life cycle changes in stars?
   Implicit: nuclear reactions

3. What series of events causes a star to go into the red giant stage?
   Explicit: the core collapses when hydrogen is used up, it becomes denser and hotter, another kind of nuclear reaction occurs and the star expands

4. How long will the sun remain as a red giant?
   Explicit: 500 million years

5. How big is a typical white dwarf?
   Explicit: the size of Earth

6. What is the stage when the star becomes a chunk of dense matter that gives off no visible light?
   Explicit: black dwarf stage

Level: Upper Middle School

7. What causes the core of a high-mass star to collapse?
   Implicit: lack of hydrogen

8. What is one thing a star can become after a supernova explosion?
   Explicit: a neutron star or a black hole

9. Why doesn't a neutron star give out light?
   Implicit: it is too dense

10. Why have scientists been unable to prove the existence of a black hole?
    Implicit: they can't be observed directly because they do not give off light

Without Look-Backs

Number Correct Explicit: _____

Number Correct Implicit: _____

Total: _____

_____ Independent: 9–10 correct

_____ Instructional: 7–8 correct

_____ Frustration: 0–6 correct

With Look-Backs

Number Correct Explicit: _____

Number Correct Implicit: _____

Total: _____

_____ Independent: 9–10 correct

_____ Instructional: 7–8 correct

_____ Frustration: 0–6 correct

Think-Aloud Summary

Think-Aloud Statements That Indicate Understanding

Paraphrasing/Summarizing _____

Making New Meaning _____

Questioning That Indicates Understanding _____

Noting Understanding _____

Reporting Prior Knowledge _____

Identifying Personally _____

Think-Aloud Statements That Indicate Lack of Understanding

Questioning That Indicates Lack of Understanding _____

Noting Lack of Understanding _____

Where the Ashes Are—Part 1

"Wake up, wake up!" my mother shouted. "We've got to get out of here! How can you sleep through all this?" She pulled the covers off me, handed me my clothes, and rushed out of the room.

"Wait!" I cried out, throwing off my pajamas. One leg in and one out of my dark blue school trousers, I stumbled over to my sister Dieu-Ha's room. My mother was yelling, "Are you deaf? Get out! We're going downstairs!"

It was five in the morning. Explosions and gunfire echoed through the high-ceilinged rooms of the government guesthouse. Arched corridors surrounded the twenty bedrooms on the second floor of the massive French-style mansion. My parents had taken the master suite at the end of the hall while my two sisters and I had large rooms next to one another. We had arrived at the end of January 1968, two days before the lunar New Year. Our family were the only guests in the building. Rather than having us stay at my grandfather's small house, my father felt we would be safer at the guesthouse, where extra platoons of local soldiers had been assigned to protect him. He also preferred the guesthouse because it was built along the bank of the river in Hue, the old imperial city, and away from the town's noisy center. The nearby train station was defunct, since the war had disrupted all but a few railway lines.

For many years my father had been working for the government of South Vietnam. Assigned to central Vietnam as a civilian deputy to the military governor, he was based in Da Nang, a coastal town just over an hour's drive from Hue. He sent us to visit his parents there regularly, especially at holidays. He came along on this holiday visit—for the lunar New Year, Tet, in 1968.

Although my father had been warned about a possible escalation in the fighting, he said to my mother: "There's a ceasefire. It's New Year's. We'll be safe." But he abandoned his plan to drive and instead arranged for a flight to Hue. We'd landed at the Phu Bai airport in midafternoon.

The road into town had been taken over by an endless convoy of tanks and army trucks transporting U.S. soldiers, most likely toward Khe Sanh, an American base that had been under siege for several months. Along with a few other civilian cars, small trucks, and innumerable motorcycles, we inched our way toward Hue. I kept looking out the car window, glimpsing rice fields here and there. Mostly, though, the view was blocked by the olive green steel of tanks and trucks.

My mother sought to distract us. "You kids are going to be spoiled this year. I bet your grandparents will have lots of treats for you. But I want you to behave."

Settled in at the guesthouse, on the second night of our stay my mother and sisters and I fell asleep just after twelve, insulated by its thick walls and heavy curtains. Endless rounds of firecrackers went off as the people of Hue celebrated the arrival of Tet. No one knew that along with the Year of the Monkey, the dreaded Viet Cong soldiers had also arrived. No one could tell when the firecrackers stopped and the gunfire began.

Dieu-Ha and I followed my mother into my other sister's room. Dieu-Quynh hid herself under a pile of blankets. Ma shook her. "Come on, we're going downstairs!" As she started to rifle through Dieu-Quynh's drawers, grabbing clothes for her to change into, she said to Dieu-Ha and me, "Go see if your father's downstairs and stay with him!"

We rushed down the corridors toward the double staircase. Its marble steps formed a half-circle framed by an intricately carved banister. A bullet shattered a porthole as we skipped down the steps. Dieu-Ha screamed. Pieces of glass and marble flew by. We raced past the elephant tusks in the huge vestibule and toward the reception hall. A chilly wind blew through the huge room. Someone had opened the drapes and shutters of the dozens of windows rising from knee level to ten feet above my head, each framing a view of the River of Perfume, Song Hu'o'ng.

Where the Ashes Are—Part 2

In the somber light I could make out dark foliage swaying by the riverbank as a coat of morning mist rose above the water. Nature paints winter scenes in Hue in shades of gray, but this morning I could see rapid bursts of orange and red fire coming from behind the bushes. A flare shot out from the far distance. Exploding with a thud, it hung from a small parachute and cast a brilliant mid-day light over a large area of the river as it floated down. Rockets exploded across the burning sky and fell to the ground in rapid succession. Deafened, Dieu-Ha and I dove behind an antique cabinet at the end of the room. My father had been nowhere in sight.

That night he had stayed up late to read a French book that contrasted two warriors: North Vietnam's famed general Vo Nguyen Giap and William Westmore-land, commander of the U.S. ground troops in South Vietnam. Just before four o'clock Cha (father in Vietnamese) had left his bed and gone up to the rooftop terrace, where he marveled at the red and green tracers flying across the sky like shooting stars. Despite his interest in the generals, he had little understanding of the role of flares and tracers as tools of warfare. They were simply a beautiful sight as they burst over the night sky.

"Your father's still up there. Been on that roof an hour! He'll get killed!" Ma wailed as she came down the staircase. Seeing the open windows, she took us into a chamber behind the reception room. "Where's Dieu-Quynh?" she ex-claimed. "She was just on the stairs with me!"

In the midst of the gunfire and explosions, my sister had gone back to bed—a mad thing to, since bullets were now flying indoors. By 1968, however, most of what Dieu-Quynh did was irrational. For four years she had been show-ing signs of mental illness. Ordering Dieu-Ha and me to sit still, my mother dashed back upstairs. A bullet came through Dieu-Quynh's room, hitting the lamp on her bedstand. Sparks flew in all directions. Ma grabbed my older sister by the wrist and led her downstairs, calling out to my father all the while.

"We shouldn't worry too much," he said in his usual unruffled tone when he entered the room a few minutes later. When he had finally left the roof, he went downstairs to look for the butler, then into an office off the living room. "I called the provincial office; they say the fighting is far away."

"Look out the windows!" my mother shot back.

"I did," Cha replied, still calm and composed. "Our soldiers are still at their posts." From the rooftop he had been able to see men in green surrounding the guesthouse.

We gathered together, crouching on the floor. No one spoke. My father glanced at the spacious desk and heavy armchairs, hoping to hide behind the furniture until the gunfire died down.

Between explosions came the sound of someone knocking at the front door. My parents put out their arms. We sat still. The pounding grew louder. After a moment of hesitation, Ma stood up. "It's our soldiers," she declared. "Come on!" My sisters followed her through the reception area to the vestibule. As my father and I reached the door to the reception room, we heard her scream.

My father led me back to the office in the back, locking the door behind him as quietly as possible. We went to the desk, and I held his hand as we low-ered ourselves behind it. My father didn't know what else to do. Spotting a steel safe in the corner of the room, he went over to open it, then without a word closed it again. Not even a nine-year-old boy could fit inside.

"I have a young son in the house," my mother was explaining to the intruders in the vestibule, Viet Cong soldiers in olive green uniforms. They wore no insignia or badges that showed affiliation or rank. Whether because of the darkness or distance, his poor eyesight, or his unfamiliarity with military matters, my father had mistaken them for our own Southern Republican Army troops.

One of the soldiers now threatened to shoot anyone still hiding in the house. "Tell us where everyone is and you'll be safe, sister," he assured my mother." "Please don't hurt us, please!" she begged. "Just let me go find my son."

Cha groped behind the heavy dark green drapes along the office wall, where a set of double doors opened onto a hallway. We tiptoed through the hall to the doors that led outside. My father motioned me out first, then carefully closed the doors behind him. I ran down the steps and turned toward the hedges that separated the guesthouse grounds from the riverbank. "Hey, boy!" someone cried. I turned. A Viet Cong soldier sitting cross-legged pointed his rifle at me. I ran back to my father.

Back in the hallway inside the house, Cha quietly approached each door to the offices surrounding the reception area. A gun muzzle protruded from one, and we backed off. The doorway to yet another office also had a gun muzzle poking out from it. There was no escape.

Out in the courtyard it was still dark. Dozens of people in nightclothes shivered in the early morning dampness. Slowly the soldiers separated families from one another. The guesthouse was to be used as a temporary holding center. More people were brought into the courtyard. A disheveled Frenchman of about thirty entered the area barefooted, a trench coat thrown on over his pajamas. Hands clasped together, he tried to explain his situation to two Viet Cong soldiers. "De Gaulle, Ho Chi Minh, amis," he kept saying. "Friends."

The two Viet Cong waved him away. One of them shouted, "Khong biet tieng dtiu!" They did not speak any foreign languages.

"They're regular soldiers," my father whispered to a man next to him, whose crisp white shirt was tucked into pajama trousers. "Such a strong northern accent."

"You're right," the man whispered back. "The way they call everybody 'Sister' and 'Brother' is strange." The men and women before us were not part of the so-called National Liberation Front within South Viet Nam. Ho Chi Minh was now sending in troops from the North for an outright offensive, a full invasion.

In the confusion our family took refuge in a small temple just off the grounds of the guesthouse. Searching through his wallet, my father took out all his business cards and hid them under a mat. "Just say you're a teacher," whispered my mother.

He never had the chance. When a Viet Cong woman found us in the temple a little more than an hour later, she jabbed her index finger into his chest. "You, Brother, I know who you are," she said. "The Party and the Revolution will be generous to all those willing to confess their crimes against the People."

"The Party" could only be the Communist party headquartered in Ha Noi. The enemy's arm had now reached into the heart of Hue. "Don't lie!" the woman continued. Putting her finger up to my father's nose, she said, "Brother, we know—you're the general staying in this house. Such opulence. We'll take care of you."

Where the Ashes Are—Part 3

We lost track of the time as the soldiers sorted out all the people gathered in front of the guesthouse. At last, however, they accepted my father's protestations that he was not a general but a government functionary. He and the other men were taken inside the mansion. Women and children were sent to a neighboring building, down into a long rectangular basement with extremely thick walls and a single narrow door at one end. The rocket explosions had ceased, but the sound of gunfire continued. We had become accustomed to it and no longer jumped at the bursts from automatic weapons. Ten families followed each other below ground. I ended up leading the way into the darkness. **STOP**

"Go to the far end. Go!" my mother urged me, and made sure that Dieu-Quynh stayed with us. She knew that, on capturing a town, the Communists would use residents as workers to support military operations. Women would be sent to look for food, or nurse the wounded. If not required to take up arms themselves, men would have to gather the wounded and the dead. Dieu-Quynh, a tall girl of eighteen, was at risk of being drafted for such service. Turning to the family behind her, my mother explained. "My daughter is ill. A big girl, but not all that wise." It was an explanation she would feel compelled to repeat often in the next days. I finally settled for a spot below a minuscule window with iron bars. In the damp, cavernous basement, the tiny hole let in a faint ray of the light that signaled the first day of the Year of the Monkey. **STOP**

Throughout that day and most of the next night the adults carried on a whispered debate, trying to make sense out of what had happened. "They can't win," the guesthouse chauffeur pronounced. "I bet they'll retreat soon. The Americans will bomb, and our troops will rescue us in a few days." My mother listened dispassionately. She sighed often and refused to eat any of the food the family next to us offered. Busy with their prisoners in the mansion, the soldiers left us alone. **STOP**

In our second day of captivity, a female voice shouted into the basement. "Mrs. Dai! Is there a Mrs. Dai down there?" My mother picked her way toward the door. "Your husband's up in the house. He wants to see you," the voice announced. My mother went up alone, warning me to keep my sister Dieu-Quynh from wandering out. During the night, Dieu-Quynh had been difficult, continually demanding hot water. For the last year or so she had been obsessed with matters of hygiene, compulsively washing her hands as well as any household utensils before she would use them. Finally realizing that this was a luxury, she now sat silent and withdrawn. I asked Dieu-Ha to stay with her, then went to sit at the door to wait for my mother. **STOP**

The guns had gone quiet at some point without anyone noticing. More soldiers had arrived in the compound and were now setting up a crude hospital. A stretched-out army poncho served as an awning, sheltering three bamboo cots that had been shoved together. The soldiers put a mat of woven branches and leaves on top of the cots, enlarging the surface to accommodate five wounded men. Looking like pallbearers carrying a white porcelain coffin, three young men and a woman in civilian clothes brought in an ancient French bathtub. They filled the tub half full of water, warning us not to use it. No one seemed to be in charge, yet a lot of orders were being issued. Sitting by the door of the basement, I watched the men and women from the North while waiting for my mother. **STOP**

"What are you doing here?" she asked when she returned, roughing up my hair. "We're going up to see your father in a while." She did not sound excited. After checking on my sisters, she set about looking for food for my father.

"Ma, what are they going to do with him?" I asked. I repeated the question again and again, but my mother would only shake her head; finally she responded, "Oh, he'll be all right. They said all he needed was a few days of re-education. They're taking him somewhere, but he'll be back."

Taken where? Would we be rescued first? Would they let him go? I didn't think she knew the answers to my questions. I tugged at her sleeve. "Ma, what's 're-education'?" She glanced at the wounded Viet Cong lying beneath the poncho. "It's like school, that's all. Now help me with this pot." **STOP**

Spoiled since her youth by household servants, my mother had rarely gone near a kitchen. Now she was cooking a big pot of rice she had secured from a woman in the basement. The Viet Cong had set up a few clay burners and gave us some coal. Other than the rice, there was nothing to cook. We ate it with pickled leeks and cucumber, which normally accompanied fancier foods during Tet. The rice tasted of the river water my mother had used to cook it in. The Viet Cong had allowed her only a small amount of water from the bathtub to take to my father. She was happy to have cleaner water for him to drink—until she tasted it. It smelled of Mercurochrome, the red disinfectant common in Viet Nam. The soldiers had used the water to wash the wounds of injured men, then poured back unused portions, now laced with Mercurochrome. She found a tiny bit of tea to steep in the water and packed some rice into a big bowl for my father. **STOP**

I sensed that my father was happy to see us, but his face showed no such emotion. He took the woven basket Ma handed him, which contained a towel, two T-shirts, and a pair of pants she had found on her previous trip to the guesthouse to see him. "There's no need—you will be well provided for," a Viet Cong cadre said. "You'll be in re-education for just a short time. Now that the region is liberated, you'll be allowed to come back soon."

In the big hall across from the master suite, my father kept caressing my head. I couldn't think of much to say. Some prisoners crouched along the wall, watching us. Others were curled up on the floor like shrimps. My mother gave my father the bowl of rice and the tea. I waited to see if he could taste the Mercurochrome, but I couldn't tell from his expression. **STOP**

I glanced around my parents' bedroom. It had been turned upside down. The book my father had been reading about Giap and Westmoreland still lay by his bed. My mother's jewelry and toilet case had had a hole gashed through it with a crude knife.

"Your mother will take you over to your grandparents' in a few days," Cha said. "I'll be back after a time."

Later, sometime past midnight, Communist soldiers took my father and a dozen other men away. Standing on a stool with my mother at my side, I watched through the tiny basement window. A rope was hooked through my father's elbows and tied behind his back, while his wrists were bound together in front of his chest. He was also tied to the man in front of him. It would be sixteen years before I saw him again. **STOP**

World War I—Part 1

World War I, also known as the Great War, drew in not only the major powers of Europe, but those of America and Asia as well. Many economic and political factors caused the war. Newly industrialized nations competed with one another for trade and markets for their goods. Also, the urge for national power and independence from other nations came from old and new powers. When a new nation tried to increase its power by building a strong military, an older nation perceived the new nation as a threat to its power. Such tensions led to the division of Europe into two groups for security: one composed of Britain, France, and Russia, the other of Austria, Hungary, and Germany.

Although the factors discussed above caused the war, the final breaking point was a local conflict between Austria and Serbia, a tiny kingdom in southeastern Europe. Serbia, supported by Russia, wanted to unite with the Serbs living in the Austro-Hungarian Empire and create a Greater Serbia. Austria, supported by Germany, did not want Serbia cutting into its empire. The war officially started in August of 1914, after the assassination of the Austrian heir to the throne, who was visiting Sarajevo, near Serbia's border. The assassin was a young man with connections to the military intelligence branch of the Serbian government. Austria's attempt to punish Serbia drew Russia and its allies Britain and France into a war against Austria–Hungary and Germany. The map below illustrates the geographical location of the countries in Europe and surrounding regions in 1914.

The War Raged on Two Fronts

Germany hoped to defeat France by striking quickly through Belgium and, therefore, to minimize the danger of a two-front war. The highly trained German troops nearly reached Paris before the French stopped them. However, the Russians aided France by suddenly attacking Germany on its eastern front, and Germany sent troops from western Europe to face the attack. With the German forces diminished, the French were able to force the weakened Germans back. The war in the west became a stalemate with neither side able to achieve a victory. As a result, both sides sought new allies to help them gain victory, and the war became a world war as Japan, Italy, Portugal, Rumania, and other countries joined Britain, France, and Russia. Germany and Austria–Hungary drew in Bulgaria and the Ottoman Empire, which included Turkey.

On the eastern front Russia kept part of the German army busy. Although Russia fought valiantly, it had not been prepared for war and thus was unable to defeat the Germans. Russian defeats led to a revolution that toppled the tsar of Russia. In late 1917 the new leader of Russia, Lenin, offered to make peace with Germany. As part of the treaty agreement, Germany gained coal mines and oil fields from Russia, which gave Germany power to fuel its army. More important, it allowed the war to be fought on only one front—the western front.

The United States entered the war when Germany began attacking American ships that were taking supplies to Britain and France. U.S. President Woodrow Wilson warned the Germans to stop the attacks, and for a while they did. But they announced an unrestricted submarine warfare after the British blockade shut off supplies to Germany. The final event that caused the United States to join the Allies was the interception of a telegram from the German foreign secretary to Mexico asking Mexico to ally itself with Germany and help fight the United States. Germany promised Mexico financial aid and the recovery of Texas, New Mexico, and Arizona when the Allies were defeated.

From *History and Life* by T. W. Wallbank, A. Schrier, D. Maier, and P. Gutierrez-Smith. Copyright © 1993 by Scott Foresman and Company. Used by permission of Pearson Education, Inc. All Rights Reserved.

World War I—Part 2

In the fall of 1918, German military leaders realized they could not win. One by one Germany's allies quit. On November 3, German sailors mutinied at Kiel, a city and port in northwest Germany. Four days later a revolution broke out in Germany. A republic was founded, and the kaiser fled to Holland.

Leaders of the new German government agreed to an armistice, which is an agreement to stop fighting. They asked that the peace settlement be based on President Wilson's Fourteen Points, which he had described in a speech to Congress in 1918. The Fourteen Points outlined the president's ideas for solving the problems that led to the war. Wilson wanted an end to secret agreements, freedom of the seas in peace and war, the reduction of armaments, the right of nationality groups to form their own nations, and an association of nations to keep the peace. In other speeches Wilson called for a negotiated peace with reasonable demands made on the losers. The Allies agreed to model the peace settlement on the Fourteen Points.

Early in the morning of November 11, 1918, the war ended. In a railroad car in the Compiègne Forest in northern France, two German delegates met Allied officials to sign the armistice. The guns were silent.

The Victors Tried to Build a Lasting Peace

No previous war had caused such widespread horror. More than 10 million troops were killed in battle, and 20 million more were wounded. Thirteen million civilians died from war-related famine, disease, and injuries. The cost of the war was estimated at more than $350 billion. Destruction was everywhere.

Three Leaders Dominated the Paris Peace Conference

After the armistice had been signed, the Allied nations met in Paris to discuss peace terms. Contrary to Wilson's wishes, the defeated countries were not allowed to send representatives to the peace conference. Thus, the so-called Big Three dominated the meeting: President Wilson; David Lloyd George, prime minister of Great Britain; and Georges Clemenceau, premier of France. At the conference Wilson pushed his Fourteen Points. Above all, he wanted to see a League of Nations, an international association established to keep the peace. To get the others to agree, however, he had to make compromises.

Georges Clemenceau, known as the "Old Tiger," had led France during the darkest hours of the war. He wanted Germany to pay war damages because almost all of the fighting on the western front had been on French soil. Most of all he insisted that France be made safe from attack by Germany in the future. He wanted German power destroyed even at the cost of permanently taking much of Germany's western territories from her. Clemenceau placed little faith in Wilson's proposed "League of Nations."

Lloyd George in turn wanted Germany's colonies for Britain. He also wanted the German navy destroyed. During the peace talks, he mediated between the idealism of Wilson and the severe terms of Clemenceau. In the resulting compromise, Wilson gave in on many details and agreed to form an alliance with Britain and France against future German attacks. Clemenceau and Lloyd George agreed to make the creation of the League of Nations part of the peace agreement, which was called the Versailles Treaty.

From *History and Life* by T. W. Wallbank, A. Schrier, D. Maier, and P. Gutierrez-Smith. Copyright © 1993 by Scott Foresman and Company. Used by permission of Pearson Education, Inc. All Rights Reserved.

World War I—Part 3

Germany Lost Territory and Wealth in Its Defeat

When the German delegation arrived to sign the Versailles Treaty, they found its terms harsher than they had expected. The Germans were outraged at the war-guilt clause, which placed the entire blame for the war on Germany and its allies. They were also dismayed that many of Wilson's Fourteen Points were missing or had been weakened by changes. The first delegates from Germany refused to sign the treaty. To avoid further attacks by Allied soldiers, however, a second German delegation signed it on June 28, 1919. Even though Germany signed the treaty, there was strong resentment over its harsh terms. **STOP**

In the treaty, France won back the provinces of Alsace and Lorraine, lost to Germany in the late 1800s. The German territory west of the Rhine River, called the Rhineland, was to become a buffer zone between the two enemies. It was to be occupied by Allied troops for at least 15 years. France was also given the rich coal mines of the Saar, located on the French–German border. But after 15 years, the Saarlanders could vote to have their region go back to the German government or remain under the French. In 1935 they voted to become part of Germany again. **STOP**

In the treaty the Allies required that Germany repay much of the cost of the war, or make reparations. They wanted an immediate payment of $5 billion in cash. Two years later they billed Germany for $32 billion, plus interest. The treaty reduced German military power and permitted Germany an army of no more than 100,000 men. The navy was allowed only six warships, some other vessels, and no submarines or military airplanes. The Germans were not alone in thinking such peace terms were unjust. Even David Lloyd George doubted the justice of the Versailles Treaty. President Wilson hoped that his dream, the League of Nations, could correct the unjust treaty later. **STOP**

New Independent Nations Were Formed

Four empires had fallen apart in the course of World War I: the German, the Austro-Hungarian, the Ottoman, and the Russian. Based partly on secret agreements made during the war, the Allies drew up treaties to divide the territory. The map on the next page shows how the empires were divided up. The western portion of the old Russian Empire lost to Germany during the war was reorganized. Finland, Latvia, Lithuania, and Estonia emerged from this territory, and part of this area was used to create Poland. **STOP**

The defeated Austro-Hungarian Empire was also divided into several new countries: Austria, Hungary, Czechoslovakia, and Yugoslavia. The creation of the new countries helped fulfill one of Wilson's Fourteen Points, the right of self-determination, or the right of people to form their own nations. **STOP**

The Ottoman Empire too was divided up. Syria, Iraq, Trans-Jordan, and Palestine were created from the Ottoman Empire. They became mandates, lands given to certain nations to develop. Syria was ruled by France, the other three by Britain. These mandates were promised independence at a future time. **STOP**

Redrawing the map of Europe, however, brought some new groups under foreign control. There were social, cultural, and language implications of this foreign control. For example, Austrians living in the southwestern part of the old Austro-Hungarian Empire came under the rule of Italy. Other German-speaking Austrians were placed under Czechoslovakian rule.

One of the biggest problems was the newly independent Poland, created from the Polish-language provinces of prewar Austria–Hungary, Germany, and Russia. The treaty's authors gave Poland some territory in eastern Germany known as the Polish Corridor. The Polish Corridor and other areas would prove to be problems in the future because they contained many ethnic minorities. Some Germans lived in the new Polish Corridor, and to complicate matters, many Hungarians also came under Romanian control. Few of these peoples were happy about the changes, and their discontent was a dangerous sign for the future. **STOP**

Characteristics of Viruses—Part 1

Similarities and Differences between Viruses and Cells

If you ever had a cold or the flu, you probably hosted viruses. A virus is an infectious agent made up of a core of nucleic acid and a protein coat. Viruses are not cells. Unlike plant and animal cells, a virus package does not have a nucleus, a membrane, or cellular organelles such as ribosomes, mitochondria, or chloroplasts. Although viruses are not cells, they do have organized structural parts.

Compared to even the smallest cell, a virus is tiny. The virus that causes polio, for example, measures only 20 nanometers in diameter. One nanometer is one billionth of a meter. At that size, 3000 polioviruses could line up across the period at the end of this sentence.

All viruses have at least two parts: a protective protein coat and a core of nucleic acid. The protein coat around the core of the nucleic acid is called a capsid. Depending on the virus, the capsid may consist of one or several kinds of protein. The capsid protects the viral nucleic acid core from its environment.

In cells, DNA is the hereditary material. Some viruses also contain DNA, while other viruses contain only RNA. In viruses containing RNA, the RNA functions as the hereditary material.

Compared to a cell, a virus has a relatively simple existence. Viruses do not eat, respire, or respond to environmental changes as cells do. It should not surprise you, therefore, to learn that viruses have fewer genes than cells have. While a human cell may contain about 100,000 genes and a bacterial cell about 1000, a virus may contain only 5 genes.

An Influenza Virus

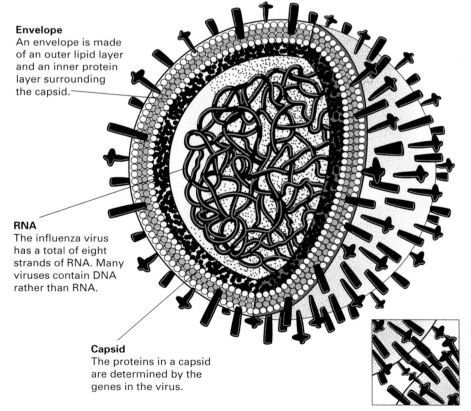

Envelope
An envelope is made of an outer lipid layer and an inner protein layer surrounding the capsid.

RNA
The influenza virus has a total of eight strands of RNA. Many viruses contain DNA rather than RNA.

Capsid
The proteins in a capsid are determined by the genes in the virus.

Projections
The spikelike projections on the viral envelope help the virus recognize and attach to a host cell.

In the figure on the previous page, you can see the parts of an influenza virus: a core of RNA, a surrounding capsid, and an outer covering called an envelope. An envelope is an additional protective coating usually made up of lipids, proteins, and carbohydrates. Envelopes are found only in viruses that infect animal cells. An envelope has spike-like projections that recognize and bind to complementary sites on the membrane of the cell being infected. Think about how a prickly burr sticks to objects.

Characteristics of Viruses—Part 2

Viral Replication: Ticking Time Bombs

Viruses do not reproduce, they replicate. Reproduction, which is characteristic of living things, involves cell division. Replication does not involve cell division. Viruses cannot replicate on their own. In order to replicate, viruses require a host. A host is an organism that shelters and nourishes something. Living cells host viruses. These host cells provide all the materials that viruses need to copy themselves.

When it enters a host cell, a virus may immediately begin to replicate, or it may remain relatively inactive. The viral replication process that rapidly kills a host cell is called the lytic cycle. You can follow the lytic cycle in the figure below. The lytic cycle begins when a virus invades a host cell and begins to replicate immediately, producing many new viruses. Eventually, the host cell lyses, or breaks apart, releasing the newly made viruses. The new viruses may then enter other cells and repeat the cycle.

As a child you may have had chicken pox, which is caused by a virus. While you were ill, most of the viruses were in the lytic cycle. Because your cells were being destroyed by the chicken pox virus, you showed symptoms of the disease.

Sometimes a virus does not start the lytic cycle immediately. Instead the virus enters the lysogenic cycle. The lysogenic cycle is a type of replication in which a virus does not immediately kill a host cell. The lysogenic cycle in a bacteria cell is shown on the right side of the figure on the next page.

During the lysogenic cycle, viral DNA inserts itself into a host cell's chromosome. A viral DNA segment that is inserted in a bacterial chromosome is called a prophage. A host cell carrying a prophage may divide many times. The prophage is replicated every time the host cell's chromosome replicates.

Lytic Cycle

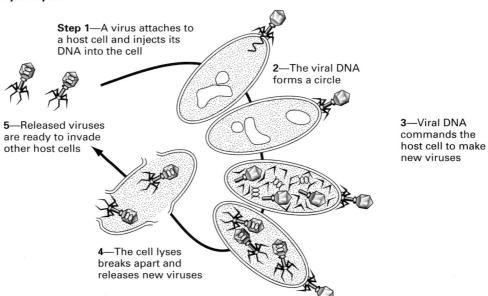

Step 1—A virus attaches to a host cell and injects its DNA into the cell

2—The viral DNA forms a circle

3—Viral DNA commands the host cell to make new viruses

4—The cell lyses breaks apart and releases new viruses

5—Released viruses are ready to invade other host cells

Lysogenic Cycle

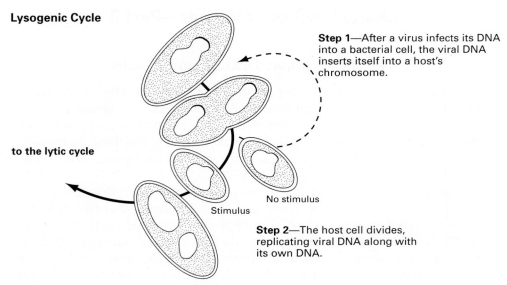

Step 1—After a virus infects its DNA into a bacterial cell, the viral DNA inserts itself into a host's chromosome.

to the lytic cycle

No stimulus

Stimulus

Step 2—The host cell divides, replicating viral DNA along with its own DNA.

Step 3—A stimulus allows the viral DNA to separate from the cell's chromosome and enter the lytic cycle. Without a stimulus, the viral DNA stays in the cell's chromosome.

Some prophages remain in the lysogenic cycle indefinitely. Usually, however, some type of environmental stimulus eventually results in the separation of a prophage from the chromosome of its host cell. The viral DNA then enters the lytic cycle. The virus that causes cold sores in humans can go through the lysogenic cycle, for example. Cold sores erupt when these viruses enter the lytic cycle.

Characteristics of Viruses—Part 3

Diversity of Viruses: An Unending Supply

Classifying viruses is difficult because they are so diverse. As a result, biologists have developed several different ways of organizing viruses. Sometimes they are organized by shape, sometimes by the host they infect. Viruses may also be classified according to the way they function inside a cell. **STOP**

Shape. The arrangement of proteins in capsids determines the shape of the viruses.

Host. Viruses can be organized according to the type of host they infect. There are animal viruses, plant viruses, and bacterial viruses. Viruses that infect only bacterial cells are referred to as bacteriophages.

Many but not all viruses invade only a specific type of organism. For example, the virus that causes polio replicates only inside human host cells. The virus that causes rabies infects only the cells of a particular animal species, such as dogs and humans. **STOP**

You may wonder how viruses can be so specific. Earlier you learned that capsids and envelopes contain specific proteins. Receptor sites on host cells also contain specific proteins. If the outer proteins in a virus do not fit with the outer proteins of a cell, the virus will not attach to the cell. Without attachment, the viral nucleic acid cannot enter the host cell to replicate. **STOP**

Function. Some viruses, such as retroviruses, can also be classified based on how they function in a host. A retrovirus is a virus that contains an RNA code that replicates by first transcribing its RNA into DNA. The prefix "retro-" means "reverse." What do you think might work in reverse in this group of viruses? **STOP**

Most viruses and all organisms make RNA from DNA in the process of transcription. Retroviruses are able to make nucleic acids in reverse order from the usual process. In retroviruses DNA is made from RNA. As you can see in the figure on the next page, retroviruses have an enzyme called reverse transcriptase, which transcribes viral RNA into viral DNA inside the host cell. You can study the figure to better understand the replication of a human immunodeficiency virus (HIV). The retrovirus causes acquired immunodeficiency syndrome (AIDS). **STOP**

Retroviruses include tumor-producing viruses as well as HIV. Tumor-producing retroviruses and HIV follow a similar invasion pattern. Many tumor-producing viruses, however, enter the lysogenic cycle after Step 3 in the figure. Tumors do not immediately appear, but the viral DNA replicates along with the host cell DNA. Eventually many host cells will contain tumor-producing viral DNA. Using what you have learned about the lysogenic cycle, you can probably predict what will happen eventually. **STOP**

Nonviral particles. Scientists have discovered two infectious agents that have simpler structures than viruses: viroids and prions. A viroid is a single strand of pure RNA. Viroids cause plant diseases. For example, viroids have killed many coconut palm trees in the Philippines. Other viroids affect the health

The Retrovirus

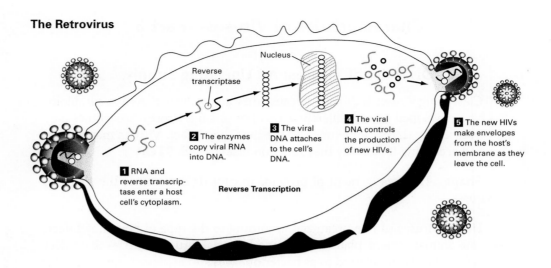

Nucleus

Reverse
transcriptase

1 RNA and
reverse transcrip-
tase enter a host
cell's cytoplasm.

2 The enzymes
copy viral RNA
into DNA.

3 The viral
DNA attaches
to the cell's
DNA.

4 The viral
DNA controls
the production
of new HIVs.

5 The new HIVs
make envelopes
from the host's
membrane as they
leave the cell.

Reverse Transcription

of crops such as potatoes and tomatoes. Unlike viruses, viroids do not have capsids protecting their nucleic acids. **STOP**

A prion is a protein molecule that can cause disease in animals. Prions are the only known infectious agents that do not contain DNA or RNA but can, nonetheless, spread throughout an organism. A prion causes a fatal disease called scrapie in sheep. Prions have also been found in the brains of cows that died from the so-called mad cow disease. Other prions are found in humans who suffer from kuru or Creutzfeldt-Jakob disease. Both of these diseases affect the central nervous system. A cure has not yet been found for diseases caused by viroids or prions. **STOP**

Level: High School

Literature

Concept Questions:

Tell me what you know about the country of Vietnam.

_____

_____

_____ (3-2-1-0)

What does "civilian" mean?

_____

_____

_____ (3-2-1-0)

What does "escalation" mean?

_____

_____

_____ (3-2-1-0)

What does "convoy" mean?

_____

_____

_____ (3-2-1-0)

What is a ceasefire?

_____

_____

_____ (3-2-1-0)

Score: _____ /15 = _____ %

_____ FAM _____ UNFAM

"Where the Ashes Are—Part 1"

"Wake up, wake up!" my mother shouted. "We've got to get out of here! How can you sleep through all this?" She pulled the covers off me, handed me my clothes, and rushed out of the room.

"Wait!" I cried out, throwing off my pajamas. One leg in and one out of my dark blue school trousers, I stumbled over to my sister Dieu-Ha's room. My mother was yelling, "Are you deaf? Get out! We're going downstairs!"

It was five in the morning. Explosions and gunfire echoed through the high-ceilinged rooms of the government guesthouse. Arched corridors surrounded the twenty bedrooms on the second floor of the massive French-style mansion. My parents had taken the master suite at the end of the hall while my two sisters and I had large rooms next to one another. We had arrived at the end of January 1968, two days before the lunar New Year. Our family were the only guests in the building. Rather than having us stay at my grandfather's small house, my father felt we would be safer at the guesthouse, where extra platoons of local soldiers had been assigned to protect him. He also preferred the guesthouse because it was built along the bank of the river in Hue, the old imperial city, and away from the town's noisy center. The nearby train station was defunct, since the war had disrupted all but a few railway lines.

Level: High School

For many years my father had been working for the government of South Vietnam. Assigned to central Vietnam as a civilian deputy to the military governor, he was based in Da Nang, a coastal town just over an hour's drive from Hue. He sent us to visit his parents there regularly, especially at holidays. He came along on this holiday visit—for the lunar New Year, Tet, in 1968.

Although my father had been warned about a possible escalation in the fighting, he said to my mother: "There's a ceasefire. It's New Year's. We'll be safe." But he abandoned his plan to drive and instead arranged for a flight to Hue. We'd landed at the Phu Bai airport in midafternoon.

The road into town had been taken over by an endless convoy of tanks and army trucks transporting U.S. soldiers, most likely toward Khe Sanh, an American base that had been under siege for several months. Along with a few other civilian cars, small trucks, and innumerable motorcycles, we inched our way toward Hue. I kept looking out the car window, glimpsing rice fields here and there. Mostly, though, the view was blocked by the olive green steel of tanks and trucks.

My mother sought to distract us. "You kids are going to be spoiled this year. I bet your grandparents will have lots of treats for you. But I want you to behave."

Settled in at the guesthouse, on the second night of our stay my mother and sisters and I fell asleep just after twelve, insulated by its thick walls and heavy curtains. Endless rounds of firecrackers went off as the people of Hue celebrated the arrival of Tet. No one knew that along with the Year of the Monkey, the dreaded Viet Cong soldiers had also arrived. No one could tell when the firecrackers stopped and the gunfire began.

Dieu-Ha and I followed my mother into my other sister's room. Dieu-Quynh hid herself under a pile of blankets. Ma shook her. "Come on, we're going downstairs!" As she started to rifle through Dieu-Quynh's drawers, grabbing clothes for her to change into, she said to Dieu-Ha and me, "Go see if your father's downstairs and stay with him!"

We rushed down the corridors toward the double staircase. Its marble steps formed a half-circle framed by an intricately carved banister. A bullet shattered a porthole as we skipped down the steps. Dieu-Ha screamed. Pieces of glass and marble flew by. We raced past the elephant tusks in the huge vestibule and toward the reception hall. A chilly wind blew through the huge room. Someone had opened the drapes and shutters of the dozens of windows rising from knee level to ten feet above my head, each framing a view of the River of Perfume, Song Hu'o'ng. (707 words)

By Nguyen Qui Duc, from *Literature and Integrated Studies*, copyright © 1997 by Scott, Foresman and Co. Reprinted by permission of the author.

Level: High School

Retelling Scoring Sheet for "Where the Ashes Are—Part 1"

Setting/Background

____ "Wake up,"
____ my mother shouted.
____ Explosions and gunfire echoed
____ through the rooms
____ of the government guesthouse.
____ It was two days
____ before the New Year.
____ Rather than stay at grandfather's house,
____ my father felt
____ we would be safer
____ where soldiers
____ had been assigned
____ to protect him.
____ My father worked for the government
____ of South Vietnam
____ as a civilian deputy
____ to the governor.

Goal

____ He sent us to visit his parents.

Events

____ Although my father had been warned
____ about a possible escalation
____ in the fighting,
____ he said,
____ "There's a ceasefire.
____ It's New Year's.
____ We'll be safe."
____ The road into town had been taken over
____ by a convoy of tanks
____ and trucks
____ transporting soldiers
____ U.S. soldiers.
____ In the guesthouse,
____ my mother,
____ my sisters,
____ and I fell asleep.
____ Firecrackers went off
____ as people celebrated the New Year.
____ No one knew

____ that along with the Year of the Monkey,
____ the soldiers had arrived
____ the Viet Cong soldiers.
____ No one could tell
____ when the firecrackers stopped
____ and the gunfire began.
____ A bullet shattered a porthole
____ as we skipped down the steps.

45 Ideas

Number of ideas recalled _____

Other ideas recalled, including summary statements and inferences:

Questions for "Where the Ashes Are—Part 1"

1. What is the story mostly about so far?
   Implicit: a family in Vietnam who are visiting relatives for the New Year and get involved in a battle or attack

2. When did the story take place?
   Explicit: January 1968 (The reader should remember both the month and the year.)

3. Describe what the road into Hue looked like from the car as the family drove into town.
   Explicit: tanks; army trucks; U.S. soldiers; cars; small trucks; motorcycles; *or* rice fields (Accept any three descriptions.)

4. Why did the mother try to distract the children from the view out of the car window?
   Implicit: she was afraid that the army trucks and tanks would scare the children

Level: High School

5. Who do you think wrote "Where the Ashes Are"?
   Implicit: one of the children (If the reader gives the author's name, ask who that was in the story.)

6. During the family's trip to Hue, why did the father choose to stay at the guesthouse instead of at the grandfather's house?
   Explicit: he thought it would be safer there because extra soldiers had been assigned to protect him; it was built on the bank of a river; *or* it was away from the town's noisy center

7. Describe the guesthouse.
   Explicit: it was large; it had high-ceilinged rooms; arched corridors; twenty bedrooms; thick walls; heavy curtains; a double staircase; marble steps; a carved banister; elephant tusks; a huge vestibule; a reception hall; and windows over ten feet (Because the author uses detail to evoke imagery, the reader should be able to describe at least three features of the guesthouse.)

8. What was father's position within the government of South Vietnam?
   Explicit: he was a civilian deputy to the military governor; *or* he worked for the government (The most important idea is that he worked for the South Vietnam government as a civilian and was not part of the military.)

9. Give two reasons why the family went on this trip despite the possibility of increased fighting.
   Implicit: they usually went during the holidays; the father believed they would be safe; *or* they visited their grandparents a lot

10. Why weren't the children afraid to go to sleep on the evening before the New Year despite all the loud noise?
    Implicit: there were so many firecrackers going off that they couldn't tell gunfire and fireworks apart; they thought all the noise was fireworks; *or* they didn't really hear it because of the insulated walls and heavy curtains

---

Without Look-Backs

Number Correct Explicit: _____

Number Correct Implicit: _____

Total: _____

_____ Independent: 9–10 correct

_____ Instructional: 7–8 correct

_____ Frustration: 0–6 correct

With Look-Backs

Number Correct Explicit: _____

Number Correct Implicit: _____

Total: _____

_____ Independent: 9–10 correct

_____ Instructional: 7–8 correct

_____ Frustration: 0–6 correct

Rate: 707 × 60 = 42,420/_____ seconds = _____ WPM

Level: High School

Literature

Concept Questions:

What does "marveled" mean?

_____

_____

_____ (3-2-1-0)

What is an invasion?

_____

_____

_____ (3-2-1-0)

What are tracers used for?

_____

_____

_____ (3-2-1-0)

What does "opulence" mean?

_____

_____

_____ (3-2-1-0)

Score: _____ /12 = _____ %

_____ FAM _____ UNFAM

"Where the Ashes Are—Part 2"

In the somber light I could make out dark foliage swaying by the riverbank as a coat of morning mist rose above the water. Nature paints winter scenes in Hue in shades of gray, but this morning I could see rapid bursts of orange and red fire coming from behind the bushes. A flare shot out from the far distance. Exploding with a thud, it hung from a small parachute and cast a brilliant midday light over a large area of the river as it floated down. Rockets exploded across the burning sky and fell to the ground in rapid succession. Deafened, Dieu-Ha and I dove behind an antique cabinet at the end of the room. My father had been nowhere in sight.

That night he had stayed up late to read a French book that contrasted two warriors: North Vietnam's famed general Vo Nguyen Giap and William Westmoreland, commander of the U.S. ground troops in South Vietnam. Just before four o'clock Cha (father in Vietnamese) had left his bed and gone up to the rooftop terrace, where he marveled at the red and green tracers flying across the sky like shooting stars. Despite his interest in the generals, he had little understanding of the role of flares and tracers as tools of warfare. They were simply a beautiful sight as they burst over the night sky.

"Your father's still up there. Been on that roof an hour! He'll get killed!" Ma wailed as she came down the staircase. Seeing the open windows, she took us into a chamber behind the reception room. "Where's Dieu-Quynh?" she exclaimed. "She was just on the stairs with me!"

Level: High School

In the midst of the gunfire and explosions, my sister had gone back to bed—a mad thing to do, since bullets were now flying indoors. By 1968, however, most of what Dieu-Quynh did was irrational. For four years she had been showing signs of mental illness. Ordering Dieu-Ha and me to sit still, my mother dashed back upstairs. A bullet came through Dieu-Quynh's room, hitting the lamp on her bedstand. Sparks flew in all directions. Ma grabbed my older sister by the wrist and led her downstairs, calling out to my father all the while.

"We shouldn't worry too much," he said in his usual unruffled tone when he entered the room a few minutes later. When he had finally left the roof, he went downstairs to look for the butler, then into an office off the living room. "I called the provincial office; they say the fighting is far away."

"Look out the windows!" my mother shot back.

"I did," Cha replied, still calm and composed. "Our soldiers are still at their posts." From the rooftop he had been able to see men in green surrounding the guesthouse.

We gathered together, crouching on the floor. No one spoke. My father glanced at the spacious desk and heavy armchairs, hoping to hide behind the furniture until the gunfire died down.

Between explosions came the sound of someone knocking at the front door. My parents put out their arms. We sat still. The pounding grew louder.

After a moment of hesitation, Ma stood up. "It's our soldiers," she declared. "Come on!" My sisters followed her through the reception area to the vestibule. As my father and I reached the door to the reception room, we heard her scream.

My father led me back to the office in the back, locking the door behind him as quietly as possible. We went to the desk, and I held his hand as we lowered ourselves behind it. My father didn't know what else to do. Spotting a steel safe in the corner of the room, he went over to open it, then without a word closed it again. Not even a nine-year-old boy could fit inside.

"I have a young son in the house," my mother was explaining to the intruders in the vestibule, Viet Cong soldiers in olive green uniforms. They wore no insignia or badges that showed affiliation or rank. Whether because of the darkness or distance, his poor eyesight, or his unfamiliarity with military matters, my father had mistaken them for our own Southern Republican Army troops.

One of the soldiers now threatened to shoot anyone still hiding in the house. "Tell us where everyone is and you'll be safe, Sister," he assured my mother. "Please, please don't hurt us, please!" she begged. "Just let me go find my son."

Cha groped behind the heavy dark green drapes along the office wall, where a set of double doors opened onto a hallway. We tiptoed through the hall to the doors that led outside. My father motioned me out first, then carefully closed the doors behind him. I ran down the steps and turned toward the hedges that separated the guesthouse grounds from the riverbank. "Hey, boy!" someone cried. I turned. A Viet Cong soldier sitting cross-legged pointed his rifle at me. I ran back to my father.

Back in the hallway inside the house, Cha quietly approached each door to the offices surrounding the reception area. A gun muzzle protruded from one, and we backed off. The doorway to yet another office also had a gun muzzle poking out from it. There was no escape.

Out in the courtyard it was still dark. Dozens of people in nightclothes shivered in the early morning dampness. Slowly the soldiers separated families from one another. The guesthouse was to be used as a temporary holding center. More people were brought into the courtyard. A disheveled Frenchman of about thirty entered the area barefooted, a trench coat thrown on over his pajamas. Hands clasped together, he tried to explain his situation to two Viet Cong soldiers. "De Gaulle, Ho Chi Minh, amis," he kept saying. "Friends."

The two Viet Cong waved him away. One of them shouted, "Khong biet tieng dtiu!" They did not speak any foreign languages.

"They're regular soldiers," my father whispered to a man next to him, whose crisp white shirt was tucked into pajama trousers. "Such a strong northern accent."

"You're right," the man whispered back. "The way they call everybody 'Sister' and 'Brother' is strange." The men and women before us were not part of the so-called National Liberation Front within South Vietnam. Ho Chi Minh was now sending in troops from the North for an outright offensive, a full invasion.

In the confusion our family took refuge in a small temple just off the grounds of the guesthouse. Searching through his wallet, my father took out all his business cards and hid them under a mat. "Just say you're a teacher," whispered my mother.

He never had the chance. When a Viet Cong woman found us in the temple a little more than an hour later, she jabbed her index finger into his chest. "You, Brother, I know who you are," she said. "The Party and the Revolution will be generous to all those willing to confess their crimes against the People."

"The Party" could only be the Communist party headquartered in Ha Noi. The enemy's arm had now reached into the heart of Hue. "Don't lie!" the woman continued. Putting her finger up to my father's nose, she said, "Brother, we know—you're the

Level: High School

general staying in this house. Such opulence. We'll

take care of you." (1,224 words)

_____

By Nguyen Qui Duc, from *Literature and Integrated Studies*, copyright © 1997 by Scott, Foresman and Co. Reprinted by permission of the author.

Retelling Scoring Sheet for "Where the Ashes Are—Part 2"

Setting/Background

___ Cha had gone to the roof
___ where he marveled at the tracers.
___ He had little understanding
___ of the roles of flares
___ and tracers.
___ My sister (Dieu-Quynh) had gone back to bed.
___ She had been showing signs of mental illness.

Goal

___ Ma grabbed my sister
___ and led her downstairs
___ calling out to my father.

Events

___ "Our soldiers are still at their posts,"
___ Cha said.
___ Between explosions
___ came the sound
___ of someone knocking
___ at the door.
___ "It's our soldiers,"
___ Ma declared.
___ "Come on."
___ We heard her scream.

Goal

___ My father led me back
___ to the office.
___ We lowered ourselves
___ behind the desk.

Events

___ "I have a young son
___ in the house,"
___ my mother was explaining
___ to the Viet Cong soldiers.
___ My father had mistaken them
___ for our own troops.
___ One of the soldiers threatened
___ to shoot anyone
___ still hiding
___ in the house.
___ My father motioned me outside.
___ A soldier pointed his rifle at me.
___ I ran back.
___ There was no escape.

Setting/Background

___ Out in the courtyard
___ dozens of people shivered.

Goal

___ The soldiers separated families.

Events

___ The guesthouse was a holding center.
___ Ho Chi Minh was sending in troops
___ for an invasion.
___ Our family took refuge
___ in a temple.
___ My father took his business cards
___ and hid them.
___ "Just say you're a teacher,"
___ whispered my mother.
___ A Viet Cong woman found us.
___ "I know who you are,"
___ she said.
___ "The Party will be generous
___ to those who confess their crimes."
___ The party could only be the
___ Communist Party.
___ "We know you're the general
___ staying in this house."

59 Ideas

Number of ideas recalled _____

Level: High School

Other ideas recalled, including summary statements and inferences:

Questions for "Where the Ashes Are—Part 2"

1. What is this segment of the story mostly about?
   Implicit: how the family is captured by soldiers

2. Describe how the river looked in the early morning light.
   Explicit: foliage was swaying on the bank; mist rose from the water; *or* orange and red fire came from behind the bushes

3. What was the content of the book that the father was reading late at night?
   Explicit: it contrasted two warriors or generals

4. What was the father watching on the roof?
   Explicit: flares or tracers or rockets (If the reader says "explosions," ask what caused the explosions.)

5. What evidence does the author present that tells us that the father doesn't know much about war?
   Implicit: he didn't understand the role of flares and tracers; he stayed on the roof to watch the war; he didn't recognize enemy troops; *or* he thought the war was far away even though bullets were coming in the guesthouse

6. Describe Cha's personality.
   Implicit: he was calm; *or* he doesn't easily get excited or worried

7. Who do you now think is the author of the story?
   Implicit: the young son

8. What did Cha try to do with his son?
   Explicit: he tried to escape

9. What happened to prevent their escape?
   Explicit: they were cut off by soldiers with guns

10. Why did the Viet Cong soldier think that Cha was a general?
    Implicit: because he was staying at the guesthouse and she figured that only an army general could stay at such a grand place

Without Look-Backs

Number Correct Explicit: _____

Number Correct Implicit: _____

Total: _____

_____ Independent: 9–10 correct

_____ Instructional: 7–8 correct

_____ Frustration: 0–6 correct

With Look-Backs

Number Correct Explicit: _____

Number Correct Implicit: _____

Total: _____

_____ Independent: 9–10 correct

_____ Instructional: 7–8 correct

_____ Frustration: 0–6 correct

Rate: $1{,}224 \times 60 = 73{,}440/$_____ seconds = _____ WPM

Level: High School

Literature

Concept Questions:

What does "captivity" mean?

_____

_____

_____ (3-2-1-0)

What does "liberated" mean?

_____

_____

_____ (3-2-1-0)

What is a disinfectant?

_____

_____

_____ (3-2-1-0)

What do you think "re-education" means in the context of this story?

_____

_____

_____ (3-2-1-0)

Score: _____ /12 = _____ %

_____ FAM _____ UNFAM

"Where the Ashes Are—Part 3"

Now I want you to read the next section, and when you come to the word STOP in the text, I want you to tell me what you are thinking. When you have finished reading, I will ask you to tell me what you remember and then I will ask you questions.

We lost track of the time as the soldiers sorted out all the people gathered in front of the guesthouse. At last, however, they accepted my father's <u>protestations</u> that he was not a general but a government functionary. He and the other men were taken inside the mansion. Women and children were sent to a neighboring building, down into a long rectangular basement with extremely thick walls and a single narrow door at one end. The rocket explosions had ceased, but the sound of gunfire continued. We had become accustomed to it and no longer jumped at the bursts from automatic weapons. Ten families followed each other below ground. I ended up leading the way into the darkness. **STOP**

_____

_____

_____

_____

_____

"Go to the far end. Go!" my mother urged me, and made sure that Dieu-Quynh stayed with us. She knew that, on capturing a town, the Communists would use residents as workers to support military operations. Women would be sent to look

Level: High School

for food, or nurse the wounded. If not required to take up arms themselves, men would have to gather the wounded and the dead. Dieu-Quynh, a tall girl of eighteen, was at risk of being drafted for such service. Turning to the family behind her, my mother explained. "My daughter is ill. A big girl, but not all that wise." It was an explanation she would feel compelled to repeat often in the next days. I finally settled for a spot below a minuscule window with iron bars. In the damp, cavernous basement, the tiny hole let in a faint ray of the light that signaled the first day of the Year of the Monkey. **STOP**

_____

_____

_____

_____

_____

Throughout that day and most of the next night the adults carried on a whispered debate, trying to make sense out of what had happened. "They can't win," the guesthouse <u>chauffeur</u> pronounced. "I bet they'll retreat soon. The Americans will bomb, and our troops will rescue us in a few days." My mother listened dispassionately. She sighed often and refused to eat any of the food the family next to us offered. Busy with their prisoners in the mansion, the soldiers left us alone. **STOP**

_____

_____

_____

_____

_____

In our second day of captivity, a female voice shouted into the basement. "Mrs. Dai! Is there a Mrs. Dai down there?" My mother picked her way toward the door. "Your husband's up in the house. He wants to see you," the voice announced. My mother went up alone, warning me to keep my sister Dieu-Quynh from wandering out. During the night, Dieu-Quynh had been difficult, continually demanding hot water. For the last year or so she had been obsessed with matters of hygiene, compulsively washing her hands as well as any household utensils before she would use them. Finally realizing that this was a luxury, she now sat silent and withdrawn. I asked Dieu-Ha to stay with her, then went to sit at the door to wait for my mother. **STOP**

_____

_____

_____

_____

The guns had gone quiet at some point without anyone noticing. More soldiers had arrived in the compound and were now setting up a crude hospital. A stretched-out army poncho served as an awning, sheltering three bamboo cots that had been shoved together. The soldiers put a mat of woven branches and leaves on top of the cots, enlarging the surface to accommodate five wounded men. Looking like pallbearers carrying a white porcelain coffin, three young men and a woman in civilian clothes brought in an ancient French bathtub. They filled the tub half full of water, warning us not to use it. No one seemed to be in charge, yet a lot of orders were being issued. Sitting by the door of the basement, I watched the men and women from the North while waiting for my mother. **STOP**

_____

_____

_____

_____

_____

"What are you doing here?" she asked when she returned, roughing up my hair. "We're going up to see your father in a while." She did not sound excited. After checking on my sisters, she set about looking for food for my father. "Ma, what are they going to do with him?" I asked. I repeated the question again and again, but my mother would only shake her head; finally she responded, "Oh, he'll be all right. They said all he needed was a few days of re-education. They're taking him somewhere, but he'll be back."

Taken where? Would we be rescued first? Would they let him go? I didn't think she knew the answers to my questions. I tugged at her sleeve. "Ma, what's 're-education'?" She glanced at the wounded Viet Cong lying beneath the poncho. "It's like school, that's all. Now help me with this pot." **STOP**

_____

_____

_____

_____

_____

Spoiled since her youth by household servants, my mother had rarely gone near a kitchen. Now she was cooking a big pot of rice she had secured from a woman in the basement. The Viet Cong had set up a few clay burners and gave us some coal. Other than the rice, there was nothing to cook. We ate it with pickled leeks and cucumber, which normally accompanied fancier foods during Tet. The rice tasted of the river water my mother had used to cook it in. The Viet Cong had allowed her only a small amount of water from the bathtub to take to my father. She was happy to have cleaner water for him to drink—until she tasted it. It smelled of Mercurochrome, the red <u>disinfectant</u> common in Vietnam. The soldiers had used the water to wash the wounds of injured men, then poured back unused portions, now laced with Mercurochrome. She found a tiny bit of tea to

Level: High School

steep in the water and packed some rice into a big bowl for my father. **STOP**

_____

_____

_____

_____

_____

I sensed that my father was happy to see us, but his face showed no such emotion. He took the woven basket Ma handed him, which contained a towel, two T-shirts, and a pair of pants she had found on her previous trip to the guesthouse to see him. "There's no need—you will be well provided for," a Viet Cong cadre said. "You'll be in re-education for just a short time. Now that the region is liberated, you'll be allowed to come back soon."

In the big hall across from the master suite, my father kept caressing my head. I couldn't think of much to say. Some prisoners crouched along the wall, watching us. Others were curled up on the floor like shrimps. My mother gave my father the bowl of rice and the tea. I waited to see if he could taste the Mercurochrome, but I couldn't tell from his expression. **STOP**

_____

_____

_____

_____

_____

I glanced around my parents' bedroom. It had been turned upside down. The book my father had been reading about Giap and Westmoreland still lay by his bed. My mother's jewelry and toilet case had had a hole gashed through it with a crude knife.

"Your mother will take you over to your grandparents' in a few days," Cha said. "I'll be back after a time."

Later, sometime past midnight, Communist soldiers took my father and a dozen other men away. Standing on a stool with my mother at my side, I watched through the tiny basement window. A rope was hooked through my father's elbows and tied behind his back, while his wrists were bound together in front of his chest. He was also tied to the man in front of him. It would be sixteen years before I saw him again. **STOP**

_____

_____

_____

_____

_____

_____

By Nguyen Qui Duc, from _Literature and Integrated Studies,_ copyright © 1997 by Scott, Foresman and Co. Reprinted by permission of the author.

Retelling Scoring Sheet for "Where the Ashes Are—Part 3"

Setting/Background

____ They accepted my father's protestations
____ that he was not a general.

Level: High School

Goal

____ He and the other men were taken
____ inside the mansion.
____ Women and children were sent
____ into a basement.

Events

____ I led the way.
____ Mother knew that
____ women would be sent
____ to look for food
____ or nurse the wounded.
____ Men would have to gather the wounded
____ and the dead.
____ Dieu-Quynh was at risk
____ of being drafted for this.
____ "My daughter is ill,"
____ mother explained.
____ The soldiers left us alone.
____ "Your husband wants to see you,"
____ a voice announced.
____ My mother went up alone.
____ She returned.

Goal

____ "We're going to see your father
____ in a while."

Events

____ "What are they going to do to him?"
____ I asked.
____ "Oh, he'll be all right.
____ They said
____ all he needed was re-education.
____ They're taking him somewhere,
____ but he'll be back."
____ "What's re-education?"
____ "It's like school."
____ Ma was happy
____ to have water
____ for my father to drink
____ until she tasted it.
____ It smelled
____ of Mercurochrome.
____ The soldiers had used the water

____ to wash the wounds
____ of men
____ and then poured back portions
____ now laced with Mercurochrome.
____ My father was happy to see us,
____ but his face showed no such emotion.
____ I glanced around my parents' bedroom.
____ It had been turned upside down.

Resolution

____ Sometime past midnight,
____ soldiers took my father away
____ with other men.
____ A rope was hooked through his elbows
____ and tied behind his back
____ while his wrists were bound together
____ in front of his chest.
____ He was also tied to the man
____ in front of him.
____ It would be years
____ sixteen years
____ before I saw him again.

60 Ideas

Number of ideas recalled _____

Other ideas recalled, including summary statements and inferences:

Questions for "Where the Ashes Are—Part 3"

1. What was this section of the story about?
   Implicit: the capture of the family and/or the separation of the father from the rest of the family

2. Describe the basement where the mother and children were kept.
Explicit: it was rectangular; it had thick walls; a single narrow door; a tiny window with bars; it was damp (The reader should remember at least two of the details.)

3. Why didn't the family jump anymore when they heard gunfire?
Explicit: they had gotten used to it

4. Why did the mother feel it necessary to protect the daughter, Dieu-Quynh?
Implicit: this daughter was suffering from a mental disorder

5. Describe the hospital that the soldiers were setting up.
Explicit: it was crude; it had a poncho as an awning; there were three cots; branches and leaves were put on the cots; there was an old bathtub filled with water (The reader should remember at least two of these details.)

6. Why was it unusual for Mrs. Dai to be cooking?
Implicit: she had been spoiled as a youth by having servants, so she had rarely been near a kitchen

7. What did it mean that the father had to have "re-education"?
Implicit: he had to learn to think like the Viet Cong

Level: High School

8. What did the mother bring to the father to eat and drink?
   Explicit: rice and tea made from water with a red disinfectant in it

9. Where was the family going to stay after the father left?
   Explicit: at their grandparents' house

10. Where do you think Cha went at the end of the story, and why?
    Implicit: to prison or to a work camp, because he was tied up and being forced to go (To get full credit, the reader should give a reason for the answer.)

Without Look-Backs

Number Correct Explicit: _____

Number Correct Implicit: _____

Total: _____

_____ Independent: 9–10 correct

_____ Instructional: 7–8 correct

_____ Frustration: 0–6 correct

With Look-Backs

Number Correct Explicit: _____

Number Correct Implicit: _____

Total: _____

_____ Independent: 9–10 correct

_____ Instructional: 7–8 correct

_____ Frustration: 0–6 correct

Think-Aloud Summary

Think-Aloud Statements That Indicate Understanding

Paraphrasing/Summarizing _____

Making New Meaning _____

Questioning That Indicates Understanding _____

Noting Understanding _____

Reporting Prior Knowledge _____

Identifying Personally _____

Think-Aloud Statements That Indicate Lack of Understanding

Questioning That Indicates Lack of Understanding _____

Noting Lack of Understanding _____

Level: High School

Social Studies

Concept Questions:

What are some causes of wars?

_____

_____

_____ (3-2-1-0)

What were the causes of World War I?

_____

_____

_____ (3-2-1-0)

What does "interception" mean?

_____

_____

_____ (3-2-1-0)

What does "unrestricted" mean?

_____

_____

_____ (3-2-1-0)

Score: _____ /12 = _____ %

_____ FAM _____ UNFAM

"World War I—Part 1"

World War I, also known as the Great War, drew in not only the major powers of Europe, but those of America and Asia as well. Many economic and political factors caused the war. Newly industrialized nations competed with one another for trade and markets for their goods. Also, the urge for national power and independence from other nations came from old and new powers. When a new nation tried to increase its power by building a strong military, an older nation perceived the new nation as a threat to its power. Such tensions led to the division of Europe into two groups for security: one composed of Britain, France, and Russia, the other of Austria, Hungary, and Germany.

Although the factors discussed above caused the war, the final breaking point was a local conflict between Austria and Serbia, a tiny kingdom in southeastern Europe. Serbia, supported by Russia, wanted to unite with the Serbs living in the Austro-Hungarian Empire and create a Greater Serbia. Austria, supported by Germany, did not want Serbia cutting into its empire. The war officially started in August of 1914, after the assassination of the Austrian heir to the throne, who was visiting Sarajevo, near Serbia's border. The assassin was a young man with connections to the military intelligence branch of the Serbian government. Austria's attempt to punish Serbia drew Russia and its allies Britain and France into a war against Austria–Hungary and Germany. The map below illustrates the geographical location of the countries in Europe and surrounding regions in 1914.

The War Raged on Two Fronts

Germany hoped to defeat France by striking quickly through Belgium and, therefore, to minimize the danger of a two-front war. The highly

Level: High School

trained German troops nearly reached Paris before the French stopped them. However, the Russians aided France by suddenly attacking Germany on its eastern front, and Germany sent troops from western Europe to face the attack. With the German forces diminished, the French were able to force the weakened Germans back. The war in the west became a stalemate with neither side able to achieve a victory. As a result, both sides sought new allies to help them gain victory, and the war became a world war as Japan, Italy, Portugal, Rumania, and other countries joined Britain, France, and Russia. Germany and Austria–Hungary drew in Bulgaria and the Ottoman Empire, which included Turkey.

On the eastern front Russia kept part of the German army busy. Although Russia fought valiantly, it had not been prepared for war and thus was unable to defeat the Germans. Russian defeats led to a revolution that toppled the tsar of Russia. In late 1917 the new leader of Russia, Lenin, offered to make peace with Germany. As part of the treaty agreement, Germany gained coal mines and oil fields from Russia, which gave Germany power to fuel its army. More important, it allowed the war to be fought on only one front—the western front.

The United States entered the war when Germany began attacking American ships that were taking supplies to Britain and France. U.S. President Woodrow Wilson warned the Germans to stop the attacks, and for a while they did. But they announced an unrestricted submarine warfare after the British blockade shut off supplies to Germany. The final event that caused the United States to join the Allies was the interception of a telegram from the German foreign secretary to Mexico asking Mexico to ally itself with Germany and help fight the United States. Germany promised Mexico financial aid and the recovery of Texas, New Mexico, and Arizona when the Allies were defeated. (607 words)

From *History and Life* by T. W. Wallbank, A. Schrier, D. Maier, and P. Gutierrez-Smith. Copyright © 1993 by Scott Foresman and Company. Used by permission of Pearson Education, Inc. All Rights Reserved.

Retelling Scoring Sheet for "World War I—Part 1"

Main Idea

____ Many economic
____ and political factors
____ caused World War I.

Details

____ Nations competed
____ for trade
____ and markets
____ and power.
____ Such tensions led to two groups:
____ one composed of Britain,
____ France,
____ and Russia,
____ the other of Austria,
____ Hungary,
____ and Germany.

Level: High School

Main Idea

___ The breaking point was a conflict
___ between Austria and Serbia.

Details

___ The war officially started
___ after the assassination of the heir
___ to the Austrian throne.
___ Austria attempted
___ to punish Serbia
___ and drew Russia
___ and its allies
___ Britain
___ and France into a war
___ against Austria–Hungary
___ and Germany.

Main Idea

___ The war raged on two fronts.

Details

___ Germany hoped to defeat France
___ and almost reached Paris
___ before the French stopped them.
___ The Russians aided France
___ and attacked Germany
___ on the eastern front.
___ The war became a stalemate
___ with neither side achieving victory.
___ Russian defeats led to a revolution
___ that toppled the tsar.
___ Lenin offered to make peace
___ with Germany.
___ It allowed the war
___ to be fought on one front
___ the western front.

Main Idea

___ The United States entered the war

Details

___ when Germany began attacking
___ American ships
___ that were taking supplies
___ to Britain

___ and France.
___ The final event was the interception
___ of a telegram
___ from Germany
___ asking Mexico
___ to ally with Germany
___ and fight the United States
___ Germany promised Mexico
___ financial aid
___ and the recovery of Texas,
___ New Mexico,
___ and Arizona.

60 Ideas

Number of ideas recalled _____

Other ideas recalled, including summary statements and inferences:

Questions for "World War I—Part 1"

1. What is this passage mostly about?
   Implicit: how and why World War I started (If
   the student says only World War I, ask "What
   about World War I?")

2. What two types of factors caused the war?
   Explicit: economic and political (The reader
   should remember both of these.)

Level: High School

3. How did the rise of new powers cause the War?
Implicit: when a new country tried to build its military, old countries perceived the new nation as a threat to their power

4. Name one set of countries in Europe and the surrounding regions that grouped together for security reasons in 1914.
Explicit: Britain, France, and Russia; *or* Austria, Hungary, and Germany (The reader should remember all three countries in one set.)

5. What event finally triggered the war?
Explicit: the assassination of the Austrian heir to the throne by a Serbian; *or* by a man with ties to the military intelligence branch of the Serbian government

6. Why do you think that Germany wanted to avoid fighting a war on two fronts?
Implicit: so its resources wouldn't be divided

7. How did the defeat of Russia on the eastern front help Germany?
Explicit: Germany gained oil fields and coal mines that gave fuel to its army; *or* it allowed the war to be fought on only one front so all their armies could be unified there

8. Why did Germany attack U.S. ships?
Implicit: because U.S. ships were taking supplies to Britain and France, who were part of the Allies

9. What final event caused the United States to join the Allies?
Explicit: the interception of a telegram from Germany to Mexico asking Mexico to ally itself with Germany and help fight the United States

10. Why might Mexico have wanted to join Germany?
Implicit: Mexico was promised financial aid from Germany; *or* it was promised it would get part of its original territory back—Texas, New Mexico, and Arizona

---

Without Look-Backs

Number Correct Explicit: _____

Number Correct Implicit: _____

Total: _____

_____ Independent: 9–10 correct

_____ Instructional: 7–8 correct

_____ Frustration: 0–6 correct

With Look-Backs

Number Correct Explicit: _____

Number Correct Implicit: _____

Total: _____

_____ Independent: 9–10 correct

_____ Instructional: 7–8 correct

_____ Frustration: 0–6 correct

Rate: $607 \times 60 = 36,420/$_____ seconds = _____ WPM

Level: High School

Social Studies

Concept Questions:

What does "idealism" mean?

_____

_____

_____ (3-2-1-0)

What does "allied" mean?

_____

_____

_____ (3-2-1-0)

What does "compromise" mean?

_____

_____

_____ (3-2-1-0)

What was the League of Nations?

_____

_____

_____ (3-2-1-0)

Score: _____ /12 = _____ %

_____ FAM _____ UNFAM

"World War I—Part 2"

In the fall of 1918, German military leaders realized they could not win. One by one Germany's allies quit. On November 3, German sailors mutinied at Kiel, a city and port in northwest Germany. Four days later a revolution broke out in Germany. A republic was founded, and the kaiser fled to Holland.

Leaders of the new German government agreed to an armistice, which is an agreement to stop fighting. They asked that the peace settlement be based on President Wilson's Fourteen Points, which he had described in a speech to Congress in 1918. The Fourteen Points outlined the president's ideas for solving the problems that led to the war. Wilson wanted an end to secret agreements, freedom of the seas in peace and war, the reduction of armaments, the right of nationality groups to form their own nations, and an association of nations to keep the peace. In other speeches Wilson called for a negotiated peace with reasonable demands made on the losers. The Allies agreed to model the peace settlement on the Fourteen Points.

Early in the morning of November 11, 1918, the war ended. In a railroad car in the Compiègne Forest in northern France, two German delegates met Allied officials to sign the armistice. The guns were silent.

The Victors Tried to Build a Lasting Peace

No previous war had caused such widespread horror. More than 10 million troops were killed in battle, and 20 million more were wounded.

Level: High School

Thirteen million civilians died from war-related famine, disease, and injuries. The cost of the war was estimated at more than $350 billion. Destruction was everywhere.

Three Leaders Dominated the Paris Peace Conference

After the armistice had been signed, the Allied nations met in Paris to discuss peace terms. Contrary to Wilson's wishes, the defeated countries were not allowed to send representatives to the peace conference. Thus, the so-called Big Three dominated the meeting: President Wilson; David Lloyd George, prime minister of Great Britain; and Georges Clemenceau, premier of France. At the conference Wilson pushed his Fourteen Points. Above all, he wanted to see a League of Nations, an international association established to keep the peace. To get the others to agree, however, he had to make compromises.

Georges Clemenceau, known as the "Old Tiger," had led France during the darkest hours of the war. He wanted Germany to pay war damages because almost all of the fighting on the western front had been on French soil. Most of all he insisted that France be made safe from attack by Germany in the future. He wanted German power destroyed even at the cost of permanently taking much of Germany's western territories from her.

Clemenceau placed little faith in Wilson's proposed "League of Nations."

Lloyd George in turn wanted Germany's colonies for Britain. He also wanted the German navy destroyed. During the peace talks, he mediated between the idealism of Wilson and the severe terms of Clemenceau. In the resulting compromise, Wilson gave in on many details and agreed to form an alliance with Britain and France against future German attacks. Clemenceau and Lloyd George agreed to make the creation of the League of Nations part of the peace agreement, which was called the Versailles Treaty. (536 words)

From *History and Life* by T. W. Wallbank, A. Schrier, D. Maier, and P. Gutierrez-Smith. Copyright © 1993 by Scott Foresman and Company. Used by permission of Pearson Education, Inc. All Rights Reserved.

Retelling Scoring Sheet for "World War I—Part 2"

Main Idea

____ In the fall of 1918,
____ German leaders realized
____ they could not win.

Details

____ Their allies quit.
____ A revolution broke out
____ in Germany.
____ A republic was founded
____ and the kaiser fled.
____ Germany agreed to an armistice.
____ Germany asked
____ that the peace settlement be based

Level: High School

____ on President Wilson's Fourteen Points.

Main Idea

____ The Fourteen Points outlined ideas
____ for solving the problems
____ that led to the war.

Details

____ Wilson wanted
____ to end secret agreements,
____ have freedom of the seas,
____ reduce armaments,
____ grant the right of nationality groups
____ to form their own nations,
____ and form an association of nations
____ to keep the peace.

Main Idea

____ The war ended
____ on November 11,
____ 1918.

Details

____ No war in previous history
____ had caused such widespread horror.
____ More than 10 million
____ troops were killed,
____ and 20 million
____ were wounded.
____ Destruction was everywhere.

Main Idea

____ The Allied nations met
____ to discuss peace terms.

Details

____ Three leaders
____ dominated the peace conference,
____ President Wilson,
____ David Lloyd George
____ of Great Britain,
____ and Georges Clemenceau
____ of France.

____ The defeated nations
____ were not allowed
____ to send representatives.
____ Wilson wanted
____ to establish a League of Nations
____ to keep the peace.
____ Clemenceau wanted Germany
____ to pay war damages
____ because most of the fighting
____ had been on French soil.
____ He insisted that France be made safe
____ from attack by Germany
____ in the future.
____ He wanted German power destroyed.
____ Lloyd George wanted
____ Germany's colonies for Britain
____ and the German navy destroyed.

Main Idea

____ The Big Three compromised.

Details

____ Wilson agreed to form an alliance
____ with Britain
____ and France.
____ Clemenceau
____ and Lloyd George
____ agreed to the League of Nations
____ as part of the Versailles Treaty.

67 Ideas

Number of ideas recalled _____

Other ideas recalled, including summary statements and inferences:

Level: High School

Questions for "World War I—Part 2"

1. What was this passage mostly about?
   Implicit: how the peace agreement was determined at the Paris Peace Conference

2. What happened on November 11, 1918?
   Explicit: World War I ended; *or* the armistice was signed

3. Name one important point in Wilson's Fourteen Points plan for solving the problems that caused the War.
   Explicit: any one of the following: a reduction in armaments, negotiated peace with reasonable demands on the losers of the war, freedom of the seas in peace and war, an end to secret agreements, right of nationality groups to form their own nations, establishment of a peace-keeping association

4. Name another important point in Wilson's plan.
   Explicit: any of the above not given as an answer to Question 3

5. Who attended the Paris Peace Conference?
   Explicit: President Wilson; David Lloyd George, prime minister of Great Britain; and Georges Clemenceau, premier of France (The reader can give either a name, such as Clemenceau, or the position, premier of France, but both are not required.)

6. Why could President Wilson be considered an idealist?
   Implicit: he thought that the League of Nations would keep permanent peace (If the reader says he or she does not know what an idealist is, define the term and then see whether the reader can answer the question.)

Level: High School

7. What did France's leader demand for France in the peace negotiations?
Explicit: that France be made safe from German attack; *or* that Germany pay war damages

8. How was the Paris Peace Conference a compromise among the United States, Britain, and France?
Implicit: each country wanted something out of the agreement, and each had to give up something

9. Which of the Fourteen Points was most important to President Wilson, and how do you know?
Implicit: the establishment of an international peace association, the League of Nations, because Wilson was willing to compromise a lot for it

10. Why would it have been appropriate for Germany to give money to France but not to the United States?
Implicit: most of the fighting in the west had been on French soil, so they had sustained damages to their country, whereas the United States did not

---

Without Look-Backs

Number Correct Explicit: _____

Number Correct Implicit: _____

Total: _____

_____ Independent: 9–10 correct

_____ Instructional: 7–8 correct

_____ Frustration: 0–6 correct

With Look-Backs

Number Correct Explicit: _____

Number Correct Implicit: _____

Total: _____

_____ Independent: 9–10 correct

_____ Instructional: 7–8 correct

_____ Frustration: 0–6 correct

Rate: $536 \times 60 = 32{,}160/$_____ seconds = _____ WPM

Level: High School

Social Studies

Concept Questions:

What happens to a country that loses a war?

_____

_____

_____ (3-2-1-0)

What is a treaty?

_____

_____

_____ (3-2-1-0)

What are reparations?

_____

_____

_____ (3-2-1-0)

What are ethnic minorities?

_____

_____

_____ (3-2-1-0)

Score: _____ /12 = _____ %

_____ FAM _____ UNFAM

"World War I—Part 3"

Now I want you to read the next section and when you come to the word **STOP** *in the text, I want you to tell me what you are thinking. When you are done reading, I will ask you to tell me what you remember and then I will ask you questions.*

Germany Lost Territory and Wealth in Its Defeat

When the German delegation arrived to sign the Versailles Treaty, they found its terms harsher than they had expected. The Germans were outraged at the war-guilt clause, which placed the entire blame for the war on Germany and its allies. They were also dismayed that many of Wilson's Fourteen Points were missing or had been weakened by changes. The first delegates from Germany refused to sign the treaty. To avoid further attacks by Allied soldiers, however, a second German delegation signed it on June 28, 1919. Even though Germany signed the treaty, there was strong resentment over its harsh terms. **STOP**

_____

_____

_____

_____

_____

In the treaty, France won back the provinces of Alsace and Lorraine, lost to Germany in the late 1800s. The German territory west of the Rhine River, called the Rhineland, was to become a buffer zone between the two enemies. It was to be occupied by Allied troops for at least 15 years. France was also given the rich coal mines of the Saar, lo-

Level: High School

cated on the French–German border. But after 15 years, the Saarlanders could vote to have their region go back to the German government or remain under the French. In 1935 they voted to become part of Germany again. **STOP**

_____

_____

_____

_____

_____

In the treaty the Allies required that Germany repay much of the cost of the war, or make reparations. They wanted an immediate payment of $5 billion in cash. Two years later they billed Germany for $32 billion, plus interest. The treaty reduced German military power and permitted Germany an army of no more than 100,000 men. The navy was allowed only six warships, some other vessels, and no submarines or military airplanes. The Germans were not alone in thinking such peace terms were unjust. Even David Lloyd George doubted the justice of the Versailles Treaty. President Wilson hoped that his dream, the League of Nations, could correct the unjust treaty later. **STOP**

_____

_____

_____

_____

New Independent Nations Were Formed

Four empires had fallen apart in the course of World War I: the German, the Austro-Hungarian, the Ottoman, and the Russian. Based partly on secret agreements made during the war, the Allies drew up treaties to divide the territory. The map on the next page shows how the empires were divided up. The western portion of the old Russian Empire lost to Germany during the war was reorganized. Finland, Latvia, Lithuania, and Estonia emerged from this territory, and part of this area was used to create Poland. **STOP**

_____

_____

_____

_____

_____

The defeated Austro-Hungarian Empire was also divided into several new countries: Austria, Hungary, Czechoslovakia, and Yugoslavia. The creation of the new countries helped fulfill one of Wilson's Fourteen Points, the right of self-determination, or the right of people to form their own nations. **STOP**

_____

_____

_____

_____

_____

Level: High School

The Ottoman Empire too was divided up. Syria, Iraq, Trans-Jordan, and Palestine were created from the Ottoman Empire. They became <u>mandates</u>, lands given to certain nations to develop. Syria was ruled by France, the other three by Britain. These <u>mandates</u> were promised independence at a future time. **STOP**

_____

_____

_____

_____

_____

Redrawing the map of Europe, however, brought some new groups under foreign control. There were social, cultural, and language implications of this foreign control. For example, Austrians living in the southwestern part of the old Austro-Hungarian Empire came under the rule of Italy. Other German-speaking Austrians were placed under Czechoslovakian rule.

One of the biggest problems was the newly independent Poland, created from the Polish-language provinces of prewar Austria–Hungary, Germany, and Russia. The treaty's authors gave Poland some territory in eastern Germany known as the Polish Corridor. The Polish Corridor and other areas would prove to be problems in the future because they contained many ethnic minorities. Some Germans

lived in the new Polish Corridor, and to complicate matters, many Hungarians also came under Romanian control. Few of these peoples were happy about the changes, and their discontent was a dangerous sign for the future. **STOP**

_____

_____

_____

_____

_____

From *History and Life* by T. W. Wallbank, A. Schrier, D. Maier, and P. Gutierrez-Smith. Copyright © 1993 by Scott Foresman and Company. Used by permission of Pearson Education, Inc. All Rights Reserved.

Retelling Scoring Sheet for "World War I—Part 3"

Main Idea

____ The German delegation found the terms
____ of the treaty
____ harsher than they expected.

Details

____ The Germans were outraged
____ at the war-guilt clause,
____ which placed the entire blame
____ for the war
____ on Germany.
____ They refused
____ to sign the treaty.
____ A second delegation
____ signed it.
____ There was resentment
____ over its terms.

Level: High School

Main Idea

____ Germany lost territory,
____ wealth,
____ and power.

Details

____ France won back the provinces
____ of Alsace and Lorraine.
____ The Rhineland became a buffer zone.
____ France was given the coal mines
____ of the Saar.
____ Germany had to repay the cost
____ of the war,
____ or make reparations.
____ The treaty reduced military power.
____ The navy was allowed
____ only six warships
____ and no submarines
____ or airplanes.

Main Idea

____ New nations were formed.

Details

____ Empires had fallen apart,
____ four empires:
____ the German,
____ the Austro-Hungarian,
____ the Ottoman,
____ and the Russian.
____ The allies divided the territory.
____ Part of Russia was reorganized into
____ Finland,
____ Latvia,
____ Lithuania,
____ Estonia,
____ and Poland.
____ The Austro-Hungarian Empire was
____ divided into Austria,
____ Hungary,
____ Czechoslovakia,
____ and Yugoslavia.
____ The Ottoman Empire was divided

____ into Syria,
____ Iraq,
____ Trans-Jordan,
____ and Palestine.
____ They became mandates,
____ lands given to nations
____ to develop.
____ The treaty gave German territory
____ to Poland
____ known as the Polish Corridor.
____ Few people were happy
____ about the changes,
____ and their discontent was a sign
____ a dangerous sign
____ for the future.

65 Ideas

Number of ideas recalled _____

Other ideas recalled, including summary statements and inferences:

Questions for "World War I—Part 3"

1. What is this passage mostly about?
   Implicit: how the empires were divided up after the war

Level: High School

2. Why didn't the Germans want to sign the Versailles Treaty?
   Implicit: the terms were too harsh; they were entirely blamed for the war; *or* many of Wilson's Fourteen points were missing or weakened

3. What would have happened if Germany hadn't signed the treaty?
   Implicit: the Allies would have attacked Germany

4. What did France gain as a result of the treaty?
   Explicit: provinces of Alsace and Lorraine; *or* the rich coal mines of the Saar

5. Why did France benefit only temporarily when it was given the rich coal mines of the Saar?
   Implicit: after 15 years the Saarlanders voted to become a part of Germany again

6. How was Germany weakened after the war?
   Implicit: it lost money, military power, and land (The reader should offer at least two of the three points.)

7. What happened to the land that Russia had lost to Germany?
   Explicit: it was reorganized into five new nations: Poland, Finland, Latvia, Lithuania, and Estonia (The reader should recall at least two of these countries.)

Level: High School

8. How was the Austro-Hungarian empire divided up?
   Explicit: into Austria, Hungary, Czechoslovakia, and Yugoslavia (The reader should remember at least two of these countries.)

9. What is the right of self-determination?
   Explicit: the right of people to form their own nations

10. What caused the problems in the Polish Corridor?
    Explicit: ethnic minorities weren't happy about living under one government

---

Without Look-Backs

Number Correct Explicit: _____

Number Correct Implicit: _____

Total: _____

_____ Independent: 9–10 correct

_____ Instructional: 7–8 correct

_____ Frustration: 0–6 correct

With Look-Backs

Number Correct Explicit: _____

Number Correct Implicit: _____

Total: _____

_____ Independent: 9–10 correct

_____ Instructional: 7–8 correct

_____ Frustration: 0–6 correct

Think-Aloud Summary

Think-Aloud Statements That Indicate Understanding

Paraphrasing/Summarizing   _____

Making New Meaning   _____

Questioning That Indicates Understanding   _____

Noting Understanding   _____

Reporting Prior Knowledge   _____

Identifying Personally   _____

Think-Aloud Statements That Indicate Lack of Understanding

Questioning That Indicates Lack of Understanding   _____

Noting Lack of Understanding   _____

Level: High School

Science

Concept Questions:

What is a virus?

_____

_____

_____ (3-2-1-0)

What is DNA?

_____

_____

_____ (3-2-1-0)

What does "infectious" mean?

_____

_____

_____ (3-2-1-0)

What is a membrane?

_____

_____

_____ (3-2-1-0)

Score: _____ /12 = _____ %

_____ FAM _____ UNFAM

"Characteristics of Viruses—Part 1"

Similarities and Differences Between Viruses and Cells

If you ever had a cold or the flu, you probably hosted viruses. A virus is an <u>infectious</u> agent made up of a core of <u>nucleic</u> acid and a protein coat. Viruses are not cells. Unlike plant and animal cells, a virus package does not have a nucleus, a membrane, or cellular organelles such as ribosomes, mitochondria, or chloroplasts. Although viruses are not cells, they do have organized structural parts.

Compared to even the smallest cell, a virus is tiny. The virus that causes polio, for example, measures only 20 nanometers in diameter. One nanometer is one billionth of a meter. At that size, 3000 polioviruses could line up across the period at the end of this sentence.

All viruses have at least two parts: a protective protein coat and a core of <u>nucleic</u> acid. The protein coat around the core of the <u>nucleic</u> acid is called a capsid. Depending on the virus, the capsid may consist of one or several kinds of protein. The capsid protects the viral <u>nucleic</u> acid core from its environment.

In cells, DNA is the <u>hereditary</u> material. Some viruses also contain DNA, while other viruses contain only RNA. In viruses containing RNA, the RNA functions as the <u>hereditary</u> material.

Level: High School

Compared to a cell, a virus has a relatively simple existence. Viruses do not eat, respire, or respond to environmental changes as cells do. It should not surprise you, therefore, to learn that viruses have fewer genes than cells have. While a human cell may contain about 100,000 genes and a bacterial cell about 1000, a virus may contain only 5 genes.

In the figure on the previous page, you can see the parts of an influenza virus: a core of RNA, a surrounding capsid, and an outer covering called an envelope. An envelope is an additional protective coating usually made up of lipids, proteins, and carbohydrates. Envelopes are found only in viruses that infect animal cells. An envelope has spike-like projections that recognize and bind to complementary sites on the membrane of the cell being infected. Think about how a prickly burr sticks to objects. (357 words)

From *Biology: The Web of Life* by Eric Strauss and Marylin Lisowski. Copyright © 1998 by Addison Wesley Longman. Used by permission of Pearson Education, Inc. All Rights Reserved.

Retelling Scoring Sheet for "Characteristics of Viruses—Part 1"

Main Idea

____ There are similarities
____ and differences
____ between viruses
____ and cells.

Details

____ A virus is an agent
____ an infectious agent

____ made up of a core
____ of nucleic acid
____ and a protein coat.
____ Viruses are not cells.
____ A virus does not have a nucleus,
____ a membrane,
____ or organelles.

Main Idea

____ A virus is tiny.

Details

____ 3000 polioviruses
____ could line up
____ across the period
____ at the end of a sentence.

Main Idea

____ All viruses have two parts.

Details

____ A virus has a protein coat
____ and a core
____ of nucleic acid
____ The coat is called a capsid.
____ The capsid protects the core.

Main Idea

____ Some viruses contain DNA,
____ while other viruses contain only RNA.

Details

____ In cells
____ DNA is the hereditary material.
____ In viruses
____ RNA is the hereditary material.

Main Idea

____ A virus has a simple existence.

Details

____ Viruses do not eat,
____ respire,
____ or respond

High School

Level: High School

____ to changes.
____ Viruses contain fewer genes
____ than a human cell.
____ A human cell has 100,000 genes
____ and a virus has 5 genes.

39 Ideas

Number of ideas recalled _____

Other ideas recalled, including summary statements and inferences:

Questions for "Characteristics of Viruses—Part 1"

1. What is this section mainly about?
   Implicit: it describes what a virus is *and* how it is different from a cell

2. What are the two parts of a virus?
   Explicit: a core of acid (nucleic not required) *and* a protein (or protective) coat

3. What is the function of the protein coat of the virus?
   Explicit: it protects the core of acid

4. Why isn't a virus a cell?
   Implicit: it doesn't have a nucleus or a membrane or organelles (Ribosomes, mitochondria, and chloroplasts are not required.)

5. If a virus contains both DNA and RNA, which functions as the hereditary material?
   Explicit: RNA

6. What determines the proteins in a capsid?
   Explicit from figure: genes in the virus

7. How is the envelope of the influenza virus different from the capsid?
   Implicit: it is an additional protective coating outside of the virus

8. What types of viruses have envelopes?
   Explicit: viruses that infect animal cells

9. How does the envelope of the virus help the virus infect a cell?
   Implicit: its projections bind to complementary sites on the cell membrane

10. How does the text suggest that the existence of a virus is less complex than that of a cell?
    Implicit: viruses have fewer genes; their genetic makeup is less complex; *or* they don't do as many things as cells do (That they don't respire or eat is correct but not required.)

Without Look-Backs

Number Correct Explicit: _____

Number Correct Implicit: _____

   Total: _____

   _____ Independent: 9–10 correct

   _____ Instructional: 7–8 correct

   _____ Frustration: 0–6 correct

With Look-Backs

Number Correct Explicit: _____

Number Correct Implicit: _____

   Total: _____

   _____ Independent: 9–10 correct

   _____ Instructional: 7–8 correct

   _____ Frustration: 0–6 correct

Rate: $357 \times 60 = 21{,}420/$_____ seconds = _____ WPM

Level: High School

Science

Concept Questions:

What does it mean to reproduce?

_____

_____

_____ (3-2-1-0)

What is a parasite?

_____

_____

_____ (3-2-1-0)

What does it mean to replicate?

_____

_____

_____ (3-2-1-0)

What is a chromosome?

_____

_____

_____ (3-2-1-0)

Score: _____ /12 = _____ %

_____ FAM _____ UNFAM

"Characteristics of Viruses—Part 2"

Viral Replication: Ticking Time Bombs

Viruses do not reproduce, they replicate. Reproduction, which is characteristic of living things, involves cell division. Replication does not involve cell division. Viruses cannot replicate on their own. In order to replicate, viruses require a host. A host is an organism that shelters and nourishes something. Living cells host viruses. These host cells provide all the materials that viruses need to copy themselves.

When it enters a host cell, a virus may immediately begin to replicate, or it may remain relatively inactive. The viral replication process that rapidly kills a host cell is called the lytic cycle. You can follow the lytic cycle in the figure below. The lytic cycle begins when a virus invades a host cell and begins to replicate immediately, producing many new viruses. Eventually, the host cell lyses, or breaks apart, releasing the newly made viruses. The new viruses may then enter other cells and repeat the cycle.

As a child you may have had chicken pox, which is caused by a virus. While you were ill, most of the viruses were in the lytic cycle. Because your cells were being destroyed by the chicken pox virus, you showed symptoms of the disease.

Level: High School

Sometimes a virus does not start the lytic cycle immediately. Instead the virus enters the lysogenic cycle. The lysogenic cycle is a type of replication in which a virus does not immediately kill a host cell. The lysogenic cycle in a bacteria cell is shown on the right side of the figure on the next page.

During the lysogenic cycle, viral DNA inserts itself into a host cell's <u>chromosome</u>. A viral DNA segment that is inserted in a bacterial <u>chromosome</u> is called a prophage. A host cell carrying a prophage may divide many times. The prophage is replicated every time the host cell's <u>chromosome</u> replicates.

Some prophages remain in the lysogenic cycle indefinitely. Usually, however, some type of environmental stimulus eventually results in the separation of a prophage from the <u>chromosome</u> of its host cell. The viral DNA then enters the lytic cycle. The virus that causes cold sores in humans can go through the lysogenic cycle, for example. Cold sores erupt when these viruses enter the lytic cycle. (371 words)

From *Biology: The Web of Life* by Eric Strauss and Marylin Lisowski. Copyright © 1998 by Addison Wesley Longman. Used by permission of Pearson Education, Inc. All Rights Reserved.

Retelling Scoring Sheet for "Characteristics of Viruses—Part 2"

Main Idea

____ Viruses do not reproduce.
____ They replicate.

Details

____ Viruses cannot replicate
____ on their own.
____ Viruses require a host.
____ A host is an organism
____ that shelters
____ and nourishes something.
____ Living cells host viruses.

Main Idea

____ The replication process
____ that kills the host cell
____ is called the lytic cycle.

Details

____ When a virus enters a cell,
____ it may replicate immediately
____ or it may remain inactive.
____ The lytic cycle begins
____ when a virus invades a cell
____ and replicates immediately,
____ producing new viruses.
____ The host cell breaks apart,
____ releasing the new viruses.
____ The new viruses enter other cells
____ and repeat the cycle.
____ Chicken pox is caused by a virus.
____ When you were ill,
____ most of the viruses were in the lytic cycle.

Main Idea

____ Some viruses do not start the cycle
____ immediately.

Details

____ The virus enters the cycle
____ the lysogenic cycle.
____ The virus does not kill the host cell
____ immediately.
____ DNA insets itself
____ into a chromosome
____ of the host cell.
____ This segment is called a prophage.
____ A cell carrying a prophage

Level: High School

____ may divide many times.

____ The prophage is replicated

____ every time.

____ An environmental stimulus results

____ in the separation of the prophage

____ from the chromosome.

____ DNA then enters the lytic cycle.

____ Cold sores erupt

____ when the virus enters the lytic cycle.

46 Ideas

Number of ideas recalled _____

Other ideas recalled, including summary statements and inferences:

Questions for "Characteristics of Viruses—Part 2"

1. What is this passage mostly about?
   Implicit: the two cycles of viral replication

2. How does a virus increase in number?
   Explicit: it replicates

3. What does a virus need to replicate?
   Explicit: a host

4. How is replication different from reproduction?
   Explicit: reproduction requires cell division, and replication does not

5. What is the major difference between the lytic cycle and the lysogenic cycle?
   Implicit: in the lytic cycle, the virus immediately begins to replicate and kill the host cell, whereas in the lysogenic cycle, it doesn't kill the host cell

6. If a virus enters your body but you show no symptoms of a disease, what cycle is the virus in?
   Implicit: the lysogenic cycle

7. In the lytic cycle, what role does DNA play in replication?
   Implicit: it tells the cell to replicate or make new viruses; *or* it carries the information necessary for replication

8. If a cell's viral DNA separates from the cell's chromosome, what can we conclude?
   Implicit: a stimulus has prompted it; *or* the lytic cycle will begin soon

9. When a cold sore erupts, what cycle is the virus in?
   Explicit: the lytic cycle

10. What happens to a prophage when the host cell divides?
    Explicit: the prophage is replicated each time

Without Look-Backs

Number Correct Explicit: _____

Number Correct Implicit: _____

Total: _____

_____ Independent: 9–10 correct

_____ Instructional: 7–8 correct

_____ Frustration: 0–6 correct

With Look-Backs

Number Correct Explicit: _____

Number Correct Implicit: _____

Total: _____

_____ Independent: 9–10 correct

_____ Instructional: 7–8 correct

_____ Frustration: 0–6 correct

Rate: 371 × 60 = 22,260/_____ seconds = _____ WPM

Science

Concept Questions:

What does it mean to classify something?

_____

_____

_____ (3-2-1-0)

What does it mean to invade something?

_____

_____

_____ (3-2-1-0)

What does the prefix "retro" mean?

_____

_____

_____ (3-2-1-0)

What is an enzyme?

_____

_____

_____ (3-2-1-0)

Score: _____ /12 = _____ %

_____ FAM _____ UNFAM

"Characteristics of Viruses—Part 3"

Now I want you to read the next section, and when you come to the word **STOP** *in the text, I want you to tell me what you are thinking. When you have finished reading, I will ask you to tell me what you remember, and then I will ask you questions.*

Diversity of Viruses: An Unending Supply

Classifying viruses is difficult because they are so diverse. As a result, biologists have developed several different ways of organizing viruses. Sometimes they are organized by shape, sometimes by the host they infect. Viruses may also be classified according to the way they function inside a cell. **STOP**

_____

_____

_____

_____

_____

Shape. The arrangement of proteins in capsids determines the shape of the viruses.

Host. Viruses can be organized according to the type of host they infect. There are animal viruses, plant viruses, and bacterial viruses. Viruses that infect only bacterial cells are referred to as bacteriophages.

Many but not all viruses invade only a specific type of organism. For example, the virus that causes polio replicates only inside human host cells. The virus that causes rabies infects only the cells of a particular animal species, such as dogs and humans. **STOP**

_____

_____

_____

_____

You may wonder how viruses can be so specific. Earlier you learned that capsids and envelopes contain specific proteins. Receptor sites on host cells also contain specific proteins. If the outer proteins in a virus do not fit with the outer proteins of a cell, the virus will not attach to the cell. Without attachment, the viral nucleic acid cannot enter the host cell to replicate. **STOP**

_____

_____

_____

_____

Function. Some viruses, such as retroviruses, can also be classified based on how they function in a host. A retrovirus is a virus that contains an RNA code that replicates by first transcribing its RNA into DNA. The prefix "retro-" means "reverse." What do you think might work in reverse in this group of viruses? **STOP**

_____

_____

_____

_____

Most viruses and all organisms make RNA from DNA in the process of transcription. Retroviruses are able to make nucleic acids in reverse order from the usual process. In retroviruses DNA is made from RNA. As you can see in the figure on the next page, retroviruses have an enzyme called reverse transcriptase, which transcribes viral RNA into viral DNA inside the host cell. You can study the figure to better understand the replication of a human immunodeficiency virus (HIV). The retrovirus causes acquired immunodeficiency syndrome (AIDS). **STOP**

_____

_____

_____

_____

Retroviruses include tumor-producing viruses as well as HIV. Tumor-producing retroviruses and HIV follow a similar invasion pattern. Many tumor-producing viruses, however, enter the lysogenic cycle after Step 3 in the figure. Tumors do not immediately appear, but the viral DNA replicates along with the host cell DNA. Eventually many host cells will contain tumor-producing viral DNA. Using what you have learned about the lysogenic cycle, you can probably predict what will happen eventually. **STOP**

_____

_____

_____

_____

Nonviral particles. Scientists have discovered two infectious agents that have simpler structures than viruses: viroids and prions. A viroid is a single strand of pure RNA. Viroids cause plant diseases. For example, viroids have killed many coconut palm trees in the Philippines. Other viroids affect the health of crops such as potatoes and tomatoes. Unlike viruses, viroids do not have capsids protecting their nucleic acids. **STOP**

_____

_____

_____

_____

_____

A prion is a protein molecule that can cause disease in animals. Prions are the only known infectious agents that do not contain DNA or RNA but can, nonetheless, spread throughout an organism. A prion causes a fatal disease called scrapie in sheep. Prions have also been found in the brains of cows that died from the so-called mad cow disease. Other prions are found in humans who suffer from kuru or Creutzfeldt-Jakob disease. Both of these diseases affect the central nervous system. A cure has not yet been found for diseases caused by viroids or prions. **STOP**

_____

_____

_____

_____

_____

_____

Retelling Scoring Sheet for "Characteristics of Viruses—Part 3"

Main Idea

____ Classifying viruses is difficult
____ because they are so diverse.

Details

____ They are organized by shape,
____ by the host they infect,
____ and according to the way
____ they function in a cell.
____ There are animal viruses,
____ plant viruses,
____ and bacterial viruses.
____ Many viruses invade only a specific type
____ of organism.

Level: High School

Main Idea

____ Some viruses are classified as retroviruses.

Details

____ A retrovirus is a virus
____ that contains an RNA code.
____ It replicates
____ by transcribing the RNA
____ into DNA.
____ Retroviruses include HIV
____ and tumor-producing viruses.

Main Idea

____ Two agents have simpler structures
____ than viruses:
____ viroids
____ and prions.

Details

____ A viroid is a strand
____ of RNA.
____ Viroids cause plant diseases.
____ A prion is a molecule
____ that can cause disease in animals.
____ Prions have been found in cows
____ that died from mad cow disease.
____ Prions have been found in humans
____ who have nervous system diseases.
____ A cure has not been found
____ for diseases
____ caused by viroids
____ or prions.

36 Ideas

Number of ideas recalled _____

Other ideas recalled, including summary statements and inferences:

Questions for "Characteristics of Viruses—Part 3"

1. What are the major topics included in this section?
Implicit: any two of the following: how viruses are classified, retroviruses, and nonviral particles

2. Name three ways in which viruses are classified.
Explicit: by shape, host, and the way they function

3. What is necessary for the virus to attach to a host?
Explicit: the outer proteins must match

4. What is a retrovirus?
Explicit: a virus that replicates by first transcribing its RNA into DNA

5. How do retroviruses and other viruses differ?
Implicit: regular viruses make RNA from DNA

Level: High School

6. What enzyme is necessary for HIV to replicate?
   Explicit in figure: reverse transcriptase

7. What are the two types of illnesses caused by a retrovirus?
   Explicit: AIDS and tumors. (Cancer is acceptable.)

8. What happens when tumor-producing viral DNA goes into the lytic cycle?
   Implicit: tumors are produced

9. If a person is found to be HIV positive but shows no symptoms of AIDS, what cycle is the HIV virus in?
   Implicit: the lysogenic cycle

10. How are viroids and prions alike, and how are they different?
    Implicit: they are both infectious agents, and no cure has been found for the diseases they produce but viroids cause plant diseases and prions cause animal diseases (Answer should include one likeness and one difference.)

Without Look-Backs

Number Correct Explicit: _____

Number Correct Implicit: _____

Total: _____

_____ Independent: 9–10 correct

_____ Instructional: 7–8 correct

_____ Frustration: 0–6 correct

With Look-Backs

Number Correct Explicit: _____

Number Correct Implicit: _____

Total: _____

_____ Independent: 9–10 correct

_____ Instructional: 7–8 correct

_____ Frustration: 0–6 correct

Think-Aloud Summary

Think-Aloud Statements That Indicate Understanding

Paraphrasing/Summarizing _____

Making New Meaning _____

Questioning That Indicates Understanding _____

Noting Understanding _____

Reporting Prior Knowledge _____

Identifying Personally _____

Think-Aloud Statements That Indicate Lack of Understanding

Questioning That Indicates Lack of Understanding _____

Noting Lack of Understanding _____

15 Technical Development of the *Qualitative Reading Inventory-5*

This section describes our rationale for the development of the *QRI-5*, including our initial decisions in designing the instrument, as well as information obtained from piloting and decisions made from pilot data. This section is divided into three parts. The first part includes the purposes for the pilot and a description of the children who formed our pilot sample. The second part describes a rationale for the development of each part of the *QRI-5* and presents the results of data analyses supporting our decisions. This section provides validity data for sections of the test. The third part discusses the reliability and validity data for the overall test.

THE PILOT

The piloting for the fifth edition of the *QRI* was focused on two major objectives:

1. Reviewers had requested that we include easier passages that assess children's ability to read basic two- or three-letter words (e.g., "can," "see," "on") and to use pictures to "read" more difficult words (e.g., "jump," "hop," "sleep"). We pilot-tested these materials to estimate their difficulty and to modify them where appropriate.

2. We also learned that school districts were using *QRI* passages to monitor students' progress four times per year. In past editions of the *QRI*, this would mean crossing genre because there were only three narratives and three expository passages at each level. The fourth assessment would require a different genre. Because of the difference in student comprehension abilities between narrative and expository text (see page 458), assessing progress across genres would not be appropriate. Therefore, we have added an additional narrative text for pre-primer through third grade levels to accommodate testing four narratives at these levels.

In addition to these major objectives, we rephrased or rewrote some of the questions and provided additional correct answers to questions that have continued to cause students difficulty. Finally, we assessed the reliability and validity of the new passages.

The initial pilot sample for the *QRI-5* comprised 153 first and second grade students from four Wisconsin school districts in the first two months of school during the fall of 2008. The schools sent permission slips home to all first and second graders; therefore, no child was excluded for any reason. We provided two-page summary reports of the students' performance on these new materials to parents and teachers. This resulted in a very high rate of permission slips being returned. The second pilot group was 16 kindergarten students from one Wisconsin school in the same district as the initial pilot. This group, which was needed to try out a revised story from the first pilot, was assessed in May of 2009.

Of the pilot sample, 48% were first graders and 52% were second graders; 47% were male and 53% were female. The racial/ethnic composition of the sample was 65% white, 27% African American, 4.6% Asian, 1.3% Hispanic, 1.3% Middle Eastern, and 0.7% Pacific Islander.

DEVELOPMENT OF THE WORD-IDENTIFICATION TESTS

The words selected for the word-identification tests came from the passages on the *QRI-5*. We used this procedure to facilitate direct comparison between words read in isolation and in context. This is particularly valuable for beginning readers who may "recognize" words in context that they are unable to recognize on word lists. The word lists were developed by choosing words in our passages that represented the most common words, that is, words with the highest Standard Frequency Index (SFI) from the *Word Frequency Book* (Carroll, Davies, & Richman, 1971). For example, the first grade list includes the words "thought" and "knew," which were in the stories "The Bear and the Rabbit" and "Marva Finds a Friend," respectively. These words are likely to be found in many stories that children read every day. In contrast we did not include words such as "softly" and "newspaper," because although they too were in these stories, they are less likely to be found in children's reading materials, and therefore less common.

We also separated the most frequent words included on the pre-primer passages. The most common ones became the pre-primer 1 (PP1) list. The mean SFI of the words on the pre-primer 1 list is 77.94 and includes many of the most frequent words in written English (e.g., "the," "a," "in," "of," "to"). The pre-primer 2/3 list also includes words from the pre-primer stories (e.g., "make," "my," "some," "people"), but these words are somewhat less frequent than those on the PP1 list, with a mean SFI of 70.02. The average SFI of each word list is presented in Table 15.1.

Table 15.1	Mean Standard Frequency Index for Word Lists										
Pre-Primer 1	Pre-Primer 2	Primer	First	Second	Third	Fourth	Fifth	Sixth	MS	HS
77.94	70.02	67.32	65.26	60.1	55.7	54.08	49.88	46.54	41.07	34.82

Analysis of the Word-List Data

1. Are the word lists of increasing difficulty? We compared the word-list scores of the first and second grade students with instructional levels in narrative text ranging from those with no instructional level (i.e., they could not read the easiest text with at least 90% accuracy and 67% comprehension) to students at the third grade instructional level. Students read more words correctly on the list with a higher SFI than the next list with a lower SFI. However, the PP2/3 versus Primer comparison did not reach statistical significance ($p < .06$). Table 15.2 illustrates comparisons of word-list difficulty between adjacent SFI levels.

Also, at each instructional level on materials new to the *QRI-4* at grade four through upper middle school, the mean number of words correctly read on the word list at the student's instructional level was 90% versus 80% on the next highest list. Therefore, the students in that sample were very capable at word identification.

2. Which is more predictive of contextual reading: words correct or words correct and automatic? We compared the total number of words on each word list that students read correctly to the total number that they read correctly and within one second (automatically). Students read 1.5 more correct words than automatic words on the PP1 list. On the PP2/3 through 2nd grade lists the average difference between automatic and correct words was five or six words. However, at the third grade level the difference was nine words.

Correlational analyses were also conducted to examine the relationships between the percentage of words read correctly and automatically or simply correct and total accuracy and CWPM on stories. For example, the percentage of pre-primer words read automatically by students with instructional reading levels of Primer or lower correlated .52 with total reading accuracy on story 1 and .61 on story 2. In comparison the correlations between percentage of pre-primer words read correctly were .50 and .60, for stories 1 and 2, respectively. The percentage of pre-primer words read automatically correlated .50 with CWPM on story 1 and .44 on story 2. Similar correlations were found for students with higher instructional levels. At each instructional level the correlation between the percentage of words read automatically on the word list and Total Accuracy and CWPM was higher than the same analysis using only the total percent of words read correctly on the word list.

Table 15.2	Mean Percent Correct on Adjacent Word Lists, PP1–Grade 3				
	PP1–PP2	PP2–Primer	Primer–First	First–Second	Second–Third
Mean	95 vs. 79	91 vs. 89	92 vs. 80	89 vs. 73	81 vs. 62
S.D.	13–28	13–16	11–22	13–21	15–26
N	152	123	116	94	72

It should be recognized that the number of words read correctly and automatically and the total read correctly on the same list are highly correlated (significant at all levels, and $r = .82+$ at all levels). Thus, although we find automaticity of word recognition in isolation to be more highly correlated with Total Accuracy and CWPM, examiners using total correct will certainly see a relationship between performance on the word lists and CWPM in context.

Reading by Analogy

Reading by analogy is assumed when a student can read a low-frequency word that contains the same spelling pattern as a high-frequency word that the student can recognize immediately. For example on the pre-primer 1 list the word "can" was the high-frequency word that represented the "-an" spelling pattern and "pan" was the lower frequency word. Analyses were conducted on the difficulty of the low-frequency words that shared the same spelling patterns with high-frequency words. Each analysis was conducted within a range of instructional levels. For example, the first analysis used data from first grade students with instructional reading levels of less than or equal to 1.35, which is the top range of pre-primer. Their performance on the PP1 and PP2/3 lists showed that the easiest patterns were "-ook," "-ee," "-an," and "in." The most difficult patterns on the PP lists were all words with the VCE pattern: "-ame," "-ace," "-ike," and "-ake." The same pattern of difficulty was found for second graders with instructional reading levels less than or equal to 1.35.

When we examined the words on the primer and first grade lists we found the same pattern among students in first and second grade if their instructional level was greater than 1.35. The easiest patterns were "-ump," "-ing," "-eep," "-eed," and "-ent." The most difficult patterns were "-ain," "-ound," and "-ew."

DEVELOPMENT OF THE PRIOR-KNOWLEDGE ASSESSMENT TASKS

Identification of Concepts

We chose the concepts, which were phrased as questions, for the conceptual-questions task on the basis of relationship to the comprehension questions. Chrystal (1991) examined the predictive validity of the understanding of concepts necessary to answer implicit comprehension questions. She examined the correlations between these concepts and comprehension of two second grade and two fifth grade texts. She found that concepts chosen because of their relationship to implicit questions correlated more highly with comprehension than did the original QRI concepts. Furthermore, concepts scored in relation to information found in the passage predicted as well for Native American as for white students. Therefore, in developing new QRI concepts, the authors (Leslie and Caldwell) and two master's degree students in reading independently chose concepts shown to be necessary to understand for answering implicit questions on each passage. For example, consider the first grade passage "The Bear and the Rabbit." The last question is a difficult one for many young readers: "Why did the bear and the rabbit become friends?" We felt that in order to answer that question, using the clues in the passage, children needed to know that one reason why people become friends is shared interests (in this particular case, their love of music). Thus, we chose the concept question "What makes a friend?" After the four of us independently chose concepts, we met to examine the consistency of our selections. We were pleased to discover that in over 90% of the cases, we chose the same concepts. Often our wording was different, so we negotiated what we thought would be the best wording, and final decisions were made after piloting.

Analyses of
Correlations
between Prior
Knowledge
and Other Test
Components

1. Does prior knowledge measured by concept questions or by prediction predict comprehension? We correlated the total conceptual-knowledge question score with comprehension, as measured by retelling and questions when the number of students who had read the passages was greater than or equal to 10.

In contrast to past piloting of PP throught first grade stories, prior knowledge correlated significantly with retelling and/or comprehension on the new pre-primer, primer, and first grade stories. On the two new pre-primer stories, prior knowledge correlated .39 and .50 with comprehension, respectively. The correlation between prior knowledge and comprehension was .61 on the primer story and .50 between prior knowledge and retelling. On the new first grade story, the correlation between prior knowledge and retelling was .38. The results on the pre-primer stories may be due to the age of the participants in the initial pilot, who were beginning first graders. Some of them with low reading ability had little to say when asked, "What does it mean to . . . (jump, hop, run, etc.)?" A few children who could demonstrate to us what these concepts meant got scores of 2. It seems as if we are measuring verbal expression to a stranger rather than prior knowledge of specific concepts on the two new pre-primer stories ("I Can" and "I See").

On the new primer and first grade stories there appears to be a true relationship between children's abilities to explain what a word means and their ability to either retell or answer comprehension questions. However, there were no correlations between prior-knowledge scores and retelling or comprehension on the new second grade story, "The Family's First Trip." On the new third grade story, "A New Friend from Europe," prior knowledge correlated with retelling at a .40 correlation and with comprehension .45 when assessed by questions.

At the fourth grade level, retelling of narrative text was predicted by conceptual-knowledge scores, as were retelling and comprehension of expository text. Leslie and Cooper (1993) found that conceptual-knowledge scores were correlated with retelling and comprehension of narrative text but that prediction scores correlated with retelling and comprehension of expository text. Our study of the upper middle school and high school texts showed strong evidence of the relationship between prior knowledge and comprehension. Prior knowledge was significantly correlated with comprehension or retelling of all six upper middle school texts, with an average of $r = .60$. At the high school level, prior knowledge correlated significantly with retelling, inferences generated during retelling, or comprehension assessed with and without look-backs *on all texts* with an average of $r = .57$.

In summary, either conceptual knowledge or prediction was significantly correlated with some form of comprehension, either retelling, inferences generated during retelling, comprehension without access to text, and/or comprehension with look-backs. These significant correlations are more consistently found as the density of the conceptual load in the texts increases. An examination of the materials on the *QRI-5* and in textbooks illustrates how this increase is noticeable in third grade materials and continues throughout the grades. In the high school texts, students are expected to learn many new concepts and vocabulary in a single chapter.

The results on the prediction task in general indicated that children reading at the third grade level and higher could use the title of the passage and the concepts, phrases, and questions to make overall predictions of passage content that correlated significantly with retelling or answers to comprehension questions. Specifically, at the third grade level, prediction correlated significantly (range of correlations was .70 to .84) with comprehension, as measured by retelling, on four out of six passages. At sixth grade, prediction was significantly correlated with retelling (.55) and comprehension (.57) of the three expository texts. On the upper middle school texts, concept knowledge best predicted comprehension.

2. Is knowledge or general reading ability more predictive of comprehension? An analysis of this question on materials new in the *QRI-4* in grade four through upper middle school found that the Terra Nova Standard Score (TNSS) of reading ability only correlated significantly with a measure of comprehension on five texts: "Early Railroads" (.61 with retelling, $n = 10$, $p < .06$); "Patricia McKissack" (.42 with comprehension, $n = 29$, $p < .01$); "How Does Your Body Take in Oxygen?" (.58 with comprehension, $n = 10$, $p < .05$); "Malcolm X" (.59 with retelling, $n = 10$, $p < .05$); and "Life Cycles of Stars—Part 1" (.78 with comprehension, $n = 10$, $p < .01$). In three of these cases the standard scores also correlated significantly with our prior-knowledge (PK) assessment on that text (on "McKissack" TNSS and PK correlated .51; on "Oxygen," .61; and on "Stars 1," .75). Therefore, although the TNSS contributed most to the prediction of comprehension in these three cases, the correlation between the two knowledge measures makes these results difficult to interpret. In contrast, our prior-knowledge assessment correlated significantly with a measure of comprehension on 12 of the 15 new passages. In conclusion, we believe that the prior-knowledge measures in the *QRI-5* provide important diagnostic information for users by measuring a factor that could influence a student's reading comprehension.

Another study of eighth graders compared the predictive validity of conceptual-knowledge scores and the Wisconsin Student Assessment System Reading Subscale scores to retelling, inferences generated during retelling, and comprehension (with and without look-backs). We examined the simple correlations among conceptual knowledge, WSAS-Reading, and measures of comprehension. If either conceptual knowledge or the WSAS-Reading score was correlated with a measure of comprehension, then partial correlations were computed. On the six middle school texts, prior knowledge was the best predictor of one or more comprehension measures. However, on "Biddy Mason," WSAS-Reading scores predicted comprehension with look-backs even after the conceptual-knowledge score was entered.

The high school passages were analyzed in separate sections because each had a different conceptual-knowledge score. On the literature selection, "Where the Ashes Are," conceptual-knowledge score predicted the number of inferences made during retelling on all sections. WSAS-Reading score was correlated only with inference generation on the third section, and when the conceptual-knowledge score was controlled for, the WSAS score was no longer significantly correlated with the number of inferences generated. On Parts 1 and 2 of "World War I," conceptual-knowledge scores and WSAS-Reading correlated with comprehension that included look-backs. When conceptual-knowledge scores were entered, WSAS-Reading remained a significant predictor of comprehension with look-backs. Only conceptual-knowledge scores correlated with retelling on the third section. On Part 1 of the biology text, "Characteristics of Viruses," only conceptual knowledge correlated with retelling, but both conceptual knowledge and WSAS-Reading were correlated with comprehension (without look-backs). When conceptual-knowledge scores were entered, WSAS-Reading did not significantly predict comprehension. On Part 2, only conceptual knowledge predicted retelling and on Part 3, only WSAS-Science predicted comprehension with and without look-backs.

In summary, prior knowledge of concepts contained in passages correlated significantly with passage comprehension more frequently than did a general measure of reading achievement. This finding illustrates the value of measuring conceptual knowledge in reading assessment.

3. How Much Prior Knowledge Is Enough? We conducted discriminant function analyses on all passages that showed significant correlations between the total-concept scores and the total-comprehension score to determine which concept score best discriminated instructional-level comprehension (70%+) from frustration-level comprehension (< 70%). The concept score that best predicted the cutoff score was obtained from the classification function coefficients. The average concept score across the passages was 55% (range 40%–66%, with 70% between 50% and 60%).

DEVELOPMENT OF THE MEASURES OF COMPREHENSION

We use three measures of comprehension: a retelling measure of what the student remembers from the passage; explicit questions (those where the answer is stated explicitly in the passage); and implicit questions (where an inference must be made in order to answer the question). We include both the retelling and question measures of comprehension, because research has indicated that the two are not measuring the same aspects of comprehension (Taft & Leslie, 1985).

A *retelling* measure allows one to examine how the memory for the text is structured. Although we do not provide a quantitative score based on the sequence of retelling, the more the student's retelling sequence conforms to the structure of the narrative, the greater the recall. Retelling indicates how the child has organized the information, and it may divulge inferences made during comprehension.

Questions, on the other hand, contain information that may drive the inferencing process, acting as scaffolds. Questions remain the primary vehicle for assessing comprehension in the classroom (Leslie & Caldwell, 2009). We have included *explicit* (or literal) *and implicit* (or inference) *questions* in order to tap both kinds of comprehension (Pearson & Johnson, 1978).

The authors designed the questions. Those from narrative texts were designed to tap the most important information in the story. According to story grammars, the goal of the main character (protagonist) is the focus around which all other information is interpreted. Therefore, in all narratives one question asks for the goal of the protagonist. The other questions were designed to tap important information the student uses to make a coherent representation of the text. That is, a detail was questioned if it was an important detail in the story, but not if it was unimportant. In expository text of third grade readability and above, the first question always asks for the implicit main idea of the passage. Again, the other questions were written to tap understanding of important information contained in the exposition. In each case the authors read each passage and questions and categorized the questions into explicit/implicit categories. If the authors disagreed on whether an answer was explicitly or implicitly stated in the passage, the question was rewritten or dropped.

One author conducted all the propositional analyses (Clark & Clark, 1977) necessary for scoring the retellings. Another judge propositionally analyzed a sample of nine passages. The interjudge reliability of the propositions identified on a passage was .98+ on the passages. After more than 20 students had read each passage below the high school level, the percentage of readers recalling each proposition on a passage was calculated. A map of each text following the story map format for narratives or the main idea format with supporting detail structure for exposition was constructed. Each map was designed on the basis of (1) theoretical considerations of importance and (2) empirical evidence from students that these propositions were recalled with some frequency.

First, one of the *QRI* authors would design a map based on the elements of a story for the narrative passages (such as setting, goal, events, resolution) or based on the main ideas with supporting details for expository passages. Then the frequency with which students recalled these propositions would be examined. Usually, propositions recalled by more than 20% of the students were placed on the map. However, there were details that many students recalled that were not important to the overall message of the passage but were interesting to the students. For example, on the Margaret Mead passage, 32% of the students recalled that "in the village in Samoa she lived in a house with no running water or bathroom." Also, there were ideas that were theoretically important but were not recalled by the students. For example, in biographical passages, even though students often did not recall resolutions of narratives that were considered important, the propositions were still placed on the map. Thus the maps are our best judgment of propositions recalled by the students and other important propositions that may not have been. After we designed the maps, a research assistant rescored all the retelling. Propositions that students frequently recalled but that were not on the map were added.

At the high school level a different procedure was used. We gave the texts to high school teachers of the relevant content (e.g., English teachers read the literature texts), and asked them to underline the segments of text they thought were important for students to remember. Then they were asked to reread the texts and underline (in a different color) the segments that they thought students would remember after one reading. If a segment of text was underlined by 50% or more of the teachers, it was put on the high school retelling map. If over 20% of students recalled a segment that the teachers had not marked, it was added to the map. Although this did not occur frequently, there were details that over 20% of students remembered that teachers did not believe were important. Thus, the maps were a combination of teachers' judgments of important propositions and students' memory of text.

Analyses of the Measures of Comprehension

1. Is retelling different in narrative and expository text? The student's retelling is evaluated in comparison to the ideas listed on the passage maps, plus appropriate inferences. Our data suggest that the amount of retelling is related to the type of text. The mean retelling of narrative texts ranged from 17 to 41%, whereas the mean retelling of expository texts ranged from 13 to 31%. The superior retelling of narrative texts was found from pre-primer through fourth grade reading levels. Differences have also been found among sixth grade average (Leslie & Cooper, 1993) and below-average readers (Leslie, unpublished). On the upper middle school texts, retelling was higher on the literature texts than on the social studies or science texts.

2. What is the relationship between retelling and comprehension as measured by questions? Correlations between retelling scores (number of propositions retold that are on the retelling scoring sheet plus relevant inferences) and total number of questions correctly answered were examined on all passages with $n = 10$ or larger. The number of statistically significant correlations ranged across readability levels. At the pre-primer level, the new story "I Can" showed a significant correlation between retelling and answering of questions, $r(30) = .48$, $p < .01$, and on the other pre-primer materials examined on the *QRI-5,* two out of the three correlations were significant. In "Just Like Mom," where the print basically describes the actions in the pictures, there was no significant correlation between retelling and comprehension. For the non-pictured pre-primer story "Lost and Found," which is a predictable sequence of goal-directed events, there was a significant correlation, $r(25) = .61$, $p < .01$, between retelling and comprehension. The expository pictured passage "People at Work" also showed a significant correlation between retelling and comprehension, $r(28) = .60$, $p < .01$.

At primer, the only statistically significant correlation between retelling and comprehension was found on the new story "A Night in the City," $r(15) = .45$, $p < .05$. At the first grade level, three out of six, and at the second grade level, two out of six, were significant. At the third and fourth grade levels, three out of six correlations were significant. At the fifth and sixth grade levels, one out of two correlations was significant. It appears that the more complex the story was for the students, the more likely retelling and comprehension were to be significantly correlated.

An examination of retelling on the *QRI-4* passages new to the grade four through upper middle school levels found that at the fourth and fifth grade levels, retelling and comprehension were significantly correlated on only one of the three passages at each level. In one case it was an expository passage ("Plant Structures for Survival"), and on the other it was a narrative text ("Patricia McKissack"). At the sixth grade level, retelling and comprehension were significantly correlated (.35–.48) on four of the five new passages. Only on "Temperature and Humidity" was there no significant correlation found. At the upper middle school level, the correlations were significant on three of the six passages, with correlations ranging from .34 to .47. We concluded that retelling and comprehension share some common variance, but there are differences between what is being measured.

3. What is the relationship between explicit and implicit comprehension? Because there are only four or five explicit questions and zero, two, four, or five implicit questions per passage, depending on the level of the passages, any conclusion about a child's ability to answer these types of questions based on the administration of *a single passage* is not recommended. In order to address this question with more reliable data, we examined the correlation between explicit and implicit comprehension on data from pairs of passages. In the *QRI-5* there are passages of the same type (i.e., narrative, expository) at each level. We collapsed data from students who read more than one of each type and examined the correlation between explicit and implicit comprehension. The correlations were significant on three of the five narrative passage sets from second grade through sixth grade, but on only one of the five sets of expository passages. Only one of the correlations was greater than .60. Based on the standard error of measurement on explicit and implicit questions on two passages (that is, eight of each type of question), if a student answered three to four explicit questions and only one or no implicit questions correctly on *two or more passages at his or her instructional level in familiar text,* then the difference is of diagnostic significance. This figure was determined by considering the standard error of measurement of these questions. The standard error of measurement of the difference between two scores is roughly equal to the square root of the sum of the squared standard errors of both tests (Thorndike, Cunningham, Thorndike, & Hagen, 1991).

4. What are the effects of look-backs? Table 15.3 presents the means and standard deviations of comprehension assessed with and without look-backs. Table 15.3 illustrates that students with a reading instructional level at third grade and higher are able to answer more questions when allowed to look back. Moreover, only on "Plant Structures for Survival" were students unable to bring their total comprehension scores (i.e., with look-backs) into instructional range when allowed to look back in text. In general, students were more able to increase their explicit comprehension because the answers to the questions were stated directly in the text, and in some cases these were complex details that taxed memory. We believe that allowing students reading at the third grade

Table 15.3

Means and Standard Deviation of Comprehension with and without Look-Backs

Passage	Level	n	Comprehension Scores	
			Without Look-Backs	With Look-Backs
"The Trip to the Zoo"	3	33	.70 (.15)	.92 (.09)
"A Special Birthday for Rosa"	3	25	.82 (.08)	.89 (.18)
"Tomie dePaola"	4	76	.47 (.22)	.68 (.12)
"Early Railroads"	4	22	.52 (.21)	.67 (.18)
"Plant Structures for Survival"	4	20	.37 (.20)	.55 (.23)
"Patricia McKissack"	5	52	.59 (.18)	.70 (.19)
"Farming on the Great Plains"	5	17	.60 (.16)	.89 (.16)
"How Does Your Body Take in Oxygen?"	5	14	.70 (.25)	.88 (.22)
"The Early Life of Lois Lowry"	6	33	.69 (.17)	.95 (.08)
"Temperature and Humidity"	6	27	.54 (.24)	.69 (.29)
"Clouds and Precipitation"	6	19	.66 (.17)	.91 (.16)
"Building Pyramids"	6	32	.79 (.19)	.89 (.13)
"The Lifeline of the Nile"	6	29	.70 (.17)	.93 (.09)
"Biddy Mason"	MS	47	.84 (.18)	.96 (.10)
"Malcolm X"	MS	33	.68 (.18)	.91 (.15)
"Immigration—Part 1"	MS	11	.77 (.26)	.98 (.04)
"Immigration—Part 2"	MS	11	.80 (.13)	1.00 (.00)
"Life Cycles of Stars—Part 1"	MS	18	.58 (.23)	.92 (.11)
"Life Cycles of Stars—Part 2"	MS	13	.58 (.19)	.92 (.09)

level and above the opportunity to look back in text provides the examiner with useful information to separate problems in comprehension versus memory.

To examine whether the comprehension or total comprehension scores (i.e., with look-backs) were more often correlated with standardized measures of reading comprehension, we compared the correlations between Terra Nova Standard Scores or Percentile Ranks and comprehension scores with and without look-backs on materials at the fourth grade through upper middle school levels. As indicated earlier, these standardized scores rarely correlated significantly with students' comprehension scores at these levels. However, when a significant correlation occurred, it was with comprehension without look-backs rather than the score with look-backs. Therefore, we recommend that the comprehension score *without* look-backs be used to estimate instructional reading level at these levels. In contrast, the standardized test scores of students reading the high school passages significantly correlated with comprehension including look-backs more frequently than without them. Therefore, we conclude that comprehension *with* look-backs should be the score to use to determine the instructional level on the high school texts on the *QRI-5*.

DEVELOPMENT OF THE THINK-ALOUD PROCEDURE

The *QRI-4* extended the think-aloud procedure into middle school. We continue this in the *QRI-5* by including one passage that the examiner reads ("The Mining Boom") while modeling seven different types of think-alouds: paraphrasing/summarizing, making new meaning, reporting prior knowledge, asking a question that indicates understanding, identifying personally, noting understanding, and noting lack of understanding. After observing the modeling, the students read one 423 word section of an expository text without thinking aloud and the next 417 word section of text while thinking aloud.

The location of **STOP** points for thinking aloud while reading varies depending on the complexity of the text and our judgment of where a think aloud (TAL) might facilitate comprehension. We include stops after the statements of main ideas and after groups of sentences that support main ideas. For example, on an upper middle school social studies text, a **STOP** was placed after 6 sentences that describe the main idea of a paragraph. Later, a **STOP** was placed between two paragraphs where the first introduced a new topic and the second expanded on the topic. In this particular text, there were 417 words, 32 sentences, and 7 **STOP**s.

Participants. Of the 77 middle school students in grades five through eight who participated in the think-aloud study, 10% were in fifth grade, 25% in sixth grade, 22% in seventh grade, and 43% were in eighth grade. There were similar numbers of male and female students: 52% were male and 48% were female. Also, 65% were white, 1% Asian American, 28% African American, and 6% Hispanic American.

Procedures. The students read a graded word list to estimate the level of text that they could read with good word identification. If a student was able to read at least 70% of the words on the list at his or her grade level, then the student read the biography text at that level. Each student's prior knowledge of four important concepts contained in the text was assessed. The student then read the biography, retold what he or she remembered, and then answered questions without looking back in the text. After *all* questions were asked, the student was encouraged to look back in the text to find information necessary to answer questions previously not answered correctly. If the student's total comprehension score (including look-backs) was 70% or above, he or she was asked to read a biography at a higher readability level. The highest-level biography on which the student scored at least 70% comprehension was chosen as the level of nonfiction text that he or she would read.

For example, if a sixth grade student read an upper middle school biography with 80% comprehension, she or he would be asked to read either a science or social studies text at the upper middle school level. The decision to read *either* a science or a social studies passage was made because we did not wish to remove students from the classroom for more than 75 minutes. Examiners randomly assigned whether science or social studies would be read. To separate the effects of thinking aloud from the content of the material, half of the participants read the first segment and thought aloud and the other students read the second segment and thought aloud. The students read the alternative section (either first or second) without thinking aloud. Again, the students first answered questions without reference to the text and then were allowed to refer to the text to answer any questions that they had forgotten or not answered correctly. All tapes were transcribed verbatim and prior knowledge, retelling, answers to questions, and think-alouds were scored according to procedures described by Leslie and Caldwell (2001).

Analysis of the Think-Aloud Results

First, as expected, no student was familiar with the think-aloud procedure, but all students were readily able to do so after modeling. This observation supports the results of the *QRI-3* pilot study. Two major goals directed the analysis of the think-aloud data:

1. Does thinking aloud while reading result in higher retelling or comprehension than reading without thinking aloud?
2. Does the quality of think-alouds produced by students correlate with their comprehension of the text?

The numbers of statements or questions generated as a result of thinking aloud were classified into nine categories: asking a question that indicated lack of understanding, reporting a conflict with prior knowledge, and the seven categories that were modeled by the examiner when reading "The Mining Boom." An analysis of the frequencies of types of think-alouds generated by students found that the most frequent type of think-aloud was *paraphrasing/summarizing*, in which a student simply rephrases or summarizes his or her understanding of what was read prior to the **STOP**. Looking across texts on which students thought aloud, anywhere from 40% ("Immigration—Part 2") to 75% ("Life Cycles of Stars—Part 2") of the think-alouds were of the paraphrasing/summarizing type. The next most frequent type of think-aloud was *making new meaning*, which ranged in frequency from 9% ("Clouds and Precipitation") to 23% ("Building Pyramids"). Other categories that had low but consistent usage were *connecting with prior knowledge* and *identifying personally*. Over 90% of the think-alouds made on all texts indicated that students understood what they were reading.

Each clause in a think-aloud was also examined for its relationship to the text that preceded the **STOP**. The clause was categorized as a paraphrase, topic statement, metacomment, or a specific type of inference: an explanation, prediction, or association. A paraphrase is a transformation of text that preserves its gist or meaning. It is not a verbatim reproduction of the text, but illustrates the student's understanding of it. A topic statement is generated when a student says, "It's about . . .". A metacomment is a statement that reports on text processing or personal connections to text content ("I saw the Egyptian exhibit in the museum this summer" or "I don't really understand what this means"). Explanatory inferences provide answers to "why" questions about states, events, or actions in narrative text and serve to explain causal relationships in exposition ("Hail is formed when ice crystals are thrown up and down within a cumulonimbus cloud"). Predictive inferences provide answers to causal consequence questions (Graesser & Clark, 1985) and may be stated as a future goal or emotional reaction in narrative text. Predictions in expository text may be stated as ideas that the author will present next ("I think I will learn about how clouds are categorized") or how a problem might be solved ("I think the author will tell me how farmers could build a pyramid"). Associative inferences occur concurrently with an event, state, or activity in narrative text (Trabasso & Magliano, 1996, p. 268). They do not explain what came before and do not predict what will come. Associative inferences provide answers to *what, how, where, when, and who questions* in narrative text (Lehnert, 1978; Graesser, Golding, & Long, 1991). In exposition, associative inferences could be connected to past text (but not in an explanatory way) or to the reader's knowledge base. For example, when reading about clouds an associative inference from text would be "The names of clouds are from another language" whereas an associative inference from world knowledge would be "Some days there are clouds and other days the sky is blue." If the think-aloud clause had been categorized as inference, we judged whether the inference originated from the student's world knowledge, which was judged when the specific information was related to the content of the text but not found *in* the text or whether it was generated using text information.

Recall was also parsed into clauses matched to the passage clauses. The clauses were again categorized into paraphrase, topic statements, metacomments, and inferences. Then the type of inference—explanatory, predictive, or associative—was determined and its origin (world or text) was assessed.

We also judged the causal coherence of the recall by examining whether clauses contained *why, when,* or *because* or other explicit causal statements either within the clause or between clauses. For example, if the student said, "Nobody wants to live in a desert because it is too dry," it would be scored as one causal statement within a clause. And if the student said, "Farmers have new machinery. Now they can grow crops faster for people," it was scored as one causal connection across two clauses. Reliability of the estimate of causal cohesion was estimated by two judges scoring 20% of the recall protocols, with exact agreement of 98%.

What Are the Effects of Thinking Aloud? Repeated measures analyses of variance were used with level of text (6, 8) as the between-subjects independent variable and think-aloud condition as the repeated measure independent variable. The dependent measures were proportion of clauses recalled, the proportion of clauses of different types (paraphrases, inferences) recalled, the causal cohesion of recall, and answers to comprehension questions. Because we counterbalanced think-aloud conditions across segments of the texts, an insufficient number of participants was available to make an analysis by text content (i.e., social studies and science) reliable. Therefore, any variance due to text effects is masked due to the averaging across participants and texts within levels.

Table 15.4 presents the mean proportions and standard deviations of prior-knowledge scores and several measures of the quantity and quality of retelling and answering of questions as a function of think-aloud condition and level of text. Thinking aloud affected the proportion of clauses recalled differently for students reading two levels of text, resulting in a TAL x Text Level interaction, $F(1, 66) = 7.34, p < .01$. Thinking aloud tended to increase the proportion of clauses retold by students reading the sixth grade texts ($M = .16$ vs. $.14$), but decreased the proportion of clauses recalled by students reading the eighth grade texts ($M = .14$ vs. $.19$). In other words, students reading the sixth grade text recalled more if they thought aloud, but students reading the eighth grade text recalled less if they thought aloud.

Despite this inexplicable result, the type of clauses recalled (paraphrase or inference) were the same on both levels of text, resulting in a significant main effect of thinking aloud. When students thought aloud they made proportionally more inferences in recall than when they did not think aloud, $F(1, 66) = 27.72, p < .001$, and conversely made fewer paraphrases when they thought aloud than when they did not, $F(1, 66) = 13.52, p < .001$.

The same type of mixed model analysis of variance examined the effects of thinking aloud on students' ability to answer comprehension questions as a function of text level. Thinking aloud was the repeated measures factor and text level was the between-subjects factor. The dependent measures were proportions of correctly answered questions. Although we had two types of questions, explicit and implicit, the number of each type was small (four or five), so the reliability of a score based on such few items would not be high enough to warrant separate analyses (Leslie & Caldwell, 2006). More questions were answered correctly after thinking aloud in the upper middle school text and fewer

Table 15.4 Mean Proportions and Standard Deviations of Prior Knowledge, Clauses Retold, Paraphrases and Types of Inferences Recalled, Causal Cohesion of Recall, and Comprehension as a Function of Think-Aloud Condition and Text Level

Level of Text		Thinking Aloud	Not Thinking Aloud
Sixth	Prior Knowledge	.65 (.28)	.66 (.32)
	Clauses Retold	.16 (.06)	.14 (.07)
	Paraphrases	.53 (.28)	.71 (.27)
	Inferences	.40 (.28)	.19 (.18)
	Explanatory	.06 (.13)	.22 (.35)
	Associative	.80 (.31)	.55 (.45)
	Predictive	.00 (.00)	.06 (.24)
	Causal Cohesion	1.10 (1.35)	.48 (.83)
	Comprehension	.64 (.17)	.69 (.26)
Upper Middle School	Prior Knowledge	.74 (.25)	.80 (.25)
	Clauses Retold	.14 (.12)	.19 (.12)
	Paraphrases	.52 (.24)	.66 (.28)
	Inferences	.39 (.26)	.20 (.17)
	Explanatory	.14 (.31)	.07 (.23)
	Associative	.73 (.40)	.69 (.40)
	Predictive	.00 (.00)	.04 (.18)
	Causal Cohesion	.54 (1.41)	.15 (.43)
	Comprehension	.74 (.18)	.70 (.21)

were answered after thinking aloud in sixth grade text, but the difference was not statistically significant, $F(1, 66) = 2.74$, $p = .10$. Finally, there was no main effect of thinking aloud, $F(1, 66) = .06$, on answering questions.

Although we were interested in a qualitative analysis of the contents of TALs and recall as well as possible differences in recall and question answering after reading with thinking aloud and reading without thinking aloud, we also wanted to address the psychometric question of whether or not to include a think-aloud measure in an assessment instrument. To answer that question, we examined the correlations among the paraphrases and inferences included in think-alouds and recall with how accurately students answered comprehension questions.

Significant negative correlations between inferences generated in recall and students' answers to comprehension questions were found on both levels of text, $r(29) = -.34$ for sixth grade and $r(39) = -.27$ for upper middle school, $ps < .05$. The finding that the more inferences made in recall, the *less* students were able to answer comprehension questions correctly surprised us and prompted further study. To understand the negative correlations we examined scores from two very different groups of students. One group had high proportions of inferences but low scores on answering questions and the other group had low proportions of inferences and high scores on answering questions. We found that the selected students had read a representative sample of our texts so the results were not due to a cluster of students reading only one text. We found that students with low scores on questions and high inference scores in recall had produced very general associative text-based inferences and were unable to answer the comprehension questions that demanded a memory of specific information from text. In contrast those students with high scores on questions and proportionately few inferences in recall had instead paraphrased the text in recall.

The first use of think-alouds as a diagnostic procedure occurred on the *QRI-3*. Results of a study of over 40 students found that the TALs that indicated understanding correlated significantly with the total comprehension score on the narrative text when lookbacks were allowed, $r(18) = .60$, $p < .01$. Also, the more inferences that occurred during think-alouds on the history text, the more literal retelling occurred, $r(17) = .40$, $p < .06$. And finally, the more inferences generated while thinking aloud on the science text, the more inferences were generated during retelling, $r(18) = .43$, $p < .05$. These findings along with our current results suggest that valuable insights into students' understanding of text can be obtained through thinking aloud.

DEVELOPMENT OF THE PASSAGES

Leveling the Difficulty of the Passages

The pre-primer through third grade passages on the *QRI-5* were developed by using leveling techniques from Gunning (1998, 2002) and Harris-Jacobson (Harris & Sipay, 1990), as well as comparing what we developed to Leveled Readers using the Fountas and Pinnell (2006) system. One advantage of the Gunning procedure is that it considers how passage length, number of different words, and pictures affect the word "reading" of beginning readers. As part of the process, Gunning has developed the Primary Word List, which is a compilation of the 810 words that occur with the highest frequency in first grade textbooks and children's books at the first grade level. Easy sight level is designated when there are no more than 35 different words in a passage no longer than 100 words, where only four to six of the words are not on the Primary Word List, and pictures illustrate more difficult words not found on the word list. Levels A and B are based on number of different words and total words. In addition, Level A contains only words with short vowel patterns, whereas Level B may include both long and short vowel patterns. Above Level B, Gunning's readability formula is used to differentiate levels by counting "hard words," or those not on the Primary Word List, as well as measuring average sentence length. These numerical estimates, which have a standard error of measurement of .3 of a school year, or three months (Gunning, 2002, p. 586), can be compared to the Harris-Jacobson procedure.

The Harris-Jacobson includes a more extensive word list that was developed using readers from pre-primer through eighth grade. It also uses the percent of hard words and average sentence length to determine readability. The standard error of measurement of the HJ is .50, or one-half a grade. Because of the SEM it is recommended that several samples of a book be used to determine its readability. Finally, the Fountas and Pinnell (2006) system uses many variables to judge the difficulty of passages, including number of different words, number of high-frequency words, sentence length, sentence complexity, predictability, language pattern and repetition, print size and number of words per page, illustration support, concept load, and familiarity. They recently reported a

SEM of one level (Fountas & Pinnell, 2008). This indicates that a passage judged to be at Level L, for example, could as well be at Levels K or M. Research on the factors that predicted level within first grade found that higher levels provide more complex sentences as measured by T-units and morphemes per book (Cunningham, Spadorcia, Erikson, Koppenhaver, Sturm, & Yoder, 2005).

Passages were included in the *QRI* if readers at a specific grade level achieved instructional level scores in word identification and/or comprehension and if piloting indicated that the passage was more difficult than the next lower level and easier than the next higher level. Thus, third grade passages were more difficult than second grade selections for our pilot sample; similarly, they were easier than those for fourth grade. Later in this section you will see how students comprehended the passages on the *QRI*.

QRI 5 passages above fourth grade were leveled using Readability Calculations, Windows version 7.0 (Micro Power and Light Company, 2007), which provides estimates based on the formula designed by Dale-Chall, the Fry Graph, and the Flesch Grade Level index, as well as many others. The results indicate some of the problems with readability formulas. One of our upper middle school passages, "Biddy Mason," was rated as fourth grade by all of the measures and its lexile (discussed later in this section) was lower than other materials at the upper middle level. We do not believe that estimate for several reasons. First, the language in the story often shows the main character thinking to herself, but it is not always marked as such. At one point in the story Biddy thinks, "These feet walked every mile from Mississippi and they remembered every step." In another section she thinks, "Someday these feet will walk me to freedom." There are no hard words in these sentences and they aren't particularly long, but they contain conventions that are not familiar to fourth graders! Because we found wide fluctuations in the levels assigned by the three formulas, we averaged the estimates to obtain a more reliable level of difficulty.

A relatively recent measure, the lexile scale, has been developed based on the readability measures of word frequency and average sentence length. What makes the lexile calculation unique is that a reader's ability and text readability are on the same developmental scale (Stenner, Burdick, Sanford, & Burdick, 2006). The lexile scale is a transformed logit scale, where 1 logit equals 180 lexiles (L). When we say that a reader has an L of 500, it means that he or she is predicted to be able to read a text of 500L and show 75% comprehension on a multiple-choice test. However, the process for determining a reader's lexile is not what most of us would consider a valid measure of reading comprehension. A text of 125 words measured at a certain difficulty is given to a student and comprehension is assessed with one question. This process continues with different segments of 125 words from various texts (there is no indication that these segments are contiguous). In a study of the accuracy of lexiles, Stenner et al. (2006) tested over 1,000 students in grade three, 893 in grade five, and 1,500 in grade eight. Each item writer developed one question on each of 30 text passages, for a total of 90 items. The standard error of measurement (SEM) is reported to be 32L for a short text (i.e., 500 words), but is reduced significantly by a much longer text (e.g., a text of 900 words would have a SEM of 2L).

As stated, to determine the lexile of a reader requires the student to read a series of 125-word text segments and answer one question on each. Then given the lexile of the segments, the average text lexile on which the student can read with 75% accuracy (on a multiple-choice test) is considered to be the student's lexile. The *QRI-5* requested lexile levels from Metametrics Corporation on each of our passages at second grade difficulty and above. Second grade was chosen because the lexile scale does not evaluate the roles of pictures or predictable text, as well as other graphic features. Therefore, we determined that a lexile is inappropriate for first grade materials. How to interpret these lexiles is a bit of a challenge. The lexile is an index of the difficulty of a text, but can we say that a student who scores 75% or higher on the most difficult passage has a lexile equal to that of the passage? That, of course, is what people want to conclude, but because we haven't obtained the student's lexile using the multiple-choice procedure used by Metametrics, such a conclusion is highly questionable.

We have had many requests for a table showing how the *QRI* levels correspond to the Guided Reading levels using either the Reading Recovery Levels, Fountas and Pinnell levels, and/or lexiles. Tables 15.5 through 15.7 present the varying estimates of passage difficulty depending on the level of material and the appropriate readability estimate.

Table 15.5 Leveling *QRI-5* Text: Comparing Two Raters' Use of Fountas and Pinnell (2005), Harris-Jacobson Readability Levels, and Gunning Classifications on Pre-Primer through Grade One Passages

	RR Level Rater		HJ Readability	Gunning
Pre-Primer: C-D-E	1	2		
Narrative: "I Can" (P)[a]	A	A	1.0	Easy Sight
Narrative: "I See"[b] (P)	B	B	1.4	Easy Sight
Narrative: "Just Like Mom" (P)	C	C	1.0	Easy Sight
Narrative: "Spring and Fall"	E	E	1.3	Easy Sight
Narrative: "Lost and Found"	F	F	1.0	Easy Sight
Expository: "People at Work" (P)	E	E	1.1	Easy Sight
Primer: F and G				
Narrative: "A Trip"	E	E	1.5	1.40
Narrative: "A Night in the City" (P)	G	G	1.5	1.65
Narrative: "Fox and Mouse" (P)	F	F	1.4	1.40
Narrative: "The Pig Who Learned to Read" (P)	G	G	1.7	1.50
Expository: "Who Lives Near Lakes?" (P)	F	G	1.3	1.3
Expository: "Living and Not Living"	G	F	1.1	1.2
First: H and I				
Narrative: "Mouse in the House"	H	H	1.8	2.40*
Narrative: "The Surprise" (P)	I	I	1.8	1.75
Narrative: "Marva Finds a Friend" (P)	H	I	1.8	2.30*
Narrative: "The Bear and the Rabbit" (P)	I	H	1.7	1.8
Expository: "Air"	I	H	1.5	1.5
Expository: "The Brain and the Five Senses" (P)	H	H	1.5	1.6

Note: Two people unknown to each other independently rated the pre-primer, primer, and first grade materials using the Fountas and Pinnell (2005) leveling system, and the ratings were identical or within one level.

* Gunning has a more restrictive word list than does the Harris-Jacobson.

[a](P) indicates a pictured passage.

[b]The rhyming pattern of this story makes it easier than the readability estimate indicates.

Table 15.6	Leveling *QRI-5* Text: Comparing Fountas and Pinnell Levels, Harris-Jacobson Readability Levels, and Lexiles for Grades 2–4		

	Level	HJ	Lexile (without Graphics)
Second: J–M			
Narrative: "What Can I Get For My Toy?"	J	2.0	410
Narrative: "The Lucky Cricket" (P)	L	2.1	510
Narrative: "Father's New Game" (P)	M	2.7	480
Narrative: "The Family's First Trip"	M	2.3	560
Expository: "Whales and Fish"	L	2.9	590
Expository: "Seasons"	M	2.4	480
Third: N–P			
Narrative: "The Trip to the Zoo"	N	3.4	670
Narrative: "A Special Birthday for Rosa"	O	3.2	750
Narrative: "The Friend"	P	3.9	710
Narrative: "A New Friend from Europe"	Q	3.8	770
Expository: "Cats: Lions and Tigers in Your House"	N	2.7	750
Expository: "Where Do People Live?"	O	2.6	500
Expository: "Wool: From Sheep to You"	P	4.6	700
Fourth			
Narrative: "Johnny Appleseed"	P	4.3	650
Narrative: "Amelia Earhart"	R	3.3	500
Narrative: "Tomie dePaola"	T	4.4	910
Expository: "Early Railroads"	Q	3.8	810
Expository: "The Busy Beaver"	R	3.2	670
Expository: "Plant Structures for Survival" (G)	T	4.6	930

Note: (P) indicates a pictured passage and (G) indicates a passage with a graphic.

The Lexile system removes all graphics, headings, bolded words, and so on when estimating a level. Therefore, to the extent that the graphics enhance comprehension the lexile may overestimate the difficulty of a selection. In addition, readability formulae and lexiles do not consider the effects of prior knowledge on comprehension. So, for example, although "Johnny Appleseed" has a readability level of 4.3 and a lexile of 650L compared to the 3.3 and 500 for "Amelia Earhart," our data indicate that "Johnny" is easier than "Amelia." (Mean comprehension scores for students at a fourth grade reading level of .79 on "Johnny Appleseed" and .64 on "Amelia Earhart.")

SEM of lexiles is estimated to be 64 divided by the square root of the number of slices of 125 words (Stenner, Burdick, Sanford, & Burdick, 2006). Therefore, passages around 250 words would be comprised of two slices of 125 words each, and the square root of 2 = 1.41, so 64/1.41 = 45.39. Most of the second through fourth grade passages are around 250 words. Passages of 350 words would have a SEM of 38.32.

Development of the Pre-Primer through Third Grade Passages

To determine concepts that were familiar to children reading at these levels, we examined basal readers, children's literature, and content-area (science and social studies) textbooks. We took ideas for passage content from these books and other children's books, and we used the lengths of passages included in basal readers and children's literature at the primer and first grade levels to guide the lengths of our passages. Our passages are purposely longer than the passages on most inventories to provide enough content to assess comprehension without asking questions on unimportant information.

The past four editions of the *QRI* have added a number of passages to the pre-primer through third grade levels, and this continues in the fifth edition. We have added two

Table 15.7	Leveling *QRI-5* Text: Mean of Three Readability Formula Estimates and Lexiles Grade 5 through HS		
		Average of Three*	Lexile (without Graphics)
Fifth			
Narrative: "Martin Luther King, Jr."		5.2	830
Narrative: "Margaret Mead"		5.0	660
Narrative: "Patricia McKissack"		7.5	970
Expository: "Farming on the Great Plains"		5.4	810
Expository: "The Octopus"		5.2	650
Expository: "How Does Your Body Take in Oxygen?" (G)		5.6	900
Sixth			
Literature: "Pele"		5.6	810
Literature: "Abraham Lincoln"		5.7	760
Literature: "The Early Life of Lois Lowry"		6.6	980
Social Studies: "The Lifeline of the Nile" (G)		6.9	850
Social Studies: "Building Pyramids" (G)		6.6	850
Science: "Temperature and Humidity"		7.5	1,030
Science: "Clouds and Precipitation" (G)		6.2	1,000
Upper Middle School			
Literature: "Biddy Mason"		4	470
Literature: "Malcolm X"		7.2	1,000
Social Studies: "Immigration—Part 1"		9.5	1,000
Social Studies: "Immigration—Part 2"		7.8	870
Science: "Life Cycles of Stars—Part 1"		7.5	820
Science: "Life Cycles of Stars—Part 2"		7.5	840
High School			
"Where the Ashes Are—Part 1"		6.8	910
"Where the Ashes Are—Part 2"		6.4	840
"Where the Ashes Are—Part 3"		6.4	850
"World War I—Part 1"		11.2	1,180
"World War I—Part 2"		8.9	950
"World War I—Part 3"		10.1	1,020
"Characteristics of Viruses—Part 1"		9.0	960
"Characteristics of Viruses—Part 2"		9.0	920
"Characteristics of Viruses—Part 3"		9.7	950

*Because of the variability among the New Dale-Chall readability formula, the Fry Readability graph, and Flesch Grade Level estimates, we averaged the three to obtain a more reliable estimate.

Note: The Lexile system removes all graphics, headings, bolded words, and so on when estimating a level. Therefore, to the extent that the graphics enhance comprehension the lexile may overestimate the difficulty of a selection. In addition, neither lexiles nor readability formulae consider the effects of prior knowledge on comprehension.

SEM of lexiles is estimated to be 64 divided by the square root of the number of slices of 125 words (Stenner, Burdick, Sanford, & Burdick, 2006). Therefore, passages around 375 words would be comprised of three slices of 125 words each, and the square root of 3 = 1.73, so 64 / 1.73 = 46.99. Passages at the fifth and sixth grade level range in length from 254 to 591 words. Passages at the upper middle school level range from 382 to 786 words. Passages at the high school level range from 354 to 1,224 words. SEM of lexiles of passages around 500 words is 32L (Stenner, Burdick, Sanford, & Burdick, 2006).

pre-primer stories, and one each at levels primer, first, second, and third. Therefore, the *QRI-5* includes both narrative and expository text and both pictured and non-pictured passages at the pre-primer through the second grade levels to allow users to compare students' abilities reading a variety of text types with and without pictures.

Based on the large sample of students from three university clinics who read the pre-primer through third grade texts, we have included Table 15.8, which presents data on instructional level reading according to the level of the passages. This table illustrates how students' reading rate and correct reading rate increase as their instructional reading level increases.

Development of the Fourth through Sixth Grade Passages

In the fourth edition we replaced one narrative passage at each level, fourth through sixth, with a biography of a children's author, written by one of the authors who first read about these writers before composing short biographies. We also replaced two of the three expository texts at the fourth and fifth grade levels and all of the expository texts at the sixth grade level. The data in Table 15.3, which illustrates the mean correct comprehension scores with and without look-backs, indicate that these texts are significantly harder than passages at the same level that were included in previous editions

Table 15.8	Means and Standard Deviations of Instructional-Level Oral Reading Accuracy, Semantic Accuracy, Corrected Rate per Minute, Retelling, and Comprehension Measure on Narrative Texts as a Function of Passage Level

	TotAcc	SemAcc	CorrRate	Retell	Comp
Pre-Primer					
"I Can" (*n* = 19)	94%	96%	42	43%	71%
"I See" (*n* = 14)	95%	96%	38	59%	93%
"Just Like Mom" (*n* = 75)	95%	98%	43	42%	86%
"Lost and Found" (*n* = 57)	94%	96%	36	38%	88%
"Spring and Fall" (*n* = 23)	94%	96%	46	35%	94%
Primer					
"A Trip" (*n* = 64)	94%	96%	37	36%	92%
"Fox and Mouse" (*n* = 26)	94%	97%	42	19%	76%
"The Pig Who Learned to Read" (*n* = 40)	95%	97%	48	31%	77%
"A Night in the City" (*n* = 10)	93%	96%	40	23%	70%
First					
"Mouse in a House" (*n* = 95)	95%	97%	54	25%	81%
"Marva Finds a Friend" (*n* = 79)	95%	98%	54	26%	85%
"The Bear and the Rabbit" (*n* = 55)	94%	97%	45	31%	75%
"The Surprise" (*n* = 14)	92%	96%	51	26%	84%
Second					
"What Can I Get for My Toy?" (*n* = 89)	96%	98%	53	28%	81%
"Father's New Game" (*n* = 54)	96%	98%	50	24%	82%
"The Lucky Cricket" (*n* = 48)	95%	98%	51	38%	79%
"The Family's First Trip" (*n* = 21)	96%	97%	71	23%	83%
Third					
"The Trip to the Zoo" (*n* = 90)	96%	98%	67	38%	83%
"A Special Birthday for Rosa" (*n* = 62)	97%	98%	51	25%	86%
" A New Friend from Europe" (*n* = 31)	96%	97%	75	18%	81%

of the *QRI*. We suspect that this reflects the increasing demand in the textbooks, rather than anything particular about the *QRI*, because 62% of the students in the pilot samples scored proficient or above on standardized tests of reading achievement. Beginning at fifth grade the look-backs allowed most students to raise their scores into instructional level range. This indicated that although students may have understood the text, they had trouble remembering some of it.

Development of the Upper Middle School and High School Passages

There were no changes in the narrative texts at these levels; however, we made major changes to the expository passages at the upper middle school level in the fourth edition. Because of the addition of the think-aloud procedure at the upper middle school level, the social studies and science texts are comprised of two segments of related text. These texts can be used together by having the student read one in the typical way and think aloud on the other, or the text can be used separately in a pre- and post-test format.

Because of the new think-aloud procedure where the examiner models thinking aloud once (see Development of the Think-Aloud Procedure), we also modified the high school materials from the fourth edition. The first two sections can be read in the typical way and the student can think aloud on the third section. The examiner can also use these texts separately.

Empirical Validation

1. Comparability of new and previous stories at the same readability level. We conducted related-means tests comparing students' total accuracy, total acceptability, correct words per minute (CWPM), retelling, and comprehension (percent of questions answered correctly) on each narrative text new to the *QRI-5* with another story of the same readability level that was part of previous editions of the *QRI*. Within the pre-primer level we compared pairs of pictured and non-pictured passages. Students' total accuracy, acceptable accuracy, and CWPM were not significantly different on "I Can" and "I See"; however, retelling and comprehension was higher on "I See." We believe that this was because of the rhyming pattern of "I See." The same pattern was observed when "I See" and "Just Like Mom" were compared. When the two non-pictured stories, "Lost and Found" and "Spring and Fall," were compared, there were no significant differences found on any of the measures.

We found no significant differences between scores on the two primer stories, "A Night in the City" and "Fox and Mouse," with the exception of retelling, where the average percent retelling was higher (32 propositions) on "Fox and Mouse" than on "A Night in the City" (23). At the first grade level we found that although the accuracy scores were at instructional level for both stories, "The Surprise" was more difficult to read accurately than "Marva Finds a Friend," and students' CWPM was lower on "The Surprise" (51) than on "Marva Finds a Friend" (61), but there were no significant differences on retelling and comprehension. Similar results were found comparing the second grade stories, "The Family's First Trip" with "The Lucky Cricket." Both stories were at instructional level for the 21 students who read them, but "Cricket" was read more accurately (97%) than "Family's First Trip" (96%). But there were no differences on CWPM, retelling, and comprehension between the two second grade stories. At third grade, "A New Friend from Europe" was more difficult to read than "A Special Birthday for Rosa" and was read at a lower CWPM, but no differences were found on retelling and comprehension.

In summary, the new *QRI-5* stories were similar in difficulty to stories previously included on the *QRI*. Students scored at instructional level on both stories; however, the new stories tended to be somewhat more difficult to read accurately and fluently.

2. Are the passages of higher readability of increasing difficulty? We assessed the difficulty of passages by comparing the performances of students reading passages of increasing readability. Specifically, we conducted multivariate analyses of variance with readability as the within-subjects factor and with total comprehension, retelling, and CWPM as the dependent measures. Also, we designated total oral reading accuracy and acceptable accuracy as dependent measures in analyses through sixth grade. The first section below compares the difficulty of the new *QRI-5* stories, and the second section compares sets of texts from previous editions. We conducted separate analyses when comparing different text types (narrative and expository) because data indicated differences in comprehension among these text types (see page 474 for a discussion of these results). We conducted sets of analyses on adjacent levels, which we will refer to as PP–P, P–1, 1–2, 2–3, 3–4, 4–5, 5–6, 6–upper middle school, and upper middle versus high school.

   a. *Comparing across readability levels on new stories.* We also conducted related-means tests on new *QRI-5* stories that were one readability level different from each other. For example, we compared students' total accuracy, total semantic acceptability, CWPM, retelling, and comprehension of the most difficult pre-primer narrative from the *QRI-4,* "Spring and Fall," with the new primer narrative, "A Night in the City," to see if the new primer story was more difficult for students than the hardest pre-primer story. All scores except retelling were significantly higher on "Spring and Fall" than on "A Night in the City." For example, the total accuracy scores were 92.5% versus 85.8%, total acceptability scores were 96% versus 92%, CWPM scores were 62% versus 34%, and comprehension scores were 90% versus 59%. These data indicate that students who were reading at instructional level on "Spring and Fall" reached frustration level on "A Night in the City." The same results were found when comparing the first grade story "The Surprise" with the second grade story "The Family's First Trip." Students' total accuracy (89%), total acceptability (94%), and comprehension (52%) were lower on "The Family's First Trip" than on "The Surprise," although there were no differences in retelling or CWPM. Students who read at instructional level on "The Surprise" were at frustration level on "The Family's First Trip." The final comparison included "A New Friend from Europe" versus "The Family's First Trip." Students who read both of these stories were less accurate (96% vs. 94%), retold less (25 ideas vs. 12 ideas), and were able to answer fewer questions (85% vs. 64%) on "A New Friend from Europe," the third grade story, than on "The Family's First Trip," the second grade story.

   b. *Narrative texts.* Table 15.9 presents means and standard deviations of rate, corrected rate, percent retelling, and percent comprehension on the following sets of narrative texts: PP–P, P–1, 1–2, 2–3, 3–4, 4–5, and 5–6. When the same students read the pre-primer and primer texts, the mean rate, corrected rate, retelling, and comprehension were significantly higher on the pre-primer text. The same results occurred when the same students read the primer and the first grade texts. However, when the first and second grade texts were compared, there were no differences in retelling among the students who read those texts. Students who read the second and third grade narratives showed higher scores on the second grade texts.

   Similar results were found when comparing the scores of students who read the third and fourth grade texts. Students who read the fourth and fifth grade texts read with more correct words per minute, retold more text, and comprehended more on the fourth grade text, but their reading rate was similar. Students who read the fifth and sixth grade texts had higher comprehension scores on the fifth grade narratives.

Table 15.9 **Means and Standard Deviations of Rate, Corrected Rate, Percent Retelling, and Percent Comprehension on Narrative Texts**

	Rate	CorrRate	Percent Retell	Comprehension
Set 1				
Pre-Primer (*n* = 182)	49 (21)	44 (24)	36 (21)	87 (18)
Primer	42 (24)	29 (29)	24 (17)	68 (22)
Set 2				
Primer (*n* = 198)	52 (20)	44 (25)	29 (18)	82 (16)
First	48 (21)	34 (29)	23 (15)	64 (23)
Set 3				
First (*n* = 280)	65 (21)	54 (26)	28 (16)	82 (15)
Second	57 (20)	40 (26)	26 (27)	57 (22)
Set 4				
Second (*n* = 242)	72 (25)	59 (30)	27 (20)	80 (16)
Third	66 (24)	49 (31)	26 (21)	67 (20)
Set 5				
Third (*n* = 228)	83 (25)	66 (33)	33 (20)	83 (14)
Fourth	67 (23)	47 (29)	18 (15)	49 (21)
Set 6				
Fourth (*n* = 84)	90 (28)	71 (41)	23 (18)	71 (18)
Fifth	86 (29)	59 (37)	18 (15)	55 (21)
Set 7				
Fifth (*n* = 64)	97 (28)	82 (37)	23 (14)	74 (18)
Sixth	100 (34)	84 (36)	22 (15)	44 (21)

Note: Standard deviations are in parentheses.

On the grade six and upper middle school narratives, comprehension and total retelling were higher on the sixth grade level than on the upper middle school passages. When compared to the high school texts, we found that the upper middle school texts were easier to comprehend both with and without look-backs than the high school texts. Specifically, the comprehension scores on "Biddy Mason" were higher than on the first segment of "Where the Ashes Are" [$t(14) = 6.23$, $p < .001$ and 2.75, $p < .02$] for comprehension without and with look-backs, respectively.

c. *Expository texts.* Generally, there were fewer students who read more than one level of expository text; therefore, we will present the general results but not include a table. On the PP–P and P–1 comparisons we found differences indicating the greater difficulty of the primer and first-level text, respectively, on all measures except rate. Comparing the 1–2 and 2–3 expository texts, we found no significant differences, likely due to the small number of students reading them. When the 3–4 expository texts were compared, significant differences were found on all dependent measures. When the 4–5 expository texts were compared, significant differences were found on corrected rate and comprehension but not retelling or rate (WPM). No differences on any measures were found on the 5–6 expository comparison. Comprehension was significantly higher on the sixth grade expository texts compared to the upper middle school expository texts. No differences were found on the other dependent measures. Comprehension scores on the upper middle school expository texts were significantly higher than scores on the high school expository texts.

There are sufficient data to conclude that the passages are of increasing difficulty. Whether all dependent measures illustrate these differences, however, depends on the level of the texts. The rate and accuracy of reading vary on adjacent passages (e.g., PP–P, P–1, etc.) through fifth grade, but comprehension differences were observed across all levels. These findings parallel the development of reading ability, where the largest changes in accuracy and fluency occur at the lower levels, but comprehension differences span all levels.

3. Are there comprehension differences on different text types? One of the theoretical foundations of the *QRI* was that it should reflect comprehension differences between narrative and expository texts. When the *QRI* was first published, instruction in the primary grades was most often based in narrative texts. Unfortunately, that practice hasn't changed a lot (Duke, 2000). To examine whether children's retelling and comprehension differed across text types, multivariate analyses of variance were conducted comparing conceptual knowledge scores, retelling, and comprehension scores for students who read at least one narrative and one expository text at a readability level. Because each student read both a narrative and an expository text, passage type was a within-subjects factor.

Results of these analyses differed according to the readability of the passages. Table 15.10 presents the means and standard deviations for proportion of correct scores on conceptual knowledge, retelling, and comprehension as a function of text type and readability level for materials at the pre-primer through third grade level. Narrative text was recalled more and comprehended more at all levels except primer. At the pre-primer level, students retold and answered more questions correctly on narrative than expository text, $F(1, 14) = 17.10$ and 5.78, $p < .001$ and $.05$, respectively, despite having more conceptual knowledge on the expository texts, $F(1, 14) = 8.96$, $p < .01$. At the first grade level, students had more conceptual knowledge, retold more, and answered more questions correctly on narrative than expository text, $F(1, 31) = 16.56$, 24.16, and 22.07, $ps < .001$. When multivariate analysis of covariance removed the variance due to conceptual knowledge ($\beta = .32$), we still found higher retelling and comprehension on narrative text, $F(1, 30) = 9.23$ and 9.50, $p < .01$. At the second grade level, students retold and comprehended more of the narrative text than the expository text, $F(1, 18) = 45.60$ and 11.53, $p < .001$ and $.01$, respectively. At the third grade level, the same pattern of results was found. Students retold and answered more questions correctly on narrative than expository text, $F(1, 25) = 21.21$ and 12.32, $p < .001$ and $.01$, respectively.

Table 15.11 on page 476 presents the means and standard deviations for proportion of correct scores on conceptual knowledge, retelling, comprehension, and total comprehension on narrative and expository text as a function of readability level from fourth through high school. Because look-backs were more common at these levels, we were able to present the data on comprehension with look-backs (i.e., total comprehension) and a different table was needed.

Differences between the retelling of narrative and expository texts were found only at the fourth and upper middle school levels. Retelling was quite low at the fifth and sixth grade levels and again at the high school level. The only comprehension differences between narrative and expository texts were found at the upper middle school and high school levels.

Table 15.10   Means and Standard Deviations for Proportion of Correct Scores on Conceptual Knowledge, Retelling, and Comprehension on Narrative and Expository Texts as a Function of Readability Level

Readability Level	Conceptual Knowledge	Retelling	Comprehension
Pre-Primer (*n* = 15)			
Narrative	.54**	.35*	.57**
	(.14)	(.16)	(.33)
Expository	.74	.15	.31
	(.23)	(.13)	(.18)
Primer (*n* = 13)			
Narrative	.58	.29	.72
	(.19)	(.16)	(.23)
Expository	.62	.33	.68
	(.11)	(.17)	(.16)
First (*n* = 32)			
Narrative	.67**	.26**	.76**
	(.14)	(.13)	(.12)
Expository	.54	.15	.50
	(.19)	(.13)	(.26)
Second (*n* = 19)			
Narrative	.69	.43**	.82**
	(.15)	(.18)	(.17)
Expository	.68	.22	.61
	(.19)	(.13)	(.19)
Third (*n* = 26)			
Narrative	.69	.34**	.77**
	(.16)	(.18)	(.16)
Expository	.66	.19	.58
	(.13)	(.11)	(.22)

Note: $*p < .05$; $**p < .01$.

THE RELATIONSHIP BETWEEN ORAL READING ACCURACY AND COMPREHENSION

1. What is the relationship between oral reading accuracy and comprehension? The correlation between oral reading accuracy (both Total Accuracy and Total Acceptability) and comprehension was examined at each readability level using two data sets. One comprises the data on the passages new to the *QRI-5*. On the new pre-primer passages, "I Can" and "I See," Total Accuracy correlated significantly with comprehension, $r(30) = .32$ and .53, respectively. On the new primer passage, "A Night in the City," Total Accuracy correlated significantly with retelling, $r = .34$. No other new story showed significant correlations between accuracy and either measure of comprehension.

The other database is the large clinical sample from which statistical analyses were conducted for the fourth edition of the *QRI*. We analyzed archived data on 898 cases from three university clinics that offered intervention programs: Marquette University,

| Table 15.11 | Means and Standard Deviations for Proportion of Correct Scores on Conceptual Knowledge, Retelling, Comprehension, and Total Comprehension on Narrative and Expository Texts as a Function of Readability Level |

Readability Level	Conceptual Knowledge	Retelling	Comp	Total Comp
Fourth (n = 12)				
Narrative	.56 (.26)	.26 (.12)*	.55 (.08)	.67 (.08)
Expository	.63 (.26)	.18 (.07)	.58 (.18)	.50 (.23)
Fifth (n = 14)				
Narrative	.57 (.29)	.19 (.13)	.72 (.10)	.81 (.10)
Expository	.62 (.42)*	.18 (.11)	.81 (.40)	.91 (.11)
Sixth (n = 32)				
Narrative	.77 (.18)*	.15 (.08)	.68 (.17)	.94 (.09)
Expository	.68 (.23)	.17 (.09)	.67 (.18)	.86 (.24)
Upper Middle School (n = 46)				
Narrative	.75 (.23)	.28 (.16)*	.84 (.17)*	.97 (.05)
Expository	.71 (.20)	.13 (.97)	.66 (.18)	.95 (.08)
High School (n = 12)				
Narrative	.42 (.25)	.16 (.12)	.49 (.21)	.81 (.16)
Social Studies	.47 (.25)	.09 (.11)	.43 (.25)	.85 (.15)
Science	.41 (.21)	.11 (.11)	.28 (.11)*	.75 (.15)

Note: * = A significant difference between narrative and expository text ($p < .05$) was found on that dependent variable.

Milwaukee ($n = 688$); Cardinal Stritch University, Milwaukee ($n = 174$); and Teachers College Columbia, New York City ($n = 36$) to provide a large sample on which to estimate the difficulty of the pre-primer through fifth grade primarily narrative passages. The demographic data from these students in the clinical samples is presented in Table 15.12.

When large databases are used, statistics can be significant but not practically useful. You will notice that many of the correlations below are not large, yet are statistically significant. Care must be taken in interpretation of these results. When the large clinical database was used, Total Accuracy and Total Acceptability both correlated significantly with comprehension, $rs(475) = .30$ and $.22$, $ps < .001$, respectively on pre-primer texts. At the primer and first grade levels, there were no statistically significant correlations between accuracy and comprehension. At the second and third grade levels, Total Acceptability correlated, $r(299) = .28$ and $r(301) = .24$, $ps < .001$ with comprehension. Similarly for fourth grade, Total Accuracy and Total Acceptability both correlated with comprehension, $r(117) = .37$ and $.33$, $ps < .001$. There were no statistically significant correlations between oral reading accuracy and comprehension when students read the fifth and sixth grade level texts. It is expected that correlations between oral reading accuracy and comprehension should exist at lower reading levels; therefore, it is difficult to explain the lack of such relationships at primer and first grade. There was enough variability in the scores at these levels to produce a significant correlation, if such a relationship existed, and certainly our sample size was sufficient.

		Sex				**Race/Ethnicity**			
Grade	*n*	M	F	White	African American	Asian American	Hispanic American	Biracial
1	66	55%	45%	48.5%	50.0%	0.0	0.0	1.5%
2	532	60%	40%	0.6%	92.4%	0.6%	1.0%	0.0
3	391	45%	50%	7.5%	88.0%	1.2%	2.5%	0.8%
4	216	50%	50%	0.9%	85.5%	0.5%	2.0%	3.0%
5	93	50%	50%	15.0%	80.0%	1.0%	2.0%	2.0%
6	60	63%	37%	12.0%	81.0%	0.0	2.0%	2.0%
7	36	44%	56%	35.0%	62.0%	0.0	3.0%	0.0
8	18	56%	44%	25.0%	69.0%	0.0	0.0	6.0%
9–11	12	75%	25%	40.0%	60.0%	0.0	0.0	0.0

Table 15.12 Demographic Data for Clinical Samples

2. How accurate does oral reading have to be for instructional-level comprehension? The traditional oral reading accuracy scores used to determine instructional level have been between 90% and 95%. We analyzed the data from each pre-primer story to determine the total accuracy level associated with the comprehension criteria for instructional level (above 67%). Instructional-level comprehension on "I Can," "I See," and "Just Like Mom" were associated with Total Accuracy scores of 95%, 89%, and 94%, respectively. This means that students could read below the 90% accuracy cut-off on "I See" and be able to answer 67% or more of the questions correctly. The best prediction of instructional-level comprehension scores on "Lost and Found" varied with the sample. In the new pilot it was 92% accuracy; however, in a previous database it was only 80%. On "Spring and Fall," instructional-level comprehension was best predicted by 90% Total Accuracy. In summary, pre-primer texts can occasionally be comprehended with Total Accuracy scores less than 90%. The two stories on which this was true are both highly predictable, "I See" on the basis of rhyme and "Lost and Found" on the predictable sentences and paragraphs in the story. However, a total accuracy score of 90% should be used to estimate instructional reading level in pre-primer texts.

RELIABILITY AND VALIDITY

An informal reading inventory should meet the requirements presented in the *Standards for Educational and Psychological Testing* (1999) written by the American Educational Research Association, American Psychological Association, and National Council on Measurement in Education. According to the *Standards,* a *test* is an instrument that evaluates some ability, and an *inventory* obtains data on which no evaluation is made (such as a personality inventory). Thus, informal reading inventories are tests, not inventories. We acknowledge this, but we call our instrument an inventory because it is structurally similar to other IRIs, however misnamed historically. No matter what it is called, there are basic standards of any instrument that must be met. Following is a discussion of reliability and validity issues as they pertain to the uses of our instrument.

Issues of Reliability of an Informal Reading Inventory

Cross and Paris (1987) present an analysis of the relationship between test purposes and the statistical evidence necessary to document the reliability and validity of the test. Perhaps the most important contribution of this work is the illustration that evidence important to one kind of test may be irrelevant or detrimental to another type of test. The purpose of the instrument should guide the author and user to determine the relevant reliability and validity data for the instrument's purposes.

Because we designed the *QRI-5* for determination of an instructional level and diagnostic purposes, the essential test properties, according to Cross and Paris, are consistency, construct representation, and penetration. Consistency is a reliability property of a test that refers to the replicability of scores for a single individual. A score is consistent if, in the absence of growth or learning, an individual repeatedly obtains the same score. The *QRI-5* measures consistency of scores in three ways: inter-scorer reliability, internal consistency reliability, and alternate-form reliability. Construct representation and penetration are validity properties and are discussed in the validity section.

Interjudge Reliability (Consistency) of Scoring. Aside from the purposes for which an instrument is used, one must have evidence that the test is scored consistently across examiners. Whenever there is a judgment, lack of consistency can develop. In our analysis of scoring reliability of the *QRI,* we examined the reliability of judges' scores on total percentage of miscues, percent of meaning-change miscues, prior-knowledge concept score, total explicit comprehension score and total implicit comprehension score, and the propositional analysis of recall. All examiners had the same scoring manual to judge these scores. However, our expert scorers (*n* = 3) were reading teachers or specialists who had master's degrees. Thus, our reliability estimates compare persons without extensive training by the test developers to those with training by the test developers. It should be noted that the experts did not receive their master's degrees from the program of either test author, but one test author trained the experts in the scoring. We did not have two judges listen to the tapes of the children's oral reading unless the examiner was an undergraduate student. Thus, we assumed that the transcription of the total number of miscues was correct. Hood (1975–1976) reports the reliability of two judges recording total miscues from tape to be .98+.

Estimates of the inter-scorer reliability of the new conceptual-knowledge questions found agreement on 299 of the 304 concepts sampled, for a 98% agreement. Scorers used the scoring instructions and examples found in Section 8. Estimates of inter-scorer reliability of total miscues, acceptable miscues, and explicit and implicit comprehension were assessed by examining data from 122 readings. These data were gathered across all readability levels and both types of text. Of the 122 readings, 49 were conducted orally. Thus, the estimate of reliability for total miscues and acceptable miscues is based on 49 observations. The estimates of inter-scorer reliability were found using Cronbach's alpha (Cronbach, 1951). Alpha reliability estimates were .99 for total miscues, .99 for meaning-change miscues, .98 for explicit comprehension, and .98 for implicit comprehension. These reliability estimates indicated a high degree of consistency between scorers. Thus, an examiner should be able to score the *QRI-5* reliably without extensive training.

We used a sample of 393 passages to estimate the reliability of scoring the list of propositions for each passage. Again, all levels and types of text were represented. The alpha estimate of inter-judge reliability was .94. This indicates that the proposition data from which we built our passage maps were scored reliably.

A recent reliability study (J. Bernstein, personal communication, August 2004) using oral reading data from the National Assessment of Adult Literacy found that different raters were able to reliably score Total Accuracy (.96) and Total Acceptability (.96). In addition, each rater was examined on the same recording twice. The mean intra-rater reliability for Total Accuracy was .97 and for Total Acceptability was .95. The raters all had undergraduate degrees, had taught for a minimum of two years, and many had advanced degrees in education or linguistics. The raters received an instruction manual that explained all aspects of the study followed by an interactive training session conducted by phone.

Internal Consistency Reliability. This form of reliability examines how reliable the score is as an estimate of the true score. For example, when we measure total comprehension, how reliable is the score as an estimate of the student's true comprehension score?

The standard error of measurement of the total comprehension score was estimated through an analysis of variance with items (1–5; 1–6; 1–8; 1–10) as the within-subject factor and subjects as the between-subjects factor. Crocker and Algina (1986) recommended the use of the standard error of measurement rather than a correlational estimate of reliability for criterion-referenced tests where there is reduced variability in the student's performance. Remember that a correlation is based, in part, on variability. In our case, we did not give harder passages to students who scored as frustrated on easier material, and so we reduced variability. Thus, a traditional correlational measure of reliability would not accurately reflect the reliability of the scores. Similarly, because the alpha coefficient is based on variability, it is subject to the same restrictions. Crocker and Algina (1986, p. 196) illustrated that the standard error of a criterion-referenced test can be very low (such as .001), indicating a highly reliable score, yet the reliability, expressed as a generalizability coefficient, could be very low (.00). This happens when there is no variability in the data. Because we have restricted variability, we chose to use the standard error of measurement. The formula for determining the standard error of measurement from analysis of variance data is:

$$\text{Standard error of measurement} = \sqrt{\frac{\dfrac{MS_i - MS_r}{n_p} + MS_r}{n_i}}$$

where
MS_i = mean square for items
MS_r = mean square residual
n_i = number of items
n_p = number of persons

Table 15.13 presents the mean, standard deviation, and standard error of measurement (SEM) of the proportion-correct total comprehension score for all passages. Consider the highest SEM for an eight-item test, .18 for "Wool: From Sheep to You" and "The Busy Beaver." A student with a score of 75% has a true score between 57% and 93%, 68% of the time. Because of the relatively large SEMs on any single passage, we recommend that an examiner give passages of the same type (such as narrative or expository) with which the student is familiar when attempting to estimate true score. When the examiner uses two passages, the percent correct is determined from 16 items. The standard error is based on 16 items and is reduced substantially. When we pooled data from children who read "The Trip to the Zoo" and "A Special Birthday for Rosa," the SEM

Table 15.13 Means and Standard Deviations and Standard Errors of Measurement of Proportional Comprehension Scores for Each Passage on the *QRI-5*

Passage Level and Name	Mean	SD	n	SEM
Pre-Primer				
"I Can"	.71	.18	23	.20
"I See"	.95	.13	23	.18
"Just Like Mom"	.82	.17	69	.21
"Lost and Found"	.90	.12	83	.13
"Lost and Found"*	.74	.24	36	.19
"Spring and Fall"	.70	.16	56	.20
"Spring and Fall"*	.60	.19	41	.22
"People at Work"	.30	.20	28	.20
Primer				
"A Trip"	.90	.12	76	.12
"A Trip"	.59	.29	63	.20
"A Night in the City"	.70	.28	14	.21
"Fox and Mouse"	.76	.30	51	.15
"Fox and Mouse"	.63	.22	48	.19
"The Pig Who Learned to Read"	.75	.28	65	.19
"The Pig Who Learned to Read"	.61	.32	50	.20
"Who Lives Near Lakes?"	.67	.19	12	.19
"Living and Not Living"	.58	.17	25	.21
First				
"The Surprise"	.86	.14	25	.15
"Mouse in a House"	.82	.17	103	.16
"Mouse in a House"	.61	.17	35	.19
"Marva Finds a Friend"	.86	.15	94	.14
"Marva Finds a Friend"	.64	.18	72	.18
"The Bear and the Rabbit"	.76	.27	57	.18
"The Bear and the Rabbit"	.54	.36	67	.21
"Air"	.55	.27	18	.19
"The Brain and the Five Senses"	.78	.16	8	.17
"The Brain and the Five Senses"	.47	.16	13	.17
Second				
"The Lucky Cricket"	.81	.10	78	.14
"The Lucky Cricket"	.58	.20	82	.17
"The Family's First Trip"	.81	.18	32	.14
"What Can I Get for My Toy?"	.80	.18	64	.14
"What Can I Get for My Toy?"	.63	.26	60	.17
"Father's New Game"	.80	.12	74	.13
"Father's New Game"	.49	.19	91	.17
"Whales and Fish"	.68	.18	17	.17
"Seasons"	.50	.22	13	.17
Third				
"The Trip to the Zoo"	.76	.17	98	.14
"The Trip to the Zoo"	.69	.24	113	.16
"A Special Birthday for Rosa"	.86	.13	72	.12
"A Special Birthday for Rosa"	.57	.19	73	.17
"A New Friend from Europe"	.83	.24	25	.17
"The Friend"	.60	.20	25	.17
"Cats: Lions and Tigers in Your House"	.69	.21	20	.16
"Where Do People Live?"	.47	.30	20	.16
"Wool: From Sheep to You"	.45	.19	15	.18

Table 15.13 *(continued)*

Passage Level and Name	Mean	SD	n	SEM
Fourth				
"Johnny Appleseed"	.79	.13	18	.14
"Johnny Appleseed"	.61	.28	36	.17
"Amelia Earhart"	.64	.16	18	.18
"Amelia Earhart"	.51	.20	43	.17
"Tomie dePaola"	.61	.21	34	.16
"Tomie dePaola"	.46	.26	108	.23
"Early Railroads"	.52	.22	22	.17
"The Busy Beaver"	.71	.13	25	.18
"Plant Structures for Survival"	.37	.17	20	.17
Fifth				
"Martin Luther King, Jr."	.65	.21	32	.17
"Margaret Mead"	.66	.18	23	.16
"Patricia McKissack"	.65	.22	17	.16
"Patricia McKissack"	.59	.20	52	.17
"Farming on the Great Plains"	.60	.23	17	.17
"The Octopus"	.66	.19	40	.16
"How Does Your Body Take in Oxygen?"	.71	.20	14	.15
Sixth				
"Pele"	.71	.17	57	.16
"Abraham Lincoln"	.75	.17	20	.16
"The Early Life of Lois Lowry"	.69	.17	33	.12
"The Early Life of Lois Lowry"	.35	.19	18	.15
"The Lifeline of the Nile"	.71	.15	22	.16
"Building Pyramids"	.79	.19	32	.14
"Temperature and Humidity"	.55	.22	23	.16
"Clouds and Precipitation"	.67	.20	17	.16
Upper Middle School				
Literature				
"Biddy Mason"	.84	.18	47	.10
"Malcolm X"	.74	.13	30	.14
Social Studies				
"Immigration—Part 1"	.77	.26	11	.11
"Immigration—Part 2"	.80	.13	11	.14
Science				
"Life Cycles of Stars—Part 1"	.58	.15	18	.16
"Life Cycles of Stars—Part 2"	.54	.18	13	.16
High School				
Literature				
"Where the Ashes Are—Part 1"	.43	.21	20	.15
"Where the Ashes Are—Part 2"	.47	.22	19	.15
"Where the Ashes Are—Part 3"	.61	.19	16	.15
Social Studies				
"World War I—Part 1"	.35	.24	22	.14
"World War I—Part 2"	.39	.26	17	.14
"World War I—Part 3"	.44	.24	17	.14
Science				
"Characteristics of Viruses—Part 1"	.20	.15	25	.12
"Characteristics of Viruses—Part 2"	.37	.20	20	.15
"Characteristics of Viruses—Part 3"	.20	.18	20	.12

*You will note that we have presented separate standard error of measurement (SEM) estimates for mean scores in the instructional-level range and also in the frustration-level range for narrative text through sixth grade. According to Standard 2.14 from the *Standards for Educational and Psychological Testing* (1999), "Where cut scores are specified for selection or classification, the standard errors of measurement should be reported in the vicinity of each cut score" (p. 35). The data presented indicate that when comprehension scores fall within the instructional-level range, the SEM is usually smaller than when scores fall in the frustration-level range.

for 16 items was .10. Thus, a child with a total score of 75% has a true score that lies between 65% and 85%, 68% of the time; this is a much more reliable estimate of true score than their separate SEMs of .15 and .14 based on eight items.

For similar reasons, we cannot recommend that users interpret scores for explicit and implicit comprehension on a single passage. First, these subtests do not contain enough items to be reliable indicators of the children's true scores in these areas if only one passage is used. Even when the examiner uses two passages, and the total number of explicit items from both passages is compared to the total number of implicit items from both passages, large differences are needed for reliable diagnostic conclusions. When we pooled explicit items from "The Trip to the Zoo" and "A Special Birthday for Rosa," we obtained a SEM of .13; the standard error for implicit items was .15. The standard error of the *difference* between these two is .20. (The formula is SEMdiff = the square root of the sum of the two squared SEMs.)

Thus, only if a student received scores of 75% to 100% correct on explicit questions and 0% to 25% correct on implicit questions can we be 95% sure that these scores do not overlap. If a student consistently receives scores that differ by as much as 50%, then conclusions that a student is better in answering one type of question than the other are reliable.

Test-Retest Reliability.   In a study of a summer reading program in the state of Michigan, researchers examined whether student scores on the *QRI-3* were reliable over time. Positive and significant test-retest reliability was reported in Paris, Pearson, Carpenter, Siebenthal, and Laier (2002).

Alternate-Form Reliability (Consistency) of Placement Decisions.   If the major purpose is to determine an instructional level, then it is important to have consistency in that level. Thus, the reliability issue becomes: "If I find an instructional level of fifth grade on this test, would I find an instructional level of fifth grade if I gave the test tomorrow or next week?" This type of reliability is called *test-retest reliability.* The interest is in the consistency of test results over time or conditions. As many test developers have learned, there is a problem in giving exactly the same test over two time periods in order to assess test-retest reliability, because the student may learn something in the first administration that raises his or her score on the second administration.

An alternative method of estimating level reliability is to examine performance on two passages similar in design; this method is called *alternate-form reliability* (Crocker & Algina, 1986). In the *QRI-5,* this means that we would examine performance on two similar passage types (such as narratives or familiar expository). If performance on these indicates the same instructional level, we have evidence for alternate-form reliability.

To obtain the best estimate of alternate-form reliability of level, we examined the reliability of the total comprehension score to estimate instructional level across passages of the same type. The procedure used to estimate alternate-form reliability of criterion-referenced tests was Livingston's (1972) K^2. This index reflects the magnitude of the discrepancy of misclassification in judging the reliability of the decision. In our case, the question is: "How close are the two comprehension scores to the cutoff of 70% for instructional level?" The formula for K^2 may be found in Crocker and Algina (1986, p. 203).

The data on the new *QRI-5* passages indicated that of the 149 students who read two passages at the same level of readability, 88% scored at instructional level in comprehension on the new story as well as a previous one in the *QRI.* When we analyzed by readability level, at the pre-primer level the new stories were written to be easier than the previously easiest story, "Just Like Mom." And as expected the new stories, "I Can" and "I See," were easier than "Just Like Mom," but were similar to each other. "I Can" is a bit easier to read accurately and "I See" is easier to retell and answer comprehension questions. At the primer level the two stories matched 100% of the time, at the first grade level matches occurred 91% of the time, at the second grade level matches occurred 84% of the time, and at the third grade level, 79% of the time.

The reliabilities of our instructional-level decisions at all other levels based on comprehension scores were all above .80; 75% were greater than or equal to .90. In addition, we examined whether the same instructional level would be indicated on the basis of the comprehension scores on each passage. Across the readability levels, 75 to 81% of the time the same instructional level would be found on both passages (specifically, at fourth, 80%; fifth, 75%; sixth, 77%; and upper middle school, 81% of the time).

Sensitivity to Change.   Sensitivity to change refers to the responsiveness of a test to change or difference on the underlying construct being measured. We have conducted research on two aspects of the *QRI* that should be sensitive to change.

Regner (1992) used the *QRI* to compare progress made by two groups of children who were experiencing reading difficulties. One group had been identified as learning disabled, and the other group, though not significantly different in reading as measured by the *QRI* and the *Woodcock Reading Mastery Test-Revised* (Woodcock, 1987) or in intelligence, had not been so identified. Regner (1992) followed the children for four months, examining their reading instruction. Pre-test and post-test performance in reading as measured by the above instruments showed significant gains for both groups but no difference between the groups. Thus, the *QRI* was capable of measuring change in word recognition and comprehension over a four-month period. It should be noted that change was assessed by weighting the word-recognition and comprehension scores. For example, the total score on a word list was multiplied by its level (primer = .5, first = 1, etc.) and added to a word-recognition accuracy score in context weighted in the same manner. Comprehension was weighted by multiplying the percentage correct by the readability of the passage. The passage chosen for this procedure was the highest-level narrative passage at the student's instructional level. This weighting made the measurements more precise and sensitive to change than simply an instructional level.

The same weighting system was used in a study of the effectiveness of an early literacy intervention program for inner-city at-risk children (Leslie & Allen, 1999). The *QRI* was used to assess students three times per year, in early September before intervention, in December to determine whether they could graduate from the program, and in May to assess final progress. Longitudinal studies of these children have also used the *QRI* and compared it to the Wisconsin Third Grade Reading Test (WTGRT). The *QRI* has been found to be a sensitive measure of growth in instructional level, and weighted scores allowed Leslie and Allen (1999) to identify factors that contributed to students' growth during and after the intervention. Furthermore, performance on the *QRI* is highly correlated with performance on the WTGRT.

A three-year longitudinal study (McCarthy, 1999) of a first grade intervention found that children in the intervention group who began significantly below their classmates at the beginning of first grade were not significantly different from them in oral reading accuracy or comprehension on the *QRI* given in April of second grade. Rate differences continued into fourth grade.

Glass (1989) examined whether students' comprehension of two first- and second-level passages would be increased if they participated in a personal, analog discussion related to themes in the story. For example, on "The Bear and the Rabbit," the researcher engaged students in a discussion of why people are afraid of real bears, why animals would like to have friends, and why people become friends. These concepts are related to the theme of the passage and directly related to the most difficult comprehension question, "Why did the bear and the rabbit become friends?" Two groups of second grade students participated: sixteen average and sixteen below-average readers reading the second- and first-level passages, respectively. Students' prior knowledge of concepts was assessed on two passages, and the analog discussion was held on one passage and not on the other. Whether the discussion was held on the first or second story was counterbalanced across students. Results showed significant improvement in comprehension when students participated in the analog discussion on a story (effect sizes were greater than 1 for students at each readability level). These results suggest that instruction directed toward the conceptual knowledge judged as important to comprehending stories can enhance comprehension on the lower-level *QRI* passages.

These findings suggest that the passages on the *QRI* are sensitive to immediate change (Glass, 1989) and long-term (3–7 months) instructional interventions (Leslie & Allen, 1999; Regner, 1992). Thus, researchers may use the *QRI* as outcome measures of instructional research. Additional studies using the *QRI* as a measure of change can be found in the References marked by an asterisk.

Issues of Validity of an Informal Reading Inventory

Content Validity.   Validity evidence can be obtained from an analysis of the relationship between a test's content and the construct it is intended to measure. "Evidence based on test content can include logical or empirical analyses of the adequacy with which the text content represents the content domain and of the relevance of the content domain to the proposed interpretation of test scores" (*Standards for Educational and Psychological Testing,* 1999, p. 11).

In our case, the research literature described in Section 2 served as the basis for test development. Thus, to review our conclusions, we sought to represent the domain of reading more systematically than other IRIs. We chose narrative and expository material to represent the reading abilities from pre-primer through high school. We included passages with pictures at the pre-primer through second grade levels to represent more fully the type of materials children encounter in school and out. Two pre-primer passages were written with rhyming text to examine children's ability to use a known rhyming word to decode a less familiar rhyming word. Passages were varied in their familiarity. In addition to presenting children with a variety of materials, we chose to measure their reading abilities in ways that reflect research findings and classroom practice.

Research suggests the powerful effects of prior knowledge, so we included a measure of prior knowledge. Oral reading research suggests that in addition to finding total miscues, examiners should attend to the proportion of uncorrected miscues that change the meaning of the passage; thus we scored oral reading accuracy in these two ways. Because of findings that comprehension may be measured by examining whether children can make inferences, remember information stated directly in text, and retain information in memory, we chose to include three ways of measuring comprehension: answers to implicit questions, answers to explicit questions, and retelling (including inferences). On the word lists we included words that can be decoded using the rules of English and those that must be memorized because their spelling is irregular. We measured children's rate of word recognition, in addition to their accuracy. In the fifth edition we also present data on students' correct words per minute (CWPM), which has also been termed *oral reading fluency*. Correct words per minute is an index of both accuracy and speed and has been described as a reliable and valid measure of reading competence (Kame'enui & Simmons, 2001).

Whether we have succeeded in our attempts to present the domain of reading depends, in part, on one's view of the importance of the factors listed above. In addition, examinations of the pilot data provided us evidence of the construct representation and penetration we have achieved. Validity data for each part of the *QRI-5* are presented in the previous parts of this section under the heading Development of the Passages.

Criterion-Related Validity.   "Analyses of the relationship of test scores to variables external to the test provide another important source of validity evidence" (*Standards for Educational and Psychological Testing,* 1999, p. 13). External variables include measures that are hypothesized to measure the same construct. Convergent evidence is expected between tests of reading comprehension using different test formats. For example, the *QRI* is an individually administered test that includes oral reading of connected text followed by retelling and comprehension. Instructional-level scores on the *QRI* should correlate with tests of reading comprehension that measure comprehension through multiple-choice formats and cloze formats.

We examined the correlation (within grade) between the instructional level obtained from the *QRI* and the student's national curve equivalent (NCE) or standard score on a group administered standardized reading test. The standardized test data from grades one, two, and three were obtained from the California Achievement Test or the Iowa Test of Basic Skills. The standardized test data from grades three through eight were Terra Nova tests. Table 15.14 presents the correlations between instructional level in and scores on standardized tests of reading achievement by grade and type of text. At the lower grade levels, we didn't have enough children reading expository text to reliably obtain a correlation. At all grade levels except seventh, where we had achievement data on only 17 students, statistically significant correlations were found between instructional level in narrative and/or expository texts and standardized test scores.

Table 15.14   **Correlations between Instructional Level in Text and Standardized Tests of Reading Achievement as a Function of Grade and Type of Text**

Grade	Correlation in Narrative Text		Correlation in Expository Text
1	.85**	n = 50	
2	.65**	n = 32	
3	.55*	n = 39	
4	.66**	n = 31	
5	.44**	n = 35	.53**
6	.27	n = 21	.45*
7	.43	n = 17	.28
8	.47*	n = 22	.55**
9	.52*	n = 19	

*Note: *p < .05; **p < .01*

In the pilot data for the fifth edition, only one school had administered standardized tests to students at the beginning of second grade. The correlations between *QRI-5* weighted instructional level (Total Accuracy score × readability level and total comprehension score × readability level) with MAPS total reading were $r(20) = .81$ for total accuracy and .80 for comprehension ($ps < .01$).

Construct Validity.   Evidence of construct validity focuses on the test scores as a measure of the psychological characteristics, or construct, of interest. The conceptual framework specifies the meaning of the construct, distinguishes it from other constructs, and indicates how measures of the construct should relate to other variables (*Standards for Educational and Psychological Testing,* 1999, p. 14). At the most general level, the *QRI-5* measures word-recognition ability and comprehension. Depending on the stage of reading development, we should find different patterns of intercorrelations. Among beginning readers, we should find greater interrelatedness among word identification on word lists, oral reading accuracy in context, and reading rate than among those factors and comprehension. On the other hand, after students have achieved some degree of automaticity of word recognition, we expect correlations between our prior-knowledge measures and retelling and comprehension.

1. **Correlations among factors on the QRI-5.** We found support for the interrelatedness and uniqueness of several factors on the *QRI.* The intercorrelations among word identification on the word lists, total oral reading accuracy, semantically acceptable accuracy, rate of reading and corrected rate were positive and statistically significant through third grade (*rs* ranged from .34 to .59 with *ns* of 275–434, all *ps* < .001). Correlations between these measures of word-identification accuracy and rate also correlated with comprehension at the pre-primer, primer, second, third, and fourth grade instructional levels. As indicated on page 476, it isn't clear why there were no statistically significant correlations between word identification and rate with comprehension at the first grade instructional level.

2. **Intercorrelations among conceptual-knowledge scores with retelling and comprehension.** The correlation between prior knowledge and comprehension was statistically significant at all levels. Using the pilot sample for the *QRI-5* prior knowledge correlated $r(30) = .39$, $p < .02$, with comprehension on the easiest passage, "I Can." Similarly, the correlation between prior knowledge and comprehension was $r(24) = .50$, $p < .01$ on "I See." On the new primer story, "A Night in the City," prior knowledge correlated $r(13) = .50$ with retelling and .61, $p < .05$ with comprehension. In addition, the correlation between prior knowledge and retelling was significant, $r(25) = .38$ with retelling of the new first grade story, "The Surprise." No statistically significant correlations were found on the new second grade story, "The Family's First Trip." However, on the new third grade story, "A New Friend from Europe," prior knowledge was correlated $r(24) = .45$ with retelling and .40 with comprehension, *ps* < .05.

Using the large clinical sample provided different results. The correlation between prior knowledge and comprehension was only $r(210) = .30$, $p < .001$ at primer level; $r(336) = .18$, $p < .01$ at first grade level; and $r(303) = .30$, $p < .001$ at second grade level. Correlations rose to $r(232) = .35$ at fourth grade level; $r(80) = .40$ at fifth grade level; and $r(64) = .48$ at sixth grade level. At the upper middle school level, prior knowledge was related to the number of inferences made while retelling "Biddy Mason," $r(30) = .47$, $p < .01$, but no statistically significant relationships were found on "Malcolm X." In expository texts, significant correlations between prior knowledge and the number of inferences made during retelling of "Immigration—Part 1," $r(11) = .62$, $p = .02$, and between prior knowledge and comprehension on "Life Cycles of Stars—Part 1," $r(18) = .86$, $p < .001$, and "Life Cycles of Stars—Part 2," $r(13) = .62$, $p < .05$.

In summary, it appears that we have evidence that the QRI-5 measures at least two constructs that have been posited to be central to the reading process—word recognition and comprehension (Gough & Tunmer, 1986), which is related to prior knowledge of concepts contained in the passages.

3. **The consequence of taking a test.** For achievement tests, of which the QRI is one type, the goal of assessment may vary from accountability to the use that teachers might put the information obtained from the students' scores. The QRI was designed to determine a student's reading level and to assess the strengths and weaknesses of the student, thereby helping the teacher determine the level and type of instruction that would best meet the student's needs. If, as we have argued earlier, a student can read a text accurately and fluently, but does not understand what he or she reads, then the implication for the teacher is that instruction in comprehension is necessary. (See Caldwell and Leslie, 2009, for instructional recommendations in such a case.) If, on the other hand, a student has difficulty reading words, but can understand a text very well if it is read to him or her, then the student needs instruction in word-identification strategies. The consequence of giving a test such as the QRI is to guide instruction.

USING THE QRI-5 TO GUIDE INSTRUCTION

In addition to the type of construct validity already presented, Cross and Paris (1987) described how a diagnostic test must represent specific constructs to be of use to teachers. Construct representation assesses how well a construct is contained in the items. Construct representation is often uncertain because one test score is the result of many cognitive processes. Often, achievement test scores have not been able to provide educators with direction for instruction. This inability is related to the fact that construct representation does not usually occur in a one-to-one relationship between a score on a test and a single cognitive process responsible for the performance on that item (Cross & Paris, 1987).

We have offered construct representation by providing the examiner with a set of passages that vary according to type of text and familiarity to the reader. In this way an examiner can determine why a child might comprehend one type of material well but not another. In addition, we have assessed comprehension in several ways: retelling, answers to questions with the text absent, and answers to the questions with the text present. Thus, an examiner can separate what a student remembers from a text from what the student comprehends with access to the text. Furthermore, on the word lists, we have represented the construct of word identification by measuring the student's rate of identification and by including words that vary in decodability.

Data Supporting the Use of QRI Results to Guide Instruction

Leslie and Allen (1999) reported a study of the effects of an early intervention project that used the QRI to assess the children's reading abilities and to group them for instruction. Their evidence suggests that different instructional procedures were correlated with growth for children who entered the project at different instructional reading levels. For readers with less than a first grade reading ability, the number of rimes taught was the best predictor of growth, but for children reading at or above first grade, the amount of story grammar instruction best predicted their growth. These data suggest that reading acquisition is a developmental process that is sensitive to different instructional methods. The students' abilities can be assessed by the *QRI*, and relevant instructional decisions can be made.

A small instructional study was also conducted in 1991 to assess whether we have been successful at providing information that will help guide instruction at the upper elementary level. Sixth graders from a single classroom were given the *QRI*. Although all students were taught, only the data from students reading at a sixth grade instructional level in narrative text ($n = 16$) were used in the analyses. The mean pre-test scores showed that students retold more information from narrative than from expository text, $F(1, 15) = 15.71, p < .001$, although there were no differences in comprehension, $F < 1$, and the prior-conceptual-knowledge scores were higher for *expository* text, $F(1, 15) = 14.64, p < .01$.

The teacher then taught four text structures to the students: cause–effect, problem–solution, sequence, and compare–contrast. The instruction in text structure occurred over one month and was integrated within a unit on Greek and Roman governments, which was particularly useful in teaching the compare–contrast structure. The instruction was composed of direct instruction on text structures, modeling how to determine structures in text, guided practice in finding structures in text, independent assessment of knowledge gained, and an application project. Post-testing with the *QRI* was conducted two months after the formal instruction had ended. Students read new (not used at pre-test) sixth grade narrative and expository texts. We also asked students to identify text structures of the expository texts. Although there were no differences between pre-test and post-test in students' abilities to identify different text structures, increases in their ability to recall expository texts were found, $F (1, 15) = 12.79, p < .01$. Mean retelling scores on expository text increased from .20 at pre-test to .30 at post-test, which made it nonsignificantly different from the retelling of narrative text (mean = .33). We cannot conclude that the instruction on text structures resulted in the improvement in retelling ability. Rather, the effect could have been a more general one. It may have been that the greater emphasis on constructing meaning in expository text was the decisive factor. The students certainly liked the unit, as we learned when one teacher came and asked what we were doing in social studies. Students had reported to her an excitement about the subject that she had not seen before. Although our results were less than conclusive, others have found that instruction in text structures can improve students' recall and comprehension of expository text (Armbruster, Anderson, & Ostertag, 1987; Richgels, McGee, Lomax, & Sheard, 1987).

References

An asterisk (*) marks published studies that used the *QRI* to document growth in reading.

Aaron, P. G. (1997). The demise of the discrepancy formula. *Review of Educational Research, 67,* 461–502.

*Abbott, S. P., & Beringer, V. W. (2000). It's never too late to remediate: Teaching word recognition skills to students with reading disability in grades 4–7. *Annals of Dyslexia, 49,* 223–250.

Adams, M. J. (1990). *Beginning to read: Thinking and learning about print.* Cambridge, MA: MIT Press.

Allington, R. L. (2001). *What really matters for struggling readers: Designing research-based programs.* New York: Longman.

*Almasi, J. J., Costanzo, Z., Crout, M., Frank, S. T., Harrison, P., Owczarzak, J., & Priddy, J. (2006–2007). An evaluation of the impact of the Kentucky reading project on teacher and student growth 2006–07. Retrieved from www.kccld.org/KRP%20Research%20PDFs/KRP%20Evaluation%202006–07.pdf

*Alvarez, L., & Corn, J. (2008). Exchanging assessment for accountability: The implications of high stakes reading for English language learners. *Language Arts, 85,* 354–366.

Alvermann, D. E., Smith, L. C., & Readance, J. E. (1985). Prior knowledge activation and the comprehension of compatible and incompatible text. *Reading Research Quarterly, 20,* 420–436.

Anderson, R. C., Reynolds, R. E., Schallert, D. L., & Goetz, E. T. (1977). Frameworks for comprehending discourse. *American Educational Research Journal, 14,* 367–382.

Applegate, M. D., Quinn, K. B., & Applegate, A. (2002). Levels of thinking required by comprehension questions in informal reading inventories. *The Reading Teacher, 56,* 174–180.

Armbruster, B. B., Anderson, T. H., & Ostertag, J. (1987). Does text structure/summarization instruction facilitate learning from expository text? *Reading Research Quarterly, 22,* 331–346.

Bader, L. (2002). *Bader reading and language inventory.* Englewood Cliffs, NJ: Prentice-Hall.

Beck, I. L. (2006). *Making sense of phonics: The hows and whys.* New York: Guilford Press.

Bender, W. N., & Shores, C. (2007). *Response to intervention: A practical guide for every teacher.* Thousand Oaks, CA: Corwin Press.

Bereiter, C., & Bird, M. (1985). Use of thinking aloud in identification and teaching of reading comprehension strategies. *Cognition and Instruction, 2,* 131–156.

Berkowitz, S., & Taylor, B. M. (1981). The effects of text type and familiarity on the nature of information recalled by readers. In M. Kamil (ed.), *Directions in reading: Research and instruction* (pp. 157–161). Washington, DC: National Reading Conference.

*Berninger, V. W., Abbott, R. D., Vermeulen, K., & Fulton, C. M. (2006). Paths to reading comprehension in at-risk second graders. *Journal of Learning Disabilities, 39,* 334–352.

Betts, F. (1946). *Foundations of reading instruction.* New York: American Book.

Blanchard, J. S., Borthwick, P., & Hall, A. (1983). Determining instructional reading level: Standardized multiple choice versus IRI improved recall questions. *Journal of Reading, 26,* 684–689.

Bowyer-Crane, C., & Snowling, M. J. (2005). Assessing children's inference generation: What do tests of reading comprehension measure? *British Journal of Educational Psychology, 7,* 189–201.

Brennan, A. D., Bridge, C., & Winograd, P. (1986). The effects of structural variation on children's recall of basal reader stories. *Reading Research Quarterly, 21,* 91–104.

Brown, C. S., & Lytle, S. L. (1988). Merging assessment and instruction: Protocols in the classroom. In S. M. Glazer, L. W. Searfoss, & L. M. Gentile (eds.), *Reexamining reading diagnoses: New trends and practices.* Newark, DE: International Reading Association.

Brown, R., Pressley, M., Van Meter, P., & Schuder, T. (1996). A quasi-experimental validation of transactional strategies instruction with low-achieving second-grade readers. *Journal of Educational Psychology, 88,* 18–37.

Brown-Chidsey, R., & Steege, M. W. (2005). *Response to intervention: Principles and strategies for effective practice.* New York: Guilford Press.

Burge, P. D. (1983). Comprehension and rate: Oral vs. silent reading for low achievers. *Reading Horizons, 23,* 201–206.

Burns, B. D., & Roe, P. C. (2002). *Burns/Roe informal reading inventory.* Itasca, IL: Riverside Publishing.

Caldwell, J. S. (2008a). *Reading assessment: A primer for teachers and coaches.* New York. Guilford Press.

Caldwell, J. S. (2008b). *Comprehension assessment: A classroom guide.* New York: Guilford Press.

*Caldwell, J., Fromm, M., & O'Connor, V. (1997–1998). Designing an intervention for poor readers: Incorporating

the best of all worlds. *Wisconsin State Reading Association Journal, 41,* 7–14.

Caldwell, J., & Leslie, L. (2003–04). Does proficiency in middle school reading assure proficiency in high school reading? The possible role of think-alouds. *Journal of Adolescent and Adult Literacy, 47,* 324–335.

Caldwell, J. S., & Leslie, L. (2009). *Intervention strategies to follow informal reading inventory assessment: So what do I do now?* Boston: Allyn & Bacon.

Caldwell, J., & Leslie, L. (in press). *Thinking aloud in expository text: Processes and outcomes. Journal of Literacy Research.*

Carroll, J. B., Davies, P., & Richman, B. (1971). *The word frequency book.* New York: American Heritage Publishing.

Carver, R. P. (1990). *Reading rate: A review of research and theory.* San Diego: Academic.

*Catts, H. W., Adlof, S. M., & Weismer, S. E. (2006). Language deficits in poor comprehenders: A case for the simple view of reading. *Journal of Speech, Language and Hearing Research, 49,* 278–294.

*Catts, H. W., Bridges, M. S., Little, T. D., & Tomblin, J. B. (2008). Reading achievement growth in children with language impairments. *Journal of Speech, Language, and Hearing Research, 51,* 1569–1580.

Chall, J. S. (1983). *Stages of reading development.* New York: McGraw-Hill.

Chard, D., McDonagh, S., Lee, S., & Reece, V. (2007). Assessing word recognition. In J. R. Paratore & R. L. McCormack (eds.), *Classroom literacy assessment* (pp. 85–100). New York: Guilford Press.

Chou-Hare, V., & Smith, D. C. (1982). Reading to remember: Studies of metacognitive reading skills in elementary school-aged children. *Journal of Educational Research, 75,* 157–164.

Chrystal, C. (1991). *Assessing prior knowledge across cultures.* Unpublished doctoral dissertation, Marquette University.

Ciardiello, A. V. (1998). Did you ask a good question today? Alternative cognitive and metacognitive strategies. *Journal of Adolescent and Adult Literacy, 42,* 210–219.

Clark, H. H., & Clark, E. V. (1977). *Psychology and language.* New York: Harcourt.

Coté, N., & Goldman, S. R. (1998). *Profiles in reading: Using verbal protocols to examine students' construction of discourse representations.* Paper presented at the American Educational Research Association Conference, San Diego.

Coté, N., Goldman, S. R., & Saul, E. U. (1998). Students making sense of informational text: Relations between processing and representation. *Discourse Processes, 25,* 1–53.

Craig, H., Thompson, C. A., Washington, J. A., & Potter, S. L. (2003). Phonological features of child African-American English. *Journal of Speech, Language and Hearing Research, 46,* 623–635.

Craig, H. K., & Washington, J. A. (2004a). Grade-related changes in the production of African American English. *Journal of Speech, Language, and Hearing Research, 47,* 450–463.

Craig, H. K., & Washington, J. A. (2004b). Language variation and literacy learning. In C. A. Stone, E. R. Silliman, B. J. Ehren, & K. Apel (eds.), *Handbook of language and literacy: Development and disorders* (pp. 228–247). New York: Guilford Press.

Crain-Thoreson, C., Lippman, M. Z., & McClendon-Magnuson, D. (1997). Windows of comprehension: Reading comprehension processes as revealed by two think-aloud procedures. *Journal of Educational Psychology, 89,* 579–591.

Crocker, L., & Algina, J. (1986). *Introduction to classical and modern test theory.* New York: Holt, Rinehart and Winston.

Cronbach, L. J. (1951). Coefficient alpha and the internal structure of tests. *Psychometrika, 16,* 297–334.

Cross, D., & Paris, S. (1987). Assessment of reading comprehension: Matching test purposes and test properties. *Educational Psychologist, 22,* 313–332.

Cunningham, J. W., Spadorcia, S. A., Erickson, K. A., Koppenhaver, D. A., Sturm, J. M., & Yoder, D. E. (2005). Investigating the instructional supportiveness of leveled text. *Reading Research Quarterly, 40,* 410–427.

*Dahl, K. L., Scharer, P. L., & Lawson, L. L. (1999). Phonics instruction and student achievement in whole language first-grade classrooms. *Reading Research Quarterly, 34,* 312–341.

Deno, S. L. (1985). Curriculum-based measurement: The emerging alternative. *Exceptional Children, 3,* 219–232.

*Duffy, A. M. (2001). Balance, literacy acceleration, and responsive teaching in a SS Literacy Program for elementary grade struggling readers. *Reading Research and Instruction, 40,* 67–100.

Duke, N. (2000). 3.6 minutes per day: The scarcity of informational texts in first grade. *Reading Research Quarterly, 35,* 202–224.

Ehri, L. C. (1991). Development of the ability to read words. In R. Barr, M. L. Kamil, P. Mosenthal, & P. D. Pearson (eds.), *Handbook of reading research* (vol. II, pp. 383–417). White Plains, NY: Longman.

Ehri, L. C. (1992). Reconceptualizing the development of sight word reading and its relationship to recoding. In P. B. Gough, L. C. Ehri, & R. Treiman (eds.), *Reading acquisition* (pp. 107–143). Mahwah, NJ: Lawrence Erlbaum Associates.

Ehri, L. C., & McCormick, S. (2004). Phases of word learning: Implications for instruction with delayed and disabled readers. In R. B. Ruddell & N. J. Unrau (eds.), *Theoretical models and processes of reading* (5th ed., pp. 365–389). Newark, DE: International Reading Association.

Englert, C. S., & Hiebert, E. H. (1984). Children's developing awareness of text structures in expository material. *Journal of Educational Psychology, 76,* 65–74.

Fountas, I., & Pinnell, G. S. (2008). *Benchmark assessment system.* Portsmouth, NH: Heinemann.

Fountas, I. C., & Pinnell, G. S. (2006). *The Fountas & Pinnell leveled book list, K-8.* Portsmouth, NH: Heinemann.

Francis, D. J., Fletcher, J. M., Catts, H. W., & Tomblin, J. B. (2005). Dimensions affecting the assessment of reading comprehension. In S. G. Paris & S. A. Stahl (eds.), *Children's reading comprehension and assessment* (pp. 369–394). Mahwah, NJ: Lawrence Erlbaum Associates.

Fry, E. (1998). The most common phonograms. *The Reading Teacher, 51,* 620–622.

Fuchs, D., & Deshler, D. D. (2007). What we need to know about responsiveness to intervention (and shouldn't be afraid to ask). *Learning Disabilities Research & Practice, 22,* 129–136.

Fuchs, L. S., & Fuchs, D. (1992). Identifying a measure for monitoring student reading progress. *School Psychology Review, 21,* 45–59.

Fuchs, L. S., & Fuchs, D. (1999). Monitoring student progress toward the development of reading competence: A review of three forms of classroom-based assessment. *School Psychology Review, 28,* 659–672.

Fuchs, L. S., Fuchs, D., & Hamlett, C. L. (1989). Monitoring reading growth using student recalls: Effects of two teacher feedback systems. *Journal of Educational Research, 83,* 103–110.

Fuchs, L. S., Fuchs, D., Hosp, M. K., & Jenkins, J. R. (2001). Oral reading fluency as an indicator of reading competence: A theoretical and historical analysis. *Scientific Studies of Reading, 5,* 239–256.

Fuchs, L. S., Fuchs, D., & Maxwell, L. (1988). The validity of informal comprehension measures. *Remedial and Special Education, 9,* 20–28.

Garner, R. (1982). Verbal-report data on reading strategies. *Journal of Reading Behavior, XIV,* 159–167.

Garner, R., & Reis, R. (1981). Monitoring and resolving comprehension obstacles: An investigation of spontaneous text lookbacks among upper grade good and poor readers. *Reading Research Quarterly, 16,* 569–582.

Gaskins, I., Downer, M., Anderson, R., Cunningham, P., Gaskins, R., & Schommer, M. (1988). A metacognitive approach to phonics: Using what you know to decode what you don't know. *Remedial and Special Education, 27,* 36–41.

Gaskins, I., Downer, M., & the teachers of Benchmark School. (1997). *The Benchmark word identification/vocabulary development program.* Media, PA: Benchmark Press.

Gaskins, I. W., Ehri, L. C., Cress, C., O'Hara, C., & Donnelly, K. (1996–1997). Procedures for word learning: Making discoveries about words. *The Reading Teacher, 50,* 312–327.

Gersten, R., & Dimino, J. A. (2006). RTI (response to intervention): Rethinking special education for students with reading difficulties (yet again). *Reading Research Quarterly, 41,* 99–108.

Glass, S. (1989). The effect of prior knowledge on reading miscues and comprehension of narrative text. Unpublished master's thesis, Marquette University.

Glenn, D. (2008). Weak results found in study of reading first program. *The Chronicle of Higher Education.* Retrieved from http://chronicle.com/daily/2008/05/2708n.htm

Goldman, S. R. (1997). Learning from text: Reflections on the past and suggestions for the future. *Discourse Processes, 23,* 357–398.

Goldman, S. R., & Rakestraw, J. A. (2000). Structural aspects of constructing meaning from text. In M. L. Kamil, P. B. Mosenthal, P. D. Pearson, & R. Barr (eds.), *Handbook of Reading Research* (vol. III, pp. 311–336). Mahwah, NJ: Lawrence Erlbaum Associates.

Good, R. H., Simmons, D. C., & Kame'enui, E. J. (2001). The importance and decision-making utility of a continuum of fluency-based indicators of foundational reading skills for third-grade high-stakes outcomes. *Scientific Studies of Reading, 5,* 257–289.

Goodman, K. S. (1965). A linguistic study of cues and miscues in reading. *Elementary English, 42,* 639–643.

Goodman, K. S. (1967). Reading: A psycholinguistic guessing game. In H. Singer & R. B. Ruddell (eds.), *Theoretical models and processes of reading* (pp. 497–503). Newark, DE: International Reading Association.

Gough, P. B., & Juel, C. (1991). The first stages of word recognition. In L. Rieben & C. A. Perfetti (eds.), *Learning to read: Basic research and its implications* (pp. 47–56). Mahwah, NJ: Lawrence Erlbaum Associates.

Gough, P. B., & Tunmer, W. E. (1986). Decoding, reading and reading disability. *Remedial and Special Education, 7,* 6–10.

Graesser, A., Golding, J. M., & Long, D. L. (1991). Narrative representation and comprehension. In R. Barr, M. L. Kamil, P. Mosenthal, & P. D. Pearson (eds.), *Handbook of reading research* (vol. II, pp. 171–205). White Plains, NY: Longman.

Graesser, A. C., Baggett, W., & Williams, K. (1996). Question-driven explanatory reasoning. *Applied Cognitive Psychology, 10,* S17–S32.

Graesser, A. C., & Clark, L. F. (1985). *Structures and procedures of implicit knowledge.* Norwich, NJ: Ablex.

Graesser, A. C., & Goodman, S. M. (1985). Implicit knowledge, question answering and the representation of expository text. In B. K. Britton & J. B. Black (eds.), *Understanding expository text* (pp. 109–171). Mahwah, NJ: Lawrence Erlbaum Associates.

Graesser, A. C., & Person, N. K. (1994). Question asking during tutoring. *American Educational Research Journal, 31,* 104–137.

Gunning, T. G. (1998). *Best books for beginning readers.* Boston: Allyn & Bacon.

Gunning, T. G. (2002). *Assessing and correcting reading and writing difficulties* (2nd ed.). Boston: Allyn & Bacon.

Hall, K. M., Markham, J. C., & Culatta, B. (2005). The development of the early expository comprehension assessment (EECA): A look at reliability. *Communication Disorders Quarterly, 26,* 195–206.

Hamilton, C., & Shinn, M. (2003). Characteristics of word callers: An investigation of the accuracy of teachers' judgments of reading comprehension and oral reading skill. *School Psychology Review, 32,* 228–240.

Hare, V. C. (1982). Preassessment of topical knowledge: A validation and extension. *Journal of Reading Behavior, 15,* 77–86.

Harris, A. J., & Sipay, E. (1985). *How to increase reading ability: A guide to developmental and remedial methods* (8th ed.). New York: Longman.

Harris, A. J., & Sipay, E. (1990). *How to increase reading ability: A guide to developmental and remedial methods* (9th ed.). New York: Longman.

Hasbrouck, J. E., & Tindal, G. (1992). Curriculum-based oral reading fluency norms for students in grades 2 through 5. *Teaching Exceptional Children,* Spring, 41–44.

Hasbrouck, J. E., & Tindal, G. A. (2006). Oral reading fluency norms: A valuable assessment tool for reading teachers. *The Reading Teacher, 59,* 636–643.

*Hoffman, J., Roser, N. L., Salas, R., & Patterson, E. (2001). Text leveling and "little-books" in first-grade reading. *Journal of Literacy Research, 33,* 507–528.

Hollenbeck, A. F. (2007). From IDEA to implementation: A discussion of foundational and future responsiveness-to-intervention research. *Learning Disabilities Research & Practice, 22,* 137–146.

Holmes, B. C., & Roser, N. L. (1987). Five ways to assess readers' prior knowledge. *The Reading Teacher, 40,* 646–649.

Hood, J. (1975–76). Qualitative analysis of oral reading errors: The interjudge reliability of scores. *Reading Research Quarterly, 11,* 577–598.

Individuals with Disabilities Education Improvement Act (IDEA). (2004). *Federal Register, 71.* Retrieved from www.ed/gov/policy/speced/guid/idea2004.html

Irwin, P. A., & Mitchell, K. N. (1983). A procedure for assessing the richness of retellings. *Journal of Reading, 28,* 391–396.

Jett-Simpson, M., & Leslie, L. (1997). *Authentic literacy assessment: An ecological approach.* New York: Longman.

Johns, J. L., & Berglund, R. L. (2002). *Fluency: Questions, answers, evidence-based strategies.* Dubuque, IA: Kendall/Hunt Publishing Company.

Johnson, N. S., & Mandler, J. M. (1980). A tale of two structures: Underlying and surface forms in stories. *Poetics, 9,* 51–86.

*Johnson-Glenberg, M. C. (1999). Training reading comprehension in adequate decoders/poor comprehenders: Verbal vs. visual strategies. *Journal of Educational Psychology, 92,* 772–782.

Johnston, P. H. (1984). Prior knowledge and reading comprehension test bias. *Reading Research Quarterly, 19,* 219–239.

Kame'enui, E. J., & Simmons, D. C. (2001). Introduction to this special issue: The DNA of reading fluency. *Scientific Studies of Reading, 5,* 203–210.

Kavale, K., & Schreiner, R. (1979). The reading process of above average and average readers: A comparison of the use of reasoning strategies in responding to standardized comprehension measures. *Reading Research Quarterly, XV,* 102–128.

Kendeou, P., & van den Broek, P. (2005). The effects of readers' misconceptions on comprehension of scientific text. *Journal of Educational Psychology, 97,* 235–245.

Kintsch, E., (2005). Comprehension theory as a guide for the design of thoughtful questions. *Topics in Language Disorders, 25,* 51–64.

Kintsch, W., & van Dijk, T. A. (1978). Towards a model of text comprehension and production. *Psychological Review, 5,* 363–394.

Kintsch, W., & Green, E. (1978). The role of culture specific schemata in the comprehension and recall of stories. *Discourse Processes, 1,* 1–13.

Kintsch, W., & Kintsch, E. (2005). Comprehension. In S. G. Paris & S. A. Stahl (eds.), *Children's reading comprehension and assessment* (pp. 71–92). Mahwah, NJ: Lawrence Erlbaum Associates.

Klingner, J. K., & Vaughm, S. (2004). Strategies for struggling second-language readers. In T. L. Jetton & J. A. Dole (eds.), *Adolescent literacy research and practice* (pp. 183–209). New York: Guilford Press.

*Kuhn, M. R. (2005). A comparative study of small group fluency instruction. *Reading Psychology, 26,* 127–146.

Kuhn, M. R., Schwanenflugel, P. J., Morris, R. D., Morrow, L. M., Woo, D. G., Meisinger, E. B., Sevcik, R. A., Bradley, B. A., & Stahl, S. A. (2006). Teaching children to become fluent and automatic readers. *Journal of Literacy Research, 38,* 357–388.

LaBerge, D., & Samuels, S. J. (1985). Toward a theory of automatic information processing. In H. Singer & R. Ruddell (eds.), *Theoretical models and processes of reading* (3rd ed., pp. 689–718). Newark, DE: International Reading Association.

Langer, J. (1984). Examining background knowledge and text comprehension. *Reading Research Quarterly, 14,* 468–481.

Lehnert, W. G. (1978). *The process of question answering.* Mahwah, NJ: Lawrence Erlbaum Associates.

Leslie, L. *Recall and comprehension of narrative vs. expository text.* Unpublished manuscript. Marquette University.

*Leslie, L., & Allen, L. (1999). Factors that predict success in an early intervention project. *Reading Research Quarterly, 34,* 404–424.

Leslie, L., & Caldwell, J. (1989). The Qualitve Reading Inventory: Issues in the development of a diagnostic reading test. In S. McCormick & J. Zutell (eds.), *Cognitive and social perspectives for literacy: Research and instruction* (pp. 413–419). Chicago: National Reading Conference.

Leslie, L., & Caldwell, J. (1990). *Qualitative Reading Inventory.* Glenview, IL: Scott Foresman.

Leslie, L., & Caldwell, J. (1995). *Qualitative Reading Inventory-II.* New York: HarperCollins.

Leslie, L., & Caldwell, J. (2001). *Qualitative Reading Inventory-3.* New York: Longman.

Leslie, L., & Caldwell, J. (2006). *Qualitative Reading Inventory-4.* Boston: Allyn & Bacon.

Leslie, L., & Caldwell, J. (2009). Formal and informal measures of reading comprehension. In S. E. Israel & G. G. Duffy (eds.), *Handbook of research on reading comprehension* (pp. 403–427). New York: Routledge.

Leslie, L., & Calhoon, J. (1995). Factors affecting children's reading of rimes: Reading ability, word frequency, and rime-neighborhood size. *Journal of Educational Psychology, 87,* 576–586.

Leslie, L., & Cooper, J. (1993). Assessing the predictive validity of prior-knowledge assessment. In D. J. Leu & C. K. Kinzer (eds.), *Examining central issues in literacy research, theory and practice* (pp. 93–100). Chicago: National Reading Conference.

Lipson, M. Y. (1983). The influence of religious affiliation on children's memory for test information. *Reading Research Quarterly, 18,* 448–457.

Livingston, S. A. (1972). Criterion-referenced applications of classical test theory. *Journal of Educational Measurement, 9,* 13–26.

Magliano, J. P., Trabasso, T., & Graesser, A. C. (1999). Strategic processes during comprehension. *Journal of Educational Psychology, 91,* 615–629.

Mahecha, N. (2003). Spanish speaking American children. In A. McCabe & L. Bliss (eds.), *Patterns of narrative discourse: A multicultural life span approach* (pp. 73–90). Boston: Allyn & Bacon.

Matsuyama, U. (1983). Can story grammar speak Japanese? *The Reading Teacher, 36,* 666–669.

McCarthy, P. (1999). The effects of balanced literacy instructional training: A longitudinal study of reading performance in the primary grades. Unpublished doctoral dissertation, Marquette University.

McCook, J. E. (2006). *The RTI guide: Developing and implementing a model in your schools.* Horsham, PA: LRP Publications.

McKenna, M. C. (1983). Informal reading inventories: A review of the issues. *The Reading Teacher, 36,* 670–679.

McKenna, M. C., & Picard, M. C. (2006/2007). Revisiting the role of miscue analysis in effective teaching. *The Reading Teacher, 60,* 378–380.

McNamara, D. S., Kintsch, E., Songer, N. B., & Kintsch, W. (1996). Are good texts always better? Interactions of text coherence, background knowledge, and levels of understanding in learning from text. *Cognition and Instruction, 14,* 1–43.

Meyer, B. J. F. (2003). Text coherence and readability. *Topics in Language Disorders, 23,* 204–224.

Meyer, B. J. F., & Rice, G. E. (1984). The structure of text. In P. D. Pearson, R. Barr, M. L. Kamil, & P. Mosenthal (eds.), *Handbook of reading research* (vol. I, pp. 319–352). White Plains, NY: Longman.

Micro Power & Light Co. (2007). *Readability calculations.* Dallas: Author.

*Milen, S. K., & Rinehart, S. D. (2000). Some of the benefits of reader's theater participation for 2nd grade Title I students. *Reading Research and Instruction, 39,* 71–88.

*Montali, J., & Lewandowski, L. (1996). Benefits of a talking computer for average and less skilled readers. *Journal of Learning Disabilities, 29,* 271–279.

*Moore, R. A., & Brantingham, K. L. (2003). Nathan: A case study in reader response and retrospective miscue analysis. *The Reading Teacher, 56,* 466–474.

Morrow, L. M., Kuhn, M. R., & Schwanenflugel, P. J. (2006/2007). The family fluency program. *The Reading Teacher, 60,* 322–333.

Mulcahy, P. I., & Samuels, S. J. (1987). Problem solving schemata for text types: A comparison of narrative and expository text structures. *Reading Psychology, 8,* 247–256.

Myers, J. (1988). Diagnosis diagnosed: Twenty years after. *Professional School Psychology, 3,* 123–134.

Myers, L., Lytle, S., Palladino, D., Devenpeck, G., & Green, M. (1990). Think-aloud protocol analysis: An investigation of reading comprehension strategies in fourth and fifth grade students. *Journal of Psychoeducational Assessment, 8,* 112–127.

Nicholson, T., Lillas, C., & Rzoska, M. A. (1988). Have we been misled by miscues? *The Reading Teacher, 42,* 6–10.

Nist, S. L., & Kirby, K. (1986). Teaching comprehension and study strategies through modeling and thinking aloud. *Reading Research and Instruction, 25,* 254–264.

Olshavsky, J. E. (1976–1977). Reading as problem solving: An investigation of strategies. *Reading Research Quarterly, 4,* 654–675.

Palincsar, A. S., Magnussen, S. J., Pesko, E., & Hamlin, M. (2005). Attending to the nature of subject matter in text comprehension assessments. In S. G. Paris & S. A. Stahl (eds.), *Children's reading comprehension and assessment.* (pp. 257–279). Mahwah, NJ: Lawrence Erlbaum Associates.

*Paris, A. H., & Paris, S. G. (2003). Assessing narrative comprehension in young children *Reading Research Quarterly, 38,* 36–76.

Paris, S. G., Carpenter, R. D., Paris, A. H., & Hamilton, E. E. (2005). Spurious and genuine correlates of children's comprehension. In S. G. Paris & S. A. Stahl (eds.), *Children's reading comprehension and assessment* (pp. 131–160). Mahwah, NJ: Lawrence Erlbaum Associates.

Paris, S. G., Pearson, P. D., Carpenter, R. D., Siebenthal, S., & Laier, B. (2002). *Evaluation of the Michigan Literacy Progress Profile (MLPP). Final Report: Year 1.* Lansing, MI: Department of Education.

Pearson, P. D., & Fielding, L. (1991). Comprehension instruction. In R. Barr, M. L. Kamil, P. Mosenthal, & P. D. Pearson (eds.), *Handbook of reading research* (vol. II, pp. 815–860). New York: Longman.

Pearson, P. D., & Hamm, D. N. (2005). The assessment of reading comprehension: A review of practices—past, present and future. In S. G. Paris & S. A. Stahl (eds.), *Children's reading comprehension and assessment* (pp. 13–70). Mahwah, NJ: Lawrence Erlbaum Associates.

Pearson, P. D., Hansen, J., & Gordon, C. (1979). The effect of background knowledge on young children's comprehension of explicit and implicit information. *Journal of Reading Behavior, 11,* 201–209.

Pearson, P. D., & Johnson, D. D. (1978). *Teaching reading comprehension.* New York: Holt, Rinehart and Winston.

Perfetti, C. A. (1985). *Reading ability.* New York: Oxford University Press.

Perfetti, C. A. (1988). Verbal efficiency in reading ability. In M. Daneman, G. E. MacKinnon, & T. G. Waller (eds.), *Reading research: Advances in theory and practice* (vol. 6, 109–143). New York: Academic.

Pikulski, J. J., & Chard, D. J. (2005). Fluency: Bridge between decoding and reading comprehension. *The Reading Teacher, 58,* 510–519.

Pressley, M., & Afflerbach, P. (1995). *Verbal protocols in reading: The nature of constructively responsive reading.* Mahwah, NJ: Lawrence Erlbaum Associates.

Rasinski, T. V., Padek, N. D., McKeon, C. A., Wilfong, L. G., Friedauer, J. A., & Heim, P. (2005). Is reading fluency a key for successful high school reading? *Journal of Adolescent and Adult Literacy, 49,* 22–27.

Rayner, K., & Pollatsek, A. (1995). *The psychology of reading.* Mahwah, NJ: Lawrence Erlbaum Associates.

Recht, D. R., & Leslie, L. (1988). The effects of prior knowledge on good and poor readers' memory for text. *Journal of Educational Psychology, 80,* 16–20.

Regner, M. (1992). Predicting growth in reading in regular and special education. Unpublished doctoral dissertation, Marquette University.

Richgels, D. J., McGee, L. M., Lomax, R. G., & Sheard, C. (1987). Awareness of four text structures: Effects on recall of expository text. *Reading Research Quarterly, 22,* 177–196.

Roberts, G., Good, R., & Corcoran, S. (2005). Story retell: A fluency-based indicator of reading comprehension. *School Psychology Quarterly, 20,* 304–318.

Rogers, T. (1991). Students as literary critics: The interpretive experiences, beliefs, and processes of ninth grade students. *Journal of Reading Behavior, 23,* 391–423.

Romero, F., Paris, S. G., & Brem, S. K. (2005). Children's comprehension and local-to-global recall of narrative and expository texts [Electronic Version]. *Current Issues in Education, 8,* 25.

Samuels, S. J. (2007). The DIBELS tests: Is speed of barking at print what we mean by reading fluency? *Reading Research Quarterly, 42,* 563–566.

Smith, W. E., & Beck, M. B. (1980). Determining instructional reading level with 1978 Metropolitan Achievement Test. *The Reading Teacher, 34,* 313–319.

Southwest Educational Development Laboratory. (2008). Reading assessment database for grades K–2. Retrieved from www.sedl.org/reading/rad/list.html

Spache, G. D. (1981). *Diagnosing and correcting reading disabilities.* Boston: Allyn & Bacon.

Spear-Swerling, L., & Sternberg, R. J. (1996). *Off-track: When poor readers become "learning disabled."* Boulder, CO: Westview Press.

Stahl, S. A. (2006). Understanding shifts in reading and its instruction. In K. A. Dougherty Stahl & M. McKenna (eds.),

Reading research at work: Foundations of effective practice (pp. 45–75). New York: Guilford Press.

Stahl, S. A., Duffy-Hester, A. M., & Dougherty Stahl, K. A. (2006). Everything you wanted to know about phonics (but were afraid to ask). In K. A. Dougherty Stahl & M. McKenna (eds.), Reading research at work: Foundations of effective practice (pp. 126–154). New York: Guilford Press.

Stahl, S. A., & Heubach, K. (2005). Fluency-oriented reading instruction. Journal of Literacy Research, 37, 25–60.

Stahl, S. A., & Hiebert, E. H. (2005). The "word factors": A problem for reading comprehension. In In S. G. Paris & S. A. Stahl (eds.), Children's reading comprehension and assessment (pp. 161–186). Mahwah, NJ: Lawrence Erlbaum Associates.

*Stahl, S. A., Pagnucco, J. R., & Stuttles, C. W. (1996). The effects of traditional and process literacy instruction on first graders' achievement and orientation toward reading. Journal of Educational Research, 89, 131–144.

Standards for education and psychological testing. (1999). Washington, DC: American Psychological Association.

Stanovich, K. E. (1980). Toward an interactive compensatory model of individual differences in the development of reading fluency. Reading Research Quarterly, 16, 32–71.

Stanovich, K. E. (1991a). Discrepancy definitions of reading disability: Has intelligence led us astray? Reading Research Quarterly, 26, 7–29.

Stanovich, K. E. (1991b). Word recognition: Changing perspectives. In R. Barr, M. L. Kamil, P. Moesenthal, & P. D. Pearson (eds.), Handbook of reading research (vol. II, pp. 418–452). White Plains, NY: Longman.

Stanovich, K. E. (1993/1994). Romance and reality. Distinguished Educator Series. The Reading Teacher, 47, 280–291.

Stanovich, K. E. (2000). Progress in understanding reading: Scientific foundations and new frontiers. New York: Guilford Press.

Stanovich, K. E. (2004). Matthew effects in reading: Some consequences of individual differences in the acquisition of literacy. In R. B. Ruddell & N. J. Unrau (eds.), Theoretical models and processes of reading, (5th ed., pp. 454–516). Newark, DE: International Reading Association.

Stanovich, K. E., Cunningham, A. E., & West, R. F. (1981). A longitudinal study of the development of automatic recognition skills in first graders. Journal of Reading Behavior, 13, 57–73.

Stein, N. L. (1979). How children understand stories: A developmental analysis. In L. Katz (ed.), Current topics in early childhood education (vol. 2, pp. 261–290). Norwood, NJ: Ablex.

Stein, N. L., & Glenn, C. (1979). An analysis of story comprehension in elementary school children. In R. O. Freedle (ed.), Advances in discourse processes: New directions in discourse processes (vol. 2, pp. 53–120). Norwood, NJ: Ablex.

Stenner, A. J., Burdick, H., Sanford, E., & Burdick, D. S. (2006). How accurate are lexile text measures? Journal of Applied Measurement, 7, 302–322.

Stevens, K. C. (1980). The effect of background knowledge on the reading comprehension of ninth graders. Journal of Reading Behavior, 12, 151–154.

Sulzby, E., & Teale, W. (1991). Emergent literacy. In R. Barr, M. L. Kamil, P. Mosenthal, & P. D. Pearson (eds.), Handbook

of Reading Research (vol. II, pp. 727–758). White Plains, NY: Longman.

Swalm, J. E. (1972). A comparison of oral reading, silent reading, and listening comprehension. Education, 92, 111–115.

Taft, M. L., & Leslie, L. (1985). The effects of prior knowledge and oral reading accuracy on miscues and comprehension. Journal of Reading Behavior, 17, 163–179.

Taylor, B. M. (1979). Good and poor readers' recall of familiar and unfamiliar text. Journal of Reading Behavior, 11, 375–380.

Thompson, C. A., Craig, H. K., & Washington, J. A. (2004). Variable production of African American English across oracy and literacy contexts. Language, Speech, and Hearing Services in Schools, 35, 269–282.

Thorndike, R. M., Cunningham, G. K., Thorndike, R. L., & Hagen, E. P. (1991). Measurement and evaluation in psychology and education (5th ed.). New York: Macmillan.

Trabasso, T., & Magliano, J. P. (1996). How do children understand what they read and what can we do to help them? In M. Graves, P. van den Broek, & B. Taylor (eds.), The first R: A right of all children (pp. 158–181). New York: Teachers College, Columbia University Press.

Valencia, S. W., & Stallman, A. C. (1989). Multiple measures of prior knowledge: Comparative predictive validity. In S. McCormick & J. Zutell (eds.), Cognitive and social perspectives for literacy: Research and instruction (pp. 427–436). Chicago: National Reading Conference.

Valencia, S. W., Stallman, A. C., Commeyras, M., Pearson, P. D., & Hartman, D. K. (1991). Four measures of topical knowledge: A study of construct validity. Reading Research Quarterly, 26, 204–233.

Van den Broek, P., Lorch, R. F., Linderholm, T., & Gustafson, M. (2001). The effects of readers' goals on inference generation and memory for texts. Memory and Cognition, 29, 1081–1087.

Walczyk, J. J., & Griffith-Ross, D. A. (2007). How important is reading skill fluency for comprehension? The Reading Teacher, 60, 560–569.

Washington, J. A., Craig, H. K., & Kushmaul, A. (1998). Variable use of African American English across two language sampling contexts. Journal of Speech, Language, and Hearing Research, 41, 1115–1124.

Weaver, C. A., & Kintsch, W. (1991). Expository text. In R. Barr, M. L. Kamil, P. Mosenthal, & P. D. Pearson (eds.), Handbook of reading research (vol. II, pp. 230–245). White Plains, NY: Longman.

Westby, C. (2004). 21st century literacy for a diverse world. Folia Phoniatrica et Logopaedica, 56, 25–271.

Woodcock, R. W. (1987). Woodcock Reading Mastery Test–Revised. Circle Pines, MN: American Guidance Service.

*Worthy, J., & Invernizzi, M. A. (1995). Linking reading with meaning. Journal of Reading Behavior, 27, 585–603.

Wright, J. (2007). RTI toolkit: A practical guide for schools. Port Chester, NY: Duke Publishing.

Zwaan, R. A., & Brown, C. M. (1996). The influence of language proficiency and comprehension skill on situation-model construction. Discourse Processes, 21, 289–327.

Index

Photo Credits

p. 157: Omers/Shutterstock; p. 184 middle left: Yoav Levy/Phototake; p. 184 bottom left: Geoff Dann/Dorling Kindersley Media Library; p. 184 top right: Jules Selmes and Debi Treloar/Dorling Kindersley Media Library; p. 184 middle right: Punchstock/Getty Images; p. 184 bottom right: Russell D. Curtis/Photo Researchers; p. 267 top: Corbis; p. 267 bottom: Daniel McGowan; p. 318: Richard Nowitz/DV/Getty Images; p. 320 top: Brian Cosgrove/Dorling Kindersley Media Library; p. 320 bottom: Robin Smith/Photolibrary; p. 321: Thierry Maffeis/Shutterstock; p. 357: Michael Moran/Dorling Kindersley Media Library; p. 359: Photodisc/Getty Images

DVDs are available for the QRI-5

The DVD prepared for the QRI-4 has been modified slightly and is available for use with the QRI-5. The administration and scoring of the QRI-4 with students of different levels of reading ability is presented. The DVD demonstrates all diagnostic options including the think-aloud procedure with middle school students.

I wish to order:

_____ DVDs @ $40.00 each $ _____ total

\+ _____ 5.6% sales tax (WI residents only)

$ _____ Total enclosed

Note: A check or money order payable to Marquette University must accompany the order. If a purchase order is used an $8 shipping and handling fee will be added to the total bill. **Purchase order number:** _____

Name: _____

School: _____

Address: _____

City: _____   State: _____   Zip Code: _____

Mail order form to:

QRI DVD
College of Education
Marquette University
P.O. Box 1881
Milwaukee, WI 53201-1881

FAX order to:

Coreen Bukowski
414-288-3945
Include purchase order number

For further information contact: lauren.leslie@marquette.edu